CHINA
A COOKBOOK

TERRY TAN

LORENZ BOOKS

CONTENTS

INTRODUCTION

I am Singapore-born Chinese, with parents whose antecedents hark back not only to eastern China, but also to southern China, mingled with South-east Asia. Our family kitchen was always perfumed with the scent of intoxicating herbs and other aromatic ingredients, such as lemon grass, ginger, chillies, limes, fresh coriander and dozens more besides. However, what ran through all the family menus, that featured Thai, Indian and Malay elements and even colonial British culinary influences, was the strong Chinese thread.

When I first came to England to run a restaurant, in the early 1980s, the public had not got their heads around the fact that I could be Chinese and yet not merely ladle out endless dishes slathered in sweet-and-sour sauce; my cooking instead incorporated many culinary influences and reflected decades of feasting on a wide range of dishes. Things have moved on so much since then, and people are much more aware and appreciative of the incredible variety of different regional dishes to be discovered and enjoyed. This book is an opportunity to look further and at the same time pay delicious homage to the vast scope of this wonderful cuisine.

Chinese food is rather a catch-all term that glosses over the provincial distinctions and fine nuances to be found in this huge and diverse country. Particular dishes may be broadly described as belonging to the Cantonese, Sichuan, Beijing or Shanghai schools of cooking – which in geographical terms can be described as being southern, western, northern and eastern respectively – and within these can be found smaller territories, each with their own identity, that feed into and draw upon the traditions of their neighbours. It is this regional cooking that I wanted to explore, uncovering and examining both what makes an area's food unique but how it links to the rest of China, too, in terms of history, tradition and of course flavour.

I hope that in the pages of this book you will not only find many tantalizing recipes that have you rushing to the kitchen, but that you will also gain insights into their background. Most importantly I hope you will be inspired to create your own deliciously good Chinese food at home.

TERRY TAN

REGIONAL SPECIALITIES

In a country as vast and varied as China, and with such a long history of migration and assimilation, it is no surprise that different regions have their own preferences when it comes to food. Nonetheless there are unifying features – the importance of using fresh produce when available, the principles of yin and yang in combining flavour and nutrition, and giving attention to producing dishes that are balanced in terms of taste, textures and colours. Certain key seasonings – soy sauce, garlic, ginger – appear repeatedly, alongside the staples of rice and noodles that form the bedrock of the nation's daily diet.

North China

The long, cold winters that grip northern China each year have shaped the culinary landscape in a variety of ways. First, the growing season is fairly short, so pickling is a common method of preserving vegetables. Second, because of the harsh climate, there is a preference for hearty, rich and warming dishes, meaning that the local menu is packed with substantial stews. Wheat is one of the main crops, and it is transformed into starchy fillers such as noodles and steamed breads.

Beijing or Mandarin-style cuisine is elegant, but in an understated way. Given its imperial history, it can be surprising to find that the ingredients are often simple, with as much influence drawn from rural Mongolia as from the great dynasties of the Forbidden City.

East China

Shanghai and the neighbouring provinces all boast their own distinctive cuisines, but notwithstanding the individual culinary identities they are united in their appreciation and use of local ingredients: the abundant fresh fish and shellfish from the sea, river and lakes; the rice grown in the lush Yangtze delta area; the alcohols, which are utilized in a plethora of recipes; the fabulous array of fresh fruits and vegetables; and the high-quality meat and poultry from the farms.

The cooking of the city of Shanghai itself is famous for featuring elegant flavour combinations and rich, fragrant dishes. The recipes take inspiration from all the surrounding provinces and incorporates their ingredients, techniques and tastes into its own unique cuisine.

South China

From bland staples such as rice and all types of noodle, to piquant and aromatic sauces and fresh vegetables, southern Cantonese-style cooks make good use of a wide range of ingredients and have absorbed many imported customs into their repertoire. Carefully prepared with minimal fuss, these ingredients are transformed into a wide variety of mouthwatering dishes, many of which are served at once as part of a communal meal in carefully thought-out combinations that adhere to the principles of fan cai – namely, providing the correct balance of nutrients, textures and colours as well as the five key flavour notes of Chinese cooking: salt, sweet, sour, bitter and hot.

West China

Farmers in western China work in a rainy, warm climate, which provides ideal conditions for growing staple crops such as rice. Wheat also grows well here, giving a different emphasis to the daily diet, with more bread and wheat-based noodle recipes than in some other parts of China. The humid climate does, however, means that many fresh foods do not keep especially well, and this has given rise to a tradition of preserving ingredients, through drying, salting, pickling, spicing and smoking.

The intense flavours of Sichuan peppercorns, chillies, onions and garlic have given the traditional cuisine of west China, and Sichuan province in particular, its reputation for boldness and fiery heat. There is also a milder side, too, which is often overlooked by the rest of the world, focusing on the fresh ingredients that are available from the local fields and rivers, and full of more subtle flavourings.

Above *The third-largest country in the world, China has a land area of about 3.7 million sq miles/9.6 million sq km, and is home to some 1.4 billion people.*

This book

Divided into regional sections that represent the broad scope of China's cooking, the chapters range from soups, dim sum, noodles and rice, to fish and shellfish, meat, poultry and vegetables, as well as a handful of sweet foods (sweet treats and desserts do not play a major role in the Chinese diet).

Each section opens with an overview of the history, geography, culinary traditions and main festivals of the four main regions (north, east, south and west), providing insight into the dishes and ingredients that are typical of each area.

The recipes then follow, grouped by type of dish. Many of these recipes are quick and easy, whereas others involve a little more time and some more unusual ingredients. These are usually available from supermarkets or Asian stores, but alternatives and variations are provided, along with preparation tips that will help you get the best from some perhaps less-familiar ingredients.

Featuring classic recipes from all around China, this book cannot of course include every dish from such a large country, but it is hoped the wide range presented will whet your appetite and equip you with the techniques you need to create a magnificent repertoire of Chinese dishes in your own home, as well as deepening your understanding of the nation's cuisine as a whole.

CLASSIC INGREDIENTS

Despite the incredible range of topographies found in China, the repertoire of favourite ingredients remains fairly consistent across the country, albeit with localized preferences and regional specialities. The foods listed here cover just some of the more typical ingredients, which are for the most part readily available in Asian stores or online. Where an ingredient may be hard to find, variations and suggested alternatives are provided in the recipes, to make the dishes more accessible.

Rice

This is grown prolifically in many parts of the country on the lush river deltas and open plains – apart from in the far north, where wheat is the staple. As a result, in most regions rice is the single most important element in almost every meal. It can come in a variety of forms, but there are two basic methods of cooking it – boiling or steaming – and when cooked and cooled, it forms the basis of fried rice.

Glutinous rice

Both long grain and short grain glutinous rice have to be soaked for several hours before they yield their fluffiness or succulence. Although the texture of cooked glutinous rice is quite firm, it is nevertheless sticky and it is this that makes it popular as a wrap-around for a range of filled rice dishes. Black glutinous rice is also available.

Below *Rice is the foundation of most meals in China, except in the north, where steamed breads take over.*

Jasmine rice

This is very popular in eastern China, with its subtly delicate scent and dry, thin yet firm grains that are translucent when raw.

Ground rice or rice flour

Many desserts have their basis in rice flour, which is made into a sort of pastry then wrapped around bean, almond and lotus seed pastes, to make tasty little sweet cakes that are steamed or boiled. Ground rice flour is also made into rice noodles or dim sum dumpling skins, as well as dumplings and pancakes, and is used as a thickener for soups and stews.

Rice papers

These fragile triangular or circular papers are used to make delicate spring rolls or as wrappers for deep-fried seafood.

Congee

Rice porridge or congee is a main staple in family meals in western and eastern China. Short grain or broken rice is cooked until it resembles porridge, with a lot of milky liquid. Congee is served with a wide range of pickles, stir-fries and simple dishes, and is often topped with hard-boiled or century eggs.

Steamed breads and pancakes

Whereas rice is central to meals elsewhere in China, steamed breads made with low-gluten wheat flour are found in those northern provinces where no rice can be grown, and form the bedrock of the daily diet there. Pancakes, also made with wheat flour, are used as wrappers for all manner of tasty fillings, both sweet and savoury, including of course the inimitable Peking Duck.

Noodles

Although rice remains the staple starch of a Chinese meal, noodles are ideal when time is short as they make a complete meal in one dish, simply stir-fried with combinations of meat, fish and vegetables.

Wheat flour noodles

These are generally yellow in colour, ranging from pale to deep golden in hue. Factories all over China produce many varieties of wheat flour noodles in a great many shapes and sizes. These noodles come either dried, to be reconstituted in warm water, or fresh, to be blanched before use in stir-fries or soup. They are especially popular in the north and west.

Fine rice noodles

There are several dried types of fine rice noodle, including rice vermicelli, or mi fun. They are usually used in soup dishes.

Above *Cheap, sustaining and quick to cook, noodles are a key feature of many Chinese dishes.*

Fresh rice noodles

The Cantonese stir up an iconic dish with fresh rice noodles called hor fun, which are low-starch, thin tapered noodles that pick up succulent sauces.

Mung bean noodles

Also known as transparent noodles, translucent vermicelli, cellophane noodles or glass noodles, these are made from mung bean flour (the same bean that yields beansprouts). These always come in dried skeins that reconstitute rapidly when soaked in warm water. Their delicate looks belie their resilience: mung bean noodles remain firm and crunchy no matter how long you cook them, so they are a great choice for many dishes, and are regarded as a vegetable ingredient rather than a carbohydrate.

Vegetables and herbs

Throughout China, vegetables are the most fundamental ingredient. Virtually every meal, no matter how grand or humble, contains some vegetables for flavour and texture as well as for their nutritional value.

Bamboo shoots

Technically a giant grass, bamboo enjoys a revered status in Chinese culture, and it grows prolifically in many areas. The shoots are pale yellow or creamy white, crunchy in texture, and have a slightly astringent taste. They absorb flavourings well and keep their texture when cooked. Bamboo shoots tend to be used fresh in China, but are also available pickled or dried. They are sold in cans or jars outside of China, either as whole shoots or in slices or chunks. Soak them for 30 minutes before use.

Bell peppers

Crunchy, colourful, tasty, quick to cook and very nutritious, bell peppers are the perfect ingredient for many Chinese dishes, especially stir-fries.

Corn

Eaten fresh as individual kernels in soups and stir-fries, corn is also preserved by drying in the sun. Sometimes you will see it spread out on highways!

Pak choi/bok choy

With pale green stalks and dark, thin leaves, pak choi is usually about 13cm/5in long. It is excellent in stir-fries and stews.

Chinese leaves/Chinese cabbage

Sometimes known as Napa cabbage, this commonly used vegetable has a delicate, sweet aroma. The broad stalks are pale green to ivory white, with a crunchy texture, and the light green leaves are slightly frilly. Chinese leaves are used in stir-fries, stews and soups, and sometimes raw in salads.

Kai lan

This is a dark green vegetable that is often described as Chinese broccoli but is actually a member of the kale family. The stalks have a robust texture and taste.

Right *Hanging up corn cobs by their husks to dry; preserving food for storage is a time-honoured practice.*

Mustard greens

These are large, pale green leaves known as gai choy in Cantonese. They have a sharp and robust flavour, and make a classic dish when poached with egg white and crab meat.

Leeks

Holding a special place in Chinese cuisine, leeks are eaten for symbolic reasons (the Mandarin name, 'suan', is phonetically similar to the word for 'count' – as in counting money). The white part is sliced or chopped, for an aromatic and versatile addition to many dishes. Leeks are often regarded as a good alternative to garlic.

Spring onions/scallions

In China, these are regarded more as a vegetable than a mere garnish. They are used in quantity in many poultry dishes; are fundamental to dumplings; and often appear stir-fried with diced meat.

Chinese chives

These chives are found in three forms throughout China: green chives with flat, slim-bladed leaves; yellow chives, which are grown under a cloche or in the dark; and flowering chives (also known as garlic chives) with sturdy round stems tipped with pointed green buds. All have a pronounced onion-garlic flavour. Green chives are usually stir-fried or used to enliven dumpling and spring roll fillings, whereas yellow chives are more delicate in flavour and are ideally suited to soups.

Gourds, squashes and melons

The Chinese are particularly fond of cooking with gourds and squashes. These range from bitter melon with its green ridged skin, or luffa squash, which has fluffy white flesh hiding within a hard green case, to the more familiar squashes, such as courgettes or zucchini. The winter melon is a large gourd-like vine fruit, treated as a vegetable in cooking. Chinese melons are best steamed or cooked in stews and soups, though they are also candied.

Aubergines/eggplants
The typical Chinese aubergine is long and thin, in shades of pale green or purple with a faintly sweet flavour. It is an incredibly versatile vegetable – it can be steamed, fried or stuffed. The fine-textured flesh readily absorbs spices and seasonings.

Mangetouts/snow peas
One of the most common Chinese vegetables, mangetouts are flat, green peas, the size of a thumb; they are very crunchy and sweet and need minimal cooking. The French name, mangetout, literally means 'eat all', so these beans require no preparation. They make good fillings for spring rolls.

Beansprouts
These are ubiquitous throughout most of the country, with the exception of the most northerly areas. They can be eaten raw but are usually added to stir-fried noodles and cooked very briefly to give some crunch to the dish. Their flavour is delicate and watery. They are available fresh in most supermarkets – ensure they are not past their best or they can be toxic.

Below *Beansprouts are sold at markets from barrels of water to ensure they are absolutely fresh.*

Jicama
This sweet turnip has a thin brown skin that needs to be removed using a vegetable peeler, and tastes faintly of water chestnuts.

Mooli/daikon
This root vegetable looks very similar to a large white carrot. It is crisp, juicy and slightly spicy in flavour. It can be eaten raw or cooked and is often ground and made into a savoury cake that is served as part of a dim sum selection.

Taro
This root vegetable, also known as yam, generally comes in regular and baby varieties. Baby taros are small and egg-shaped; others are about 25cm/10in long and barrel-shaped. Both are covered in short hairs, with white, purple-flecked flesh. Taro is used in much the same way as potatoes – mashed, baked or added to soups, stews and curries. The larger variety is firm with a nutty flavour; the smaller one is creamier and sweeter, lending itself to sweet dishes.

Cassava
Also known as manioc or tapioca, this is a large tuber with a rough, dark brown skin. Cassava is extremely versatile, but is mostly used in sweet dishes. It should not be eaten raw.

Water chestnuts
These are sold fresh in Chinese markets, with brown skins that peel away to reveal a crunchy white nut inside. Also available canned, they can be eaten raw or cooked.

Dried and preserved vegetables
At times of bumper harvests in China, many vegetables are dried or salted for cooking in the winter months when fresh food is scarce. Many types of dried vegetables are traditionally used, both for their nutritional qualities and for their concentrated flavour. These include dried cole and lily buds, preserved mustard greens, preserved winter vegetables and salted vegetables. Mixed vegetables are also pickled and kept for many months, adding a spicy, rich flavour to winter dishes.

Above *Shiitake mushrooms are extremely popular in Chinese cuisine and feature in all manner of dishes.*

Mushrooms

In China, mushrooms come in all shapes, sizes, colours and textures. They are sometimes used fresh, but dried mushrooms are more common; when reconstituted, they have wonderful depths of flavour.

Shiitake

Also known as Chinese black mushrooms, these have a distinctively husky flavour and are usually sold dried. They are not all black – they vary from a pale peach colour to dark greyish-brown, depending on the variety. They must be softened in warm water for about 30 minutes, after which the tough stems are removed and the caps are chopped up and added to stews, stir-fries and fillings for dim sum.

Oyster mushrooms

These grow in clumps in tropical and temperate climes. The caps, gills and stems are all the same colour, which can be pearl grey, pink or yellow. Large ones should be torn, rather than cut, into pieces.

Straw mushrooms

Once peeled, small dark brown caps and cream-coloured stems are revealed, which look beautiful in clear broths. The flavour and texture are very delicate. These are available in cans in Asian stores if you are unable to find them fresh.

Cloud ear/wood ear mushrooms

Thin and brittle in their dried form, cloud ears need to be soaked in water, when they swell up and resemble frilly clumps of rubbery seaweed. They expand to six or eight times their volume after soaking. When cooked, they become translucent and gelatinous, but still retain a bite. Silver ear fungus goes by the same name in Mandarin, and is used in the same way. The generic name is 'mu er'.

White fungus

This type of edible fungus is similar to cloud ear mushrooms, but is peachy white in colour. It is called 'bai mu er' in Mandarin, meaning 'white cloud ear'. It needs to be soaked before it can be used, until it is soft with a jelly-like texture. White fungus is often added to soups.

Left *Fruit is sometimes candied in a sugar syrup and served on sticks as a sweet treat.*
Right *Fruit trees, such as this red plum, burst into bloom in springtime.*

Fruit, nuts and seeds

Many deciduous fruit trees such as peach, apricot, plum and chestnut have their origins in China and lots of regions have the favourable climatic conditions and rich soils to be able to support a plethora of temperate and sub-tropical fruits, including apples, pears, peaches, grapes, apricots, plums, persimmons and kiwi fruit. Fruit tends to be eaten on its own as a snack; fruity desserts are very rare, although fruits are candied and served on sticks at street stalls.

Nuts and seeds also grow well in many parts of China, and gingko nuts and sesame seeds in particular appear in countless dishes, both sweet and savoury.

Apples and pears

China is the world's biggest producer of apples – accounting for almost half of the global total – and is in the top three producers of pears. Many of these fruits are exported, though some do end up being eaten, usually raw as a snack, in China itself. They are also commonly coated in sugar syrup and candied, or turned into fritters.

Apricots

This tasty, soft fruit is grown widely in China. The seeds or kernels are so sweet that they can be substituted for almonds in some recipes. The fruit is also preserved in sugar or salted as a snack.

Plums

Chinese plums are sometimes eaten fresh, but most often end up pickled, dried, salted or puréed into plum sauce. Salted, and glacé or candied, plums are favourite snacks throughout China.

Bananas

These are usually eaten fresh or fried as fritters. A number of savoury dishes include the blossoms of the banana plant.

Coconuts

The flesh of ripe coconuts is squeezed for a rich white milk that is essential in Chinese desserts and cakes, and that is also used as a marinade for meat.

Chinese dates

These are usually sold with the stones or pits in, but they are easy to remove with a knife. Dates can be bought in dried form, and are used in sweet dishes.

Guavas

This fruit is the size of a large plum and the whole fruit is edible, from its seeds to its rind. In the west of China people love to dip slices of guava in preserved prune powder and salt.

Mangoes, papayas and pineapples

These sweet, juicy fruits are usually eaten raw as a refreshing snack. Pineapples are are also used in sweet-and-sour dishes.

Jackfruits

This large fruit tastes rather like ripe mango, and the flesh is both creamy and chewy.

囍
囍
囍

Star fruits/carambolas
This pretty fruit has a mildly floral flavour, similar to an Asian pear, but juicier. In south China it is often dried and salted to be enjoyed as a snack. The green immature fruit is frequently sliced and served as part of a salad or added to stir-fries.

Limes
These are used fresh or preserved in salt, as a snack. They can also be used in marinades and dressings.

Mandarin oranges
These have been cultivated for centuries in temperate China and symbolize prosperity during Lunar New Year. They are eaten fresh, or dried to add a citrus flavour to many savoury stews and sweet dishes. In western provinces, dried tangerine peel is often used as a seasoning in both stews and sweet drinks. Unripe mandarins are green; ripe ones are orange.

Persimmons
Also known as Sharon fruit, the persimmon is widely cultivated in sub-temperate China. They are orange in colour and the size of a mandarin. They come in two types: hard and crunchy, and soft and mushy with lots of juice. Dried persimmon has been an integral ingredient in Chinese cooking for centuries, and is especially popular in herbal drinks.

Lychees
These sweet, fragrant fruits have bumpy skins that are terracotta-pink in colour. They are easily peeled to reveal juicy white flesh, which covers a shiny, coffee-coloured seed. Sweet and fragrant, lychees are usually eaten as a refreshing snack on their own.

Longans
Related to and resembling lychees, this fruit comes in several varieties. The name derives from the Cantonese for 'dragon's eye'. The Chinese set much store by dried longan as a sweet ingredient in herbal drinks.

Left *Mandarin oranges are a symbol of good luck, and feature at Lunar New Year and also at weddings.*
Right *Ginkgo nuts are available in cans or vacuum-packed, which makes them more convenient.*

Ginkgo nuts
Popular in sweet and savoury dishes, ginkgo nuts can be bought vacuum-packed or canned, which saves the lengthy process of soaking and boiling to make them tender. They are believed to have many health benefits and contain restorative nutrients.

Other nuts
Cashew nuts, walnuts, pine nuts and peanuts (the latter is actually a legume, but is generally treated as a nut) all add crunch, flavour and protein to dishes, and are delicious toasted and sprinkled over a stir-fry or noodle dish to provide contrast. Chestnuts, meanwhile, are made into a paste that is used as a sweet filling for Pearl Balls.

Lotus seeds
Like ginkgo nuts, dried lotus seeds require lengthy soaking and boiling before use, so it is best to buy them canned so that they are ready to use. They are added to sweet soups and other desserts.

Sesame seeds
These tiny seeds come in a variety of colours, from creamy white to charcoal black. They can be ground to a paste, imparting a subtle perfume, but are most often sprinkled on stir-fries just before serving, such as the delicious Sesame Beef from Hubei, or rolled with rice to make sweet dishes.

Meat, poultry and eggs

Although many provincial dishes feature lamb, mutton, goat, beef and game – especially in the northern provinces, where there is a large Muslim population – pork and chicken remain the main performers in the wide repertoire of meat recipes found in China.

Pork

The way that pork is cut dictates how it is cooked in Chinese cuisine, with specific ratios of lean meat to fat to skin. Roast pork is made from a rib cut that is streaked with fat and cut as a long strip. For slow-cooking or braising, the hock or leg cut is usually used. Suckling pig is a festive delicacy and no wedding banquet is considered complete without this scrumptious centrepiece. Lesser cuts are used for minced or ground pork, the mainstay of dim sum fillings; and pork fat is rendered down to lard, in which many stir-fried dishes are cooked, giving them a distinct flavour.

Beef

Expensive and hard to come by in southern China, beef is mainly eaten on special occasions. In the west, stir-fries with beef often contain bamboo shoots, that quintessential Chinese vegetable, as well as fiery Sichuan chillies and peppercorns. Fillet steak or beef tenderloin, rump or round steak, sirloin, rib-eye and stewing steak are all used, often having first been tenderized.

Game

Although rare in much of China, some dishes of the northern provinces, particularly Hebei, feature game.

Offal/variety meats

Chinese cooks have elevated the art of cooking offal to great heights. Lungs with shredded bamboo shoots, liver with wine and garlic, kidney in soup redolent with ginger, trotters braised in soy sauce – these great dishes take pride of place in most Chinese homes.

Poultry

Many rural homes have backyards where chickens and ducks are reared, and chicken is probably the most widely eaten meat in China; the range of chicken dishes throughout the country is virtually endless, with hundreds of different recipes. If cooked whole, chicken is usually braised, steamed or simmered gently in a stew with ginseng or other herbs. More often, chicken is cut into small pieces before cooking. Symbolizing good tidings, it is always the featured dish during the Lunar New Year.

As it is tougher than chicken, duck is confined to fewer dishes, and recipes tend to involve lengthy marinating and cooking times, but these processes yield wonderful results, such as that icon of Chinese cooking around the world, Aromatic Crispy Duck.

Pigeons and quail are often steamed, deep-fried or stewed with medicinal herbs.

Below *Chicken is China's most popular meat, and birds are commonly reared by countryside dwellers.*

Eggs

In addition to hen's eggs, which are used in many dishes, duck's eggs and quail's eggs are also enjoyed. Duck's eggs are available salted or as century eggs. The latter are coated in a mixture of tea, alkaline clay, salt and wood ash, then rolled in rice chaff. These are placed in cloth-covered jars or woven baskets. In about three months, the mud hardens into a crust, and the eggs are ready for consumption. The yolk becomes a dark green, cream-like substance with a strong odour of sulphur and ammonia, while the white becomes a dark brown, transparent jelly with little taste. They may be difficult to find outside of China. Quail's eggs usually end up in soups.

Hard-boiled eggs of all types are served to elders on their birthdays as symbols of completeness and respect. These are cooked with noodles in a sugary broth as the sweetness also denotes a good life ahead.

Below *Eggs – hen's, duck's or quail's – are often hard-boiled and used to top noodles or soups.*

Fish and shellfish

In many parts of China – whether by the coast or the inland rivers and tributaries – wet markets are a common feature, where fishmongers sell absolutely fresh fish and seafood of a bewildering variety. This is cooked as soon as possible after being caught, and any leftovers are processed into cakes or balls that are then steamed or fried and served as savoury complements to a range of noodle and rice dishes.

Sea fish

Sea bass, snapper, threadfin and mullet thrive in abundance in the coastal waters off China. Snapper has a fine texture and mild-tasting flesh, and it can be grilled, fried or steamed. The term whitefish usually refers to mullet, pomfret (which come in two types: black or white), porgy, or other similar white-fleshed fish. Whitebait and sprats (young fish of any species) are also popular, as are anchovies – one of China's favourite foods – which are best known in their dried form and are used extensively as a seasoning agent, especially in soup.

River fish

In the river tributaries of China, freshwater fish are plentiful. From the inland rivers come freshwater wrasse, mudfish, perch, trout, pike, carp and sturgeon, as well as their sprats. The latter are so small they can be eaten whole, or they can be dried and stored for the winter months to be used in soups and stews. Red snappers are distinctive brightly coloured fish, with a delicate flavour and soft flesh, and are often simply steamed with a few aromatics. Snakeheads are eel-like fish that are enjoyed for their meaty flesh and rich flavour, and often feature in a soup dish made with fish and rice vermicelli.

Eels

Plump adult eels – especially female ones, which tend to be larger – are highly prized and popular in stewed dishes containing lots of wine and ginger. They are almost always sold alive as they spoil quickly.

Below *Many fishermen, such as this one on the Li River, still use the traditional method of casting a fishing net.*

Right *Stinky tofu is enjoyed as a snack in many parts of China, often accompanied by some pickled vegetables.*

Seafood
Both marine and freshwater prawns are prized by the Chinese. Juicy and meaty, the bigger ones are often grilled whole, or added to stir-fries and curries; the small ones are dried and added to stocks to enhance the flavour. There are several varieties of crab, the most common being 'mottled' or 'flower' crabs. These are cooked and flaked to be added to stir-fries or used as a filling for dumplings.

Squid, too, are an important and plentiful seafood, and can be cooked in a variety of ways, including being quickly stir-fried or simmered in soup.

In the world of crustaceans, mussels and scallops are both popular, and are simply steamed or cooked in Chinese wine with garlic and ginger.

Tofu and tofu products

Few other foods stimulate the creativity of Chinese chefs more than humble tofu and its variations. Tofu, or beancurd, is made from soaked, mashed and strained soya beans, and is white in colour. As old as Chinese culinary history itself, tofu is a highly nutritious product that lends itself to a multitude of recipes, especially as it comes in many forms.

Fresh tofu
The soft variety of fresh tofu, sometimes branded as silken tofu, can be eaten just as it is, requiring no more than gentle blanching or steaming. It is delicate and so cannot withstand harsh cooking techniques. The firm variety is best in stir-fries and as fillings, as it is much more robust.

Pressed tofu
Cubes of fresh tofu are dried and pressed until they become firm cakes with a light brown skin. These are then sliced and added to stir-fries.

Dried tofu
Also known as beancurd sticks in China, this is made by simmering soy bean milk until a thin skin forms on top. This skin is then lifted off very carefully and hung out to dry. It features in many soups and stews.

Fried tofu
This type of tofu is made by deep-frying firm tofu until a brown skin forms. It can form a pocket for meat or seafood stuffing, or is simply shredded and added to congee. In Sichuan and Hubei, fried tofu is a main ingredient in many vegetarian stews.

Fermented tofu
This is a favourite condiment in many parts of China, which is traditionally served with rice congee, in a marinade for poultry or as a rich seasoning that is used in braised dishes. It comes in two types: red and white, both of which taste extremely salty and pungent. Red fermented beancurd is essential for red-cooked dishes, and as a seasoning and colourant for roasted meats such as pork.

Stinky tofu
Aptly named, this type of fermented tofu comes in many different types, depending on what was added to the brining liquid and for how long it was brined. Colours range from golden to black.

Tofu skins
These processed brown, wrinkly sheets are often used as spring roll and dim sum wrappers, and can also be fried as a garnish for stir-fried noodles or added to vegetable stews.

Condiments, spices and flavourings

Chinese cuisine is full of strong and surprising tastes, often derived from a subtle combination of seasoning ingredients. The appearance of the dish is also a major consideration, and herb and spice garnishes are central to Chinese food.

Garlic

This aromatic bulb is used in myriad ways, filling the kitchen with its distinctive aroma.

Ginger

This is available in two forms: young tender stems of a pale yellow colour with green stalks, or ginger roots with a light brown thin skin. The tender stems of root ginger are ground, chopped or puréed, and are integral to stir-fries and as a condiment in dips.

Chillies

Fresh or dried, red or green, chillies are fundamental to the cooking of western China in particular. They come in many varieties, from the mild and bland to the incredibly hot. Fresh chillies are typically chopped finely and added to many stir-fries, lending the dishes a fiery kick and a dash of vivid colour. Sichuan cooking is almost synonymous with the spiciness of chillies.

Chilli bean paste

This thick, spicy mixture is made of a purée of ground dried chillies blended with yellow bean paste. It is originally from Sichuan, where it is known as dou banchiang.

Black bean sauce

Soy beans are roasted and fermented with salt, and sometimes also with ginger, until black and very pungent. They are then left whole or ground into a thick paste to be used as a condiment.

Yellow bean sauce

This salty sauce is actually brown in colour, and is made from fermented soya beans.

Left *Soy sauce, vinegar, aromatic sauces, garlic and ginger paste appear constantly in Chinese cooking.*

Hoisin sauce

This is made from a blend of yellow bean paste and sugar, and is coloured a rich, dark mahogany. Its most common use is as a rub on pancakes with crispy duck, but it is also used as a seasoning for stews and roast pork.

Soy sauce

This has become a major part of all regional Chinese cooking. It is made of soy beans and comes in dark, light, reduced salt, thick or thin varieties. It adds colour and flavour to stews, casseroles and marinades, and features in a vast range of braised poultry and pork dishes. This is one Chinese staple that you will definitely need in your store cupboard: it is to the East what salt is to the West.

Sichuan peppercorns

These reddish-brown pungent peppercorns are indigenous to western China. They are very strong, with a hint of liquorice flavour. They are used in many recipes, and also make an attractive garnish when ground and sprinkled on top of the dish.

Five-spice powder

Indispensable in Cantonese stews and as a spice for spring roll fillings, this is a blend of powdered aniseed, fennel, cloves, cinnamon and pepper.

Fresh herbs

Usually used as a garnish to add flavour and colour to a dish, the most common herb used in Chinese cooking is fresh coriander or cilantro.

Vinegars

Black and red vinegars are essential seasonings and are used widely as the basic souring agent in soups, or are served on their own as tasty dips for dumplings and fried foods. Clear and clean-tasting, rice vinegar is ubiquitous in Fujian cuisine due to its lovely aroma and subtle acidity.

Sesame oil

Widely used, this oil has an intense nutty fragrance that can overpower other seasonings, so a teaspoon or two is sufficient.

BEVERAGES

Tea is the main non-alcoholic beverage of many parts of China, alongside water, fruit juices, soft drinks and sometimes soybean milk, although coffee is increasingly popular – especially in cities – as cafe culture continues its global march. In terms of alcohol, Chinese wine made from grains is much enjoyed, especially when served hot to keep out the chill during the winter months, alongside beer and warming liquors and, more recently, wine made from grapes, which grow well in some parts of China.

Tea

China is one of the world's largest producers and consumers of tea, and its history dates back thousands of years, when it was initially drunk as a tonic. Yunnan, the south-western province closest to Myanmar and Vietnam, is the birthplace of tea; it has the ideal climate, with a perfect rooting medium in the red clay soil. In Hunan province, too, red and black teas are grown along the foothills of the mountains. Tea is used for steaming fish, poultry and meat, with each tea providing a distinctive flavour.

Although there are hundreds of varieties of tea, they all fall into two basic categories, black (sometimes called red) and green. Both types come from the same plant and the chief differences lie in processing. Black tea is first fermented, or oxidized, which is the technical term for this process. When it is only semi-fermented, or semi-oxidized, it is called oolong tea. The name is derived from 'wu long', meaning 'black dragon', and the strongest of these is Tie Guan Yin, meaning 'iron goddess of mercy'.

Green tea is unfermented and is dried in the sun or in special drying kilns, where the leaves may also be steamed to make them soft. They are then rolled and fired in the kilns until they turn a yellowish-green and take on their unique curled shape. The finest teas are still hand-processed, especially the rare teas such as Gunpowder and Dragon Well.

Alcoholic drinks

Archaeological digs in China have dated the existence of alcohol as far back as 4,000 years ago. Certainly by the 11th century, winemaking from fruits and grains was an industry all over present-day China. The Chinese production of alcohol is split between beer, wine and grain alcohol.

Beer

Although historical records show that both wine and beer have been made in China for thousands of years, beer drinking has only become really popular in the last 30 years. Today, probably the best-known Chinese beer is from Qingdao: it is commercially known as Tsingtao, and it is available worldwide.

Wines and liquors

Broadly, Chinese wines come under two main headings – yellow and white grain liquor. These are both made from glutinous rice and are either fermented (huang jiu – yellow liquor), or distilled (mi jiu – white liquor). White liquor is called shaojiu or 'burned liquor', because of the sensation it produces in the mouth or the fact that it is served warm.

Perhaps the most famous Chinese liquor, Maotai is known as the spirit of China. Its name literally means 'thatched terrace', and it originated during the Qing dynasty in a village of the same name situated in the Guizhou province – an area famous for winemaking.

Many types of flavoured wines are used in the cooking of southern China. Wu Liang Ye (five-grain liquor) is a heady spirit; the five grains are sorghum, rice, glutinous rice, sweet corn and unhusked wheat. To Mei Jau is a Cantonese liquor produced from rice wine, with added 'to mei', a flower found locally, and crystal sugar syrup. Mui Kwai Lo is aromatic and rose-flavoured; sweet sherry makes a good substitute.

Wine – mostly red – made with grapes is also produced in some regions of China (and has been for thousands of years), with cabernet sauvignon being the most popular grape variety.

Right *Many types of tea are produced and drunk in China, such as oolong, pu'er, tie guan yin, and sencha.*

KITCHEN EQUIPMENT

Chinese cooks have long used pans and utensils, such as the wok, where the shape and function have remained almost unchanged for centuries. The natural materials of clay, metal and bamboo are still preferred for the preparation and serving of food, and the most popular cooking methods, such as stir-frying or steaming, rely on direct heat; convection ovens are not often used in Chinese kitchen. The few modern culinary inventions found in Chinese kitchens, such as electric rice cookers, tend to be updated versions of traditional equipment and techniques.

Woks

The wok dates back centuries to the time of the nomadic tribes in northern China. These people were always on the move with their animals, searching for the best grazing sites, so they needed a utensil with a rounded base that could sit on a few rocks over a fire. The wok was born and has not changed its basic shape since then. It does multiple duties in most Chinese households as a steamer, a braising pan, a frying pan and even a shallow boiler.

The best woks are made of heavy cast iron. Non-stick ones are not ideal for rapid stir-frying as the action may chip the coating. Stainless steel is not the best material either, as it conducts heat too rapidly and may burn food. The heat in electric woks is not sufficiently high for quick stir-frying; they are good for slow braising and steaming, however. Cast iron is considered to be the best material for woks, although cast aluminium, being much lighter and less expensive, is increasingly used.

Frying pans
Although a wok can be used for most purposes, a frying pan is useful for pancakes and other things that require a flat-bottomed pan.

Ladles
The traditional wok ladle is shaped at an angle relative to the curvature of the wok for better scooping and more efficient stir-frying, as the blade has a broader area than a wooden spoon or conventional ladles.

Cleavers
This is a unique Chinese knife made of tempered iron or steel, honed to razor sharpness, the best size being about 30cm/12in in length and 10cm/4in wide. It usually has a wooden handle, although they are also often made from a single piece of metal. The cleaver provides essential leverage for cutting through bone and large pieces of meat, and is a versatile implement – it can be used as a carver, crusher, slicer and chopper. The blunt end serves as a mallet for tenderizing meats.

Clay or sand pots
This Chinese vessel comes with a single handle and functions as an oven-to-table utensil when food is to be served piping hot or sizzling. Traditional clay pots have a wire frame to support the structure, as the intense heat can sometimes cause cracks to form. This kind of pot is never used for the whole cooking process; dishes are cooked in a wok or other cooking vessel and then transferred to the clay pot, which is preheated just enough to maintain the temperature.

Steamers
These are traditionally made of woven bamboo, but they may also be made of aluminium, with multiple perforated trays to allow the steam to come through each layer. Steamers come in many sizes, small enough to contain bitesize morsels (as in dim sum) or large enough to contain several chickens. Multiple stack steamers are ideal for cooking several dishes at the same time and are a common sight at street food stalls and restaurants in China.

Left *Bamboo steamers that can be stacked enable you to steam several dishes at the same time.*

Steamboats
This kind of cooking pot originated in Mongolia, in the far north of the country. It is sometimes called a fire pot or a hot pot, and is usually made of brass-coated or enamel-coated metal, with a funnel in the centre of a moat which contains stock or water. It used to be heated over charcoal, although it is common these days to see electric models with thermostatic controls. Various foods are cut up and placed around the steamboat so that diners can cook the food themselves in the stock, using brass wire spoons, which ensures everybody gets what they want and cooked how they like it.

Bamboo draining baskets
Ubiquitous in all Asian countries, these versatile utensils are used for many purposes – as sieves or strainers, for draining soaked rice, or even as food covers that allow air circulation and keep out flying insects. They are, in fact, simply the Chinese version of a colander.

Chopsticks
For many centuries, the Chinese have used bamboo chopsticks as they have a slightly rough texture, which is best for picking up slippery foods such as noodles and sauces. Normal chopsticks are 23cm/9in long, but longer ones – up to twice this length – are used for turning deep-fried foods, keeping the user at a safe distance from spitting hot oil.

Rice cookers
These are common in Asian homes, and are no longer regarded as a novelty in the West, as many restaurants have made use of this marvellous Japanese invention. Electric models now also have clever features for keeping rice warm for up to an hour. These work on the principle of weight – when all the liquid evaporates, the inner container, which sits on a spring-loaded element, rises automatically, switching the appliance off.

Serving dishes
Many Chinese dishes are served with a variety of accompaniments, such as dips or sauces. It is good to have a few tiny dishes in which to present them.

NORTHERN CHINA

Cooking from Beijing, Hebei, Tianjin, Henan, Shanxi, Shandong, Liaoning, Jilin and Heilongjiang

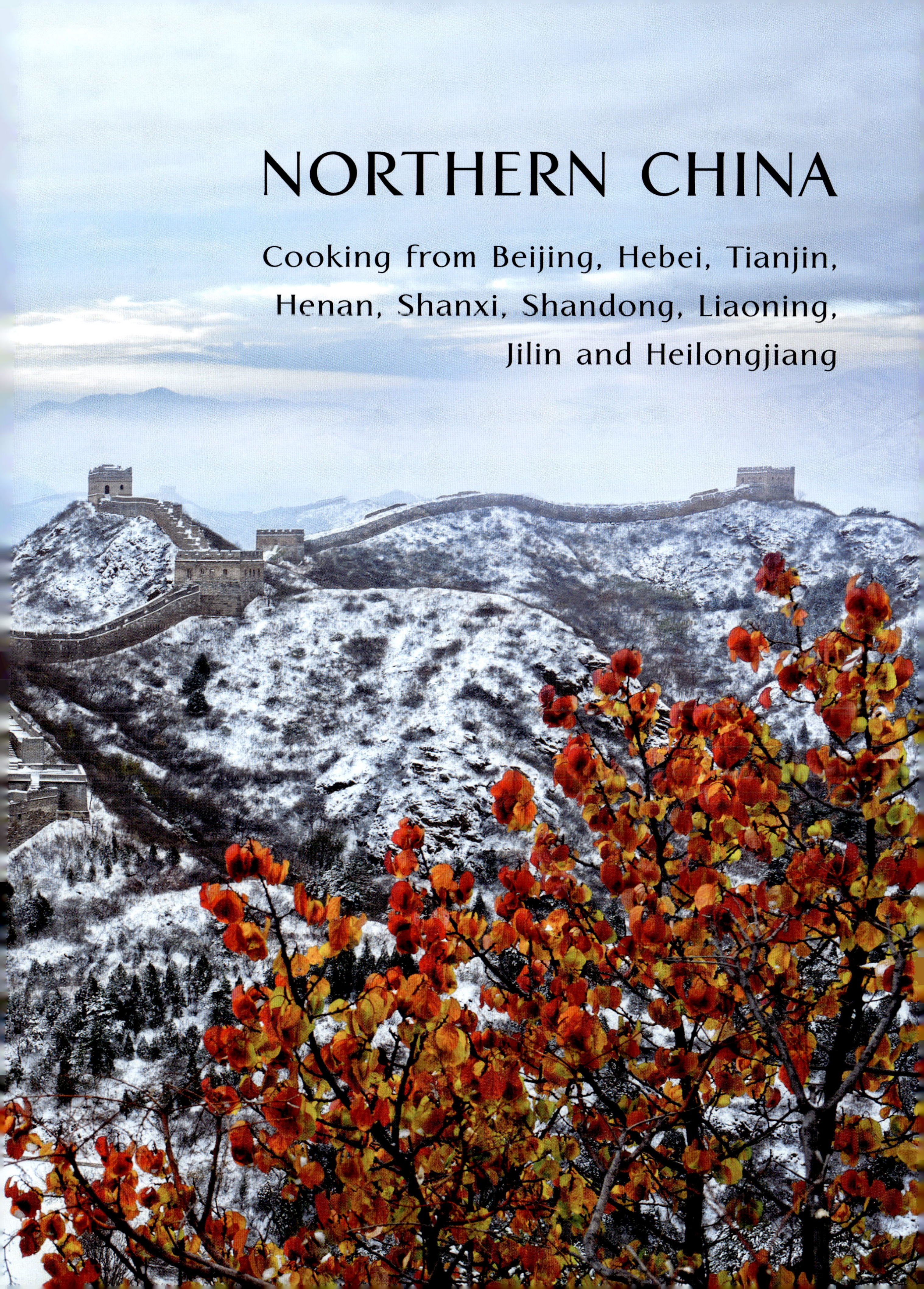

LAND OF ICE & SNOW

The expansive land mass of northern China stretches from Heilongjiang province in the far north, which borders Russia, all the way to Shanxi province in central China. Bustling, modern Beijing is the heart of this region, being both the cultural and culinary capital. This book focuses on the Beijing school of cooking, as well as on the traditional food of the surrounding area: Hebei, Tianjin, Henan, Shanxi, Shandong, Liaoning, Jilin and Heilongjiang. This northern area is unified by an unforgiving climate and landscape, which has shaped the cuisine found in these parts.

The undulating landscape of China's northern provinces is varied and impressive, comprising grasslands, rivers, mountains and forests. It is an important agricultural area, feeding a colossal population (much of which is clustered in and around the municipality of Beijing), but there are still remote and inhospitable lands in the far north of this region.

Topography of northern China

The valleys, hills and mountains are blanketed metres deep in a fine-grained soil known as loess, a pale mixture of clay and silt deposited by strong winds during the last Ice Age. This fertile substance makes the region a farming heartland.

Below *Encompassing what was Manchuria, the region stretches far north and north-east beyond Beijing.*

The north-eastern part of this region, containing Heilongjiang, Jilin and Liaoning, is covered with vast forests full of tall pines and cedars, dense bamboos and flamboyant rhododendrons. Between the fields and woods lie plateaux that are incised by gorges and ravines containing rushing rivers. Further south, on the densely populated North China Plain, the land is flat, with fields of grain stretching for miles.

Farming lands

Wheat is grown in most parts of China, particularly on the North China Plain (which covers parts of Hebei and Shandong, and is formed from deposits from the Yellow River) and in the Fen River valley in Shanxi. Other grains include corn, millet and oats. The diet of the northern people has been shaped by local agriculture, and their staple foods are bread and noodles made from these grains. Rice is not grown.

The Yellow River

Named for the large quantities of yellowish silt deposited along its banks and in its waters, the famous Yellow River begins in Qinghai in the north-west, flows through many provinces, and empties into the Bo Hai Basin north of the Shandong Peninsula. It runs for an amazing 4,700km (2,940 miles), and has been the cause of many catastrophic floods throughout China's history.

Despite this, the Yellow River is also known as the 'Mother River' of China and the 'cradle of Chinese civilization'. The agricultural areas of Shandong and Henan provinces are irrigated by the Yellow River on its way to the sea. The river also forms the border of Shanxi province, whose central valley is its economic heart, with rich farmlands and flourishing livestock.

This area is also steeped in history, and the many temples and monasteries that are present are a reminder that this province was once the political and cultural pulse of China.

Further north lies the historical area of Manchuria, which today comprises the modern provinces of Heilongjiang, Liaoning and Jilin, as well as some of Inner Mongolia. Its varied landscape ranges from bustling seaports to vast expanses of uninhabited land that is unsuited to agriculture. These areas contain towering rock formations, volcanic lakes and dense forests.

The capital city and Hebei

Beijing municipality (formerly known as Peking), the national capital, is carved out of Hebei province, which is largely a farming and industrial area. Beijing is a magnet for tourists, and millions of people visit each year to see the Forbidden City, the Great Wall and Tiananmen Square, and to enjoy the culinary delicacies. Within the city, the ancient settlements

Above *Preserving food is essential for survival in rural areas of Heilongjiang in north-east China.*

of Hutong – a maze of alleyways with distinctive courtyards – sit alongside today's modern flyovers and handsome boulevards.

An extreme climate

The climate in much of northern China is harsh and unforgiving. Summers can reach 45°C/113°F, while winter temperatures fall to -20°C/-4°F, with bitterly cold winds coursing through from the Mongolian steppes. The growing season diminishes the further north you go; in Manchuria there are only 90 frost-free days per year. The old saying that the northern Chinese will eat 'anything with legs, except a table; and anything that flies, except an aeroplane' refers to the inventiveness of the cuisine and the people who developed it, who have to just make the best of whatever can be grown in the difficult climate: this they manage with panache.

A POWERHOUSE OF PROGRESS

The history of the northern provinces in China is a long and fascinating one. The most remote, sparsely populated areas, with their colder and harsher topography, have had relatively little influence on the evolution of present-day China. On the other hand, Beijing and the surrounding provinces, with their more benign climates and burgeoning populations, have become the driving force of Chinese progress in many diverse areas – cuisine, politics, the arts, agriculture and industry.

The earliest known settlements, built around 8000BCE, were largely primitive villages based on an agricultural economy, and found in the coastal regions of the Shandong peninsula and along the rich deltas of the Yangtze River. The people were hunter-gatherers and fishermen. Archaeological sites in Henan have yielded evidence of carnivore diets, such as fossilized pork bones; that millet, wheat, barley and rice were grown; and that these grains were also turned into alcoholic beverages such as rice wine. Soy beans have been cultivated for more than 3,000 years, and products such as tofu and soy sauce were developed many centuries ago.

The development of the capital city

The emergence of the Song Dynasty in the 10th century saw a period of astounding social, political and culinary advancement. A new middle class emerged, with a consequent increase in demand for the finest materials, food and drink. The sprawling capital city became the domain of the seat of power. Today, Beijing still hosts a wealth of awe-inspiring dynastic sites from centuries ago.

Below *One of the many palaces that, together with lakes and gardens, comprise the Qing-Dynasty Summer Palace in Beijing.*

Right *Tea and the making of it has been part of daily life in China since the Qing dynasty.*

The influence of Mongols and Muslims

By the time of the powerful Mongol leader Genghis Khan in the 13th century, Mongol influences were strong in northern Chinese cuisine. From the earliest times, traditional Mongolian cuisine relied primarily on dairy products and meat. These nomadic people sustained their lives directly from the products of their work animals: horses, cattle, yaks, camels, sheep and goats. Milk, cream, cheese and mutton were important in their diet, and their favourite beverage was fermented mare's milk.

Meanwhile, Chinese Muslims were settling in the region. These settlers came mostly from the Hui, the Uyghur and the Mongolian minority tribes. As Muslims, they do not eat pork, and therefore lamb, beef and mutton historically made up their diet, and still do today. Hand-made noodles also originated among the Hui, who passed the skills on to imperial chefs, and these skills in turn filtered down to the general populace by the time of the late Qing Dynasty in the 19th century.

China opens up to the world

The 15th century saw China's emergence as a maritime power, and trade links were forged with other nations. Many foreign ingredients were brought back by seafarers and incorporated in the local cuisine. The Portuguese brought chilli peppers, which were embraced with relish, especially in the western areas. The construction of the Grand Canal in the 17th century facilitated the transportation of rice from the south.

The excesses of the Qing Dynasty

The Qing Dynasty, China's last dynasty, was founded by Nurhachi, and lasted nearly 300 years, from 1644 to 1912. As the first Qing Emperor, Nurhachi unified the scattered tribes of the north, and, under his rule, the Manchus and the Chinese were able to work peacefully together while maintaining their own distinct cultural traditions. The end of the Qing Dynasty in the 19th century was a turbulent period in Chinese history, with many uprisings.

One of the most interesting characters was the ruthless Empress Dowager Cixi (1835–1908). Her epicurean demands famously bordered on the obscene – she lived in such fear that she would be killed, she demanded that meals consist of up to 100 dishes, on the premise that it would have been difficult for someone to poison every dish! An appreciation for the art of cooking, eating and drinking tea became part of everyday Chinese life.

North China in modern times

The Qing Dynasty was overthrown in the early 20th century and a republic was created. Radical thinking would dominate Chinese history from now until the demise of Chairman Mao. He had reorganized the Communist Party of China (CPC) and initiated the Long March. After the Sino-Japanese War, during World War II, the CPC occupied most of the country from 1949 onwards.

By the end of the 20th century and into the 21st century, the People's Republic of China had changed the way Chinese people thought about their history. There was much social, cultural, land and economic reform. By the 1970s, most Western nations had established diplomatic ties with the republic.

Beijing is now one of the world's largest cities and the centre of China's political, artistic and culinary culture. China looks set to become the largest and most industrialized economy in the world, with Beijing at its heart. It continues to develop by looking outwards and to the future while respecting and preserving its own traditions.

MANDARIN CUISINE

Chinese regional cooking can be said to fall into four categories that roughly correspond to the four points of the compass: north, south, east and west. However, since it is in the nature of cooks to enjoy sharing ideas and recipes, these distinctions are not clear-cut. The northern school of Chinese cuisine is often termed Mandarin cuisine or Beijing-style cooking. Each individual province has its own food history and collection of recipes, but they have influenced each other for centuries, with similar ingredients dotting the menus.

A Tang Dynasty official once said: 'There is nothing that cannot be eaten. Making things edible is only a question of skilfully blending sweet, sour, bitter, salty and peppery flavours while cooking.' He was said to have stewed an old saddle and declared it very tasty. Apocryphal perhaps, but the story certainly sums up Chinese attitudes to food.

Beijing cuisine

The focus of northern Chinese cuisine is, of course, the Beijing school. Due to its imperial heritage of excess and affluence, Beijing cuisine came to be regarded as the most sophisticated yet robust style, using simple ingredients in an elaborate way. The elegance of Beijing cooking may not be apparent to the uninitiated; its simplicity masks clever techniques and a close understanding of the best produce of the region. Beijing cuisine is more influenced by the vast hinterland of Mongolia and beyond than it is by the sea on its eastern shores. Menus are thus rich in lamb, game and poultry, roasted or barbecued to tender perfection, as well as some fresh fish and shellfish from the ocean and rivers.

During the Manchu Dynasty, some 2,000 chefs were employed in the palace kitchens of the Forbidden City. The kitchens were divided into separate departments to make special food for picnics and travelling (emperors journeyed far and wide surveying their kingdom), and dawn and dusk sacrifices (Taoism and ancestor worship ruled the Chinese household), as well as having divisions just for rice and noodles, pickles and so on. Modern Beijing chefs are proud of their traditional hand-tossed noodles, and in the streets of Beijing you can still see noodle sellers dexterously balancing lumps of dough in their hands, kneading and transforming them into noodles before your eyes.

Further afield in northern China

The culinary traditions of this region include recipes from as far north as historical Manchuria, all the way down to Henan and Shandong.

A chief characteristic of northern cooking is the frequent and lavish use of soy bean paste. This is the basis of many other pastes, such as hoisin and yellow bean, which are used to enrich sauces.

Chefs in the northern regions attach great importance to the use of fresh meat and young

Left *Steamed breads made from wheat flour are a staple food in Shandong culinary tradition.*

vegetables when they are in season, because in the harsh terrain, with difficult transportation and no refrigeration, they needed to make the most of their local products.

Historically, rice was not used in northern China, but in more recent decades, due to modern transportation, northerners have discovered the versatility of this grain and adapted some of their traditional dishes to include rice.

Shandong cuisine is one of the most influential in China. The Beijing school, as well as other northern provincial styles, is thought to be a branch of Shandong style. Seafood is common, as well as wheat, millet, and other grains. Steamed breads are the choice staple.

Tianjin shares a similar cuisine with Beijing, though it uses more fish due to its coastal location. The flavours here are less heavy and rich than in Beijing.

Liaoning cuisine is derived from traditional native cooking styles, but it is also heavily influenced by Beijing and features strong tastes with much interplay of sweet and sour flavours. Winters here can be severe, resulting in a short growing season, and the difficult climate has helped to shape the cuisine. Most dishes are rich and hearty, with wine sauces and bean pastes. The cooks here coax much from wheat, millet and soybeans, transforming them into a wide range of breads, noodles and other starchy fillers that insulate the body against the cold winter.

Above *Street stalls can serve fabulously fresh foods; this seafood dish is offered in a Beijing night market.*

Jilin cuisine relies heavily on preserved foods and hearty fare owing to the harsh winters and relatively short growing seasons. Pickling is a common method of food preservation, and many households have large urns of pickled cabbage or mustard greens steeping away in their kitchens, as they do in Korea just across the border. Noodles tend to be the most common staple in Jilin cuisine.

Heilongjiang is a province criss-crossed by rivers, and its cuisine is famed for its fish.

ANCIENT RITUALS

All traditional Chinese festivals are based around the lunar calendar rather than the Gregorian calendar, and they hold a special place in the lives of the people. Many celebrations have remained unchanged for centuries, with traditional dress, music and dancing. The foods that accompany the festivals are also entrenched in age-old ritual. Whether in the form of special snacks, sweet cakes or savoury dishes, food plays an important role in many of the festivities.

Spring Festival or Lunar New Year

The most important festival in northern China is the Spring Festival or Lunar New Year. This falls between 21 January and 19 February, depending on the phases of the new moon. It heralds the beginning of the season of fruitfulness and anticipates the harvest to come. There are many ancient and colourful rites associated with the festival, as the various regional ethnic groups celebrate it differently.

Below *The Lantern Festival is the culmination of the Lunar New Year in northern China.*

Preparing the house

During the period from the 23rd day of the previous lunar month to the festival itself, every family cleans the house from top to bottom, and stocks up on fish, meat, nuts, seeds, sweets and fruits. Every market in northern China is ablaze with vibrant colours, from the plum blossoms, oranges and tangerines to red lanterns, whole roast pigs and melon seeds dyed red for good fortune.

Chinese characters for prosperity, luck and longevity are written on red scrolls and then pasted on doors and gates, and paper pictures adorn

windows. These messages originated in the Song dynasty (960–1279), and are written in a literary form that is characterized by concise sentences expressing wishes for the coming year.

The family reunion

On the eve of the Lunar Festival, every family will try their best to assemble at the home of the eldest member, where they enjoy the family reunion feast in which dumplings (jiaozi) are the most typical food. It is a time for old debts to be settled and differences smoothed over. It is an important Chinese belief that no one should go into the New Year bearing grudges or do anything that disrupts family harmony.

Devout Taoists burn joss sticks at ancestral altars and offer special dishes, nuts, fruits and flowers to the dead. Prayers are said to determine if the food has been received by the departed. As a mark of filial piety and respect, no one else can eat until it is agreed that the dead have received their gifts.

Festival food and flowers

At home, families cook a special chicken soup called 'broth of prosperity', filled with egg dumplings and pigeon eggs symbolizing gold and silver ingots. The chicken represents the phoenix rising from the ashes, or rebirth and rejuvenation. Pork, duck, chicken and fish constitute the 'four heroes of the table'. Braised, seasoned pork shoulder is known as 'mist of harmony'; a combination of sea cucumber, squid and seaweed is named 'jade of ink' or 'gold of darkness'; vermicelli noodles (fun si) are referred to as 'silvery threads of longevity'; platters of chicken wings are thought 'to soar one thousand miles'; and bamboo shoots are eaten because they grow so tall and inspire people to 'year after year, ascend to great heights'.

Floral tributes are another important feature of the festival. Two particularly popular flowers are narcissi, which stand for good fortune, and camellias, with their waxy blooms, which herald the coming of spring and symbolize youth and rebirth.

Lantern Festival

In the north of China, the Lunar New Year culminates in the Lantern Festival on the 15th day. Tianguan, the Taoist deity responsible for good fortune, loved all kinds of entertainment and celebrated his birthday on the 15th day of the first lunar month. In homage, fun-filled activities take place and lanterns are lit to create the ambience of gaiety that he so loved.

Above *Good luck messages for the Spring Festival are even painted on to chillies and fireworks.*

Moon Cake Festival

This mid-autumn festival is celebrated by both the Han people and many minority nationalities in North China. Moon worship can be traced back as far as the ancient Xia and Shang dynasties (2000–1066BCE). In subsequent years, Chinese people started the custom of baking 'moon cakes' stuffed with lotus seed paste as gifts for their relatives. As night falls, people come outside to gaze at the full moon, or walk by the lakes to celebrate the festival by watching the moon and its reflection.

Dragon Boat Festival

In northern China, as elsewhere in the country, this is celebrated on the fifth day of the fifth lunar month. Dumplings wrapped in lotus leaves are made and eaten; in these northern provinces, the dumplings are typically filled with both savoury meat mixtures and sweet bean paste.

NORTHERN CHINA

SOUPS & DIM SUM

ELEGANT SOUPS & FESTIVAL SNACKS

These days, Beijing is the political and economic hub of modern China. However, barely a decade ago, the soaring high-rises of the exuberant capital rose from a ground that was still busy with scenes from an agrarian past. Farmers pulled their ploughs across fields just a stone's throw from the urban concrete jungle, and it is this juxtaposition of old and new that underscores the essence of Mandarin cooking.

Whether simple or grand, every dish has its beginnings in the pastoral history of the region, and soups such as White Fungus & Chicken Soup, or Sour-and-Hot Lamb Soup, grace the farmer's table just as easily as the imperial dining room.

Some dim sum items like Prawn & Crab Wontons and Little Dragon Dumplings are now star items on menus in Chinese restaurants across the world. Each dim sum has been the result of a long culinary evolution, with connections to the magnificent dynasties for whom Beijing was the seat of power. The fact that they are simple and inexpensive to prepare explains their universal popularity. They do, however, require good-quality ingredients and skilful preparation, which is why they are so often associated with joyful festivals and time-honoured celebrations.

Steamed, shallow-fried or deep-fried, the dim sum offerings are usually also served with a dip that complements the flavours of the individual parcel, providing the perfect balance between sweet, salty, sour and spicy.

添丁甜醋
Black Vinegar
BLACK RICE VINEGAR)
VINAIGRE DOUCE
750g 600mL POIDS NET

CHICKEN & BAMBOO SHOOT SOUP

Bamboo shoots, especially when cooked from raw, have a strong husky taste that needs to be tempered. Even when using canned shoots, you should soak them in cold water for a few minutes before use so their aroma and taste is more subtle. They contrast well with the chicken here.

SERVES 4

1 egg white
1 skinless chicken breast, sliced into thin strips
115g/4oz bamboo shoots, sliced into fine julienne strips
1 chicken stock/bouillon cube
15ml/1 tbsp lard or white cooking fat, or vegetable oil
5ml/1 tsp grated fresh root ginger
15ml/1 tbsp light soy sauce
2.5ml/½ tsp ground black pepper
15ml/1 tbsp cornflour/cornstarch

1 Whisk the egg white until slightly frothy, then add the chicken strips and coat them in the egg white. Soak the bamboo shoots in cold water for 15 minutes, then rinse and drain.

2 Bring 800ml/scant 1½ pints/3½ cups water to the boil in a large pan and add the stock cube. Turn down to a simmer.

3 Meanwhile, heat the lard, cooking fat or oil in a wok and fry the ginger for 1 minute, then add the chicken. Stir-fry for 1 minute, then transfer to the hot stock. Add the bamboo shoots and simmer for 10 minutes. Add the soy sauce and pepper, and simmer for 5 minutes.

4 Blend the cornflour with 30ml/2 tbsp water and add to the soup. Stir until it thickens a little, then serve immediately.

Cook's Tips

- If you have fresh stock, use instead of the measured water and stock cube.
- Pork strips also work well; use a cut with streaky fat for flavour.

SERVES 4

40g/1½oz white fungus, soaked until very soft and with a jelly-like texture
800ml/scant 1½ pints/3½ cups boiling water
1 skinless chicken breast
2 garlic cloves, chopped
30ml/2 tbsp vegetable oil
30ml/2 tbsp light soy sauce
15ml/1 tbsp sesame oil
2.5ml/½ tsp ground white pepper

Cook's Tip

White fungus expands greatly and you will not need much. Any excess can be chilled for up to one week to be used in stir-fries and stews.

WHITE FUNGUS & CHICKEN SOUP

The rather odd-looking white fungus used here looks nothing like the rest of the mushroom family to which it belongs. Peachy white in colour, it could pass itself off as a natural sea sponge, but it is similar in texture to the more common cloud ear or wood ear mushrooms. Called bai mu er (or white cloud ears in translation), it is a characteristic ingredient of this soup from Beijing.

1 Strain the white fungus from its soaking liquid and trim off the brown woody parts. Cut the fungus into bitesize pieces.

2 Put the water into a large pan, add the chicken and cook for 15 minutes. Remove using a slotted spoon, and slice it thinly, then return to the stock and add the fungus. Simmer for 10 minutes.

3 Meanwhile, fry the garlic in the oil in a wok until it is light brown and fragrant, then add it to the soup along with the soy sauce, sesame oil and pepper. Adjust the seasoning to taste, and serve hot.

CHICKEN, PEA & TOMATO SOUP

This soup, also known as Three Pearls Soup, is a typical offering from Shandong province that is usually served during the cold winter months – Shandong winters can plunge to a shivering -15°C/5°F!

SERVES 4

1 skinless chicken breast
2.5ml/½ tsp salt
5ml/1 tsp cornflour/cornstarch
1 egg white
2 large tomatoes
30ml/2 tbsp sesame oil
1 chicken stock/bouillon cube
30ml/2 tbsp light soy sauce
45ml/3 tbsp Shaoxing wine or dry sherry
75g/3oz/¾ cup green peas

1 Mince or grind the chicken and mix it with the salt and cornflour. Whisk the egg white until slightly frothy, then add the ground chicken mixture and combine well.

2 Plunge the tomatoes into boiling water for 30 seconds, then refresh in cold water. Peel away the skins, remove the seeds and chop the flesh into small dice.

3 Bring 800ml/scant 1½ pints/3½ cups water to the boil in a pan, then add the sesame oil, stock cube, soy sauce and wine or sherry. When it is bubbling, use two teaspoons to drop in nuggets of chicken mixture so that they form small chicken balls.

4 Once all the chicken has been added, cook for 5 minutes. Add the tomatoes and peas and simmer for 5 minutes more. Serve hot.

Cook's Tips

- If you have it, use fresh stock instead of the measured water and stock cube.
- Tomatoes can be substituted with something of a similar colour, such as diced ham or some sliced red radishes.

SERVES 4

30ml/2 tbsp vegetable oil
2 garlic cloves, crushed
1 chicken stock/bouillon cube
1 skinless chicken breast, cut into 1cm/½in dice
250g/9oz raw prawns/shrimp, shelled
5ml/1 tsp cornflour/cornstarch
15ml/1 tbsp sesame oil
2.5ml/½ tsp salt
15ml/1 tbsp light soy sauce
30ml/2 tbsp Shaoxing wine or dry sherry
sliced spring onions/scallions, to garnish

Cook's Tip

Use fresh stock instead of the measured water and stock cube if you have it.

CHICKEN & PRAWN BALL SOUP

Chinese cuisine is known for combining unlikely ingredients, like the chicken and seafood used here – and the result is fabulous. This unusual soup hails from Henan and blends the two distinct flavours really well. Adding cornflour to minced meat or fish gives a smooth texture.

1 Heat the oil in a wok and fry the garlic for 2 minutes, then drain, reserving the oil, and set aside.

2 Bring 800ml/scant 1½ pints/3½ cups water to the boil in a large pan and add the reserved garlic-flavoured oil and the stock cube. Add the chicken and simmer for 15 minutes.

3 Meanwhile, mince the prawns and mix with the cornflour, sesame oil and salt. Shape the mixture into small balls and drop into the soup. Cook for 5 minutes more.

4 Add the soy sauce and wine or sherry, then simmer for a further 5 minutes, until the chicken and prawn balls are cooked through. Adjust the seasoning, then serve hot, garnished with spring onions.

TOFU & MINCED PORK SOUP

This classic blend of ingredients makes a style of soup that is popular not only regionally but also nationally. In Henan, Hunan and Sichuan, this soup is cooked with various seasonings, and some will be thickened with cornflour whereas others are enriched with wine. The Sichuan version is usually fiery with chopped chillies. It is a dish that allows a chef to use his or her ingenuity.

SERVES 4

- 250g/9oz/generous 1 cup minced/ground pork
- 5ml/1 tsp cornflour/cornstarch
- 2.5ml/½ tsp ground black pepper
- 30ml/2 tbsp light soy sauce
- 30ml/2 tbsp sesame oil
- 250g/9oz firm tofu, cut into 1cm/½in cubes
- 2 eggs, lightly beaten
- 1 spring onion/scallion, finely sliced on the diagonal, and 5ml/1 tsp preserved winter vegetable (tung cai or tong choy), to garnish

1 Mix the minced pork with the cornflour and pepper. Bring 800ml/scant 1½ pints/3½ cups water to the boil in a large pan and add the soy sauce and sesame oil. Add the tofu and pork, stirring vigorously with a pair of chopsticks to separate the pork so that it does not form uneven lumps. Simmer for 5 minutes.

2 When the pork is properly distributed, add the eggs to the soup, stirring. Cook for 5 minutes, or until the soup is thick and the egg is incorporated. You might get some streaks of egg, but this is fine.

3 Garnish with spring onion and winter vegetable, and serve.

Variation

If you like, you can garnish with fried garlic or shallots to give the soup a crispy and aromatic edge.

SERVES 4

1 meat stock/bouillon cube
200g/7oz lamb fillet, cut into 1cm/½in cubes
200g/7oz white radish or mooli/daikon, peeled and cut into 1cm/½in cubes
30ml/2 tbsp black or red rice vinegar
5ml/1 tsp Sichuan peppercorns, finely ground
30ml/2 tbsp dark soy sauce
2.5ml/½ tsp salt
15ml/1 tbsp cornflour/cornstarch
crispy fried onions, to garnish

Variation

For a less intense sourness, use malt or balsamic vinegar instead of Chinese red or black vinegar.

SOUR-AND-HOT LAMB SOUP

As hearty soups go, this Henan staple echoes that of Sichuan with its blend of hot and sour flavours. Lamb is the preferred meat in the north, but this soup is usually made with local goat, termed 'mutton', which can be a somewhat tough meat. In the West, 'mutton' refers to the meat of older sheep. Ordinary lamb will do as well and it also takes less time to cook.

1 Bring 1 litre/1¾ pints/4 cups water and the stock cube to the boil in a large pan. Add the lamb and cook, uncovered, for 25 minutes over a high heat. The stock will have reduced to about 800ml/scant 1½ pints/3½ cups and the lamb will be almost tender. Reduce the heat and simmer until tender to your liking.

2 Add the radish to the pan and simmer for 10 minutes, then add the vinegar, Sichuan peppercorns, soy sauce and salt.

3 Just before serving, blend the cornflour with a little water and add to the soup. Stir until thickened, garnish with the onions and serve.

PRAWN & CRAB WONTONS

Wontons are a Cantonese invention but, over time, they have become ubiquitous throughout China, with many different fillings. They are easy to make and lend themselves to deep-frying, steaming or adding to soups. It is important to work quickly when using wonton skins – do not let them stand for too long before cooking, as the skins can become brittle when exposed to the air.

MAKES 16 WONTONS

250g/9oz raw prawns/shrimp, shelled
250g/9oz white crab meat
115g/4oz tofu, finely mashed
1 egg, lightly beaten
30ml/2 tbsp light soy sauce
15ml/1 tbsp sesame oil
2.5ml/½ tsp ground black pepper
5ml/1 tsp cornflour/cornstarch
16 wonton skins
vegetable oil, for deep-frying (optional)
chilli sauce, to serve

1 Mince the prawns very finely. Mix with the white crab meat and mashed tofu, then mix in the beaten egg to combine well.Add the soy sauce, sesame oil, black pepper and cornflour. Stir again and divide into 16 equal portions.

2 Put one portion on to a wonton skin and fold up into a half-moon shape, sealing the edge with a little water. (If the skins are square, fold into triangles.) Repeat with the remaining skins.

3 Either deep-fry the wontons until golden brown, or steam them for 10 minutes. Serve with a chilli sauce dip.

Cook's Tip

Wonton skins are made from flour and are available in all Chinese stores, either as 7.5cm/3in squares or circles of the same diameter.

SERVES 4

2 skinless chicken breasts
15ml/1 tbsp sesame oil
15ml/1 tbsp light soy sauce
1 egg, beaten
25g/1oz/¼ cup sesame seeds
vegetable oil, for deep-frying

FOR THE DIP
4 garlic cloves, crushed
60ml/4 tbsp black or rice vinegar
a pinch of salt

Variation

You can also use minced chicken or pork. Shape into small balls and coat in sesame seeds before frying.

SESAME-COATED CHICKEN

The use of aromatic little sesame seeds is common all over China. They appear in dim sum, sprinkled on stir-fries, ground into a cream or, as here, are used to coat pieces of meat or chicken for deep frying. They have a delicate, nutty fragrance. Sesame seeds are either pale beige or jet black in colour. They brown quickly so watch your oil temperature when frying these delicious morsels.

1 To make the dip, mix the garlic with the vinegar in a small serving bowl and add the salt. Set aside.

2 Slice through each chicken breast horizontally to make 8 thin pieces (4 from each breast). Place between sheets of clear film and tenderize lightly by beating with a rolling pin. Season with sesame oil and soy sauce.

3 Place the egg in a shallow dish and the sesame seeds on to a plate. Coat each slice of chicken liberally with egg, then roll it in the sesame seeds to coat evenly. Pat the seeds on firmly.

4 Deep-fry the chicken rolls in the vegetable oil over a medium heat until golden brown. Serve with the vinegar and garlic dip.

LITTLE DRAGON DUMPLINGS

Within the dim sum menu, these dumplings, called xiao long bau in Mandarin, are among the most popular. How their name came about remains a mystery, but the dragon reigns supreme in Chinese culture as the most noble of heraldic beasts. Traditionally, these dumplings encase a small quantity of soup, the inclusion of which requires years of training. Imagine biting into a steamed dumpling that contains a tablespoon or two of hot soup! I'm afraid this is beyond all but the most expert chefs, and even dim sum houses rarely sell the soup – but this version is just as delicious and much simpler to make. High-gluten flour is necessary for making the dough; it is available in most Chinese stores.

1 To make the filling, roughly mince the prawns, then combine with the minced pork and cornflour.

2 Add 60ml/4 tbsp water, the Chinese celery, spring onions, soy sauce, sesame oil, pepper and sugar. Stir well until the flavours are incorporated, and set aside.

3 Mix the flours in a large bowl and pour over the boiling water. Add the oil or fat and stir with a wooden spoon. As soon as the mixture is cool enough to handle, knead it on a floured work surface for 5 minutes. You may find the dough rather crumbly, but, as you work, keep scooping up the floury parts and kneading them into the dough. Continue to knead until the dough is smooth and elastic (like bread dough).

4 Roll out the dough into a long sausage shape, 2cm/¾in in diameter. Cut it into 12 pieces and shape into small balls.

5 With a rolling pin, flatten each piece until it is paper-thin. The dough is very elastic, and will not break. Put a tablespoonful of filling on to each 'skin' and wrap it into a half-moon shape.

6 Seal and crimp the edges; shape each dumpling so that the crimped edge is lying across the top of the dumpling, rather like a Cornish pasty.

7 Place the dumplings on a lightly oiled plate that will fit into your steamer and steam for 15 minutes, or until the skins become slightly translucent. Serve warm with a soy or chilli sauce dip.

MAKES 12 DUMPLINGS

200g/7oz/1¾ cups high-gluten flour (gou garn fun), plus extra for dusting
75g/3oz/⅔ cup plain/all-purpose flour
200ml/7fl oz/scant 1 cup boiling water
30ml/2 tbsp vegetable oil, lard or white cooking fat
soy sauce or chilli sauce, to serve

FOR THE FILLING

200g/7oz raw prawns/shrimp, shelled
200g/7oz/1¾ cups minced/ground pork
5ml/1 tsp cornflour/cornstarch
15ml/1 tbsp chopped Chinese celery
3 spring onions/scallions, roughly chopped
30ml/2 tbsp light soy sauce
30ml/2 tbsp sesame oil
2.5ml/½ tsp ground black pepper
a pinch of sugar

Cook's Tip

This is a basic dough that can be used for a whole range of dim sum dumplings. The consistency of the cooked dough depends on how thinly you roll it out.

LOTUS LEAF PARCELS

Rice, fish, shellfish, meat and all manner of other ingredients are cooked, wrapped in lotus leaves and steamed. Dim sum is made all over China; Cantonese dim sum menus invariably feature lotus leaf-wrapped glutinous rice, but other regional cuisines use lotus leaves to wrap sweet desserts and, in Beijing, they encase delectable savoury fillings, as here. The leaves are very large but can be trimmed to make more dainty parcels, each one a delicious combination of pork, lotus seeds and succulent quail's eggs.

MAKES 4 PARCELS

30ml/2 tbsp vegetable oil
2 garlic cloves, crushed
200g/7oz belly pork, diced
8 Chinese mushrooms, soaked and chopped
16 canned lotus seeds
16 quail's eggs, hard-boiled and peeled
20g/¾oz chopped Chinese celery leaves
30ml/2 tbsp oyster sauce
30ml/2 tbsp Shaoxing wine or dry sherry
5ml/1 tsp ground black pepper
15ml/1 tbsp dark soy sauce
10ml/2 tsp cornflour/cornstarch
2 lotus leaves, soaked until soft

Cook's Tips

• Quail's eggs take about 3 minutes to hard-boil.

• If the lotus leaves appear to be brittle, use a double layer for extra strength. They are actually quite resilient and do not tear easily.

1 Heat the oil in a wok and fry the garlic for 2 minutes. Add the pork and stir-fry for 3 minutes, or until sealed all over.

2 Add the mushrooms and lotus seeds, then fry for 2 minutes.

3 Add the quail's eggs, celery leaves, oyster sauce, wine or dry sherry, pepper and soy sauce, then stir gently so that you do not break up the delicate quail's eggs.

4 Blend the cornflour with 75ml/5 tbsp water and add to the pan. Stir until the cornflour thickens the sauce and binds all the ingredients together. Transfer the filling to a bowl and set aside.

5 Trim the lotus leaves and cut each into two fan-shaped halves. Divide the mixture between the four leaf halves (there should be about 45ml/3 tbsp on each), making sure there is a good mixture of pork, mushrooms, lotus seeds and quail's eggs in each parcel.

6 Wrap each parcel securely, folding over the sides. Steam for 15 minutes, then serve immediately – the parcels should be opened at the table.

BEEF & MUSHROOM DUMPLINGS

This is a typical steamed dim sum dish from Henan. It is sometimes made with minced lamb, here, however, minced beef is used. Seasonings for dumplings in northern China tend to be on the heavy, heady side with the addition of wine to give a rich flavour.

MAKES 12 DUMPLINGS

200g/7oz/1¾ cups high-gluten flour (gou garn fun), plus extra for dusting
75g/3oz/⅔ cup plain/all-purpose flour
200ml/7fl oz/scant 1 cup boiling water
30ml/2 tbsp vegetable oil, lard or white cooking fat

FOR THE DIP

25g/1oz fresh root ginger
1 spring onion/scallion
75ml/5 tbsp black vinegar
a pinch of salt

FOR THE FILLING

400g/14oz/3½ cups minced/ground beef
5ml/1 tsp cornflour/cornstarch
30ml/2 tbsp oyster sauce
15ml/1 tbsp Shaoxing wine or dry sherry
2.5ml/½ tsp ground black pepper
1 spring onion/scallion, finely chopped
15ml/1 tbsp ground ginger
8 Chinese mushrooms, soaked until soft

1 To make the dip, peel and grate the ginger, and chop the spring onion very finely. Place them in a bowl with the black vinegar and salt. Mix well, then set aside.

2 To make the filling, mix the beef with the cornflour, oyster sauce, wine or sherry, pepper, onion and ginger. Chop the mushrooms finely and stir into the beef mixture. Set aside.

3 Mix the flours in a mixing bowl, and pour over the boiling water. Add the oil or fat and stir with a wooden spoon. As soon as the mixture is cool enough to handle, transfer it to a floured work surface and knead for 5 minutes. You may find the dough rather crumbly, but, as you work, keep scooping up the floury parts and kneading them into the dough. Continue to knead until the dough is smooth and elastic (it should have the consistency of bread dough).

4 Roll out the dough into a long sausage shape, 2cm/¾in in diameter. Cut it into 12 pieces and shape into small balls.

5 With a rolling pin, flatten each piece until it is paper-thin. It will not break, as the dough is very elastic. Put a tablespoonful of filling on to each 'skin' and fold it over into a half-moon shape.

6 Seal and crimp the edges; shape each dumpling so that the crimped edge is lying across the top of the dumpling, rather like a Cornish pasty.

7 Place the dumplings on a lightly oiled plate that will fit into your steamer and steam for 15 minutes, or until the skins become slightly translucent. Serve warm with the dip.

BEEF CAKES

Usually served at festive occasions, these are a meaty variation of onion pancakes, which are more common on international dim sum menus. Beef cakes make hearty snacks and can be made well in advance, then warmed up or lightly re-fried. They go very well with the vinegar, ginger and spring onion dip on page 54. The traditional recipe uses solid pork fat, chopped and added to the beef for crunch and succulence. This may be hard to find, so use bacon rind as a substitute – it gives a nice, smoky flavour.

MAKES 8 CAKES

200g/7oz/1¾ cups plain/all-purpose flour, plus extra for dusting
45g/1½oz/⅓ cup tapioca flour
a pinch of salt
200ml/7fl oz/scant 1 cup boiling water
15ml/1 tbsp vegetable oil, plus about 75ml/5 tbsp for frying

FOR THE FILLING
200g/7oz/1¾ cups minced/ground beef
75g/3oz pork fat or bacon fat, finely chopped
45ml/3 tbsp water
30ml/2 tbsp light soy sauce
2.5ml/½ tsp ground black pepper
2 spring onions/scallions, finely chopped
25g/1oz fresh root ginger, grated
a pinch of sugar
30ml/2 tbsp sesame oil

1 Place all the filling ingredients in a bowl and mix together thoroughly. Pinch off a small ball, cook it quickly in a small pan, then taste to check the seasoning. Adjust the seasoning, if necessary. Cook the rest of the mixture in the pan for about 5 minutes, until the beef is cooked through, then set it aside to cool.

2 Sift the flours into a mixing bowl and add the salt. Mix well and gradually add the boiling water, stirring well. Add the 15ml/1 tbsp vegetable oil. When cool enough to handle, transfer the dough to a floured surface and knead for 5 minutes, until smooth.

3 Roll out the dough into a long sausage shape and cut it into eight pieces. Flatten each piece into a thin circle about 9cm/3½in in diameter, or as thin as you can make them without breaking them.

4 Divide the beef filling mixture between the eight circles (there should be a heaped tablespoonful on each). Draw the sides in to the centre, then pinch to seal firmly. Smooth the sealed sides, then shape and flatten them gently into round, flat cakes with the sealed side underneath.

5 Heat a frying pan with the 75ml/5 tbsp oil and fry the cakes, in batches, for 3 minutes on each side, or until golden brown. Add more oil, if necessary, for each batch, but heat it up before adding the remaining cakes. Serve hot.

NORTHERN CHINA

FISH & SHELLFISH

DELICATE RIVER & OCEAN CATCHES

I am lucky enough to have spent much time in Beijing, and had the pleasure of dining in some of the city's most famous restaurants, as well as sampling various dishes from its street food menus; I came away as sated with one as the other. Throughout history, the cuisine of Beijing has been influenced greatly by that of Shandong, so good-quality fish and shellfish dishes take pride of place on many a restaurant menu. Prawns and scallops are cooked to perfection, and both sea and river fish are given special treatment by top chefs.

At the other end of the spectrum is the wonderful street food; the glorious sights, smells and sounds showcasing the vendors' deft wok skills as they stir up fiery concoctions of succulent fish and shellfish. From Sweet-and-sour Prawns to scrumptious Fish & Tofu Mock Crab Cakes, the seafood plates from this region are exemplary. Carp, trout, snapper and grouper get the most refined treatment wherever they are cooked, regardless of having a street or restaurant backdrop.

With chefs becoming more travel-wise, and learning from each other, there is today a stronger influence from other regions being displayed in Mandarin food. A perfect example is the Mongolian Seafood Steamboat, which is now cooked in restaurants across the country. Its beginnings, in the remote northern areas, may have been traditionally rustic, but as a dining experience it has become the epitome of creative Chinese cooking. It makes a truly memorable meal.

RAW FISH SALAD

In the past, I must admit that the provinces in the extreme north-east did not hold much fascination for me. This is possibly because so little is known about Liaoning, Heilongjiang and Jilin. Several years ago, however, two doctors from Liaoning moved in next door to me, and from them I learned about this far-flung region and sampled the wonderful food. Liaoning cuisine is heavily influenced by Beijing and features strong tastes, with interplay between sweet-and-sour flavours. This Liaoning raw fish salad is integral to Lunar New Year repasts, as its name, yu sheng, means 'rebirth' in Mandarin.

SERVES 4

450g/1lb salmon fillet, skin removed (wild salmon is best)
20g/¾oz pickled ginger
75g/3oz green carrot (see Cook's Tip)
75g/3oz iceberg lettuce
75g/3oz white radish or mooli/daikon
2 spring onions/scallions
fried garlic or shallots, to garnish

FOR THE DRESSING
a pinch of ground cinnamon
2.5ml/½ tsp Chinese five-spice powder
45ml/3 tbsp rice vinegar
2.5ml/½ tsp sugar
2.5ml/½ tsp salt
15ml/1 tbsp sesame oil
30ml/2 tbsp plum sauce

1 Freeze the salmon for 20 minutes so that it firms up – this will make slicing it much easier. Using a sharp knife, slice the fillet thinly across the grain, then chill the fish slices while you prepare the vegetables.

2 Slice the pickled ginger, green carrot, iceberg lettuce, radish or mooli and spring onions into extremely fine pieces and soak them in cold water for 15 minutes.

3 Drain the vegetables thoroughly and transfer them to a serving bowl. Add the sliced salmon, and toss everything together.

4 Mix all the dressing ingredients together in a small bowl, then taste and adjust the seasonings as necessary. Pour the dressing over the fish and vegetables, and toss to coat everything.

5 Serve, garnished with fried garlic or shallots.

Cook's Tips

• Green carrots are not unripe carrots but a specific genus. They are a seasonal ingredient and therefore not always available. Use normal carrots instead, if you cannot find them.
• For any raw fish dish it is essential to buy the freshest fish possible. Always check with your fishmonger first that it is suitable for eating raw.

SWEET-AND-SOUR PRAWNS

Shandong is believed to be the birthplace of sweet-and-sour dishes but, being such an enticing blend, the technique has crossed many borders, and is a particular favourite in Shanxi. Northern chefs insist that the sauce should contain kaoliang wine vinegar made from sorghum and millet. If unavailable, use any rice wine vinegar.

SERVES 4

- 450g/1lb king prawns/jumbo shrimp, shelled, but with tails left on
- 30ml/2 tbsp cornflour/cornstarch
- 45ml/3 tbsp vegetable oil
- 15ml/1 tbsp crushed garlic
- 1 onion, quartered
- 12 water chestnuts, drained and sliced in half
- ½ red bell pepper, thinly sliced

FOR THE SAUCE

- 60ml/4 tbsp kaoliang wine vinegar or rice wine vinegar
- 45ml/3 tbsp plum sauce
- 2.5ml/½ tsp sugar
- 200ml/7fl oz/scant 1 cup water or stock

1 Make a cut down back of each prawn. Pull out the vein then rinse. Dust the prawns with cornflour, then shake off the excess. Heat the oil in a wok and fry the prawns until they are just cooked and have a crispy coating. Remove with a slotted spoon, and set aside.

2 Fry the garlic in the oil remaining in the wok for 2 minutes, then add the onion. Fry for 2 minutes, then add the water chestnuts and red pepper. Fry for 1 minute.

3 Blend the sauce ingredients together, then add to the pan. Bring to the boil and cook for 1 minute. Add the prawns and stir to incorporate. Cook for 2 minutes, then serve hot.

SERVES 4

450g/1lb prawns/shrimp, shelled
200g/7oz firm tofu
15ml/1 tbsp sesame oil
15ml/1 tbsp light soy sauce
5ml/1 tsp ground black pepper
2 eggs, lightly beaten
45ml/3 tbsp cornflour/cornstarch
vegetable oil, for deep-frying

FOR THE ACCOMPANIMENTS
English (hot) or Dijon mustard
chilli sauce
black vinegar
1 cucumber, sliced into thin rounds
75g/3oz pickled ginger

Variation

You could also use good-quality thawed frozen prawns/shrimp to make these cutlets.

PRAWN CUTLETS

In the inland areas of northern China, you can see fishermen in small boats throwing large nets into the rivers and dragging them to catch prawns, as well as squid and fish. The catches are often sold immediately on the riverbanks. Prawns this fresh have an extra-special flavour when they are cooked. Most of us are not able to buy prawns direct from the fishing boat, but do try to buy the freshest ones you can.

1 Place the dips and accompaniments into bowls and set aside.

2 Mince or grind the prawns finely. Mash the tofu with a fork until smooth, then mix with the prawns. Add the sesame oil, soy sauce and pepper and blend well, then add the egg and stir to combine.

3 Shape into four patties, each about 6cm/2½in in diameter and 1cm/½in thick.

4 Heat the oil for deep-frying in a wok or deep-fryer. Coat the patties with cornflour and deep-fry until golden and cooked through. Serve immediately with the dips and accompaniments.

FRESH SCALLOPS & PAK CHOI

Here is a dish with a true imperial flavour, one that Shandong citizens are extremely proud of as a banqueting dish. Use the best scallops you can find – each one large and about 1cm/½in thick. The pak choi here is of the smaller variety, sometimes called Taiwan pak choi, with pale green stalks and dark green leaves. This dish is sometimes served with the pak choi arranged to look like the spokes of a wheel, with the scallops on top.

SERVES 4

300g/11oz pak choi/bok choy
300g/11oz fresh scallops
15ml/1 tbsp vegetable oil
15ml/1 tbsp crushed ginger
15ml/1 tbsp crushed garlic
15ml/1 tbsp sesame oil
30ml/2 tbsp Shaoxing wine or dry sherry
2.5ml/½ tsp salt
2.5ml/½ tsp ground black pepper
a pinch of sugar

1 Trim off the hard root end of the pak choi, while leaving them whole and as complete stalks. Bring a pan of water to the boil and blanch the pak choi for 1 minute, then lift out using tongs and drain. Blanch the scallops in the water for 20 seconds, then drain.

2 Heat the oil in a wok and fry the ginger and garlic for 2 minutes. Add the sesame oil, wine or sherry, salt, pepper and sugar. Stir for 30 seconds, then add the pak choi and scallops.

3 Continue to stir-fry for 1 minute, then serve immediately.

Variation

Vegetables such as mangetouts/snow peas, courgettes/zucchini and green beans also make a good contrast. Blanch them in place of the pak choi.

SERVES 4

350g/12oz meaty white fish, such as cod or halibut
115g/4oz tofu, mashed
1 egg, lightly beaten
15ml/1 tbsp cornflour/cornstarch
15ml/1 tbsp rice flour
2 spring onions/scallions, finely chopped
3 garlic cloves, crushed
15ml/1 tbsp sesame oil
15ml/1 tbsp light soy sauce
2.5ml/½ tsp ground black pepper
vegetable oil, for deep-frying
thinly sliced cucumber and a chilli sauce dip, to serve

Variation

You can use a mixture of vegetables: mushrooms, marrow or large zucchini, and carrots are particularly suitable.

FISH & TOFU MOCK CRAB CAKES

The Chinese believe that a 'mock' anything is better than none at all. These patties were concocted for the Empress Dowager of the Qing Dynasty who, being fond of crab that was unfortunately then out of season, was served a fishy version. Her Imperial Majesty loved it, and no heads rolled.

1 Steam the fish for 10 minutes, until opaque and cooked through, then cool, flake and mash until fine. Thoroughly mix the tofu and egg with the fish, cornflour and rice flour.

2 Add the spring onions, garlic, sesame oil, soy sauce and pepper. Stir well and shape into small patties about 4cm/1½in in diameter and 1cm/½in thick.

3 Deep-fry until golden brown, and serve with sliced cucumber and a chilli sauce dip.

MONGOLIAN SEAFOOD STEAMBOAT

Probably one of the oldest forms of social entertainment, a Mongolian steamboat is a really festive winter warmer, a convivial repast meant for at least six people, all seated around the bubbling centrepiece. Steamboats are also called hot-pots and date back to early Mongolian times. The technique also appears in Japan and Korea, both countries having their own styles, known as shabu shabu and sinsulo respectively. The traditional utensil is a large brass pan with a built-in funnel in the centre; charcoal is put in the space directly under the funnel and lit. Stock is then poured into the moat and, when it boils, diners immerse the foods of their choice to cook in the stock, using wire mesh spoons. Today, steamboats may be charcoal or electric with a thermostatic control.

SERVES 8–10

2 litres/3½ pints/9 cups boiling water (plus extra on the boil)
2 meat stock/bouillon cubes

FOR THE SEASONINGS, DIPS AND GARNISHES

a small bottle of light soy sauce
Chinese wine or sherry
6 garlic cloves, crushed and fried until golden brown
6 spring onions/scallions, chopped
small dishes of chilli sauce
small dishes of black vinegar
ground black pepper

FOR THE STEAMBOAT

250g/9oz tofu, cubed
450g/1lb skinless chicken breast, thinly sliced
450g/1lb prawns/shrimp, shelled
30 prepared fish balls
4 pieces of fish cake
100g/3¾oz mung bean noodles, soaked
1 large Chinese cabbage, sliced into small pieces
50g/2oz golden needles (or dried lily buds), soaked and trimmed
200g/7oz pig's liver, thinly sliced

1 Preheat the steamboat and fill the moat with boiling water. Add the stock cubes. Have a kettle standing by with more water for topping up as the meal goes on.

2 While the stock is simmering, arrange all the seasonings, dips, garnishes and the main ingredients in plates and bowls set around the steamboat. Provide a wire mesh spoon, a porcelain soup spoon, chopsticks and a soup bowl for each person.

3 To cook and eat, each person puts a few pieces of selected raw foods into their wire mesh spoon and dunks it into the boiling stock until cooked, then they transfer it to their individual soup bowl and add seasonings, dips and garnishes to their liking.

4 When all the ingredients are eaten, the stock will be extremely rich. It can then be ladled into each bowl to be drunk with a spoon.

Cook's Tips

• Stock/bouillon cubes are handy, but for better flavour it pays to make your own stock.

• The selection of ingredients is entirely personal and there is no set formula. Meat, seafood, poultry, vegetables – anything you fancy can be used as a steamboat ingredient.

GARLIC EEL CUTLETS

In Hebei, garlic is used generously in dishes and is particularly suited to fish with strong flavours, such as mackerel and tuna steaks. In northern China the favoured fish is carp or eels. The latter are used in this dish because the aromatics enhance without overpowering the flavour of the fish. Always buy eels absolutely fresh and ask the fishmonger to gut and fillet them for you.

SERVES 4

450g/1lb prepared eel cutlets
45ml/3 tbsp vegetable oil
6 garlic cloves, sliced
3 spring onions/scallions, sliced into 5cm/2in lengths
15ml/1 tbsp black bean sauce
5ml/1 tsp sugar
15ml/1 tbsp Shaoxing wine or dry sherry
4 dried Chinese mushrooms, soaked and sliced
shredded lettuce, to serve

1 Wash and pat the eel pieces dry on kitchen paper. Heat the oil in a wok and fry the garlic until golden brown. Drain and set aside.

2 In the remaining oil, fry the spring onions for 1 minute, then add the black bean sauce, sugar, wine or sherry, and the mushrooms. Stir for 1 minute, then add 200ml/7fl oz/scant 1 cup water.

3 Bring to the boil, then add the eel and simmer for 10 minutes, or until well soused. Sprinkle fried garlic all over, then serve on a bed of shredded lettuce.

Variation

For a less intense sourness, use malt or balsamic vinegar instead of Chinese red or black vinegar.

SERVES 4

2 large river trout
5ml/1 tsp salt
15ml/1 tbsp cornflour/cornstarch
vegetable oil, for deep-frying
15ml/1 tbsp vegetable oil
4 garlic cloves, crushed
1 green bell pepper, thinly sliced
2 spring onions/scallions, white parts only, finely chopped
45ml/3 tbsp strong Chinese wine, such as kaoliang or rose-flavoured wine, or dry sherry
5ml/1 tsp sugar
15ml/1 tbsp sesame oil
2.5ml/½ tsp ground black pepper

Variations

You could also use trout fillets; you will need about 400g/14oz. Any other firm-fleshed fish fillets can be cooked in the same way.

TROUT IN WINE SAUCE

River trout are plentiful in the tributaries of northern China. In Jilin, the fish is often soused with wine, ginger and bean sauces. Trout is a fish with a subtle taste and it fries well. It has a slippery skin, but rubbing it vigorously with salt improves the texture. A strong Chinese wine, such as kaoliang or rose-flavoured wine, will give the best flavour, but you can use dry sherry at a push.

1 Rub the trout with salt and rinse. Pat dry with kitchen paper, then coat with cornflour. Heat the oil for deep-frying in a wok or deep-fryer. Deep-fry the fish until crisp, then set aside.

2 Heat the 15ml/1 tbsp oil in a wok and gently fry the garlic for 2 minutes. Add the pepper and spring onions and fry for 1 minute.

3 Add the wine or sherry, sugar, sesame oil, pepper and 200ml/7fl oz/scant 1 cup water, and bring to the boil. Add the trout and simmer for about 3 minutes, until the fish is cooked through and the cornflour coating has thickened the sauce. Serve immediately.

STEAMED FISH WITH GINGER

When fish is absolutely fresh, the best way to cook it is by steaming it with hints of fresh ginger. A few pickled sour plums will heighten the subtle flavour of delicate fish such as sea bass, mullet or snapper, and a few shreds of salted mustard greens add a salty touch to the ensuing 'soup' that is created after steaming. This is a classic dish of Tianjin, a municipality that borders Hebei province and Beijing.

SERVES 4

- 2 whole sea bass, mullet or red snapper, cleaned
- 25g/1oz fresh root ginger, finely shredded
- 2 pickled sour plums
- 50g/2oz salted mustard greens, finely shredded
- 30ml/2 tbsp sesame oil
- 15ml/1 tbsp light soy sauce
- 2.5ml/½ tsp ground black pepper

Cook's Tips

- The soup from this dish is delicious spooned over plain boiled rice.
- For special occasions, drizzle 30ml/1 tbsp cognac or brandy over the fish before serving.

1 Pat the fish dry on kitchen paper, then make several deep cuts diagonally into the thickest part of each one and place them into a deep plate or dish that will fit into your steamer.

2 Sprinkle the ginger all over the fish and put the sour plums on top. Add the salted mustard greens around the edge, tucking them in under the fish, with a few shreds on top.

3 Drizzle the sesame oil and soy sauce all over, then sprinkle over the ground black pepper. Sprinkle water along the sides of the plate or dish.

4 Steam the fish for 15 minutes, until it is cooked through. There will be a small amount of soup in the bottom of the plate or dish. Serve immediately.

MONKFISH IN YELLOW BEAN SAUCE

Yellow bean sauce is a favourite seasoning in Chinese cooking, and it is often used in the north, where soya beans are widely grown. It is less salty than black bean sauce, and it marries well with vinegar, sugar and pepper. Whole preserved yellow beans can be used instead of the sauce – crush them with a fork before using.

SERVES 4

- 450g/1lb monkfish tail, filleted and membrane removed
- 45ml/3 tbsp vegetable oil
- 25g/1oz fresh root ginger, grated
- 2.5ml/½ tsp ground black pepper
- 30ml/2 tbsp yellow bean sauce
- 15ml/1 tbsp rice vinegar
- 2 spring onions/scallions, sliced
- 5ml/1 tsp cornflour/cornstarch (optional)

1 Cut the monkfish into medallions about 2cm/¾in thick. Heat the oil in a wok and shallow-fry the fish for 3 minutes, turning once so that each piece is well sealed. Set aside.

2 In the remaining oil, fry the ginger for 2 minutes and add the pepper, yellow bean sauce and vinegar. Stir for 1 minute then add the fish, spring onions and 300ml/½ pint/1¼ cups water.

3 Simmer for 10 minutes, or until the sauce is slightly thick. If you prefer it thicker, blend the cornflour with water and add it to the sauce, then cook for 1 minute. Serve hot.

Variation

Other firm-fleshed fish such as halibut, cod and snapper can be used in this dish, but you may need to reduce the cooking time.

SERVES 4

2 whole snappers, about 450g/1lb total weight, cleaned
30ml/2 tbsp tapioca flour
vegetable oil, for deep-frying

FOR THE FIRST DIP
25g/1oz fresh root ginger
3 garlic cloves
2 spring onions/scallions
30ml/2 tbsp rice vinegar
15ml/1 tbsp yellow bean sauce
5ml/1 tsp sugar
45ml/3 tbsp warm water
5ml/1 tsp oil

FOR THE SECOND DIP
15ml/1 tbsp plum sauce
15ml/1 tbsp rice vinegar
15ml/1 tbsp hoisin sauce
15ml/1 tbsp crushed garlic
45ml/3 tbsp warm water

CRISPY FISH

Most northern fish dishes are bathed in some sort of sauce; unadorned deep-fried fish is not common within the cuisine. There are exceptions, however, when the fish is of a superior quality and absolutely fresh. Even then, there is always a dip or two, or even a pouring sauce.

1 To make the first dip, chop the ginger, garlic and spring onions until very fine, then mix with the vinegar, yellow bean sauce, sugar, water and oil. Set aside in a small serving bowl.

2 To make the second dip or sauce, mix all the ingredients in a small pan and warm over gentle heat for 2 minutes. Set aside in another small serving bowl.

3 Snip off any protruding fins from the fish, then coat in flour.

4 Heat the oil for deep-frying in a wok or deep-fryer, then deep-fry the fish until golden brown. (You may need to do this in batches.) Fillet and serve, either with the two dips on the side or with the second dip poured over as a sauce.

RED COOKED FISH

The technique of cooking seafood in a rich red sauce is typical of North China, especially Beijing. The colour is created through a mixture of hoisin sauce, preserved red beancurd and Shaoxing wine. This is a well-travelled dish and, in other regions, it takes on whatever indigenous ingredients are available. The term hong shao is also applied to many meat and poultry dishes that are cooked in a similar sauce to this.

SERVES 4

- 450g/1lb snapper or grouper fillets
- 5ml/1 tsp cornflour/cornstarch, plus extra to coat
- 45ml/3 tbsp vegetable oil
- 3 garlic cloves, sliced
- 75g/3oz leeks, thinly sliced
- 30ml/2 tbsp Shaoxing wine or dry sherry
- 15ml/1 tbsp preserved red beancurd, mashed
- 15ml/1 tbsp hoisin sauce
- 15ml/1 tbsp rice vinegar
- 2.5ml/½ tsp sugar
- plain rice, to serve

Variation

For a more traditional dish, deep-fry a whole fish, head and tail intact, and then pour the sauce over while the fish is still hot.

1 Cut the fillets into bitesize pieces, then coat lightly with cornflour.

2 Heat the oil in a wok and shallow-fry the fish pieces until they are cooked through and have a crisp coating. Set aside and keep warm.

3 In the remaining oil, fry the garlic for 2 minutes, then add the leeks. Stir-fry for 1 minute.

4 In a small bowl mix together the wine or sherry, preserved red beancurd, hoisin sauce, rice vinegar, sugar and 200ml/7fl oz/scant 1 cup water, then add the mixture to the pan.

5 Cook, stirring, for 1 minute, then add the fish. Allow the fish to heat through for 30 seconds.

6 Blend the teaspoonful of cornflour with a little water, and add it to the pan. Stir for 1 minute, or until the sauce thickens, then serve hot, with plain rice.

HOT-AND-SOUR CARP

This strongly flavoured Hebei dish is typical of the region's cooking. The national capital of Beijing is situated within Hebei, and this province is also where the Great Wall ends. Hebei is a mountainous plateau, traversed by tributaries of the Yellow River, which explains the area's fondness for freshwater fish.

SERVES 4

- 1 large whole carp, about 450g/1lb
- 5ml/1 tsp salt
- vegetable oil, for deep-frying
- 25g/1oz cloud ear/wood ear mushrooms, soaked until soft
- 25g/1oz fresh root ginger, grated
- 2 garlic cloves, crushed
- 15ml/1 tbsp chilli oil
- 30ml/2 tbsp rice vinegar
- 15ml/1 tbsp yellow bean sauce
- 2.5ml/½ tsp sugar
- 2 spring onions/scallions, chopped

1 Clean the carp but leave it whole. Make diagonal cuts across the thickest part of the fish and rub the skin and cuts with salt. Heat the oil for deep-frying in a wok or deep-fryer, then deep-fry the carp until crisp and cooked through. Set it aside and keep warm. Reserve 30ml/2 tbsp of the deep-frying oil in the wok.

2 Slice off and discard the woody parts from the cloud ears, then chop the fungus. In a wok, heat the reserved deep-frying oil, and fry the ginger and garlic for 2 minutes.

3 In a small bowl, blend the chilli oil with the vinegar, yellow bean sauce, sugar and 200ml/7fl oz/scant 1 cup water, then add it to the wok. Bring to the boil and add the cloud ears and spring onions. Cook for 1 minute, then pour over the fried fish. Serve immediately.

Variation

You can coat the fish in cornflour before deep-frying to give it a crisp coating. When the sauce is hot, add the fish and simmer until cooked through. The cornflour will thicken the sauce.

SERVES 4

1 large carp, about 450g/1lb (head removed, if you like)
5ml/1 tsp salt
vegetable oil, for deep-frying, plus 30ml/2 tbsp
25g/1oz fresh root ginger, grated
3 garlic cloves, sliced
30ml/2 tbsp sesame paste (see Cook's Tip) or tahini
15ml/1 tbsp Shaoxing wine or dry sherry
2.5ml/½ tsp sugar
chopped spring onions/ scallions, to garnish

Cook's Tip

Make sesame paste by finely grinding 40g/1½oz sesame seeds. Cook over low heat in 30ml/2 tbsp oil and a little water to form a paste.

CARP IN GINGER SESAME SAUCE

The sesame sauce used in this Beijing dish is made from sesame paste, which is sold in all Chinese stores. Sesame paste has the same consistency as smooth peanut butter and it has a strong flavour. It blends well with aromatics like ginger or garlic. In this recipe, it gives the fish a subtle and slightly spicy flavour, accentuated by the wine or sherry.

1 Clean the carp. Make diagonal cuts across the thickest part of the fish and rub the skin and cuts with salt. Heat the oil for deep-frying in a wok or deep-fryer, then deep-fry the carp until crisp and cooked through. Set it aside and keep warm.

2 Heat the 30ml/2 tbsp oil in a wok or frying pan and fry the ginger and garlic for 2 minutes. Add the sesame paste, wine or sherry, sugar and 200ml/7fl oz/scant 1 cup water, and bring to the boil.

3 Lower the fish into the wok or pan and simmer for 2 minutes, then turn it over once so that every part of the fish is bathed in the sauce. Serve hot, garnished with chopped spring onions.

NORTHERN CHINA
POULTRY

SMOKED, STEAMED & STIR-FRIED

Symbolism is hugely important in Chinese culture, and it is particularly apparent in the culinary arts. Chicken is often inextricably linked with the mythical phoenix, and is a popular choice at Chinese New Year banquets and weddings, the heraldic creature giving its symbolic name to the dish known as Phoenix Chicken.

In the northern provinces, much use is made of smoking as a special technique, and chefs particularly embrace the flavour imparted by tea leaves which are often used as an aromatic smoking material.

Flavoursome ingredients such as chestnuts, ginger and rice wine add many dimensions of taste to a humble chicken, duck or game bird. Kwei-Fei Chicken, commonly known as 'drunken chicken', is a firm favourite and a shining example of the northern love of poultry soused in plenty of wine.

While game is quite rare in much of China's provincial cooking, quail is a favourite bird in the rural northern areas. It is usually cooked in a marinade of wine, ginger, garlic and sesame oil, which lifts the taste of the bird to great heights.

The most famous Mandarin dish has to be Peking Duck. Although the city is now known as Beijing, the older English spelling of Peking is preserved in the name of this age-old recipe. Although the ingredients list is very short (just duck and Chinese maltose or clear honey), it takes a long time to prepare, and there are many restaurants in Beijing that specialize in producing it.

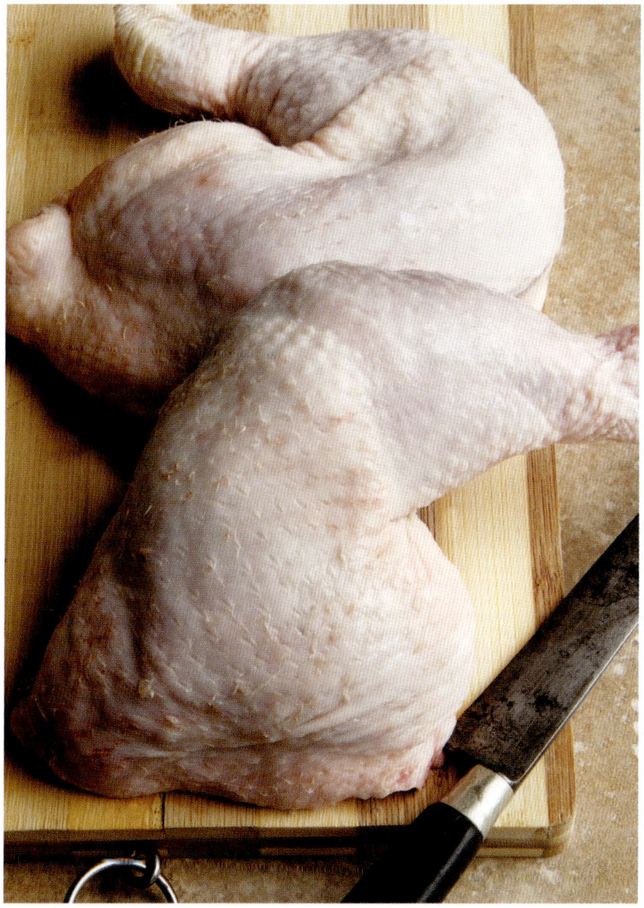

CHICKEN WITH WALNUTS

Although they do not appear often in Chinese cooking, walnuts are a particular favourite of the northern regions, as they are farmed widely there. The indentations in walnuts make an attractive contrast to the smoothness of sliced chicken, and they soak up the rich yellow bean sauce beautifully. This Shandong dish has influenced the cuisine of Guangzhou, where chicken is fried with cashew nuts. This is a fairly sweet dish because of the inclusion of Chinese maltose, which is normally used as a rub for Peking Duck. Use clear honey if this is unavailable.

SERVES 4

115g/4oz/1 cup walnuts
15ml/1 tbsp vegetable oil
3 garlic cloves, sliced
400g/14oz skinless chicken breast, cut into 1cm/½in cubes
5ml/1 tsp sugar
5ml/1 tsp rice vinegar
15ml/1 tbsp Chinese maltose or clear honey
15ml/1 tbsp yellow bean sauce
shredded lettuce, to serve

1 Wash and drain the walnuts, removing any excess skins. Heat the oil in a wok and fry the garlic for 2 minutes, or until golden brown.

2 Add the chicken and stir-fry for 2 minutes. Add the walnuts and sugar, then stir-fry until the walnuts are slightly caramelized.

3 Add the rice vinegar, maltose or honey, yellow bean sauce and 75ml/5 tbsp water, then stir vigorously until the sauce is fairly thick and the chicken and walnuts are well coated. Serve immediately, on a bed of shredded lettuce.

Variations

- You can replace the walnuts with diced carrots, celery or water chestnuts, if you like.
- You could also use cubed pork or duck in place of chicken.

SERVES 4

150g/5oz water chestnuts, ginkgo nuts, lotus seeds or lychees (see Cook's Tip)
15ml/1 tbsp vegetable oil
½ large onion, sliced or chopped
400g/14oz skinless chicken breast, cut into 1cm/½in cubes
30ml/2 tbsp hoisin sauce
2.5ml/½ tsp ground black pepper
15ml/1 tbsp rice vinegar
5ml/1 tsp cornflour/cornstarch
fresh coriander/cilantro, to garnish
plain boiled rice, to serve

Cook's Tip

If you are using canned lychees, add 15–30ml/1–2 tbsp of the juice to the sauce for extra fragrance.

CHICKEN WITH HOISIN SAUCE

From Henan comes a dish that uses hoisin sauce (also called sweet bean sauce) to wonderful effect. Many northern chefs make their own hoisin sauce by blending yellow bean sauce with sugar until the correct level of sweetness is achieved. For this dish, you can choose the complementary ingredient to work with the chicken – water chestnuts, ginkgo nuts, lotus seeds or lychees, for example – all of which will give delicious results.

1 Cut the water chestnuts, ginkgo nuts, and lotus seeds or lychees into bitesize pieces. Heat the oil in a wok, add the onion and stir-fry for 3 minutes.

2 Add the chicken and stir-fry for 2 minutes. Add the hoisin sauce, black pepper and rice vinegar, and cook, stirring, for 2 minutes.

3 Blend the cornflour with 90ml/6 tbsp water and add to the wok. Stir until the sauce has thickened slightly.

4 Serve immediately with rice, garnished with fresh coriander.

TEA-SMOKED CHICKEN

Not only is tea fundamental to Chinese cuisine, this beverage is also central to Chinese culture. Infusing foods with the delicate perfume of different teas is practised throughout the country, despite the complicated method involved. Five-star restaurants in major cities offer this dish, but it is within the reach of home cooks with some adaptation. What is important is the length of time needed to chill the seasoned chicken – about 2 hours. Semi-fermented oolong tea from the Fujian province gives the best flavour.

SERVES 4

5ml/1 tsp salt
1 whole chicken, about 1.5kg/3¼lb
45ml/3 tbsp Shaoxing wine or dry sherry
30ml/2 tbsp sesame oil
25g/1oz fresh root ginger, crushed
noodles, to serve (optional)
fresh coriander/cilantro, to garnish (optional)

FOR THE SMOKING MATERIALS
50g/2oz tea leaves of your choice
150g/5oz/1¼ cups plain/all-purpose flour
115g/4oz/½ cup demerara/raw sugar
75g/3oz barley

1 Rub the salt all over the breast of the chicken, then chill it for about 2 hours.

2 Rinse the chicken thoroughly and pat it dry with kitchen paper. Cut down the breastbone to spatchcock the chicken, and press it down to flatten it out. Make several deep scores into the breast.

3 Line a large wok with a double sheet of foil. Prepare the smoking materials by mixing the tea leaves with the flour, sugar and barley, and spread the mixture out evenly on top of the foil.

4 Place a bamboo steamer (large enough to take the chicken) over the top of the smoking materials so that there is space between the tea mixture and the steamer. Put the chicken directly on to the bamboo steamer and cover with the lid.

5 Turn the heat to high and, when you see smoke emanating from the lid, adjust the heat so that there is no scorching. Smoke the chicken, covered, for 25 minutes, until cooked through, turning the chicken halfway through. Transfer the chicken to a plate.

6 Mix the wine or sherry, sesame oil and ginger in a bowl, then rub this mixture over the chicken. Leave to marinate for 15 minutes.

7 Place the chicken in a steamer placed over a pan of simmering water and steam for 1 hour, until fragrant.

8 Serve immediately with some cooked noodles and garnished with fresh coriander, if you like.

FIVE-SPICE SMOKED CHICKEN

Smoking foods does not always involve tea – smoked seafoods, for example, are infused with the fragrance of different materials such as barley grains, Sichuan peppercorns, aromatic woods and pungent spices. It is a blank canvas, and you can create your own flavours for different foods. My particular favourite smoking materials for chicken are Sichuan peppercorns, cloves, cinnamon and coriander seeds, which mirror the Chinese five-spice powder in the marinade. This combination is a personal preference rather than a traditional one, but the method and resulting taste are quintessentially Chinese.

SERVES 4

5ml/1 tsp salt
2 skinless chicken breasts
15ml/1 tbsp soy sauce
30ml/2 tbsp Shaoxing wine or dry sherry
3 garlic cloves, crushed
a pinch of Chinese five-spice powder
15ml/1 tbsp sesame oil
shredded spring onion/scallion, to garnish
chilli sauce dip, to serve

FOR THE SMOKING MATERIALS
15 cloves
2 sticks cinnamon, broken
150g/5oz/1¼ cups plain/all-purpose flour
115g/4oz/½ cup demerara/raw sugar
15ml/1 tbsp coriander seeds

1 Rub the salt all over the chicken breasts, then chill them for about 15 minutes.

2 Pat the chicken with kitchen paper to dry it thoroughly. Make a few gashes into the thickest part and rub with soy sauce and wine or sherry.

3 Line a large wok with a double sheet of foil. Mix together all the smoking materials, then spread the mixture evenly on top of the foil.

4 Put a bamboo steamer in the wok. It should be large enough to hold the chicken on top while leaving space between the smoking mixture and the steamer.

5 Put the chicken directly on to the bamboo steamer and cover with the lid. Turn the heat to high and, when you see smoke emanating, adjust the heat so that there is no scorching.

6 Smoke the chicken, covered, for 15 minutes, until partially cooked, turning the chicken halfway through. Transfer the chicken to a plate.

7 Mix the garlic, Chinese five-spice powder and sesame oil in a bowl, and rub this mixture over the chicken. Leave to marinate for 15 minutes.

8 Place the chicken in a steamer placed over a pan of boiling water and steam for 20 minutes, until fragrant.

9 Slice and serve, garnished with shredded spring onions and accompanied by a chilli sauce dip.

Variation

For a different flavour profile, replace the smoking materials suggested here with a selection of woody herbs and aromatics, such as thyme, lavender and rosemary.

PHOENIX CHICKEN

The 'phoenix' in this dish is a symbolic name for chicken; dim sum restaurants sometimes feature 'phoenix claws', and I have amusing recollections of unwary Western friends ordering what they thought was a grand delicacy and receiving chicken feet! This recipe uses chicken joints.

SERVES 4

1 chicken, about 1.5kg/3¼lb, cut into 8 large joints and trimmed of fat or protruding bones
5ml/1 tsp salt
45ml/3 tbsp vegetable oil
3 garlic cloves, sliced
40g/1½oz fresh root ginger, grated
15ml/1 tbsp black bean sauce
5ml/1 tsp sugar
2.5ml/½ tsp ground black pepper
1 leek, finely sliced
15ml/1 tbsp cornflour/cornstarch

1 Rub the chicken pieces with salt. Heat 30ml/2 tbsp of the oil in a wok and shallow-fry the chicken for 5 minutes, turning constantly until well sealed and the skin shrinks a little. Remove and set aside.

2 Clean the wok and heat the remaining oil. Fry the garlic and ginger for 2 minutes. Add the black bean sauce, sugar and pepper, and cook for 1 minute.

3 Return the chicken and add 250ml/8fl oz/1 cup water. Cook over high heat for 5 minutes, then add the leek. Reduce the sauce by half.

4 Blend the cornflour with a little water and add this to the sauce. Stir and cook for a further 2 minutes, until the chicken is cooked through and the sauce is thickened. Serve hot.

Variation

Other sauces can be used instead of black bean sauce to create different flavours: try plum sauce for a slightly sweet hint or oyster sauce for a more savoury finish.

SERVES 4

1 whole chicken, about 1.5kg/3¼lb
120ml/4fl oz/½ cup Shaoxing wine or dry sherry
45ml/3 tbsp light soy sauce
vegetable oil, for deep-frying
45ml/3 tbsp port
4 spring onions/scallions
2.5ml/½ tsp salt
1 chicken stock/bouillon cube

Cook's Tip

Use a pan that just cradles the bird; most Chinese chefs prefer to slow-cook in a wok, as the curved shape is ideal for this.

Variation

As a final touch, you could add some sliced mushrooms during the last 5 minutes of cooking.

KWEI-FEI CHICKEN

Commonly called 'drunken chicken', this is a Beijing classic. Yang Kwei-Fei was an empress of the Tang Dynasty in the 7th century, noted not only for her beauty but also for her fondness for a tipple. If legend is to be believed, she was known to instruct her palace chefs to souse chicken with huge quantities of wine.

1 Rub the chicken inside and out with 15ml/1 tbsp each of the Shaoxing wine or sherry, and the soy sauce. Set aside for 20 minutes.

2 Heat the oil in a wok and deep-fry the chicken until the skin takes on a crisp, golden-brown hue. Lift out the chicken and drain.

3 Boil a large pan of water, and blanch the chicken for 4 minutes, then drain again. Transfer to a deep pan or wok with the remaining wine or sherry and soy sauce, port, spring onions and salt.

4 Add the stock cube and enough water to just cover the chicken. Simmer, covered, for 1½ hours, turning once or twice. Serve hot.

OIL-SOAKED CHICKEN

This classic Beijing dish actually originated in Fujian – it was probably poached by visiting emperors from the capital city. Although the name might imply greasiness, it simply means that the chicken has been deep-fried after an initial steaming. This 'twice-cooked' method is commonly used and produces an incredibly crisp yet succulent bird.

SERVES 4

- 4 chicken thighs and 4 chicken drumsticks
- 5ml/1 tsp salt
- 30ml/2 tbsp strong Chinese wine or sherry
- 15ml/1 tbsp cornflour/cornstarch
- vegetable oil, for deep-frying
- sliced pineapple or cucumber, to serve

FOR THE SAUCE

- 30ml/2 tbsp hoisin sauce
- 45ml/3 tbsp pineapple juice
- 15ml/1 tbsp rice vinegar
- 15ml/1 tbsp light soy sauce
- 120ml/4fl oz/½ cup water
- 15ml/1 tbsp cornflour/cornstarch

1 Rub the chicken all over with salt and wine or sherry. Place into a steamer and steam for 15 minutes, until partially cooked. Set aside.

2 When the chicken is cool enough to handle, coat each piece with cornflour. Heat the oil for deep-frying, and deep-fry the chicken for 8 minutes, until golden brown and cooked. Remove and keep warm.

3 To make the sauce, blend all the sauce ingredients in a wok. Bring to a gentle boil.

4 Pour the sauce over the chicken and serve immediately, with sliced pineapple or cucumber.

SERVES 4

1 chicken, about 1.5kg/3¼lb (or 450g/1lb joints or breasts)
plain noodles or rice, to serve

FOR THE MARINADE
30ml/2 tbsp Shaoxing wine or dry sherry
30ml/2 tbsp light soy sauce
15ml/1 tbsp sesame oil
2.5ml/½ tsp ground black pepper
2 spring onions/scallions, halved
15ml/1 tbsp ginger purée
15ml/1 tbsp garlic purée

Cook's Tip

You can add a few tablespoonfuls of water to the chicken when it steams, if you like, to give you a light soup to serve alongside the chicken to moisten the noodles or rice, and to give extra fragrance.

STEAMED CHICKEN WITH WINE

This is a northern Chinese favourite that has transcended borders, and even the seas – steamed chicken with wine is now a staple in just about every Chinese home, wherever it may be. It is a simple dish; if you have all the ingredients, all you need to do is sit and watch it steam. The results belie the simplicity of preparation. A whole chicken is used here, but you can use joints or breasts, if you prefer.

1 If using a whole chicken, cut down the breastbone to spatchcock it and press it down to flatten it out. Combine all the marinade ingredients in a deep bowl (big enough to take the chicken).

2 Add the chicken and cover it with the marinade, then leave it to marinate for 15 minutes. Transfer the chicken to a deep plate or ceramic dish that will fit into your steamer. Spread the spring onions from the marinade on top.

3 Steam, covered, for 1 hour, or until cooked through. Serve with plain rice or noodles, and with any liquid left in the bottom of the plate, if you like (see Cook's Tip).

BRAISED CHICKEN & CHESTNUTS

This all-time favourite combination of flavours can also be used with duck, but chicken is equally tasty and it takes half the time to cook. The floury texture and sweetness of chestnuts complements chicken superbly. These are commonly sold canned or vacuum-packed. Raw chestnuts are time-consuming and fiddly to prepare, with only a slight difference in taste, though you can use raw chestnuts, if you like (see Cook's Tip).

1 Remove the skin from the chicken thighs and cut each thigh in half. Heat the vegetable oil in a wok, add the garlic and stir-fry for 2 minutes, or until golden brown.

2 Add the sesame oil and the chicken and stir-fry for 2 minutes or until the chicken is sealed all over. Add the chestnuts, spring onions, hoisin sauce, oyster sauce and preserved red beancurd, and cook, stirring vigorously, for 2 minutes, until well blended.

3 Add 200ml/7fl oz/scant 1 cup water and bring to the boil. Simmer for 20 minutes, or until the sauce is very thick and the chicken pieces are cooked through. Serve immediately.

SERVES 4

450g/1lb boneless chicken thighs
30ml/2 tbsp vegetable oil
3 garlic cloves, chopped
15ml/1 tbsp sesame oil
20 cooked and peeled chestnuts, canned or vacuum-packed (see Cook's Tip)
2 spring onions/scallions, chopped
15ml/1 tbsp hoisin sauce
30ml/2 tbsp oyster sauce
1 cube preserved red beancurd, mashed

Cook's Tip

If you prefer to prepare your own chestnuts, soak them overnight, then boil for 15 minutes. Cool and remove the skins – this can be fiddly, as the skins are buried in the crevices of each nut.

SERVES 2–4

4 prepared quails
15ml/1 tbsp dark soy sauce
30ml/2 tbsp vegetable oil
3 garlic cloves, chopped
25g/1oz fresh root ginger, chopped
15ml/1 tbsp sesame oil
30ml/2 tbsp oyster sauce
15ml/1 tbsp Chinese wine or sherry
5ml/1 tsp sugar
5ml/1 tsp ground black pepper
15ml/1 tbsp cornflour/cornstarch
plain rice, to serve

Cook's Tip

If you deep-fry the marinated quails briefly, it will shorten the simmering time and also result in the skin having a crispier texture.

BRAISED QUAILS

Game birds are more popular in China's rural north (where quail, partridge and other wild birds thrive) than they are in towns. Quails, however, often appear on banquet menus today. They are very small birds and you need two for an adult main course portion or one as an appetizer. The important thing to remember with game is that the meat is quite dry and needs slow cooking to moisten and tenderize it. Braising does this perfectly.

1 Rub the quails with the dark soy sauce. Heat the oil in a wok, add the garlic and ginger and stir-fry for 2 minutes, until golden.

2 Add the sesame oil, oyster sauce, wine or sherry, sugar and pepper, and cook, stirring, for 1 minute. Add the quails and cook, turning them a few times, for 3 minutes.

3 Add 500ml/scant 1 pint/2 cups water and cook over high heat for 20 minutes, until the sauce is slightly reduced. Blend the cornflour with a little water and add to the wok to thicken the sauce. If you like your quails a little pink, they should be ready to serve now; if you like them more well-done, continue cooking a little longer.

4 Serve the quails hot, with the sauce poured over, accompanied by plain rice.

BRAISED DUCK IN PEPPERY SOY SAUCE

The sauce in this dish is similar to the southern Chinese pork dish called Mists of Harmony, which uses caramelized dark soy sauce and pepper. As duck is richer than pork, here the fattiness is cut with pepper and cloves. It does take time to cook, but is well worth the effort. If you have a pressure cooker, this will take about half the time and requires half the quantity of water. Use the thickest dark soy sauce you can find; the variety labelled sweet soy sauce (kecap manis in Indonesian) is excellent.

SERVES 6–8

1 oven-ready duck
5ml/1 tsp salt
30ml/2 tbsp vegetable oil
15ml/1 tbsp sugar
75ml/5 tbsp dark soy sauce
5ml/1 tsp Chinese five-spice powder
10ml/2 tsp ground black pepper
6 cloves
2 thumb-sized pieces of fresh root ginger, bruised
chilli and garlic sauce, sliced cucumber and plain boiled rice, to serve

Cook's Tip

If you make this dish the day before, chill the sauce overnight The next day the duck fat will have solidified and can be scooped off.

1 Pat the duck dry with kitchen paper, then rub salt all over, inside and out. Heat the oil in the largest wok you have and caramelize the sugar until it froths and turns a dark brown.

2 Roll the duck in the hot sugar, turning over once or twice until the skin is coated in the sugar. Add the soy sauce and continue to cook, bathing the duck in it, for 3 minutes.

3 Add the remaining ingredients and 2 litres/3½ pints/9 cups water, and bring to the boil. Transfer to a deep, high-sided pan and simmer the duck, covered, for at least 2 hours, checking regularly to see if you need to top up with hot water.

4 When the duck is tender, remove it from the sauce. Turn up the heat and boil to reduce the sauce by about half.

5 Allow the duck to cool enough so that you can chop it into smaller pieces or debone it. Serve with the reduced sauce on the side, a sharp chilli and garlic sauce, sliced cucumber, and plain rice.

PEKING DUCK

If ever there was a dish that won international plaudits, this is the one. It is completely different from crispy aromatic duck, which hails from Sichuan province and is often confused with its Beijing cousin. Why the name has never been changed to Beijing Duck is purely due to tradition. Few restaurants outside of China serve true Peking Duck, as it requires around 48 hours of preparation and does not lend itself to short-order cooking, unlike the Sichuan recipe. Regardless, it is worth all the effort. Many restaurants in Beijing specialize in nothing but this dish, and it is served over a three-course meal – duck with pancakes, then stir-fried duck with vegetables, and, lastly, the meaty carcass goes into the kitchen to emerge as a soup to finish the meal.

SERVES 8

1 oven-ready duck
30ml/2 tbsp Chinese maltose or clear honey

TO SERVE
hoisin sauce
5 spring onions/scallions, sliced very finely into 5cm/2in strips
½ cucumber, peeled and sliced very finely into 5cm/2in strips
24 Mandarin pancakes (see recipe pages 126–7, or use store-bought ones)

1 A day or two before serving, wipe the duck dry with kitchen paper both inside and out, and hang it in a warm place to dry overnight or for up to 2 days.

2 On the morning of roasting, use a hair-dryer to thoroughly dry the duck skin all over. This will result in really crispy skin that pops away from the meat when you carve the duck.

3 Boil a kettleful of water. Put the duck in a large colander and pour boiling water all over and inside the duck. Do this twice so that the duck skin shrinks and some fat is removed.

4 Melt the honey or maltose in a small pan and add 200ml/7fl oz/scant 1 cup water. Bathe the duck with this mixture, then leave it to dry for at least 6 hours.

5 Preheat the oven to 200°C/400°F/Gas 6. Put the duck on a rack in a roasting pan and roast for 1¼ hours. The duck meat should still be a little pink inside; do not overcook.

6 Meanwhile, put the hoisin sauce into several small sauce dishes and arrange the spring onions and cucumber on small serving plates on the table. Lightly steam each stack of 8 pancakes for 3 minutes.

7 Serve the duck displayed in all its dark gold glory (see the picture on page 80), and carve at the table, taking away squares or strips of skin and meat. Each diner then spreads a pancake with a little hoisin sauce, tops it with spring onions and cucumber, adds some Peking duck, and rolls the pancake up to eat.

Cook's Tips

- Mandarin pancakes are sold frozen in Chinese stores. They can be microwaved individually for 10 seconds.
- Any leftover duck is delicious when shredded and stir-fried with crunchy vegetables.
- Boil the carcass in a large pan of water to use as a stock or for soup.

NORTHERN CHINA
MEAT

HEARTY STEWS & WARMING SPICES

While Chinese city-dwellers today have the privilege of buying meat at large wet markets or modern supermarkets, many people in rural northern China depend on local butchers or their own small herds. With poverty still widespread in these areas, many of the cuts of meat available to locals are the cheaper, tougher ones. This explains why many dishes are marinated with wine, bean sauces and aromatics, and stewed until fork-tender.

Being China's favourite meat, pork features on the menu in the form of perfectly cooked Stewed Spare Ribs, which have earned their cachet world-wide, and Mu Shu Pork, which has become a signature dish in nearly every Chinese restaurant around the globe.

Lamb and mutton are put to excellent use in northern Chinese cookery. Locally, the word mutton is often used to refer to goat meat, rather than to meat from older sheep, though goat can be difficult to get hold of and mutton can work just as well.

Offal meats like liver and kidney get special treatment, with wine and herbs cutting their strong flavours. Spices like cumin, caraway, cloves and pepper have been employed by chefs in the region for hundreds of years, as they have been available here since the first century.

This is a region that is home to many Chinese Muslims, for example the Uyghur peoples of Xinjiang, who eschew the eating of pork. Lamb, mutton, goat and beef are their meat mainstays, which is another reason why they have become quintessential to the regional cuisine.

STEWED SPARE RIBS

With pork being the most popular meat throughout China, there is never any shortage of spare ribs cut in precisely the way they should be, with every rib having the perfect ratio of lean meat to fat. The best way to coax maximum succulence from them is to braise or stew them in a rich seasoning; deep-frying, as many restaurants tend to do, can render them quite dry. If you marinate them for a few hours, they will be ambrosial.

SERVES 4

500g/1¼lb spare ribs, cut into 5cm/2in lengths
15ml/1 tbsp vegetable oil
3 garlic cloves, crushed
25g/1oz fresh root ginger, grated
shredded spring onion/scallion, to garnish

FOR THE MARINADE

30ml/2 tbsp dark soy sauce
5ml/1 tsp sugar
30ml/2 tbsp oyster sauce
30ml/2 tbsp Shaoxing wine or dry sherry
30ml/2 tbsp plum sauce
2.5ml/½ tsp ground black pepper
a pinch of Chinese five-spice powder

1 Combine the marinade ingredients in a bowl, add the ribs and coat in the marinade. Leave to marinate for 4–6 hours or overnight.

2 Heat the oil in a wok, then add the garlic and ginger and stir-fry for 2 minutes. Add 450ml/¾ pint/scant 2 cups water, the ribs and all the marinade, and cook, stirring, for 2 minutes.

3 Transfer all the contents to a pan with a tight-fitting lid and bring to the boil. Cook over high heat for 15 minutes, then turn down to medium heat and simmer for 40 minutes, until the sauce is very thick and glossy. Serve garnished with shredded spring onion.

SERVES 4

450g/1lb boneless leg of pork
5ml/1 tsp salt
150g/5oz turnip, cut into bitesize pieces
15ml/1 tbsp vegetable oil
2 garlic cloves, crushed
30ml/2 tbsp black bean sauce
15ml/1 tbsp sesame oil
5ml/1 tsp sugar
noodles or plain boiled rice, to serve

Variation

Root vegetables, such as swede/rutabaga, carrots or mooli/daikon, can be used instead of turnip, for a tasty alternative.

PORK & TURNIPS

Like other root vegetables, turnips are used in numerous ways in China: boiled, steamed, mashed, dried and pickled. Chopped and salted turnips are a favourite garnish in Chinese regional cuisines – imparting a salty and smoky tang to congee, soups and stir-fries. When stir-fried, they have a lovely crunch with a subtle, sweet flavour.

1 Remove the skin from the pork and slice the meat into thin strips. Rub salt all over the turnips and set aside to sweat for 20 minutes. Squeeze handfuls of turnip to remove as much moisture as possible.

2 Heat the oil in a wok, add the garlic and stir-fry for 2 minutes. Add the pork and continue to stir-fry vigorously for 2–3 minutes.

3 Add the black bean sauce, sesame oil and sugar, and stir-fry for 1 minute. Add 120ml/4fl oz/½ cup water and bring to a boil. Stir for 3 minutes, or until the pork is nearly cooked and turning opaque.

4 Add the turnip and cook, stirring, for 2 minutes, until the pork and turnips are cooked through. Serve hot with noodles or rice.

MU SHU PORK

Also known as 'egg flower pork', this dish plays an important role as a filling for pancake rolls and other northern breads in Mandarin cooking. Mu shu is the name for the dried lily buds, or golden needles, that are integral to the dish, together with cloud ear mushrooms. The name also reflects the hint of gold in the eggs that are added. This is a time-honoured dish that features on the menus of restaurants within and beyond China.

SERVES 4

- 350g/12oz lean pork with a little fat
- about 120ml/4fl oz/½ cup vegetable oil
- 25g/1oz cloud ear/wood ear mushrooms, soaked until soft
- 25g/1oz golden needles, soaked and trimmed
- 15ml/1 tbsp light soy sauce
- 15ml/1 tbsp dark soy sauce
- 2.5ml/½ tsp sugar
- 4 eggs, lightly beaten
- 10 Chinese yellow chives, cut into 5cm/2in lengths
- 15ml/1 tbsp Shaoxing wine or dry sherry
- 15ml/1 tbsp sesame oil
- plain boiled rice, to serve

FOR THE MARINADE

- 2.5ml/½ tsp salt
- 5ml/1 tsp light soy sauce
- 2.5ml/½ tsp ground black pepper
- 15ml/1 tbsp Shaoxing wine or dry sherry
- 5ml/1 tsp cornflour/cornstarch
- 30ml/2 tbsp water

1 Cut the pork into thin strips, each about 6cm/2½in long. Mix the marinade ingredients together in a shallow dish, then add the pork and mix to coat all the strips thoroughly. Marinate for 15 minutes.

2 Heat half the vegetable oil in a wok, add the pork and stir-fry for 3 minutes, until it is sealed all over and almost cooked through. Transfer the pork to a heatproof bowl and set aside.

3 Add a little more oil to the wok, if needed, then add the cloud ear mushrooms and golden needles and stir-fry for 1 minute.

4 Add the soy sauces and sugar, and cook, stirring, for 1 minute. Transfer the mixture to the heatproof bowl containing the pork.

5 Clean the wok and add a little more oil. Add the eggs and stir (as you would for scrambled eggs) until they start to solidify. Add the chives, wine or sherry, and sesame oil, and cook, stirring, for 1 minute.

6 Add the fried pork, cloud ears and golden needles, then continue to cook, stirring, for 1–2 minutes, until the pork is cooked through and everything is incorporated. Serve with plain boiled rice.

Cook's Tip

The different ingredients are partly cooked, then combined at the end so that they will cook evenly.

Variation

This pork dish can also be used as a filling for Mandarin pancakes – see pages 126–7.

SWEET-AND-SOUR LAMB

Although lamb is not normally associated with sweet-and-sour flavours, this is popular in Shanxi province among the Chinese Muslims, who don't eat pork. The origin of 'sweet-and-sour' is usually attributed to eastern chefs, though northerners refute this, claiming it to be an invention of palace chefs in the Forbidden City. No one knows for sure, but every chef has their own version.

SERVES 4

300g/11oz lean lamb, cut into 1cm/½in cubes
15ml/1 tbsp cornflour/cornstarch
vegetable oil, for deep-frying, plus 30ml/2 tbsp
15ml/1 tbsp sliced fresh root ginger
15ml/1 tbsp sliced garlic
1 large onion, quartered
15ml/1 tbsp yellow bean sauce
15ml/1 tbsp sugar
15ml/1 tbsp plum sauce

1 Coat the lamb cubes with cornflour. Heat the oil for deep-frying in a wok or deep-fryer and fry the lamb until golden brown and cooked through. Set aside.

2 In a clean wok, heat the 30ml/2 tbsp oil, add the ginger and garlic, and stir-fry for 1 minute. Add the onion and fry for 2 minutes, or until soft and the onion layers separate.

3 Blend the yellow bean sauce with the sugar, plum sauce and 200ml/7fl oz/scant 1 cup water, then add to the pan. Bring to the boil, then add the fried lamb. Simmer for 2–3 minutes, or until well incorporated and the sauce is glossy and thick. Serve hot.

Variation

Add ingredients such as carrots, mushrooms or even lychees to bulk up the dish. To strike a proper balance, use about 75g/3oz of each vegetable or fruit and the dish will feed up to six people.

SERVES 4

200g/7oz lamb fillet
3 eggs, lightly beaten
15ml/1 tbsp fresh root ginger, grated
15ml/1 tbsp lard, white cooking fat or vegetable oil
15ml/1 tbsp Shaoxing wine or dry sherry
15ml/1 tbsp light soy sauce
2.5ml/½ tsp ground black pepper
shredded spring onion/scallion, to garnish
plain boiled rice or steamed bread, to serve

Cook's Tip

A pair of chopsticks, with the aid of your wok ladle, will break up and scramble the eggs as they should be.

CASSIA LAMB

The evergreen tree cassia is indigenous to southern China and South-east Asia. It has tiny, yellow flowers with four petals, and it has a close relative, known as 'true cinnamon', which is primarily used for its aromatic bark. In fact, there is neither cassia nor cinnamon in this dish – the name alludes to the colour of the cooked eggs only. Such is Chinese symbolism that the recipe name can tell an entirely different story from the ingredients list!

1 Cut the lamb into thin strips and tenderize it with a meat mallet or the blunt edge of a cleaver, until it is almost shredded. Place the lamb in a bowl, add the eggs and ginger, and mix well.

2 Heat the lard, white cooking fat or vegetable oil in a wok, add the lamb mixture and stir-fry over high heat for 1 minute, or until the eggs are scrambled.

3 Add the wine or sherry, soy sauce and pepper, and cook, stirring, for 1 minute more. The dish will have a distinct yellow hue. Garnish with shredded spring onions and serve with rice or steamed bread.

CUMIN & CARAWAY LAMB

Spices have been used in northern Chinese cooking for centuries. After all, the silk and spice routes were opened as far back as the 1st century BCE, and spices such as cumin, caraway, pepper, cloves and cinnamon were traded like precious stones. The Uyghur people in Xinjiang and the nomadic Mongols have been using spices in their cooking for a long time. Collectively, they are known as the Hui, and are affiliated historically to the Sunni branch of Islam.

SERVES 4

300g/11oz lean lamb
5ml/1 tsp ground cumin
vegetable oil, for deep-frying, plus 30ml/2 tbsp
15ml/1 tbsp cornflour/cornstarch
175g/6oz Chinese cabbage, sliced into strips
15ml/1 tbsp ground ginger
2.5ml/½ tsp caraway seeds, finely ground
15ml/1 tbsp yellow bean sauce
15ml/1 tbsp sugar
2 large tomatoes, quartered

1 Cut the lamb into thin strips and rub them with the cumin and 2 tbsp of oil. Heat the oil for frying in a wok or deep-fryer, then coat the lamb with the cornflour and deep-fry until crisp. Set aside to drain on kitchen paper.

2 Blanch the cabbage in boiling water for 2 minutes, then drain and set aside.

3 In a clean wok, heat the 30ml/2 tbsp oil and fry the ginger and caraway seeds for 1 minute. Add the yellow bean sauce and the sugar and stir-fry for 30 seconds.

4 Add the lamb and cabbage and stir for 1 minute. Add 200ml/7fl oz/scant 1 cup water and bring to the boil. Simmer for 5 minutes, then add the tomatoes. Cook until the tomatoes are just soft, then serve hot.

Variation

Caraway seeds have a distinctive liquorice flavour and can be overpowering if over-used. Ground cloves makes a good substitute, if you prefer.

TUNG-PO MUTTON

Su Tung-Po was a famous poet and gourmet of the Song Dynasty who lived in Hangzhou. This dish, which is attributed to him, has crossed many borders. Muslims from Shandong tweaked the original pork dish to suit their tastes, eschewing pork and alcohol, both of which are forbidden by Islam edict. They also bulked it up with potatoes and carrots to make a substantial winter dish. Curiously, the mutton version seems to have become more mainstream than the pork in many restaurants. In northern China, goat meat would be used for this dish.

SERVES 4

400g/14oz lean mutton or lamb
vegetable oil, for deep-frying
130g/4½ oz potatoes, cut into bitesize pieces
5ml/1 tsp sugar
30ml/2 tbsp soy sauce
15ml/1 tbsp vegetable oil
25g/1oz grated fresh root ginger
2 garlic cloves, crushed
2.5ml/½ tsp ground Sichuan peppercorns
a pinch of Chinese five-spice powder
4 spring onions/scallions, cut into 5cm/2in lengths
1 meat stock/bouillon cube
130g/4½ oz carrots, cut into bitesize pieces

1 Cut the mutton or lamb into 2.5cm/1in cubes. Heat the oil for frying in a wok or deep-fryer, and deep-fry the mutton or lamb for 4 minutes. Transfer to a plate lined with kitchen paper and set aside.

2 Deep-fry the potatoes in the hot oil for 4 minutes, then drain on kitchen paper and set aside.

3 Transfer the fried mutton or lamb to a deep pan and add all the remaining ingredients except the fried potatoes and the carrots. Add 1.2 litres/2 pints/5 cups water. Bring to the boil, and simmer for 50 minutes.

4 Add the potatoes and carrots, then cook for a further 10 minutes, until the meat and vegetables are tender.

Variation

You can give a lift to the dish by adding 30ml/2 tbsp Shaoxing wine or dry sherry in the last 5 minutes of cooking time, if you like.

SLICED BEEF & BAMBOO SHOOTS

Beef and bamboo shoots have an affinity that is utilized in many dishes, particularly in northern China. In Henan, this dish has pride of place for special occasions and festive days, perhaps because beef is quite expensive, whereas lamb or mutton are the meats that are served every day. When beef is to be stir-fried, it benefits from being tenderized, either by being beaten with a mallet or sprinkled with bicarbonate of soda.

1 Cut the beef across the grain into thin slices about 6cm/2½in long. Tenderize them with a meat mallet on both sides until the slices are extremely thin. Alternatively, mix the non-tenderized beef slices with the bicarbonate of soda.

2 Put the soy sauce, pepper and wine or sherry in a shallow glass bowl, add the beef, mix to coat it well, then leave it to marinate for 15 minutes.

3 Slice the bamboo shoots into pieces the same size as the beef, then rinse and drain. Heat the oil in a wok, add the garlic and ginger and stir-fry for 2 minutes.

4 Add the beef and its marinade and stir-fry over high heat for 2 minutes. Add the bamboo shoots, yellow bean sauce and sugar, then stir-fry for 1 minute.

5 Blend the cornflour with 120ml/4fl oz/½ cup water and add to the pan. Cook, stirring, for 2 minutes, or until the sauce is thickened. Serve hot, garnished with shredded spring onion.

SERVES 4

350g/12oz rump/round or sirloin steak
5ml/1 tsp bicarbonate of soda/baking soda (optional)
15ml/1 tbsp dark soy sauce
5ml/1 tsp ground black pepper
15ml/1 tbsp strong Chinese wine, such as kaoliang, or dry sherry
175g/6oz bamboo shoots
30ml/2 tbsp vegetable oil
2 garlic cloves, crushed
25g/1oz fresh root ginger, shredded
30ml/2 tbsp yellow bean sauce
5ml/1 tsp sugar
10ml/2 tsp cornflour/cornstarch
shredded spring onion/scallion, to garnish

Cook's Tip

If you use bicarbonate of soda/baking soda, even tough cuts of beef, such as stewing steak, will be tender enough for stir-frying.

STIR-FRIED VENISON

Game meats are not commonly cooked outside northern and western China, as they are not widely available (apart from in places such as Yunnan, where deer are plentiful, and Hong Kong, where a sophisticated clientele expect restaurants to source exotic ingredients). In Hebei, venison is served as an occasional treat.

1 Slice the venison thinly and mix with the bicarbonate of soda and wine or sherry. Set aside for at least 3 hours, or preferably overnight.

2 Heat the oil in a wok, add the garlic and stir-fry for 2 minutes. Add the venison and stir-fry over a high heat for 2 minutes, then add the soy sauce, oyster sauce and pepper. Stir-fry for 1 minute more Add the mushrooms to the wok and stir-fry for 1 minute.

3 Blend the cornflour with 120ml/4fl oz/½ cup water, then add to the wok. Stir over high heat until the sauce thickens. Serve hot, sprinkled with sesame seeds and spring onion, with noodles.

SERVES 4

350g/12oz venison
5ml/1 tsp bicarbonate of soda/ baking soda
15ml/1 tbsp Shaoxing wine or dry sherry
30ml/2 tbsp vegetable oil
2 garlic cloves, crushed
15ml/1 tbsp dark soy sauce
15ml/1 tbsp oyster sauce
2.5ml/½ tsp ground black pepper
8 Chinese mushrooms, soaked until soft, or canned mushrooms, sliced in half
5ml/1 tsp cornflour/cornstarch
15ml/1 tbsp sesame seeds, to garnish
chopped spring onion/scallion, to garnish
noodles, to serve

SERVES 4

900g/2lb trimmed oxtail pieces
1.2 litres/2 pints/5 cups boiling water
15ml/1 tbsp vegetable oil
25g/1oz fresh root ginger, sliced
150g/5oz onions, quartered
120ml/4fl oz/½ cup Shaoxing wine or dry sherry
30ml/2 tbsp oyster sauce
5ml/1 tsp salt
2.5ml/½ tsp ground black pepper
1 beef stock/bouillon cube

Cook's Tip

This dish is suitable for cooking in a pressure cooker. You will need half the quantity of water and it will cook in 1 hour.

OXTAIL STEW

When oxtail is cooked in northern China, it tends to be in a thick soup or casserole, sometimes with the addition of herbs such as wolf or boxthorn berries for their nutritive properties. Whether you serve it as a soup or a stew depends on the amount of water you use, so add more or less liquid depending on your preference.

1 Blanch the oxtail pieces in the boiling water for 3 minutes, then drain. This will remove some of the fattiness.

2 Heat the oil in a wok, add the ginger and stir-fry for 2 minutes. Add the oxtail pieces and stir-fry for 2 minutes, or until well coated. Add the onion, wine or sherry, oyster sauce, salt, pepper, 1.2 litres/2 pints/5 cups water and the stock cube, then transfer to a deep pan.

3 Bring to the boil and simmer, covered, for 1½ hours or until tender. Top it up with hot water, if necessary.

4 If the dish is intended to be soupy, allow 200ml/7fl oz/scant 1 cup of liquid per serving with the pieces of the oxtail. Otherwise, serve as a stew by boiling the liquid to reduce the stock.

LIVER IN FIVE SPICES

Liver demands careful cooking because it toughens up when overcooked by even a few minutes. Here, it is bathed in a piquant thick sauce.

SERVES 4

- 450g/1lb pig's liver
- 2.5ml/½ tsp Chinese five-spice powder
- 30ml/2 tbsp crushed garlic
- 30ml/2 tbsp rice wine
- 15ml/1 tbsp vegetable oil
- 30ml/2 tbsp fresh root ginger, cut into thin strips
- 15ml/1 tbsp oyster sauce
- 30ml/2 tbsp dark soy sauce
- 2.5ml/½ tsp ground black pepper
- 30ml/2 tbsp sesame oil
- 5ml/1 tsp cornflour/cornstarch
- 3 spring onions/scallions, cut into 5cm/2in pieces

1 Put the liver in the freezer until it firms up, then slice it thinly. Mix the Chinese five-spice powder, garlic and rice wine in a bowl, then add the liver. Mix well, then leave to marinate for 25 minutes.

2 Heat the oil in a wok, add the ginger and stir-fry until crisp and golden brown. Add the liver and its marinade, the oyster sauce, soy sauce, pepper and sesame oil, and cook, stirring, for 2 minutes.

3 Blend 105ml/7 tbsp water with the cornflour and add to the wok. Cook, stirring, until the sauce thickens and the liver is cooked. Stir in the spring onions during the last 30 seconds. Serve hot.

SHREDDED KIDNEYS IN WINE

SERVES 4

2 pig's kidneys
30ml/2 tbsp Shaoxing wine or dry sherry
3 garlic cloves, crushed
30ml/2 tbsp vegetable oil
3 spring onions/scallions, cut into 5cm/2in pieces
4 slices pickled ginger, sliced into strips
a pinch of Chinese five-spice powder
15ml/1 tbsp dark soy sauce
fresh coriander/cilantro and shredded spring onion/scallion, to garnish
boiled rice, to serve

Cook's Tip

Make sure you remove every bit of the white membrane, and allow enought time to soak the kidneys for an hour before cooking them.

The kidneys in this dish are cut in such a way that each piece becomes a frill, although it is described in the recipe name as 'shredded'. The recipe is a close cousin of Liver in Five Spices, and the two are often cooked at the same time, making a robust pair of dishes with restorative properties.

1 Slice each kidney in half. With a sharp knife, remove all the white membrane and core. Cut each half into four pieces, then make slices about 1cm/½in away from your fingers, right through the kidney and tapering at each end. This makes a frill on each piece. Soak the pieces in cold water for at least 15 minutes.

2 Mix the wine or sherry and garlic in a shallow bowl, add the kidney pieces, mix well and leave to marinate for 1 hour.

3 Heat the oil in a wok, add the onions and stir-fry for 1 minute. Add the ginger, five-spice powder and soy sauce. Stir-fry for 1 minute, then add 120ml/4fl oz/½ cup water and bring to the boil.

4 Add the kidney and stir over medium heat until cooked through. Garnish with coriander and spring onion, and serve with rice.

FOUR TREASURES MEAT

Numerology can have different meanings from one region to the next. It tends to be a dialectic thing: the number four is avoided at all costs in Guangzhou, as in Cantonese it is phonetically the same as the word 'death'. In Mandarin and other regional dialects, the number four does not have any negative symbolism, and the Four Treasures Meat dish is popular in Beijing. Traditionally, the 'four treasures' refer to poultry feets, wings, tongues and viscera – a mixture that would not go down well with conservative diners! Here, I have taken a modern approach and used alternatives that taste excellent together.

SERVES 4

150g/5oz duck breast
150g/5oz belly pork
vegetable oil, for deep-frying, plus 15ml/1 tbsp
115g/4oz chicken livers
1 pig's kidney
2 spring onions/scallions, chopped
25g/1oz fresh root ginger, grated
30ml/2 tbsp dark soy sauce
15ml/1 tbsp yellow bean sauce
15ml/1 tbsp rice wine
2.5ml/½ tsp sugar
2.5ml/½ tsp ground black pepper
5ml/1 tsp tapioca flour
sliced spring onion/scallion, to garnish

1 Remove the skin from the duck breast and slice it into 1cm/½in-wide pieces. Remove the skin from the belly pork and slice as for the duck.

2 Heat the oil for frying in a wok or deep-fryer, and deep-fry the duck and belly pork pieces for 3 minutes (in batches, if necessary), then drain on kitchen paper and set aside.

3 Wash and drain the chicken livers, then cut the larger pieces into two. Slice through the pig's kidney, and cut out the white core and membrane. Cut into 4cm/1½in pieces and make surface criss-cross cuts in each. (When they are cooked, each piece will open up like a flower.)

4 Heat the 15ml/1 tbsp oil in a clean wok, add the spring onions and ginger and stir-fry for 2 minutes. Add the duck, pork, livers and kidney and stir-fry for 2 minutes.

5 Add the soy sauce, yellow bean sauce, rice wine, sugar and pepper, and cook, stirring, for 1 minute. Add 200ml/7fl oz/scant 1 cup water, bring to the boil, and simmer for 5 minutes.

6 Blend the tapioca flour with a little water until smooth and add to the wok. Stir until the sauce thickens, then serve hot, garnished with some sliced spring onion.

Cook's Tip

You can choose four kinds of any other meat, fish, shellfish or vegetable for this stir-fry.

NORTHERN CHINA

PANCAKES, BREAD & NOODLES

STARCHY FILLERS & FESTIVAL TREATS

Since the climate of the northern provinces is not suited to growing rice, the grain (ubiquitous in the rest of China) has never formed part of the local menus. Today, rice is enjoyed here as it is in the rest of the world, but the local favourites remain breads and noodles.

Apart from Mandarin Pancakes, which are traditionally served with Peking Duck, very few pancakes are offered plain; they are usually filled with a meat-based or sweet mixture. Bean paste is a common filler, and can be either savoury or sweet.

Steamed breads form the carbohydrate staple in the northern provinces, no matter what else is on the table. They are made from low-gluten wheat flour, which is available in Chinese stores.

During festive occasions, noodles are prepared with great pride, and families sit down to delicious offerings, often with eels, minced beef or lamb. Throughout China, noodles have always been regarded as symbolic of longevity, though many modernists today regard this with some bemusement. Nevertheless, it is still traditional for noodles to make a grand appearance at every special event.

In Beijing, hand-pulled noodles are especially famous, and they are on sale every day from street food stalls. They are to northern China what pasta is to Italy, and the cooking of noodles has not changed greatly for centuries. Many dishes have become iconic in Chinese restaurants around the world, and there does not seem to be a limit to the dishes chefs can create with noodles.

MANDARIN PANCAKES

Peking duck would not be the same without these pancakes. I learned how to make them many moons ago from the master of Chinese cuisine, the late, venerable Kenneth Lo, when I was teaching at his culinary institute in London. They are extremely easy to make, requiring no special skill, but a lot of patience. Of course, the easy option is to buy them ready-made, but think how impressed your guests will be when you next entertain and serve your own Peking duck, accompanied by your own pancakes!

MAKES 12 PANCAKES

200g/7oz/1¾ cups plain/all-purpose flour
150ml/¼ pint/⅔ cup boiling water
15ml/1 tbsp vegetable oil
Peking Duck, to serve (see pages 98–9)

Cook's Tips

- Any unused pancakes can be wrapped and frozen, or chilled for up to 5 days.
- When using them from frozen, always steam the pancakes rather than frying or heating them in the microwave.

1 Sift the flour into a large heatproof bowl, then gradually pour in the boiling water, stirring with a pair of chopsticks or a wooden spoon. Do not add any more water, even if the dough appears rather dry. Set aside to cool.

2 Turn out the dough on to a floured work surface and knead for 10 minutes, or until it is firm and slightly elastic. Set aside for 30 minutes to rest.

3 Roll out the dough into a long sausage about 2.5cm/1in in diameter. Slice into 12 pieces and roll each one into a small ball.

4 Flatten each ball with the palm of your hand and roll out into a paper-thin circle, about 13cm/5in in diameter. Repeat with the remaining balls of dough.

5 Brush each pancake with oil on one side and pair them up, one on top of another, oiled sides facing together.

6 Heat a frying pan with a little oil and fry each double pancake for 1 minute, or until brown bubbles begin to appear. Flip over and cook the other side for 1 minute.

7 Gently peel the pancakes apart. Fold each in half and stack them on a large plate that will fit inside your steamer. Steam for 25 minutes, then serve with Peking Duck.

BEAN PASTE CAKES

The bean paste here is not the sweet variety made from red beans, but a paste made from shelled mung beans, which is cooked as a savoury filling. The beans are sold ready-shelled, but they do have to be soaked overnight. The dish is not known in most of China, coming as it does from Tianjin, a large municipality that borders Beijing. I was introduced to this savoury cake by my neighbours from Liaoning and found it most unusual, with its blend of crispy pork fat and soft mung bean paste.

MAKES 4 CAKES

150g/5oz/1¼ cups plain/all-purpose flour
15ml/1 tbsp cornflour/cornstarch
a pinch of salt
120ml/4fl oz/½ cup boiling water
90ml/6 tbsp vegetable oil
chilli sauce dip, to serve

FOR THE FILLING
90g/3½oz shelled mung beans, soaked overnight (see Cook's Tip)
75g/3oz pork fat or bacon fat, finely chopped
2 spring onions/scallions, finely chopped
15ml/1 tbsp light soy sauce
2.5ml/½ tsp ground black pepper
30ml/2 tbsp sesame oil

1 To make the filling, boil the mung beans in 300ml/½ pint/1¼ cups water for 15 minutes. Drain in a colander until nearly dry, then transfer to a mixing bowl and mash with a potato masher to make a smooth paste.

2 Heat a wok and fry the pork or bacon fat for 2 minutes, then add the spring onions. Stir-fry for 1 minute, then add the soy sauce, pepper and sesame oil. Cook, stirring, for a further 1 minute, then transfer to a large bowl.

3 Add the mashed mung beans and stir well. Set aside while you make the batter.

4 Sift the flour and cornflour into a mixing bowl and add the salt. Stir to mix, then gradually add the boiling water, stirring well. Stir in 15ml/1 tbsp oil. Allow to cool, then transfer to a floured work surface and knead for 5 minutes.

5 Roll out the dough into a long sausage shape and cut into four pieces. Flatten each piece into a thin round about 3mm/⅛in thick. Divide the mung bean mixture between the rounds – there should be about 15ml/1 tbsp on each. Fold and draw the sides into the centre. Twist and pinch off any excess. Seal with a dab of water and shape into a round, flat cake.

6 Place the cakes on a lightly oiled plate that will fit into your steamer, and steam for 10 minutes. Remove and allow to cool.

7 Heat a frying pan with the remaining oil and cook the cakes, sealed side down, until golden brown, then flip them over to fry the other side. You will need to do this in batches.

8 When brown and crispy, remove and drain on kitchen paper. Serve with a chilli sauce dip.

Cook's Tip

When soaking overnight, use enough water to just cover the beans. By the next day, all the water will have been absorbed.

STEAMED BREADS

Made from wheat flour, steamed breads account for much of the carbohydrates eaten in the north of China. This popular bread, called man tou, is believed to have originated here during the Song Dynasty (960–1279). The cooks of Sichuan refute this, however, claiming it was their invention. Until food distribution became more efficient in modern China, rice was not integral to northern cuisine; steamed breads were the staple of choice. Today, they are still central to many meals.

MAKES ABOUT 20 BREADS

15ml/1 tbsp sugar
15ml/1 tbsp active dried yeast
450g/1lb/4 cups low-gluten wheat flour, plus extra for dusting
lard, white cooking fat or vegetable oil, for greasing

Cook's Tips

- Any unused rolls can be chilled, covered and then resteamed for 5 minutes before serving.
- You can also use 1 sachet (7g/¼oz) of easy bake/rapid-rise dried yeast instead of active dried yeast; omit the sugar and frothing step and add it with the flour.

1 Mix the sugar with the yeast in a bowl and add 100ml/3½fl oz/scant ½ cup lukewarm water. Put in a warm place. After about 15 minutes it will begin to froth.

2 Put the flour into a large bowl and make a well in the middle. Pour in the yeast mixture and mix well. Add more lukewarm water, a little at a time, up to about 200ml/7fl oz/scant 1 cup. Add just enough to make a pliable dough.

3 Transfer the dough to a well-floured work surface and knead vigorously for 10 minutes, or until the dough is elastic and smooth. Put it into a lightly oiled bowl, cover with a damp dish towel and leave in a warm place to rise for 1 hour, or until doubled in bulk.

4 Knock back/punch down the dough to its original size, then leave for a further 30 minutes to rise again.

5 Knead the dough on a floured work surface for about another 15 minutes before shaping.

6 There are many ways you can shape man tou. The most basic is to roll the dough into a sausage, then press it into a flat rectangle about 5mm/¼in thick. Lift up the long side and roll it up tightly like a roulade. Press the end to seal, and slice into 2cm/¾in rounds.

7 Grease a plate that will fit into your steamer with the lard, fat or oil. Place the dough rounds on the plate and steam for 10 minutes, or until they have puffed up. You may need to do this in batches, depending on the size of your steamer.

8 Serve with any braised or roasted meat dish.

BEIJING EEL NOODLES

As a fish with scarcely any bones, eel is undeservedly maligned and often passed over. Eel flesh is smooth and firm – excellent cooked in a wine sauce and served with noodles. Beansprouts and celery give the requisite crunch.

SERVES 4

- 400g/14oz fresh yellow egg noodles
- 200g/7oz eel cutlets
- 5ml/1 tsp ground black pepper
- 30ml/2 tbsp sesame oil
- 30ml/2 tbsp Shaoxing wine or dry sherry
- 30ml/2 tbsp vegetable oil
- 15ml/1 tbsp crushed garlic
- 2 spring onions/scallions, cut into 2.5cm/1in strips
- 90g/3½oz beansprouts
- 30ml/2 tbsp oyster sauce

1 Blanch the noodles in boiling water, then drain. Cut the eel into strips. Mix the pepper, sesame oil and wine or sherry in a bowl, add the eel strips and leave to marinate for 15 minutes.

2 Heat the oil in a wok, add the garlic and stir-fry until golden brown. Add the spring onions and stir-fry for 1 minute. Add the eels and their marinade and cook, stirring, over high heat for 2 minutes. Remove the eels from the wok using a slotted spoon and set aside.

3 Add the noodles and beansprouts and stir-fry for 2 minutes. Add 200ml/7fl oz/scant 1 cup water, the oyster sauce and eels, and cook, stirring, for 3 minutes, until the eels are cooked. Serve immediately.

Cook's Tip

Ask your fishmonger to cut each eel into chunks, so it will be easier to slice them into strips.

SERVES 4

175g/6oz/1½ cups lean minced/ground lamb
30ml/2 tbsp Shaoxing wine or dry sherry
15ml/1 tbsp sesame oil
5ml/1 tsp cornflour/cornstarch
2.5ml/½ tsp salt
15ml/1 tbsp vegetable oil
3 garlic cloves, crushed
15ml/1 tbsp dark soy sauce
200g/7oz fresh wheat or egg noodles
4 spring onions/scallions, cut into 5cm/2in pieces
2.5ml/½ tsp ground black pepper

Variation

Minced pork or beef can be cooked in exactly the same way as the lamb.

MINCED LAMB NOODLES

In the province of Liaoning, minced lamb takes the place of pork in many dishes, with noodles being the favourite accompaniment. The province, together with Jilin and Heilongjiang, as well as a part of Inner Mongolia, is within the region that was formerly known as Manchuria. Liaoning cuisine is heavily influenced by that of the Manchus, as well as that of Beijing. As a result, much of its cooking is refined and elegant.

1 In a bowl, mix the lamb with the wine or sherry, sesame oil, cornflour and salt, then set aside for 15 minutes.

2 Heat the oil in a wok, add the garlic and stir-fry for 2 minutes. Add the lamb and its marinade and stir-fry for 2 minutes. Add 200ml/7fl oz/scant 1 cup water and the dark soy sauce, and cook, stirring, for a further 2 minutes.

3 Add the noodles, spring onions and pepper and cook, stirring, for 3 minutes more, or until the noodles and lamb are well mixed, the lamb is cooked through and the spring onions are soft. Serve.

STIR-FRIED NOODLES & LAMB

This dish is reputed to have been invented by the first of the Manchurian emperors of the Qing Dynasty. While they reigned, the arts flourished and the Mandarinate was filled with educated people, gourmets and cultured officials. As this is a Muslim dish, rice vinegar is used instead of wine.

SERVES 4

15ml/1 tbsp vegetable oil
2 garlic cloves, crushed
25g/1oz fresh root ginger, shredded
175g/6oz lean lamb, cut into thin strips
15ml/1 tbsp rice vinegar
15ml/1 tbsp sesame oil
15ml/1 tbsp dark soy sauce
1 leek, thinly sliced
200g/7oz fresh wheat or egg noodles
2.5ml/½ tsp ground black pepper

1 Heat the oil in a wok, add the garlic and ginger and stir-fry for 2 minutes. Add the lamb and stir-fry for 2 minutes.

2 Add 200ml/7fl oz/scant 1 cup water, bring to the boil and simmer for 5 minutes, until the lamb is cooked through. Remove the lamb with a slotted spoon and set aside.

3 In the same wok, add the rice vinegar, sesame oil, soy sauce and leek and cook, stirring, for 2 minutes, or until the leek is soft. Add the noodles and pepper and continue to stir until well mixed. The sauce should be just thick enough to coat the noodles.

4 Return the lamb to the wok and heat through, stirring as little as possible, so that you can then serve the lamb on top of the noodles.

Cook's Tip

You can also use a tougher cut of lamb or mutton. If so, mix it with 5ml/1 tsp bicarbonate of soda/baking soda before cooking to tenderize it.

SERVES 4

200g/7oz dried wheat noodles
15ml/1 tbsp vegetable oil
2 garlic cloves, crushed
150g/5oz/generous 1 cup minced/ground beef
30ml/2 tbsp oyster sauce
15ml/1 tbsp sesame oil
15ml/1 tbsp dark soy sauce
90g/3½oz Chinese cabbage, thinly sliced
2.5ml/½ tsp ground black pepper
15ml/1 tbsp cornflour/cornstarch
2 spring onions/scallions, shredded, to garnish

NOODLES WITH MINCED BEEF

Although not as famous as Sichuan's dan dan noodles, Shanxi takes pride in the glorious minced beef noodles that appear on local menus. This recipe makes a one-dish meal that contains all the nutritional constituents: starch, protein and vegetables.

1 Blanch or cook the noodles according to the packet instructions. Drain and set aside.

2 Heat the oil in a wok and fry the garlic for 2 minutes, then add the beef and fry for 2 minutes. Add the oyster sauce, sesame oil, soy sauce, Chinese cabbage and pepper and fry for 2 minutes.

3 Mix the cornflour with 90ml/6 tbsp water and add to the wok. Stir until the sauce is thick. Add the noodles and continue to stir until the noodles, beef and vegetables are well mixed.

4 Garnish with spring onions and serve.

NORTHERN CHINA

VEGETABLES, EGGS, TOFU & NUTS

CRISP, CRUNCHY, FRESH & HEALTHY

As in the rest of China, the tenet of yin-yang (or universal balance) comes into play whenever vegetables are prepared. The symbiosis of textures, flavours and colours underscores the essence of vegetable dishes, whether served as a main meal or something to accompany meat, poultry, fish or shellfish. Humble though they may be, vegetables such as beansprouts, bamboo shoots, cabbage, pak choi, mushrooms, and aubergines or egglants are combined and prepared in such skilful ways, that they can often overshadow the grandest meat and poultry dishes.

Peanuts are grown in the northern provinces, and are seen as much more than a crunchy snack: they can be used in recipes, and are seasoned and boiled to make tasty nibbles.

Eggs also feature – a favourite ingredient of thrifty cooks, who can use them to whip up nutritious meals when fresh vegetables are scarce. They are combined with tofu and preserved vegetables in the Steamed Egg Custard recipe from Hebei.

Tofu is one of China's best-loved ingredients, and it is put to good use in the northern provinces. Being relatively inexpensive and very nutritious, it is a useful food for vegetarians and meat-eaters alike. During Taoist and Buddhist festivals, tofu is especially popular. Along with vegetables like beans, aubergines and leafy greens, it takes centre-stage in stews and stir-fries. In China, vegetable dishes aren't reserved for vegetarians; they simply make good eating.

PICKLED CHINESE CABBAGE

Chinese cabbage – also known as napa cabbage – is a large, leafy vegetable with firm, white stalks and pale leaves that are similar to cos or romaine lettuce in texture. This pickle is typical of Jilin cooking. It has a very crisp texture and a tangy, clean taste. Make it 2 days in advance.

SERVES 6–8

- 1 large Chinese cabbage
- 15ml/1 tbsp salt
- 500ml/scant 1 pint/2 cups white vinegar
- 3 fresh red chillies, stalks removed, sliced lengthways and seeded
- 5ml/1 tsp sugar

1 Cut the cabbage into 1cm/½in wide strips and shred the leaves into small pieces. Place in a bowl and sprinkle the salt all over. Toss well, then cover and leave overnight to soften.

2 Take out a handful of cabbage at a time and squeeze out any moisture. Pat dry with kitchen paper.

3 Pour the vinegar into a pan and bring to the boil. Add the cabbage and simmer for 2 minutes, in batches if necessary. Remove using a slotted spoon and drain in a colander. Leave the vinegar on the heat.

4 Add the chillies to the boiling vinegar, and cook for 1 minute, then drain in a colander. Mix the cabbage and chillies together, add the sugar and toss. Cover and set aside overnight, then stir and serve.

Variation

For an even spicier pickle, much like Korean kimchi, add 30ml/2 tbsp chilli paste to the blanched Chinese cabbage and steep for 2 days before serving.

SERVES 4

1 whole green cabbage, cut into strips 1cm/½in wide
15ml/1 tbsp sugar
30ml/2 tbsp rice vinegar
15ml/1 tbsp light soy sauce
5ml/1 tsp cornflour/cornstarch
3 pickled plums or limes, sliced into small pieces

Variation

Root vegetables and mustard greens also work well with a sweet-and-sour sauce. Slice and blanch until soft in the same way before mixing with the sauce.

SWEET-AND-SOUR CABBAGE

As a rule, sweet-and-sour sauces are cooked with meat or seafood, but in Shandong province, local vegetables such as green cabbage, pak choi and root vegetables often get the sweet-tart treatment. This recipe includes some pickled limes or plums for an extra kick of flavour.

1 Bring a pan of water to the boil and blanch the cabbage for 2–3 minutes, until just soft but not mushy. Drain until quite dry.

2 In a pan, mix the sugar with the rice vinegar, 120ml/4fl oz/½ cup water and the soy sauce, and warm until the sugar has dissolved. Increase the heat and bring to the boil. Simmer for 2 minutes.

3 Meanwhile, mix the cornflour with a little water. Add to the sauce and stir until it thickens. Add the pickled plums or limes.

4 Place the cabbage in a pan and warm it up a little. Add the sauce and toss well to blend, then heat through without boiling. Serve.

COLD AUBERGINE SALAD

In the chilly northern provinces cold vegetable dishes or salads are not overly popular, but when summer arrives, such dishes do appear on menus. Even if a vegetable dish is served cold, though, it is very rarely raw; there is always at least some gentle cooking before assembly. Aubergine is a good choice for this process, as it has a texture and taste that are not diminished when served chilled. This recipe comes from Tianjin.

SERVES 4

400g/14oz aubergine/eggplant
2.5ml/½ tsp salt
350ml/12fl oz/1½ cups water
30ml/2 tbsp sesame oil
15ml/1 tbsp rice vinegar
2.5ml/½ tsp sugar
15ml/1 tbsp sesame seeds
5ml/1 tsp preserved sweet turnip, chopped

1 Cut off the aubergine stalks, and slice the aubergines in half lengthways. Slice them horizontally into semi-circles, each 1cm/½in wide.

2 Place the aubergine slices in a colander, sprinkle with salt and set them aside for 15 minutes.

3 Taking a handful at a time, squeeze out the moisture from the aubergines, and pat them dry with kitchen paper.

4 Place the water in a pan, bring to the boil, add the aubergines and simmer for 5 minutes. Drain thoroughly.

5 In a bowl, mix the sesame oil with the vinegar and sugar and stir until the sugar dissolves. Add the boiled aubergine slices and toss well.

6 Transfer to a serving bowl, and garnish with sesame seeds. Serve at room temperature or chilled, with preserved sweet turnip.

Variation
Courgettes or zucchini can be prepared in the same way.

STEAMED EGG CUSTARD

This is a delicious, light dish that is ideal with congee and is very easy to prepare. It requires only eggs and tofu: two products that have a great affinity with each other. In Hebei province it is a favourite summer dish that provides a perfect contrast to deep-fried meat and chicken dishes. The seasonings and toppings can be varied to taste, but sesame oil and pepper are typical of northern China. Use soft or silken tofu for the best results.

SERVES 4

4 eggs
2.5ml/½ tsp ground white pepper
15ml/1 tbsp light soy sauce
a pinch of sugar
275g/10oz soft tofu
15ml/1 tbsp sesame oil
1 spring onion/scallion, chopped
5ml/1 tsp chopped preserved winter vegetable (tung chai)

1 Lightly beat the eggs (do not over-beat) and season with pepper, soy sauce and sugar.

2 In a separate bowl, mash the tofu with a fork, add the sesame oil and 45ml/3 tbsp water, then mash again until smooth. Add the egg mixture and spring onion and stir well to incorporate.

3 Transfer to a deep plate or shallow bowl that will fit into your steamer. Sprinkle the winter vegetable over the top, and steam for 10 minutes, or until the custard is set.

Cook's Tip

If you are not serving this to vegetarians, you can add 30ml/2 tbsp minced pork or chicken to the egg mixture and mix well. Continue the recipe, but steam for 15 minutes, until the meat is cooked through.

SERVES 4

4 leeks, white parts only
30ml/2 tbsp vegetable oil
15ml/1 tbsp chilli paste
15ml/1 tbsp light soy sauce
2.5ml/½ tsp sugar
15ml/1 tbsp Shaoxing wine or dry sherry
5ml/1 tsp cornflour/cornstarch

FRIED LEEKS WITH HOT SAUCE

In markets all over Beijing, vegetable vendors sell stacked heaps of leeks, many with damp soil still clinging to the roots, amongst other local produce. Leeks are a member of the allium family, with garlic and onions, and share much the same pungency. In southern China, they are eaten for symbolic reasons: in the Cantonese dialect, the word for 'leeks' rhymes with the word for 'count', so it bodes well for prosperity. In northern China, however, they are popular merely for their delicious taste and texture, both of which are showcased in this dish.

1 Slice the leeks, diagonally, into pieces 2.5cm/1in wide. Wash them in plenty of cold water to remove any soil that often clings to the insides of the white stalks. Drain thoroughly.

2 Heat the oil in a wok and, when smoking, add the leeks. Stir-fry over high heat for 2 minutes. Add the chilli paste, soy sauce, sugar and wine or sherry, and stir-fry for a further 2 minutes.

3 Blend the cornflour with 60ml/4 tbsp water and add to the wok. Stir until thickened slightly, then serve hot.

Cook's Tip

Wash the green parts of the leeks thoroughly to remove any dirt, then use them to make vegetable stock, if you like. Use 100g/3¾oz leeks to 200ml/7fl oz/scant 1 cup water.

FRIED BEANS IN GARLIC SAUCE

The beans used here are normal green beans, about 7.5cm/3in long; however, any other type of fresh bean, such as broad or fava beans, can be cooked in the same way. When blanched, they retain their crunch and green colour. In Hebei, yellow bean sauce is the key seasoning, and is salty enough that no additional salt is required.

SERVES 4

- 4 garlic cloves, crushed
- 25g/1oz fresh root ginger, grated
- 1.5ml/¼ tsp ground Sichuan peppercorns
- 15ml/1 tbsp yellow bean sauce
- 2.5ml/½ tsp sugar
- 30ml/2 tbsp sesame oil
- 400g/14oz green beans, trimmed
- 15ml/1 tbsp vegetable oil
- plain boiled rice or noodles, to serve

1 Put the garlic in a small bowl with the ginger, peppercorns, yellow bean sauce, sugar and sesame oil, then mix together.

2 Bring a small pan of water to the boil and blanch the beans in it for 2 minutes. Drain.

3 Heat the oil in a wok, add the sauce and stir-fry for 1 minute. Add the beans, and cook, stirring, over high heat for 2 minutes.

4 Add 100ml/3½fl oz/scant ½ cup water. Continue to cook, stirring, for 1 minute, or until well mixed and aromatic. Serve hot with plain rice or noodles.

Variation

Replace the yellow bean sauce with Sichuan chilli bean sauce for a fiery kick.

SERVES 4

450g/1lb/2 cups beansprouts
15ml/1 tbsp vegetable oil
3 garlic cloves, crushed
2 spring onions/scallions, cut into 5cm/2in lengths
2.5ml/½ tsp salt

Variation

Beansprouts are grown from soaked mung beans. If you can find soy beansprouts, which have larger heads and slightly thicker sprouts, they can be used in this dish instead.

STIR-FRIED BEANSPROUTS

Of all stir-fried vegetable dishes, this is truly the most universal one. Although of peasant origins, it has transcended all social barriers and is now ensconced in every Chinese home and restaurant around the world. The beansprouts are usually given a hint of salt or soy sauce, and include aromatics like garlic, spring onion, ginger and chillies. Beansprouts have a short shelf life, so choose those that are crisp and firm, and avoid them if they look waterlogged. If they are slightly limp, soak them in ice-cold water for 20 minutes to revive their crispness.

1 Wash the beansprouts and discard any roots or green bean husks.

2 Heat the oil in a wok, add the garlic and stir-fry for 2 minutes. Add the beansprouts and toss to coat.

3 Stir-fry over high heat for 2 minutes, then add the spring onions and salt. Stir-fry for 30 seconds, then serve immediately.

BRAISED BAMBOO SHOOTS

SERVES 4

450g/1lb canned bamboo shoots
15ml/1 tbsp vegetable oil
2 garlic cloves, crushed
2 spring onions/scallions, chopped
30ml/2 tbsp yellow bean sauce
15ml/1 tbsp hoisin sauce
5ml/1 tsp sugar
30ml/2 tbsp sesame oil
2.5ml/½ tsp ground black pepper

For this Henan dish, use the whole canned shoots rather than ones that have been pre-cut, so you can cut them to the shape or size you like. They have already been processed and boiled, so the cooking time is not lengthy.

1 Cut the bamboo shoots into bitesize chunks (or slices, if you prefer) and soak them in cold water for 30 minutes. This will reduce the scent and taste of the pickling liquid from the canned shoots.

2 Heat the oil in a wok, add the garlic and stir-fry for 2 minutes. Drain the bamboo shoots and add them to the pan. Stir-fry for 2 minutes, then add the spring onions.

3 Cook, stirring, for 1 minute, then add the yellow bean sauce, hoisin sauce, sugar, sesame oil, black pepper and 450ml/¾ pint/ scant 2 cups water.

4 Bring to the boil, and simmer over a high heat for 5 minutes. Reduce the heat to medium and simmer gently for 30 minutes, or until the sauce has reduced by about half. Serve immediately.

Cook's Tip

In China, most chefs and home cooks use fresh bamboo shoots, as they are readily available; many rural homes will have a patch for growing bamboo. When the shoots are mature, they are pulled up, the outer husks are removed, and the shoots are boiled. This can take several hours.

SERVES 4

350g/12oz dried or fried tofu
115g/4oz canned straw mushrooms
1 leek, white part only
15ml/1 tbsp vegetable oil
30ml/2 tbsp hoisin sauce
15ml/1 tbsp dark soy sauce
2.5ml/½ tsp ground black pepper
15ml/1 tbsp Shaoxing wine or dry sherry
2.5ml/½ tsp sugar
15ml/1 tbsp sesame oil
5ml/1 tsp cornflour/cornstarch

Cook's Tip

To make your own fried tofu, buy the firm white variety and cut it into cubes. Heat plenty of oil until smoking, then lower in and deep-fry the tofu, in batches, until a golden skin forms.

BRAISED TOFU

In China, tofu is not regarded as a meat substitute, but with reverence for its own nutritional and chameleon-like qualities. Using the dried or fried variety will save one step, as you do not need to pre-fry them. They come as squares or cubes with a light brown, wrinkled skin. Use fresh tofu, if you like, but you need to fry it first (see Cook's Tip). With complementary ingredients such as mushrooms and vegetables, this dish achieves banquet status.

1 If using dried tofu, cut each square into two triangles. If using fried tofu cubes, leave them whole, as they are usually already bite-size.

2 Drain the straw mushrooms. Slice the leek diagonally into 1cm/½in slices. Wash in plenty of cold water and drain well.

3 Heat the oil in a wok, add the leek and stir-fry for 1 minute. Add the hoisin sauce, dark soy sauce, pepper, wine or sherry, sugar, sesame oil and 350ml/12fl oz/1½ cups water, and bring to the boil.

4 Add the tofu, and simmer for 10 minutes over medium heat. Just before serving, blend the cornflour with a little water and add to the pan. Stir until the sauce thickens. Serve immediately.

VEGETARIAN STEW

A quintessential northern vegetarian dish from Henan, this stew is a signature dish for many Taoist and Buddhist festivals, when meat is not allowed. Most Chinese families, however, serve vegetable dishes as part of every meal, as they demand a good balance of all the food groups. This dish is similar to the eastern Chinese dish, Buddha's Vegetarian Stew, which hails from Fujian.

SERVES 4

4 Chinese black mushrooms
100g/3¾oz button/white mushrooms
40g/1½oz cloud ear/wood ear mushrooms, soaked until soft
30ml/2 tbsp vegetable oil
3 garlic cloves, crushed
25g/1oz fresh root ginger, grated
1 cube preserved red beancurd
30ml/2 tbsp hoisin sauce
5ml/1 tsp salt
200g/7oz pak choi/bok choy, sliced into strips
10 mangetouts/snow peas

1 Bring 400ml/14fl oz/1⅔ cups water to the boil in a pan, add the black and button mushrooms and simmer for 10 minutes or until soft.

2 Remove the mushrooms with a slotted spoon and slice them, then strain and reserve the liquid. Trim off the woody parts from the cloud ear mushrooms.

3 Heat the oil in a wok, add the garlic and ginger and stir-fry for 2 minutes, then add the preserved red beancurd. Cook, stirring and mashing it a little, for 1 minute.

4 Add the hoisin sauce, salt, pak choi, mangetouts and all the mushrooms. Cook, stirring, for 2 minutes, then add the reserved strained mushroom liquid.

5 Simmer for 15 minutes, or until the sauce is thick and coats the vegetables and mushrooms. Serve immediately.

BOILED PEANUTS

Peanuts are not considered to be merely a crunchy snack. In northern provinces they take starring roles, possibly because there is some symbolism attached to them: the Chinese word for peanuts, hua shen, is a synonym for 'success'. They are boiled, fried and roasted, as well as processed into oil. Buy them raw, with their skins on, and they can be cooked in a seasoned broth.

SERVES 4

450g/1lb raw peanuts
5ml/1 tsp Sichuan peppercorns
1 small cinnamon stick
a pinch of ground cloves
2 star anise
25g/1oz fresh root ginger, grated
5ml/1 tsp sugar

1 Place the peanuts in a pan of water, bring to the boil and simmer for 30 minutes. Allow to cool, then drain. Take handfuls of the nuts and rub them together gently to remove the skins. Rinse and drain.

2 Bring 1.2 litres/2 pints/5 cups water to the boil and add the nuts. Put the peppercorns, cinnamon, cloves, star anise and ginger in a piece of muslin/cheesecloth and tie with cook's string. Add to the pan.

3 Simmer for 45 minutes, then remove the spices and drain the peanuts. Leave to cool before serving.

Cook's Tip

If you do not have any muslin/cheesecloth, the spices can be added directly to the water. Drain the nuts carefully to make sure the spices are all removed.

SERVES 4

450g/1lb potatoes, peeled and cut into 5mm/¼in slices
45ml/3 tbsp vegetable oil
30ml/2 tbsp dark soy sauce
a pinch of Chinese five-spice powder
2.5ml/½ tsp ground Sichuan peppercorns
15ml/1 tbsp sesame oil

Variations

- Cut the potatoes into 2cm/¾in dice instead of slices for a more chunky texture, if you like.
- Root vegetables like swede/rutabaga, turnip and sweet potato work very well cooked this way.

SOY SAUCE POTATOES

I was served this unusual Beijing dish at a dinner hosted by a friend who said his grandfather had been a chef in the court of the last emperor, Pu Yi, before the fall of the Qing Dynasty. I was curious about the use of potatoes, as they are not a typical Chinese ingredient. It it thought the dish was brought to Beijing from Shanghai, which has been an bustling international centre for many centuries.

1 Boil the potatoes in plenty of water for 5 minutes, or until just soft. Gently lift out with a slotted spoon to prevent them from breaking up. Place in a colander to drain thoroughly.

2 Heat the oil in a wok until smoking. Working in batches, add the potato slices and fry until golden. Do not crowd the wok or they will not become brown. Remove and drain on kitchen paper.

3 Remove all but 15ml/1 tbsp oil and add the soy sauce, Chinese five-spice powder, pepper, sesame oil and 45ml/3 tbsp water.

4 Add the potatoes and stir gently, turning them over so that they are thoroughly coated with the sauce. Serve hot.

NORTHERN CHINA
SWEET THINGS

SWEET SNACKS & FESTIVE BITES

From afternoon snacks to festival food, the tastes and textures of northern Chinese sweet dishes may be a new experience for many people. The fruity, creamy and chocolatey flavours of the West are not found here – intensely sugary morsels are the traditional choices. Many of these are served during festivals and celebrations.

Several types of dates feature in north Chinese sweet dishes and they range from plain, dried ones to cloying honeyed bites. They are often mashed and used as a delicious filling in pancakes.

Apples are often caramelized, and this is one sweet treat that does appear on menus outside of China. Taros (pictured opposite, bottom right) can be given the same treatment, and are also boiled, mashed and sweetened.

Sesame seeds, black or white, are used frequently as a crunchy coating for sticky taro slices and steamed glutinous rice, bringing colour, flavour and texture.

Although the sweet menu is short, any chef or cook with ingenuity can create their own signature dishes with understanding of the basic ingredients: date pancakes can be tweaked with a dried fruit paste filling, and taro can be replaced by pumpkin or sweet potato for a starchy substitute.

Some may find the rather intense, cloying sweetness of the recipes a bit too much; if so, although this is the traditional flavour of Mandarin sweet snacks, you can of course adjust the amount of sugar to suit your own palate. Enjoy!

CARAMELIZED APPLES

The origin of this dish is obscure, and it seems to have a higher profile in Chinese restaurants outside of China than within it. During festival times, however, children in Beijing can be seen munching candied fruits of various kinds, which are sold on sticks for ease of eating during the celebrations. In this recipe, the apples are cored and cut into pieces before being coated in batter and sugar, for serving on a plate. Chinese chefs have an ingenious way of caramelizing sugar in a little lard or oil.

1 To make the batter, sift the flour into a mixing bowl and stir in the beaten egg. Gradually add 120ml/4fl oz/½ cup cold water, and stir to make a smooth batter the consistency of cream. Set aside for 20 minutes.

2 Fill a bowl with iced water, and set aside. Peel and core the apples, and cut each into eight pieces.

3 Heat the oil for deep-frying in a wok or deep-fryer. Working in batches, quickly dip the apple pieces in the batter, then deep-fry them for 2–3 minutes, until golden brown. Remove with a slotted spoon, and drain on kitchen paper.

4 In a separate non-stick wok, heat the 30ml/2 tbsp vegetable oil until smoking, then add the sugar. Swirl the wok around until the sugar becomes a light brown caramel.

5 Immediately, add the apple pieces, a couple at a time, and toss them in the caramel with a pair of wooden spoons. When well coated, lift each piece with a slotted spoon and dunk into the iced water for a few seconds. You will notice the sugar being pulled into threads. Drain and serve immediately.

SERVES 4

75g/3oz/¾ cup self-raising/ self-rising flour
1 egg, lightly beaten
4 large eating apples
vegetable oil, for deep-frying, plus 30ml/2 tbsp
250g/9oz soft dark brown sugar

Variation

Banana slices can be caramelized in the same way, or you could experiment and try out other fruits, such as pear, pineapple, plums – anything that will hold its shape when briefly cooked.

CARAMELIZED TAROS

Here, taros are cooked in much the same way as Caramelized Apples, but with the addition of sesame seeds to give extra crunch. This is much less sweet than caramelized apples, but equally delicious.

SERVES 4

- 450g/1lb taros, cut into bitesize pieces
- vegetable oil, for deep-frying, plus 15ml/1 tbsp
- 130g/4½oz/scant ¾ cup caster/superfine sugar
- 30ml/2 tbsp sesame seeds

Variation

You can also toast the sesame seeds before using, to impart a nutty flavour. Spread them out on a foil-lined baking tray, and place under a hot grill for a few minutes, until the seeds are a light brown.

1 Fill a bowl with iced water, and set aside. Wash the taro pieces, then pat them very dry with kitchen paper.

2 Heat the oil for deep-frying in a wok or deep-fryer, and deep-fry the taro pieces, in batches, for about 3 minutes, until cooked through and golden brown.

3 In a clean wok, heat the 15ml/1 tbsp oil and add the sugar. Swirl the wok around until the sugar becomes a light brown caramel.

4 Add the fried taro pieces, in batches, and stir for 1 minute with a pair of wooden spoons. Add the sesame seeds and stir gently for 1 minute, or until each piece of taro is coated.

5 Lift each piece with a slotted spoon and dunk into the iced water for a few seconds. You will notice the sugar being pulled into threads. Drain and serve immediately.

DATE PANCAKES

Two main types of Chinese dates are used in cooking: small red, dried dates, which are unsweetened, and black, boiled dates. There is also a third, less common, variety called mi zao in Mandarin, which is coated with honey and eaten as a snack, but it is also ideal for making sweet pastries like this Henan date cake. This variety can be hard to find, even within China, so you can use dried red dates, which are sold in all Chinese stores.

SERVES 6–8

125g/4¼oz/1 cup plain/all-purpose flour
1 egg, lightly beaten
vegetable oil, for deep-frying, plus extra for the pancakes

FOR THE FILLING
175g/6oz Chinese red dates
30ml/2 tbsp lard or white cooking fat
45g/1½oz/3 tbsp caster/superfine sugar

1 Sift the flour into a large bowl and make a well in the centre. Add the egg, and stir to mix. Gradually add 200ml/7fl oz/scant 1 cup water. Stir to make a smooth pouring batter. Set aside.

2 For the filling, put the dates into a small pan and add water to just cover. Boil for 10 minutes, or until the dates are completely soft. Drain the dates, reserving the liquid. Remove any skins that might have come away from the dates and remove the stones or pits.

3 Press the dates through a sieve or strainer and discard the skins. Using a fork, mash the dates a little more, then add a little of the reserved liquid – enough to make a creamy paste.

4 Heat the lard or white cooking fat in a clean wok and cook the sugar until it is golden brown. Add the date mash, stir well to combine, then remove from the wok and set aside to cool.

5 Heat a small frying pan with a little oil and pour in 30ml/2 tbsp of the pancake batter. Swirl the pan around to create a thin pancake. Cook until the underside is set, then flip it over to cook the other side. Slide on to a plate and repeat with the remaining batter.

6 Spread 15ml/1 tbsp of the date mash on to each pancake, and fold over to encase the paste. Tuck the loose sides underneath and seal with a little water.

7 In the same pan, add a little more oil and fry each folded pancake for 1 minute on each side.

8 Heat the oil for deep-frying in a wok or deep-fryer and deep-fry each pancake until bubbly and golden brown. Cut into pieces and serve warm.

Variations

- Mediterranean dates can be used if you can't find Chinese red dates. If they are sugar-coated, reduce the sugar quantity by half.
- Sweet pastes made from sesame seeds or almonds can be used for this snack. If you can find the canned pastes, using them will save you a lot of time.

SWEET SESAME ROLLS

Sesame seeds are used to make an outer coating for these rolls, made from glutinous rice with a filling of sweet red bean paste, which is sold in cans in Chinese stores. Sesame seeds come in two types: white or black. This favourite Beijing snack traditionally uses the white type, but you can use either, since, apart from their colour, there is no difference in taste. These look very pretty with a mixture of white and black seeds, as here.

SERVES 4

150g/5oz/generous ⅔ cup glutinous rice, soaked for 3 hours
115g/4oz sweet red bean paste
115g/4oz/1 cup white or black sesame seeds, or a mixture

Cook's Tips

- Sweet red bean paste straight from the can is usually a little stiff, so it helps to heat it in the microwave briefly.
- If not serving immediately, do not keep the rolls warm, as this can cause bacteria to grow in the rice. Allow to cool, then chill.
- A mixture of both white and black sesame seeds gives an attractive effect, but you can just use one or the other, if you like.

1 Thoroughly rinse and then drain the soaked glutinous rice and put it on to a plate that will fit into your steamer. Steam for 30 minutes, or until very soft.

2 Meanwhile, warm the sweet bean paste in a microwave on medium power for 1–2 minutes, or until just soft, to make it more manageable. Divide the sweet bean paste into two portions. Divide the cooked rice into two portions.

3 Spread a piece of clear film/plastic wrap about 15 x 18cm/6 x 7in on to a Japanese bamboo mat for rolling sushi, if you have one, or a piece of baking parchment.

4 Spread the glutinous rice in a layer on the clear film and top it with the warm sweet bean paste. Spread the paste into an even layer with a moistened butter knife or metal spatula.

5 Roll up like a roulade, using the the mat or baking parchment to help you.

6 Put the sesame seeds on to a large plate. Gently lift the roll and place it on to the sesame seeds. Roll it gently to coat it all over in the seeds.

7 Cut into 2.5cm/1in slices to serve warm. The rolls can also be chilled and served cold.

TARO CREAM

When it comes to tubers such as taros, potatoes or sweet potatoes, the Chinese do not make a clear distinction between them. They are all regarded as starchy bases and are used in similar ways, though taro is by far the most popular. Taro cream is believed to have originated in the Fujian province, but has since been adopted by chefs of many provinces, particularly in the northern areas. It is sweet, smooth and comforting, and is served as a dessert or snack. You can adjust the amount of sugar to taste, or use a sugar substitute, if you like. This nourishing dish is normally served lip-scaldingly hot.

SERVES 4

450g/1lb taro or yam, peeled and cut into large chunks
100g/3¾oz/7 tbsp lard or white cooking fat
150g/5oz/¾ cup caster/superfine sugar

Cook's Tip

There are two common types of taro: a large tuber about the size of a grapefruit and a smaller one like a plum. Both have white flesh flecked with purple, but the smaller variety has the better flavour.

1 Put the taro in a pan, add just enough water to cover, and bring to the boil. Simmer for 25 minutes, then allow to cool. Mash into a smooth paste.

2 Mix the paste with lard or white cooking fat and sugar in a bowl that will fit into your steamer, and cover with a plate or clear film/plastic wrap.

3 Steam for 20 minutes, stirring once or twice, until the sugar has completely dissolved. Serve immediately.

EASTERN CHINA

The cooking of Shanghai, Zhejiang, Fujian, Anhui, Jiangsu and Jiangxi

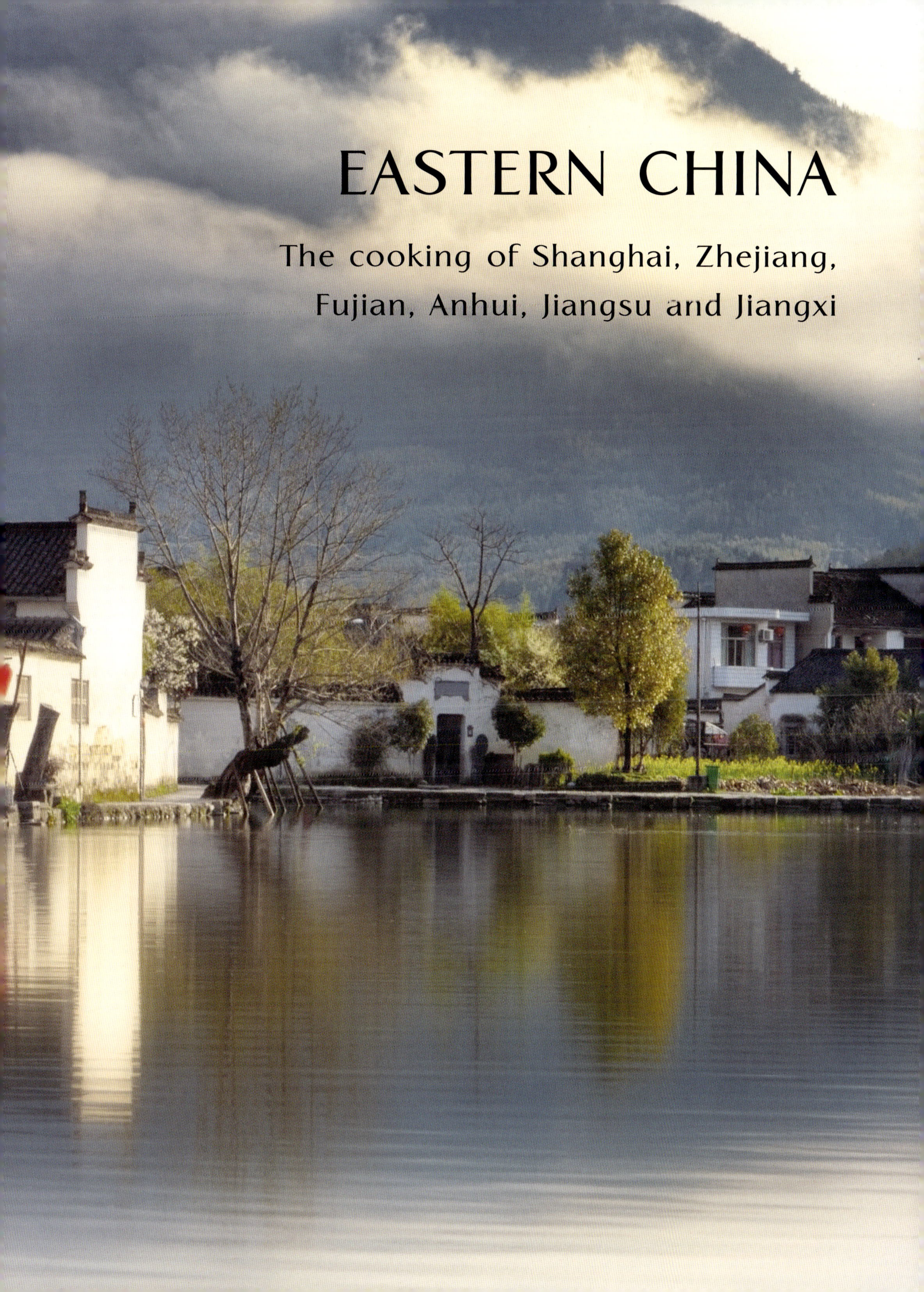

LUSH WETLANDS & FERTILE DELTAS

Eastern China comprises the huge metropolis of Shanghai, and the surrounding provinces of Jiangsu, Anhui, Zhejiang, Fujian and Jiangxi. The most notable feature of the region is the Yangtze River Delta, and water is the predominant element of the landscape. This area is largely low-lying, with ancient irrigated rice fields traversed by a vast network of canals, many of which date back centuries. Jiangsu, Shanghai, Fujian and Zhejiang all share a coastal position, meaning that the sea also plays a huge part in the culinary culture.

The Yangtze River Delta, also known as the Chang Jiang Delta, or the Golden Triangle of the Yangtze, generally comprises the triangular-shaped territory of Shanghai, southern Jiangsu Province and northern Zhejiang Province. The area lies at the heart of the region traditionally called Jiangnan (literally, 'south of the Yangtze River'). The Yangtze River is China's longest waterway, running over 6,300km (nearly 4,000 miles) on its epic journey from the Tibetan Plateau, past the Sichuan basin, then through the deep Yangtze gorges and the basins of Hubei and Anhui before it drains into the East China Sea.

A vast network of lakes and tributaries slows down its progress as it winds its way through Jiangsu Province. Most of this vast river is navigable, and trade routes have existed for many centuries between the different provinces of China along the river. Not surprisingly, therefore, the cuisine of eastern China makes a clear distinction between the flavours of ocean fish and river fish, and freshwater fishing is extremely important. In Qingpu, 50 ponds containing five different species of fish yield 29,000 tons of fish each year.

Below *The fertile eastern and coastal regions of China are famous for their rice and fish dishes.*

Climate and farming

Eastern China has a marine monsoon sub-tropical climate, and the weather is generally warm and humid. However, winter temperatures can drop as low as -10°C/14°F and, even in springtime, large temperature fluctuations can occur. The Yangtze River Delta contains the most fertile soils in all of China. Rice is the dominant crop of the delta, but further inland, fishing rivals it for supremacy.

The other major crops of this region are tea and silk, both of which have been farmed here for hundreds of years.

Eastern provinces

Jiangsu is probably the most blessed province in eastern China, with lush wetlands and fertile land that supports abundant agriculture. It has been dubbed 'the land of fish and rice' ever since its ancient beginnings. This small area of China, only about 5 per cent of the land mass, provides about 40 per cent of China's wealth. This wealth comes mainly from the waterways of the mighty Yangtze and the stupendous Grand Canal that slices its way from the north into the lower reaches of the lower delta region. Jiangsu is hot and humid in summer with cold, misty winters and plenty of rain – an ideal climate for growing rice.

Above *Water defines much of eastern China, with its extensive coastline and profusion of inland waterways.*

Fujian's topography is dominated by soaring mountains, river valleys and a sub-tropical coastline. The coastal ports have been magnets for international trade for centuries, but the forbidding, mountainous inland areas of this province were relatively inaccessible until the 1960s, when roads were built through the thick jungle. Sea fishing has been the main livelihood of Fujian's inhabitants for centuries.

Zhejiang is one of China's smallest provinces and is divided into two distinct areas. The flatter delta area north of Hangzhou, the capital of Zhejiang, is a verdant region of rolling hills, tea plantations and meandering rivers; the mountainous area to the south where it joins Fujian province is far less suited to agriculture. The benefits of this terrain are that southern Zhejiang offers much unspoilt beauty, with rugged mountains, lofty peaks and expansive valleys. Hangzhou's tea plantations yield one of the world's most sensuous teas, Dragon Well Tea (Long Qing Cha). Near Hangzhou is the waterside city of Shaoxing, famous for its eponymous wine (often spelt Xiaoxing). While this wine may be imperfect by Western wine standards, it is nonetheless much loved by locals for its robust flavour. It is also ideal for cooking.

Urban development

The urban centres of eastern China are the major cities of Shanghai, Nanjing, Hangzhou, Suzhou and Ningpo. These share much the same climate – cold winters, contrasted with summers that often reach highs of a searing 40°C (over 100°F) with humidity to match.

In modern times the area has developed tremendously fast, and has become known as the Yangtze Delta Metropolitan Area, the largest built-up area in China, covering some 99,600sq km (38,500 square miles). It is home to more than 115 million residents, of whom an estimated 80 million are part of the urban population.

A THRIVING AGRICULTURAL HUB

Eastern China has a long history of farming, fishing and trade. This is a fertile region, suited to agriculture, and the population is correspondingly large and relatively prosperous. From the time of the Han dynasty (206BCE–CE220) onwards, the Yangtze River Delta has been an area of high productivity, with its own traditions of culture, food and farming. Today, Shanghai is one of the world's largest cities, buzzing with modern technology, architecture and transport, and an ever-expanding population.

The biggest city and most important port in China's eastern region, Shanghai dates back to the 10th century. It is a municipality with provincial status (in other words, it is big enough to have its own local government). Located in the Yangtze valley, it was a small market town with only 12,000 families living there until 1127, when sudden migration and refugee movements swelled the population twentyfold to some 250,000 people.

By the 13th century, Shanghai and the surrounding area became one of China's richest regions, producing cotton, the backbone of Shanghai's economy until the early 19th century. By the time of the Ming Dynasty, between the 14th and 17th centuries, the first shoots of capitalism in East China appeared and were nurtured in this area. Shanghai continued to grow throughout the rest of the Qing Dynasty (1644–1911), and became a large financial centre that gave important support to both large-scale agriculture and smaller farming enterprises.

Shanghai reached an economic peak in the early 19th century. The Qing rulers of China were not well organized and had little government control, so

Below *Zhujiajiao is a famous ancient town on the outskirts of Shanghai that was established 1,700 years ago.*

Right *Cotton and tea are important crops in Jiangxi, which was once a key stop on the overland trade route.*

provincial guilds, termed Native Place Associations, used their extensive networks to control the city and began to compete with each other. During the Opium War of 1840, British forces temporarily held Shanghai. The war ended with the 1842 Treaty of Nanking, which saw Shanghai opened for international trade. The Taiping Rebellion broke out in 1850 and devastated the countryside but left the foreign settlements untouched.

From this uneasy situation two cities emerged: a chaotic Chinese city and a Westernized city, inhabited mainly by Chinese who preferred the Western lifestyle. This Westernized part of Shanghai has always been seen as one of the world's most modern cities. New inventions such as trams were introduced, and Shanghai was turned into a huge metropolis. British and American businessmen made a great deal of money in trade and finance here, and Germany used Shanghai as a base for investing in China. Today, the city vibrates with a lively ambience that draws thousands of visitors from all over the world.

Jiangxi – 21st-century backwater

When the Grand Canal was built in the 7th century, linking China's major waterways, the inland province of Jiangxi suddenly became an important transit point on the overland trade route from Guangdong. Tea growing and silver mining soon created a wealthy merchant class. However by the 19th century, many coastal ports in this region created competition and Jiangxi's role became less prominent. Traditional and ancient Chinese junks, which made up most of the river craft, slowly disappeared. The province had a rather dubious reputation of being an important Communist guerrilla base in the 20th century, but after many years, the Kuomintang drove the Communists out and on to their 'Long March' to Shaanxi.

Fujian – trading province

The coastal areas of Fujian had been part of the Chinese empire since the Qin Dynasty (221–207BCE). From its early beginnings as a frontier region it grew into a major commercial centre with important ports for the maritime silk route. Other commodities traded were precious stones, textiles, porcelain and food products, which were magnets to Arab merchants and other traders. Missionaries also came to the area.

When the Ming emperors forced restrictions in the 16th century that affected this maritime trade, Fujian people began to emigrate to Taiwan, Singapore, the Philippines, Malaysia and Indonesia; Fujian cuisine still exists today in these countries. The capital city, Fouzhou, is now a flourishing, bustling boom town with incredible skyscrapers and endless construction projects. The historical port of Xiamen (Amoy) is said to have been the birthplace of soy sauce, an ingredient that now enjoys a global status.

Anhui – the quiet province

Probably the least known among China's eastern provinces, Anhui has seen little of the frantic development permeating the rest of urban China today. The borders were defined by the Qing government in the 17th century and have remained largely unchanged over the centuries, although its location, set between the warring factions of northern and southern China, has meant the province has seen more than its fair share of fighting and government changes.

This inland province contains fertile agricultural land in the north, where it consists mainly of flat river plains, and a far more mountainous region in the south. The contrast is so marked that the province was divided into two at the founding of the People's Republic of China, but Anhui was merged into one again in 1952.

SHANGHAI CUISINE

The vibrant and modern city of Shanghai, situated on the Yangtze estuary, has spread its culinary culture well into the eastern provinces of Jiangsu, Zhejiang and even further south into Fujian. It is a municipality with provincial status and much influence, and is blessed by being located in an extremely fertile lower valley of the Yangtze River. The immense river and long coastline mean that, unsurprisingly, the amazing diversity of eastern recipes includes many exquisite fish and shellfish dishes.

The delta region is an enormously prolific rice bowl, providing this basic food for the whole of China. Shanghai dishes tend to be richer and heavier than those of Beijing or Cantonese cuisine, but the emphasis is still on freshness, with pure and natural flavours. The Yangtze River puts fish and shellfish at the heart of the food culture, and locally caught shrimps, crab, wild duck and carp feature strongly.

Shanghai cuisine

The culinary style of Shanghai is elegant, with fragrant sauces. Some Chinese cooks are of the opinion that Shanghai does not have its own definitive cuisine, but adopts and adapts those from the surrounding provinces, so that the resulting marriage of styles and ingredients is a hybrid with Shanghai soul. Shanghai chefs can be heavy-handed with alcohol, resulting in many 'drunken' dishes. Almost every creature that flies, swims or crawls is fair game for this delicious sousing.

Salted meats and preserved vegetables are commonly used to enhance dishes, and sugar is used with abandon, especially in tandem with soy sauce. 'Red cooking' (Hong Shao) is a popular style of stewing meats and vegetables in an intoxicating blend of wine, preserved beancurd and soy sauce.

There are many well-known and almost legendary recipes from Shanghai, such as Beggar's Chicken, a whole chicken wrapped in lotus leaves, covered in

Below *Distilled rice liquor, aged in clay pots, is used with abandon in many a 'drunken' dish in Shanghai.*

clay and oven-baked. Lime-and-ginger-flavoured 'hundred year eggs' are another popular Shanghai creation. Some may draw the line at eating 'Stinky Tofu', but it remains a delicacy of this region. There are many more: Lion's Head Pork Balls, an exquisite treat of succulent pork in a rich wine sauce; Sweet-and-Sour Spare Ribs, so well known in the West; and Stir-fried Eels in Hoisin Sauce – all rich and delicious products of Shanghai cuisine.

Cuisine of the other eastern provinces

The eastern school of cooking has more distinct provincial styles than other parts of China, the most high-profile being the Huai Yang style, which has its centre in Yangzhou. This gave the world the famous Yangzhou Fried Rice.

Jiangxi and Zhejiang share a border, and they also share many culinary elements, creating a food sub-school called the Jiangzhe style, which has an emphasis on grand banquet dishes served at festivals.

Hangzhou, in Zhejiang province, is famed for its Dragon Well Tea, Xiaoxing for its eponymous wine and Jinhua or Kin Hua for its superb ham. Rice wine goes into many dishes, in a style similar to that of Beijing cooking. Indigenous vegetables such as Chinese kale and cabbage appear in numerous dishes, often pickled in brine. Soy-braised duck and goose are regional specialities.

The use of seasoning is quite restrained, allowing the natural flavours of the ingredients to shine. For richer and saltier meat dishes, honey and maltose are used to flavour pork, sliced ham and chicken.

Above *Lotus leaves are typically used for wrapping various fillings in Fujian cooking.*

Fujian – a fresh style

In Fujian, cooking tends to be on the light side, with an emphasis on steaming food. As Fujian borders Guangdong, many dishes reflect Cantonese elements. Fish, which is a predominant ingredient in this coastal region, is touched only lightly with ginger, sesame oil, soy sauce and pepper. The same restraint applies to meat and poultry dishes. The lotus plant grows profusely in ponds, lakes and streams in this area, and its leaves are used for wrapping many fillings. Lotus nuts are also used in cooking, while lotus blossom is revered in Taoism.

EASTERN TRADITIONS

While the Gregorian calendar is followed for all practical purposes in China, it is the lunar calendar that governs the cultural, festive, religious and spiritual life of Chinese people. Most of the important celebrations, such as Lunar New Year and the Moon Cake Festival, have evolved over thousands of years and are intrinsic to life throughout China. However, there are some less well-known festivals, such as the Cold Food Festival described below, that are closely tied to local history and traditions.

Lunar New Year

Shanghai sees in the Lunar New Year with a veritable explosion of fireworks all over the city. Family and friends get together and indulge in Yangge dancing and lion dancing. The origins of the Yangge dance can be traced back 2,000 years to a religious activity to greet the gods and dispel evil. Today, it is less allied with its religious past, and has become more of a party in this most outward-looking of Chinese cities. Fireworks have spiritual significance – they are meant to see out the old and bring in the new. Everyone in the family must wear new clothes on the morning of Lunar New Year's Day and the older population will visit temples, bringing offerings of food, wine and even live poultry to appease the gods.

Below *Pyrotechnics light up the night sky above the iconic cityscape of Shanghai at Lunar New Year.*

Moon Cake Festival

There are many legends about this festival, but one in particular is singled out for its charm. A Taoist priest boasted that he could take his Tang emperor to the moon palace, then threw his walking stick into the

sky. It turned into a bridge and they both went to the moon palace, where they spent many joyous years, and on their return the people celebrated by making round cakes to signify this lunar journey.

Another oddity of the eastern provinces is Moon Cake Gambling, a game invented by a former Fujian pirate-cum-patriot to keep his buccaneers from being homesick. Every mid-autumn festival, a game of dice is played in a large porcelain bowl to compete for moon cakes. The prizes range from tiny cookies to large moon cakes, the different sizes representing the official positions won in the imperial examinations. While few people take this history seriously, they enjoy going through the motions of the game, though fruits, wine and other foods are often awarded as prizes, rather than moon cakes.

Above *Moon cakes are used for a gambling game, as well as being simply eaten, in eastern China.*

Tin Hau Festival

While mostly celebrated in Guangdong and Hong Kong, this festival is also popular in Fujian Province due to its fishing heritage. Tin Hau, the Goddess of the Sea, is known as the Queen of Heaven and the Mother of all fishermen, and was supposed to have been born in Fujian in 1093. There is an interesting story behind this holy figure: one day, as usual, her father and brothers went far out to sea to fish, but at home, Tin Hau had a dream that they were drowning. She flew over the deep sea on clouds and rescued her family. It is also believed that Tin Hau predicted storms and told travellers' fortunes.

Ching Ming (Clear and Bright) Festival

One particular festival is followed with reverence in eastern provinces. In death, as in life, Chinese people celebrate or commiserate with special foods. The Ching Ming Festival falls in early April and is a day when families visit graveyards to pay respects to their ancestors, offer food to the God of the Earth and spend a day picnicking on the site. There is great veneration in these festivities, for Taoism embraces ancestor worship and filial piety extends to the afterlife.

Cold Food Festival

This is an unusual celebration, hardly known outside Fujian. It has its origins in Taiwan, as most Taiwanese are of Fujian extraction. On 4 April each year, fire and smoke are taboo. According to legend, a court official from 2,000 years ago was burned to death on that day, and in remembrance, the Fujian Chinese used to forgo the use of fire for an entire month.

This abstinence has now become just a single day, on which the residents of Fujian will eat only cold food, such as spring rolls and even cold noodles. Interestingly, these days some people regard the day as a quirky challenge and eat only rather less traditional foods, such as cold cheeseburgers.

Eat Leizaisu

It is believed that the birthday of Leizun, an important personage of Suzhou, falls on 24 June. The festival of Eat Leizaisu dictates that everyone goes vegetarian for one day out of respect for this man and because doing so is believed to prevent disaster, avoid epidemic disease and ensure everlasting peace. In the past, the people of Suzhou celebrated this festival for a whole month, generally in June, but today they are more likely to celebrate it for just a few days. The end of the festival is marked with a special noodle dish known as Luya Noodles.

EASTERN CHINA

SOUPS & DIM SUM

VERSATILE SOUPS & DUMPLINGS

Soups in eastern China can range from the very light to broths of substance. Tofu and vegetables play important roles, with Shanghai offerings such as Tofu & Spinach Soup, for example. Pork, fish and shellfish are also favourite ingredients, especially in the hearty fare that is prepared during the winter months.

In rural areas of eastern China, thick soups packed with seafood, meat, tofu and root vegetables are often served as evening meals in themselves.

Soup bases are like blank canvases to which just about anything can be added. In eastern China, it is common for lard or white cooking fat to be stirred into soups, giving them a silky smooth feeling in the mouth and a higher calorific value.

Congee, or rice porridge, often falls into the dim sum category, even though it is not a dumpling. Salted Duck Egg Congee is one such example, and is served both in the eastern provinces and elsewhere in China. Pumpkin Cake and Steamed Prawn Dumplings are also very typical eastern Chinese snacks.

Today, most Chinese people consider eating at a dim sum restaurant a special treat, and very few families are inclined to prepare so many small dishes themselves at home. Most restaurants feature as many as 50 items on the menu, many of which are fiddly to prepare and require skills learned over years of dim sum-making. The selection of recipes here, however, will allow even the novice Chinese cook to create stunning translucent dumplings at home.

FISH BALL & NOODLE SOUP

A dish with a long history and peasant beginnings, fish ball noodles are considered to be comfort food. This particular noodle soup is sold by hawkers all over China and South-east Asia. Traditionally regarded as a late-night supper dish, it has been known to soothe the hunger pangs of mahjong players, who clatter their tiles through the night in Hong Kong, Singapore, New York and around the world.

SERVES 4

150g/5oz mung bean noodles
800ml/scant 1½ pints/3½ cups boiling water
1 fish stock/bouillon cube
24 store-bought fish balls
15ml/1 tbsp light soy sauce
15g/½oz/1 tbsp preserved winter vegetable (tung choy)
2.5ml/½ tsp ground black pepper
15ml/1 tbsp sesame oil
2 spring onions/scallions, chopped
fresh coriander/cilantro leaves, to garnish
sliced fresh red or green chillies and light soy sauce, to serve

1 Soak the mung bean noodles in warm water for about 15 minutes until they swell and become gelatinous. Drain.

2 Pour the boiling water into a large pan, add the stock cube and bring back to the boil. Add the fish balls, and boil for 5 minutes. They will swell slightly and become a little crunchy.

3 Add the noodles and simmer for 3 minutes, then add all the other ingredients.

4 Garnish with fresh coriander and serve with fresh chillies and light soy sauce, allowing each diner to add them to taste.

Cook's Tip

Do use home-made fish stock instead of the measured water and stock cube, if you have it.

SERVES 4

30ml/2 tbsp vegetable oil
3 garlic cloves, roughly chopped
25g/1oz ginger, shredded
300g/11oz carp fillets
800ml/scant 1½ pints/3½ cups boiling water
1 fish stock/bouillon cube
150g/5oz mooli/daikon or white radish, cut into 1cm/½in cubes
30ml/2 tbsp light soy sauce
30ml/2 tbsp sesame oil
2.5ml/½ tsp ground black pepper
fresh coriander/cilantro leaves, to garnish

Variation

Any firm-fleshed fish, such as halibut, cod or haddock, can also be used.

CARP & MOOLI SOUP

The people of Shanghai are famously skilled at preparing and cooking seafood. Carp are prized for their ornamental beauty, symbolism (gold and silver carp are believed to be the bringers of good fortune), and wonderful taste and texture. Whenever there is a meal requiring fish, the bones and carcass are simmered with aromatics to make a stock for another day – for ease you can also use a stock cube.

1 Heat the oil in a wok, add the garlic and ginger and fry until golden brown. Drain, reserving the oil, and set the garlic and ginger aside. Cut the carp into 5mm/¼in thick slices.

2 Pour the water into a large pan and add the stock cube. Bring back to the boil, then add the reserved garlic and ginger oil, the carp and mooli or radish. Simmer for 5 minutes, then add the soy sauce, sesame oil and pepper.

3 Simmer for 3 minutes, then serve hot, garnished with the fried garlic and ginger, and fresh coriander leaves.

TOFU & SPINACH SOUP

Although Chinese spinach comes from the same botanical family as regular spinach, and is similar to it, it is more robust and fibrous in texture with purple streaks running all the way from the stem to the leaves. It is believed to be restorative for the blood. Chinese spinach is usually sold with the roots still on, and is becoming more easily available. Salt fish is widely used in Shanghai cooking as a salting and flavouring agent.

SERVES 4

- 150g/5oz spinach, preferably Chinese spinach, if available
- 800ml/scant 1½ pints/3½ cups boiling water
- 75g/3oz salt fish
- 30ml/2 tbsp vegetable oil
- 2 garlic cloves, crushed
- 30ml/2 tbsp light soy sauce
- 2.5ml/½ tsp ground black pepper
- 15ml/1 tbsp sesame oil
- 115g/4oz tofu, cut into 1cm/½in cubes

1 Tear the spinach leaves into small pieces and slice the stalks thinly. Set aside. Pour the boiling water into a large pan and return to the boil. Add the salt fish and simmer for 10 minutes.

2 Meanwhile, heat the oil in a small frying pan and fry the garlic for 30 seconds. Pour the garlic and oil into the stock and add the soy sauce, pepper and sesame oil.

3 Simmer for 2 minutes, then add the tofu and spinach. Stir and cook for 2 minutes, then serve hot.

Variation

If salt fish is not to your liking, soak 15ml/1 tbsp dried shrimps or anchovies and add to the soup

SERVES 4

800ml/scant 1½ pints/3½ cups boiling water
115g/4oz/¾ cup processed soya beans, soaked overnight, rinsed and drained
150g/5oz/generous 1 cup minced/ground pork
30ml/2 tbsp vegetable oil
2 garlic cloves, crushed
15ml/1 tbsp yellow bean sauce
2.5ml/½ tsp ground black pepper
15ml/1 tbsp sesame oil
2.5ml/½ tsp sugar
2 spring onions/scallions, chopped
coriander/cilantro leaves, to garnish

PORK & SOYA BEAN SOUP

Soya beans grow profusely throughout most of China and, when not used to make various kinds of tofu, are cooked much like normal pulses. Chinese stores sell them dried and they have to be soaked overnight, but many stores also sell processed soya beans that require no soaking. They are frequently used as a stock base because they impart a distinctive, almost meaty, flavour.

1 Pour the boiling water into a large pan and add the soya beans. Bring to the boil and simmer for 15 minutes.

2 Break up the pork with a fork, then add to the stock so that it forms lumps when it comes in contact with the boiling liquid.

3 Simmer for 5 minutes, then add all the other ingredients except the spring onions. Cook for 3 minutes. Just before serving, add the spring onions. Serve, garnished with fresh coriander.

HAM & BAMBOO SHOOT SOUP

SERVES 4

800ml/scant 1½ pints/3½ cups meat stock or water
115g/4oz ham, diced into 1cm/½in cubes
150g/5oz young bamboo shoots, cut into thin strips
30ml/2 tbsp vegetable oil
2 garlic cloves, crushed
30ml/2 tbsp Shaoxing wine or dry sherry
30ml/2 tbsp light soy sauce
5ml/1 tsp lard or white cooking fat
1 egg, lightly beaten
25g/1oz/¼ cup peas, thawed if frozen

This fragrant soup hails from Hangzhou in Zhejiang Province, which has been known as a popular beauty spot for centuries. There is an old Chinese saying: 'In Heaven there is Paradise; in China we have Hangzhou.' This beautiful city also offers many gastronomic delights. Chinese ham is very different from the Western kind and the best is reputed to come from Jinhua, also in the same province. If this is unavailable, use good smoked ham.

1 Put the stock or water into a large pan and bring to the boil. Add the ham and bamboo shoots and simmer for 15 minutes.

2 Heat the oil in a small pan and fry the garlic for 30 seconds, then pour the garlic and oil into the stock. Add the wine or sherry, soy sauce and lard or white cooking fat. Simmer for 2 minutes.

3 Swirl the egg into the stock mixture and stir until the stock is streaked with the egg. Add the peas and cook for 2 minutes. Serve.

SERVES 4

300g/11oz meaty pork ribs
1 bitter melon
1.2 litres/2 pints/5 cups boiling water
30ml/2 tbsp light soy sauce
2.5ml/½ tsp ground black pepper
15g/½oz dried shrimps, soaked until soft, minced
2.5ml/½ tsp sugar
5ml/1 tsp lard or white cooking fat
chilli sauce, for dipping

Variation

If you are short of time, use fairly lean pork, thinly sliced, instead of ribs. Cook it for 30 minutes before adding the other ingredients.

SPARE RIB & BITTER MELON SOUP

When cooking, chefs recommend that you can temper some of the bitterness of bitter melon by steeping cut slices in a little salt and then squeezing out the moisture. Fujian bitter melon lovers, however, would never do such a thing, as it is the very bitterness that is its intrinsic allure.

1 Cut the pork ribs into 2.5cm/1in pieces. Cut the bitter melon lengthways and remove and discard the soft core and red seeds. Scrape away and discard any white pith that clings to the green flesh. Cut the flesh into half-moon slices, 1cm/½in wide.

2 Pour the boiling water into a large pan, add the pork rib pieces and simmer for 45 minutes, until the meat comes away from the bones easily (simmer for a further 15 minutes if the ribs are not tender enough). The stock will reduce to about 800ml/scant 1½ pints/3½ cups. Skim off any fatty froth floating on top.

3 Add the remaining ingredients (except for the chilli sauce) and simmer for 5 minutes. Serve with chilli sauce for dipping.

SALTED DUCK EGG CONGEE

A watery rice porridge, congee has been a staple dish throughout China and South-east Asia for centuries. The word 'congee' is believed to have derived from the Dravidian word 'kanji' (an Indian rice porridge). Its history is rooted in peasant farming communities where a little rice had to feed many people. Over time many things have been thrown into the congee pan – from vegetables to salt fish, eggs and meat. Today, expensive ingredients such as lobster, scallops and oysters are added. True congee, such as this simple egg one, uses broken rice, which is available in Chinese stores.

SERVES 4

- 100g/3¾oz/½ cup broken rice
- 2 salted duck eggs
- 5ml/1 tsp preserved winter vegetable (tung choy)
- 15ml/1 tbsp sesame oil
- 5ml/1 tsp salt
- 5ml/1 tsp white pepper, plus extra to serve
- 2 spring onions/scallions, roughly chopped

Variation

This simple but warming dish can be dressed up by adding cooked minced pork, salt fish or chicken – in fact, anything you fancy.

1 Bring the rice and 1 litre/1¾ pints/4 cups water to the boil and simmer for 30 minutes, or until the rice grains are mushy and the liquid is milky. If the consistency is too thick, add a drop more boiling water.

2 Hard-boil the salted duck eggs for 10 minutes. Cool in cold water, then peel off the shells. Cut into quarters.

3 Set aside four of the duck egg quarters and half the chopped spring onions for garnishing, then add the rest and all of the other ingredients to the rice porridge.

4 Bring to a gentle boil over low heat. Cook for a further 5 minutes, or until well incorporated.

5 Remove from the heat and allow to cool a little before serving warm. Garnish each dish with the reserved spring onions and a quarter of duck egg. Sprinkle with a little extra white pepper and serve immediately.

QUAIL'S EGG SESAME TOAST

Sesame toast is a favourite on dim sum menus everywhere and makes a good choice of finger food when you are entertaining. This recipe has a hard-boiled quail's egg sitting beneath the usual filling of minced pork. When coated with sesame seeds and deep-fried, these have an intriguing flavour and texture.

MAKES 8 TOASTS

4 quail's eggs, hard-boiled
4 slices of white bread, crusts removed
2 eggs, lightly beaten
250g/9oz/generous 1 cup minced/ground pork
15ml/1 tbsp light soy sauce
2.5ml/½ tsp white pepper
5ml/1 tsp cornflour/cornstarch
sesame seeds, for coating
vegetable oil, for deep-frying
sliced cucumber and hoisin sauce or chilli sauce, to serve

Variations

- You can use minced chicken, prawns or shrimp instead of the pork, if you like.
- For a quicker version, omit the hard-boiled quail's eggs.

1 Put the quail's eggs in a small pan of boiling water and cook for 5 minutes. Drain, then cool in cold water. Shell the eggs and cut each in half.

2 Cut each slice of bread into two triangles. Brush with beaten egg. Mix the pork with the soy sauce, pepper and cornflour, stirring well.

3 Place a halved quail's egg, cut side down, on each bread triangle and spread minced pork over the top, patting it in firmly. Brush with beaten egg.

4 Spread a generous amount of sesame seeds over a plate and carefully coat the top of each covered toast liberally. Shake off the excess.

5 Heat the oil to 180°C/350°F (test by frying a small cube of bread; it should brown in 40 seconds) and fry the toasts, a few at a time, until golden brown. Set aside to drain on kitchen paper while you cook the remaining toasts in the same way.

6 Once all the toasts are cooked, serve immediately with sliced cucumber and hoisin sauce or chilli sauce, for dipping.

SWEET TURNIP DUMPLINGS

Also known as jicama, sweet turnips are similar in texture to the common swede or rutabaga but with the sweetness of a conference pear and a hint of water chestnuts. They have a light tan-coloured skin and are shaped like spinning tops. The flesh is white and crunchy, and is often used in Fujian as a filling ingredient for spring rolls or stir-fried as a vegetable. Sweet turnips are not common outside of China, but they are sold fresh by some Chinese and Thai stores. Each dumpling should about 7.5cm/3in long, and half as wide.

MAKES 10–12 DUMPLINGS

- 60g/2¼oz/generous ½ cup wheat starch, plus extra for dusting
- 75g/3oz/⅔ cup cornflour/cornstarch
- a pinch of salt
- 200ml/7fl oz/scant 1 cup hot water
- 15ml/1 tbsp vegetable oil
- sweet soy sauce dip, to serve

FOR THE FILLING

- 450g/1lb sweet turnip or jicama, peeled
- 30ml/2 tbsp vegetable oil
- 2 garlic cloves, crushed
- 15ml/1 tbsp yellow bean sauce
- 5ml/1 tsp sugar
- 15ml/1 tbsp light soy sauce
- 15ml/1 tbsp sesame oil
- 150g/5oz small prawns/shrimp, peeled and chopped

Variation

In Guangdong, bamboo shoots are used instead of sweet turnip. Slice canned bamboo shoots into similar-sized pieces as the turnip but cook them for 15 minutes.

1 To make the filling, cut the sweet turnip into matchstick strips about 5mm/¼in thick. Heat the oil and fry the garlic for 20 seconds, then add the yellow bean sauce, sugar, soy sauce and sesame oil. Stir for 30 seconds and then add the turnip and 500ml/scant 1 pint/2 cups water.

2 Simmer over medium heat for 25 minutes, or until nearly dry and the turnip pieces have broken up. Add the prawns and cook for 2 minutes. Allow to cool.

3 Mix the wheat starch, cornflour and salt together in a bowl and slowly add the hot water, stirring well to mix and form a soft dough. Add the oil and continue to knead a little until the mixture is the consistency of bread dough but less springy.

4 Roll out the dough into a cylinder shape on a board sprinkled with wheat starch. Cut into 10–12 equal pieces and form into sausage shapes. With a small rolling pin, flatten each piece into a round and roll out to 9cm/3½in in diameter.

5 Drain the turnip mixture well. Put one heaped tablespoonful of the mixture in the centre of a piece of dough. Fold in half to make a half-moon shape. Seal the edge with a little dab of water, and crimp. Trim off any floppy edges. Repeat with the other dough pieces.

6 Arrange the dumplings on a lightly oiled plate that will fit into your steamer and steam over a pan of boiling water for 15 minutes on high heat. The cooked dumplings will have a translucent and glossy appearance. Serve with a sweet soy sauce dip.

STEAMED PRAWN DUMPLINGS

The batter for these dumplings uses wheat starch (known as mien fen in Mandarin), mixed with cornflour or tapioca flour to achieve the typical exquisite translucence. Dim sum originated in south China, and any batter that steams to a translucent thinness is known as Ha Gau (Cantonese) pastry, but the dumplings are popular all over China. The dough dries out quickly, so it needs to be filled and cooked immediately.

MAKES 20 DUMPLINGS

60g/2¼oz/generous ½ cup wheat starch, plus extra for dusting
75g/3oz/⅔ cup cornflour/cornstarch
a pinch of salt
200ml/7fl oz/scant 1 cup hot water
soy sauce dip or chilli sauce dip, to serve

FOR THE FILLING

675g/1½lb prawns/shrimp
5ml/1 tsp sugar
5ml/1 tsp cornflour/cornstarch
1 spring onion/scallion, finely chopped
5ml/1 tsp salt
2.5ml/½ tsp sugar
2.5ml/½ tsp ground white pepper

1 To make the filling, peel and wash the prawns and cut each into small dice. Mix the sugar and cornflour in a bowl and rub the prawn pieces gently in the mixture to coat thoroughly. Wash off the cornflour and sugar by putting the prawns in a colander and rinsing them under running water for 10 minutes. Drain well. This gives the prawns a delicious crunch.

2 In a bowl, combine the prawn pieces, spring onion, salt, sugar and pepper. Put into a pan and cook over a low heat for 5 minutes, stirring often, or until the prawns turn pink with a fairly thick coating. Allow to cool.

3 In a bowl, mix the wheat starch, cornflour and salt together, then slowly add the hot water, mixing well to form a soft dough. The consistency should be similar to bread dough but less springy.

4 Roll the dough into a cylinder shape on a board sprinkled with wheat starch flour. Cut into 20 equal pieces and form into sausage shapes. With a small rolling pin, flatten each piece into a round and roll out until it is about 7.5cm/3in in diameter and the thinness of parchment.

5 Put one heaped teaspoonful of prawn mixture into the centre of a piece of dough. Fold in half to make a half-moon shape. Pinch the ends together, then pleat and shape into a closed dumpling. Trim off any floppy edges. Repeat with the other dough pieces.

6 Arrange the dumplings on a lightly oiled plate and steam over a pan of boiling water for 15 minutes on high heat. The cooked dumplings will have a glossy, pearly appearance. Serve with a soy sauce or chilli sauce dip.

Cook's Tip

Wheat starch has a fine consistency that's similar to that of cornflour. It is especially good for making dim sum dough and is widely available in Chinese stores.

PUMPKIN CAKE

This delicious Fujian snack is often made during festive occasions. It is one of the most comforting foods on the eastern Chinese menu and a lovely way to use pumpkin. This is a savoury, and yet sweet, concoction that bears much similarity to the Yam Cake of South China, which is a more famous dim sum offering. It is usually served during Chinese New Year, but is a tempting mouthful on any day.

MAKES 6–8 WEDGES

- 1kg/2¼lb pumpkin, peeled and cut into chunks
- 300g/11oz/2⅔ cups rice flour
- 30ml/2 tbsp tapioca flour
- 50g/2oz dried shrimps, soaked and drained
- 8 Chinese dried mushrooms, soaked until soft
- 45ml/3 tbsp vegetable oil
- 4 garlic cloves, crushed
- 1 Chinese sausage, cut into very small dice
- 15ml/1 tbsp sesame oil
- 30ml/2 tbsp light soy sauce
- 2.5ml/½ tsp ground white pepper
- sliced cucumber and a spicy dip, to serve

1 Steam the pumpkin for 20 minutes, or until soft enough to mash easily. Allow the pumpkin to cool, then process it to a fine paste using a food processor or potato masher.

2 Mix the rice flour, tapioca flour and mashed pumpkin together. Stir to mix thoroughly until the mixture is a smooth paste, the consistency of thick batter.

3 Chop the soaked dried shrimps roughly. Snip off and discard the mushroom stems, then slice the caps.

4 Heat the oil in a wok and fry the garlic for 30 seconds until light brown. Add the dried shrimps, mushrooms and sausage, and fry for 1 minute. Add the sesame oil, soy sauce and pepper, and stir for 30 seconds until well mixed.

5 Add the prepared pumpkin mash and mix well, making sure the ingredients are well distributed.

6 Transfer the mixture to a lightly oiled steaming tray and press gently with a spatula to form a firm, round cake. Steam for about 25 minutes or until cooked through.

7 Allow to cool completely, then chill. Cut into wedges and serve with cucumber slices and a spicy dip.

EASTERN CHINA

FISH & SHELLFISH

STEAMED, SMOKED, BRAISED OR FRIED

In this region of abundant fish and shellfish, chefs distinguish between each type of fish when selecting the flavourings to go with them, and when deciding upon the best cooking methods. Robust fish such as carp, eel, pomfret and porgy are particularly popular, as they can withstand aromatics and seasonings that maximize their flavour. The coastal regions that stretch from Jiangsu to Fujian yield a magnificent array of these types of fish, and they are typically combined with bold ingredients such as black bean sauce.

In Hangzhou, chefs are insistent on using only fish from the famous West Lake, as they believe the quality to be unbeatable. Dishes such as Fish in Vinegar Sauce, made using West Lake fish, demonstrate this penchant for local products. When cooking this dish at home, you can use any good fresh fish.

Rice wine is used in many of the fish and shellfish recipes of the region, with Shaoxing wine from Zhejiang being the most popular type. This adds wonderful depth of flavour.

Excess fish is transformed into delightful morsels, such as fish balls, which can be added to many a dish. These can be bought from Chinese stores along with a whole host of other processed fish shapes. They can also be made at home, such as in the recipe for Fried Prawn Balls, and these have a superior flavour to bought ones.

Sweet crab meat is combined with mild tofu for the Huaiyang dish of Braised Tofu with Crab, a dish of peasant origins transformed to make it fit for emperors.

SEAWEED FISH

The seaweed reference in the name of this dish is misleading, as no seaweed is used, though the thinly sliced cloud ears, once cooked, do resemble seaweed in texture. Many Chinese dishes have names that are not reflected in the ingredients used – usually the result of symbolism, which plays a large part in Chinese culinary culture.

SERVES 4

- 600g/1lb 5oz monkfish or any firm-fleshed fish, filleted
- 15ml/1 tbsp cornflour/cornstarch, plus 5ml/1 tsp for the sauce
- vegetable oil, for deep-frying
- 30g/1¼oz cloud ear/wood ear mushrooms, soaked in cold water for 20 minutes
- 30ml/2 tbsp vegetable oil
- 2 garlic cloves, chopped
- 25g/1oz fresh root ginger, chopped
- 15ml/1 tbsp oyster sauce
- 15ml/1 tbsp hoisin sauce
- 30ml/2 tbsp Chinese wine
- 2.5ml/½ tsp ground white or black pepper
- chopped Chinese celery leaves, to garnish

1 Cut the fish into 2.5cm/1in chunks and coat with 15ml/1 tbsp cornflour. Dust off the excess. Heat the oil for deep-frying in a wok or deep-fryer. Deep-fry the fish until golden. Set aside.

2 Using scissors, trim off any hard woody parts from the cloud ears and cut into fine strips.

3 Heat 30ml/2 tbsp oil in a wok and fry the garlic and ginger for 30 seconds until golden. Add the oyster sauce, hoisin sauce, wine, 175ml/6fl oz/¾ cup water and the pepper, and bring to the boil.

4 Add the fish and simmer for 3 minutes, or until nearly cooked. Add the cloud ears and simmer for 2 minutes more.

5 Blend the 5ml/1 tsp cornflour with a little water and stir it into the sauce. Serve, garnished with Chinese celery leaves.

SERVES 4

2 red mullet or snapper, about 675g/1½lb total weight
2.5ml/½ tsp salt
30ml/2 tbsp cornflour/cornstarch
vegetable oil, for deep-frying, plus 30ml/2 tbsp
25g/1oz fresh root ginger, shredded
4 garlic cloves, sliced
15ml/1 tbsp sesame oil
15ml/1 tbsp Fuzhou wine lees, or 1 cube preserved red beancurd (tofu ru) mashed with 30ml/2 tbsp Chinese wine
15ml/1 tbsp light soy sauce
1 leek, white part only, thinly sliced
5ml/1 tsp sugar
fried slices of garlic or shallots, to garnish

WINE-BRAISED FISH & LEEKS

Leeks are eaten in China for their crunchy texture and pungent taste as well as for their symbolic representation of good fortune; the vegetable's Chinese name rhymes with the word for 'counting'.

1 Clean the fish and trim off any protruding sharp fins and the tail. Make several deep cuts along the deepest part of the body. Rub with salt. Dust with 15ml/1 tbsp cornflour and shake off the excess.

2 Heat the oil for frying in a wok or deep-fryer, then deep-fry the fish until crisp. Drain, set aside and keep warm.

3 Heat the 30ml/2 tbsp oil in a wok and fry the ginger and garlic for 30 seconds. Add the sesame oil, wine lees or beancurd and wine mixture. Add the soy sauce and stir for 1 minute, then add the leek, 300ml/½ pint/1¼ cups water and the sugar, and bring to the boil.

4 Blend the remaining cornflour with a little water and stir it into the sauce until smooth and slightly thick. Add the whole fish and bathe liberally with the sauce for about 30 seconds, or until heated through. Serve with a garnish of fried garlic or shallots.

FISH IN BLACK BEAN SAUCE

One of the most basic dishes in the Yangtze delta region is fish cooked in a black bean sauce. Black beans have been a staple seasoning in China for centuries. They are used whole, as fermented beans, or processed into a rich, aromatic paste with ginger and garlic. Commercial black bean paste comes in many grades, some with Sichuan peppercorns and others with chilli. It has an affinity with sesame oil and spring onions.

SERVES 4

450g/1lb monkfish or halibut fillets
5ml/1 tsp salt
30ml/2 tbsp cornflour/cornstarch
vegetable oil, for deep-frying

FOR THE SAUCE
2 garlic cloves, crushed
25g/1oz fresh root ginger, shredded
1 spring onion/scallion, chopped, plus extra to garnish
15ml/1 tbsp black bean sauce
5ml/1 tsp sugar
30ml/2 tbsp sesame oil
5ml/1 tsp vinegar, preferably Chinese rice wine vinegar
boiled rice, to serve

1 Cut the fish into 2.5cm/1in cubes and rub with the salt. Wash and drain, then coat with cornflour. Shake off the excess. Heat the oil for deep-frying in a wok or deep-fryer and deep-fry the fish until crisp and golden brown. Set aside.

2 To make the sauce, heat 15ml/1 tbsp of the deep-frying oil in a wok and stir-fry the garlic and ginger for 40 seconds. Add the spring onion, black bean sauce, sugar, sesame oil, vinegar and 300ml/½ pint/1¼ cups water.

3 Cook for 1 minute, or until well blended, then add the fish. Stir over high heat for 2 minutes, or until the sauce is thick. Serve with boiled rice, garnished with chopped spring onions.

Variation

You can omit the deep-frying stage and add the fish directly to the sauce to braise instead.

SMOKED POMFRET

Although smoking was traditionally a Sichuan style of food preparation, it has since spread to all regions, and in Shanghai it is fairly common. Tea leaves are great smoking material, as they give a subtle, smoky flavour that works well with seafood. Semi-fermented oolong tea from Fujian Province gives the best flavour.

1 Rub the pomfret with the salt. Line a large wok with a double sheet of foil. To make the smoking mixture, mix the tea leaves with the flour and sugar, and spread evenly on top of the foil. Place a lightly oiled bamboo steamer on the wok, leaving space between the smoking materials and the fish.

2 Put the pomfret directly on the steamer rack. Turn the heat to high and, when the smoke begins to appear, turn the heat down to medium. Smoke for 30 minutes. Remove the fish and leave to cool.

3 Drizzle with wine or sherry and sesame oil, and sprinkle the ginger over the top. Put on a deep plate in a bamboo steamer and steam for 10 minutes before serving.

SERVES 4

675g/1½lb pomfret, snapper or porgy, cleaned, with fins
5ml/1 tsp salt
vegetable oil, for greasing
45ml/3 tbsp Shaoxing wine or dry sherry
30ml/2 tbsp sesame oil
25g/1oz fresh root ginger, peeled and very thinly sliced

FOR THE SMOKING MATERIALS
50g/2oz loose-leaf tea of your choice
150g/5oz/1¼ cups plain/all-purpose flour
45ml/3 tbsp light muscovado/brown or demerara/raw sugar

SERVES 4

1 large meaty fish head, such as tuna or salmon
30ml/2 tbsp vegetable oil
3 garlic cloves, chopped
25g/1oz fresh root ginger, chopped
15ml/1 tbsp black bean sauce
800ml/scant 1½ pints/3½ cups boiling water
45ml/3 tbsp Chinese rose-flavoured wine (mei kwei lo)
a small piece of tangerine peel, about 5cm/2in square
a pinch of Chinese five-spice powder
2.5ml/½ tsp ground black pepper
200g/7oz cabbage leaves, shredded
4 spring onions/scallions, cut into 5cm/2in lengths

FISH HEAD CASSEROLE

To the Chinese, a fish head is as good as any part of the main body, as it contains a lot of tender meat, especially if the head is large. The best heads to use are salmon or tuna, but they have to weigh in at around 1kg/2¼lb to be worthy of being cooked. The meat yield is about a third of the weight, and is mostly found in the cheeks and near the gills.

1 Remove the gills and any entrails and cut the fish head into two pieces using a cleaver. Rub all over with salt, then wash and drain.

2 Heat the oil in a wok and fry the garlic and ginger for 40 seconds, then add the black bean sauce. Stir for 1 minute, then stir in the water, wine, tangerine peel, five-spice powder and pepper.

3 Bring to the boil and cook over a high heat for 5 minutes to reduce the liquid and concentrate the flavour. Add the cabbage and cook over high heat for 5 minutes.

4 Add the fish head and cook for 10 minutes over medium heat. Add the spring onions and cook for 3 minutes more. Serve immediately.

FISH IN VINEGAR SAUCE

Hangzhou restaurant chefs are purists and will only serve fish caught from the famous West Lake. The Chinese also make a distinction between freshwater and saltwater fish, since there is an intrinsic difference in taste. The most popular West Lake fish is the grass carp or mirror carp, which has a delicate flavour. You can use any fresh fish.

SERVES 4

- 600g/1lb 5oz carp or other whole firm-fleshed fish, cleaned
- 750ml/1¼ pints/3 cups boiling water
- 25g/1oz fresh root ginger, chopped
- 30ml/2 tbsp Shaoxing wine or dry sherry
- 30ml/2 tbsp dark soy sauce
- 5ml/1 tsp sugar
- ½ leek, white part only, thinly sliced
- 15ml/1 tbsp rice vinegar
- 15ml/1 tbsp cornflour/cornstarch

1 With a sharp knife, slit all the way down the fish from the gills to the tail and open out to make a butterfly shape, one half with the bone and the other without. Cut deep slits along the thickest parts of the flesh on the skin side but not all the way to the bone.

2 Pour the boiling water into a wok and bring back to the boil. Lower in the whole fish and cook for 2 minutes, then lift out carefully with a slotted spoon and put on a serving plate.

3 Remove all but 200ml/7fl oz/scant 1 cup of the water and add the ginger, wine or sherry and the soy sauce. Cook for 1 minute, then add the sugar, leek and rice vinegar. Cook for 1 minute more.

4 Blend the cornflour with a little water, then stir into the wok and cook until the sauce is thickened. Ladle over the boiled fish. Serve.

Variation

You can also deep-fry the carp instead of boiling it. Make the sauce following step 3 onwards.

SERVES 4

675g/1½lb prepared eels, bones removed
salt, for preparing the eels
15ml/1 tbsp cornflour/cornstarch
vegetable oil, for shallow frying, plus 30ml/2 tbsp
25g/1oz fresh root ginger, shredded
2 spring onions/scallions, cut into 5cm/2in lengths
30ml/2 tbsp Shaoxing wine or sherry
30ml/2 tbsp hoisin sauce
15ml/1 tbsp dark soy sauce
2.5ml/½ tsp salt
strips of red chillies, to garnish

Cook's Tip

Eels are rather difficult to prepare, so ask your fishmonger to gut them and cut them into chunks for you, if you like.

EELS IN HOISIN SAUCE

The riverine and delta areas of eastern China abound with eels that, because they are cartilaginous and boneless apart from the main vertebrae, make good eating. Eel meat is often likened to chicken, rather like monkfish – which, indeed, can be used in place of eel if you like. Eels should always be alive when bought as they don't keep well.

1 Pat the eels dry with kitchen paper and rub with a little salt to remove some of the slippery coating on the skins. Cut into 2.5cm/1in medallions. Wash and drain, then coat with cornflour.

2 Heat a pan or wok with oil for shallow frying and fry the eel for 1 minute, or until they are half-cooked. Drain well on kitchen paper.

3 Heat the 30ml/2 tbsp oil and fry the ginger for 40 seconds. Add the spring onions, stir for 30 seconds, then add the eels.

4 Stir over high heat for 1 minute, then add the wine or sherry, hoisin sauce, soy sauce, 120ml/4fl oz/½ cup water and the salt.

5 Stir over high heat for 1 minute, or until the sauce is slightly thick and glossy. Serve garnished with strips of red chillies.

FRIED PRAWN BALLS

Fujian chefs are good at processing seafood into savoury balls and cakes, often adding them to noodle dishes, many of which are grand enough to serve at banquets. This recipe uses prawns; the mixture needs a bit of work to achieve the desired consistency, but the results are superior to commercial ones, which tend to contain a lot of flour.

1 Process the prawns to a smooth paste in a blender or food processor. Transfer to a mortar and grind slowly with a pestle. As you do this, add the water and tapioca starch or cornflour a little at a time, turning the prawn paste as you work.

2 Add the salt, sesame oil and pepper and blend well using the pestle. Continue to process the prawns in this way for at least 15 minutes. This will aerate the prawn mixture until it has a slightly springy texture. Alternatively, use a food processor or blender, although the results will not be quite the same, because of the cutting action of the blade rather than the grinding action of a pestle; the latter is preferable.

3 Using scissors, trim off and discard any hard woody parts from the cloud ears, then chop them finely. Add to the prawns and continue to process until well mixed.

4 With floured fingers, shape the mixture into small balls the size of large grapes.

5 Heat the oil for frying in a wok or deep-fryer. Deep-fry the prawn balls until they are golden brown, then remove and leave to cool. The balls will shrink a little, and have slightly shrivelled skin; this is normal.

6 Serve with chilli sauce for dipping.

SERVES 4 AS AN APPETIZER OR 2 AS A MAIN

675g/1½lb prawns/shrimp, peeled and deveined (see Cook's Tip)
30ml/2 tbsp water
30ml/2 tbsp tapioca starch or cornflour/cornstarch, plus extra for dusting
5ml/1 tsp salt
15ml/1 tbsp sesame oil
2.5ml/½ tsp ground white pepper
25g/1oz cloud ear/wood ear mushrooms, soaked in cold water for 20 minutes
vegetable oil, for deep-frying
chilli sauce, for dipping

Cook's Tip

To devein a prawn or large shrimp, make a shallow cut down the centre of the curved back, pull out the black vein with a cocktail stick, toothpick or your fingers, and rinse the prawn well.

FRIED FISH BALLS

Fish balls are integral to the cuisine of Fujian, and Fuzhou chefs elevate the cooking of these delicacies to great heights. Being a coastal region, excess fish is processed into fish balls, fish cakes and pastes to be used as stuffing ingredients. Fish balls are often boiled or steamed, then fried and served with a sauce. Street food vendors sell this snack, often skewering a few on bamboo sticks. Fish balls are available in Chinese stores.

SERVES 4 AS AN APPETIZER OR 2 AS A MAIN

12 large prepared fish balls
vegetable oil, for deep-frying
½ cucumber

FOR THE SAUCE
15ml/1 tbsp chilli sauce, or to taste
30ml/2 tbsp tomato ketchup
15ml/1 tbsp oyster sauce
45ml/3 tbsp water
5ml/1 tsp vinegar

1 Bring a large pan of water to the boil and cook the fish balls for 5 minutes. Drain thoroughly and pat them dry on kitchen paper.

2 Heat the oil for frying in a wok or deep-fryer and deep-fry the fish balls until they are golden brown.

3 Blend together all of the sauce ingredients in a pan and warm gently over a low heat. Do not allow it to boil.

4 Peel and core the cucumber, then cut it into chunks, each the size of a fish ball. Skewer the fish balls alternately with the cucumber, and serve with the sauce on the side.

Variation

You could also serve the fish bowls in a deep bowl with the cucumber and with the sauce poured over the top.

SERVES 4

450g/1lb prawns/shrimp, shelled
15ml/1 tbsp vegetable oil
2 garlic cloves, chopped
1 spring onion/scallion, chopped
15ml/1 tbsp oyster sauce
2.5ml/½ tsp ground white or black pepper
15ml/1 tbsp sesame oil
24 vacuum-packed or canned ginkgo nuts, rinsed and drained
5ml/1 tsp cornflour/cornstarch
chopped spring onion, to garnish
noodles, to serve

PRAWNS & GINKGO NUTS

Ginkgo biloba nuts come from the maidenhair tree and are regarded by the Chinese with near reverence for their restorative and medicinal properties; they also add flavour and crunch to stir-fries and soups. Dried ginkgo nuts take a long time to soak and soften, so I often prefer to use the canned or vacuum-packed ones that need no preparation other than draining.

1 Devein the prawns by making a shallow cut down the centre of the curved back and pulling out the black vein. Cut the prawns into smaller pieces, if they are very large.

2 Heat the oil in a wok and fry the garlic for 20 seconds, then add the spring onion. Stir for 30 seconds, then add the oyster sauce, pepper and sesame oil. Add the prawns and ginkgo nuts. Cook, stirring, for 2 minutes, until the prawns are cooked.

3 Blend 100ml/3½fl oz/scant ½ cup water with the cornflour and add it to the wok. Stir until the sauce is thick. Serve hot, garnished with spring onion and accompanied by noodles.

DRY-FRIED PRAWNS

In Chinese cooking, there are many different types of stir-frying, ranging from flash-frying to a 'fire in the wok'. This traditional recipe from Anhui uses a dry stir-frying method, which is employed most often for delicate shellfish. For the best results, cook prawns in their shells with only the heads removed. It is traditional to use lard or white cooking fat instead of oil, to add extra flavour.

SERVES 4

- 450g/1lb large tiger prawns/ jumbo shrimp, unpeeled
- 30ml/2 tbsp lard or white cooking fat, or vegetable oil
- 2.5ml/½ tsp salt
- 2 garlic cloves, crushed
- 25g/1oz fresh root ginger, shredded
- 1 spring onion/scallion, finely chopped
- 15ml/1 tbsp rice wine
- 5ml/1 tsp sugar
- 15ml/1 tbsp light soy sauce
- 5ml/1 tsp ground black pepper
- shredded lettuce, to serve

1 Wash the prawns, then remove the heads. Heat the lard, fat or oil in a wok until very hot and stir-fry the prawns with the salt until they turn completely pink and glossy. Remove and set aside.

2 Add the garlic to the wok with the ginger and spring onion, and stir-fry for 1 minute. Add the rice wine, sugar, soy sauce and pepper, and stir to blend for 1 minute.

3 Return the prawns to the pan and toss until well coated. Serve on a bed of lettuce.

SERVES 4

450g/1lb large prawns/shrimp
30ml/2 tbsp vegetable oil
2 garlic cloves, chopped
15ml/1 tbsp light soy sauce
15ml/1 tbsp sesame oil
30g/1¼oz/2 tbsp peas, thawed if frozen
5ml/1 tsp cornflour/cornstarch
boiled rice, to serve

Variation

Give the dish a little crunchiness by adding 30ml/2 tbsp of chopped water chestnuts, if you like.

PHOENIX PRAWNS

This dish is believed to have been a creation of the Muslim Hui people, who number some 4.5 million and are scattered throughout the northern provinces. Their cuisine is regarded as a distinct entity, since Islam forbids the eating of pork, which is the main meat in China, and also alcohol. The name of the recipe is symbolic, because prawns, when cooked with their tails on, are likened to the mythical bird!

1 Peel the prawns, but leave the tails on. Devein the prawns by making a shallow cut down the centre of the curved back and pulling out the black vein.

2 Heat the oil in a pan or wok and fry the garlic for 20 seconds. Add the prawns and stir-fry for 1–2 minutes, or until they turn pink.

3 Add the soy sauce, sesame oil, peas and 90ml/6 tbsp water, and stir until it begins to simmer.

4 Blend the cornflour with a little water and add to the pan. Stir for 1 minute, or until thick, and serve hot, with boiled rice, if you like.

DRAGON WELL PRAWNS

The original version of this classic Hangzhou dish calls for the prawns to be cooked in Dragon Well tea, but it is something of an acquired taste and can be overpowering. Dragon Well tea is also hard to obtain outside China. Instead, you can use a weak tea made with jasmine tea leaves.

SERVES 4

- 450g/1lb prawns/shrimp, shelled
- 1 egg white
- 30ml/2 tbsp Shaoxing wine or dry sherry
- 2.5ml/½ tsp sugar
- 15ml/1 tbsp light soy sauce
- 5ml/1 tsp jasmine tea leaves
- 15ml/1 tbsp vegetable oil
- 1 spring onion/scallion, chopped, plus extra to garnish
- 2.5ml/½ tsp ground black pepper
- 15ml/1 tbsp sesame oil
- boiled rice, to serve

1 Devein the prawns by making a shallow cut down the centre of the curved back and pulling out the black vein. In a shallow dish, lightly beat the egg white and mix with the wine or sherry, sugar and soy sauce. Add the prawns and marinate for 30 minutes.

2 Boil 250ml/8fl oz/1 cup water and brew the jasmine tea leaves for 3 minutes, then strain. Lift the prawns from their marinade and steep in the hot tea for 10 minutes, then drain.

3 Heat the oil in a wok and fry the spring onion for 30 seconds. Add the pepper and sesame oil. Stir for 30 seconds, then add the prawns and cook for 1–2 minutes, or until they are pink.

4 Drizzle a little of the marinade over and stir for 20 seconds to blend. Serve garnished with spring onions, on a bed of boiled rice.

Cook's Tip

Experiment with different Chinese teas such as lapsang souchong or pu erh, or even try Earl Grey for an unusual result.

BRAISED TOFU WITH CRAB

From the Huaiyang school of cooking comes this delicate dish of crab and tofu that is typical of the region. It is a clay-pot dish believed to have peasant origins. It uses dried bamboo pith, which, when cooked, imparts a crunchy texture in contrast to the soft tofu and crab meat. The seasonings are a subtle mixture of yellow bean sauce, wine and hoisin sauce. If you do not have time to prepare fresh crab, use good-quality canned crab meat.

SERVES 4

450g/1lb tofu, rinsed and drained
vegetable oil, for deep-frying, plus 15ml/1 tbsp
2 garlic cloves, chopped
30ml/2 tbsp rice wine
15m/1 tbsp yellow bean sauce
15ml/1 tbsp hoisin sauce
75g/3oz bamboo pith, soaked until soft
1 egg, lightly beaten
350g/12oz white crab meat

Cook's Tips

- Scallops can also be cooked in the same way. Use frozen or fresh from the shell.
- If bamboo pith is not available, use ordinary canned bamboo shoots instead.

1 Cut the tofu into 2.5cm/1in cubes. Heat the oil in a wok or deep-fryer until smoking, then lower the tofu pieces into the oil, one at a time, and deep-fry until a brown skin forms. Lift out with a slotted spoon and set aside.

2 Heat the 15ml/1 tbsp oil in a large pan and fry the garlic for 20 seconds. Add the rice wine, yellow bean sauce and hoisin sauce, and stir for 30 seconds.

3 Cut the bamboo pith into short lengths about 4cm/1½in wide. Add to the pan with 350ml/12fl oz/1½ cups water and simmer for 3 minutes.

4 Add the tofu and beaten egg, and stir for 1 minute, or until the sauce is slightly thick. Add the crab meat and stir for 30 seconds to heat through. Serve hot.

EASTERN CHINA
POULTRY

SYMBOLIC STEWS & CULINARY ICONS

From the bustling metropolis of Shanghai to the rural villages of Jiangxi and the humid port of Amoy, cooks in eastern China have created many dishes that have since become global culinary icons. Beggar's Chicken is one such recipe, and it has aquired an almost mystical status that has stood the test of time over many centuries. Another one is a dish that has the Mandarin seal of approval: Prime Minister's Chicken Stew.

Stews and braised dishes are popular on the menus of the eastern provinces, especially during the colder winter months. Chicken, high in nutritional value, is paired with restorative ginseng in a truly warming, healthy and flavourful dish, Chicken & Ginseng Stew.

Marinated Duck is one of the stars of Zhejiang's poultry menu, with its deep flavour that develops from lengthy marinating. Even the simple dish Stir-fried Diced Chicken from Jiangxi cannot fail to impress, its fiery promise coming from the use of chillies that are borrowed from neighbouring Hunan.

Whether it is the simplest or the most elaborate dish, a marriage of flavours and textures is the key to poultry perfection in eastern China. The art of cooking chicken and duck has been handed down from generation to generation, and through centuries of imperial and home cooking. Today, in the hands of cooks and chefs who understand the importance of this culinary synergy, there is no such thing as an ordinary dish, no matter how simple or complex the ingredients and method.

BEGGAR'S CHICKEN

The story behind this curiously named dish is about a vagrant who stole a chicken. Being fearful of being discovered, he decided to wrap it in lotus leaves and wet mud before flinging the parcel into a fire he had made to warm himself. In reality, this method of cooking has been around for centuries, especially in Micronesia, and it still exists in New Zealand and other Pacific islands. The recipe no longer calls for mud, but uses a dough instead. The dough is edible but is not meant to be eaten.

1 To make the wrapping, put the flour, yeast, sugar, salt, water and egg whites in a bowl, and mix to form a dough. Cover and leave to stand for 15 minutes, then knead for 5 minutes, until soft and elastic. Leave to rise in a warm place for 1½–2 hours, until doubled in size.

2 Make the stuffing. Soak the mushrooms for 20 minutes in 150ml/¼ pint/⅔ cup warm water, then strain, reserving the liquid. Snip off and discard the stems and thinly slice the caps. Soak the dried vegetable in cold water for 10 minutes, then rinse, squeeze dry and chop finely.

3 Heat the oil in a wok over high heat. Fry the ginger, garlic and onion for 20 seconds, add the chopped dried vegetable and fry for 1 minute. Add the pork or chicken, carrot, mushrooms, spring onions, soy sauce, wine or sherry and fry vigorously for 1 minute, then add the reserved mushroom soaking liquid. Cook for 1 minute, then transfer to a bowl to cool. Stir in the sesame oil and pepper.

4 Preheat the oven to 200°C/400°F/Gas 6. Line a roasting pan with foil. Rub the inside and outside of the chicken with wine and salt. Wipe the lotus leaves with kitchen paper dipped in hot water.

5 Spoon the stuffing into the chicken, packing it in well. Secure the open end with string or sturdy wooden cocktail sticks or toothpicks. Wrap the chicken in the first lotus leaf as you would a parcel, then place seam side down on the second lotus leaf and wrap again. Tuck in the loose ends; use cocktail sticks to secure if necessary.

6 On a well-floured surface, gently roll out the dough into a large rectangle about 1cm/½in thick. Put the leaf-wrapped chicken on top and bring up the dough to enclose the chicken completely. Pinch the seams well to seal and patch any holes with dough scraps.

7 Put the chicken in the roasting pan. Brush the dough with water and bake for 30 minutes, then reduce the heat to 180°C/350°F/Gas 4 and bake for 1½ hours longer, or until the dough is brown and dry. There may be small fissures and cracks. To serve, crack open the dough and carve the chicken at the table, then serve the chicken and stuffing with rice.

SERVES 4

1 small chicken, about 900g/2lb
15ml/1 tbsp Shaoxing wine or dry sherry
2.5ml/½ tsp salt
2 dried lotus leaves
boiled rice, to serve

FOR THE DOUGH WRAPPING
800g/1¾lb/7 cups plain/all-purpose flour, plus extra for dusting
7ml/1½ tsp easy bake/rapid-rise dried yeast
5ml/1 tsp sugar
5ml/1 tsp salt
450ml/¾ pint/scant 2 cups warm water
2 egg whites, lightly beaten

FOR THE STUFFING
4 dried shiitake mushrooms
90g/3½oz dried vegetable (mui choi)
30ml/2 tbsp vegetable oil
25g/1oz fresh root ginger, grated
4 garlic cloves, chopped
1 small onion, halved and thinly sliced
150g/5oz/generous ½ cup minced/ground pork or chicken
½ small carrot, coarsely grated
2 spring onions/scallions, chopped
30ml/2 tbsp light soy sauce
15ml/1 tbsp Shaoxing wine or dry sherry
5ml/1 tsp sesame oil
2.5ml/½ tsp ground white pepper

RICE WINE CHICKEN

In Jiangxi Province, chefs are fond of steeping chicken and meat in wine overnight before it is cooked. The result is an intense alcoholic flavour, as most rice wines are 30 per cent proof. Start preparations the day before, if possible.

1 Trim off all excess fat from the chicken. Rub both the inside and outside with the salt.

2 Mix the rice wine with the garlic, sesame oil and pepper, and rub all over the chicken. Put the chicken in a sealable plastic bag, press out as much air as you can, then seal. Leave to marinate in the refrigerator for at least 4 hours or overnight. Turn the chicken every once in a while so that every part is evenly marinated.

3 When ready to cook, bruise the ginger with a pestle or a heavy rolling pin until it cracks but remains in one piece. Push the ginger and the spring onions, folded in half, into the chicken cavity.

4 Put the chicken on a deep plate that will fit into the steamer. Pour any remaining marinade over it. Steam over medium-high heat for 1 hour, until very tender. Cut into portions and serve warm or cold.

SERVES 4

1 chicken, about 1.2kg/2½lb
5ml/1 tsp salt
60ml/4 tbsp rice wine
15ml/1 tbsp crushed garlic
5ml/1 tsp sesame oil
2.5ml/½ tsp ground white pepper
large piece of fresh root ginger, the size of a plum, peeled
3 spring onions/scallions

Cook's Tip

Many cooking wines are made from rice, usually glutinous, and are generally termed bai jiu or mi chiu (white liquor)

SERVES 4

1 chicken, about 1.2kg/2½lb
3 slices of ginseng root
40g/1½oz fresh root ginger
5ml/1 tsp salt
1.2 litres/2 pints/5 cups water
6 cloves
dark soy sauce, for dipping
finely sliced spring onions/ scallions, to garnish

Cook's Tips

- Ginseng can be worth its weight in gold but most Chinese herbal stores sell a range that is not too prohibitively expensive.
- You can use ginseng granules instead of root, though they do not have the restorative properties of the latter.

CHICKEN & GINSENG STEW

Ginseng is a strange-looking root known the world over as an elixir. It is a strong herb and you need only a few shreds to impart its intoxicating flavour (you don't actually eat the ginseng, as it has a fibrous texture – it just flavours the stock). Cloves are added to the dish to heighten the flavour and temper the bitterness of the ginseng.

1 Trim the chicken of all excess fat. Combine all the ingredients except the soy sauce and spring onions in a heavy pan and bring to the boil over medium heat. Reduce the heat, then cover and simmer gently for 1½ hours, or until the chicken is falling off the bone.

2 Carefully transfer the chicken to a platter. Leave to cool slightly, then remove the bones and coarsely shred the meat. Strain the cooking liquid into a clean pan and add the chicken meat, then return to a gentle simmer over medium heat.

3 Serve hot, garnished with sliced spring onion and with a dish of dark soy sauce as a dip for the chicken.

PRIME MINISTER'S CHICKEN STEW

History does not identify which prime minister this dish was in honour of, only that it is a banquet offering that no doubt pleased one Chinese premier enough for it to go down in history. It is still common practice, especially in Taiwan, for chefs to prepare a particular dish for certain politicians. In ancient Shanghai, this dish was cooked to please an imperial Mandarin. It is a hearty stew containing chicken, pork and Chinese ham (Jinhua) braised in Chinese rice wine, and could grace any grand banquet today. If you cannot find Chinese ham, substitute with Spanish Serrano ham, or similar smoked varieties.

SERVES 6–8

1 chicken, about 1.2kg/2½lb
165g/5½oz belly pork, without skin
250g/9oz smoked ham joint
30ml/2 tbsp vegetable oil
40g/1½oz fresh root ginger, sliced
5ml/1 tsp salt, or to taste
2.5ml/½ tsp sugar
2.5ml/½ tsp ground white pepper
800ml/27fl oz/scant 3¼ cups water
100ml/3½fl oz/scant ½ cup rice wine
12 quail's eggs
3 spring onions/scallions, cut into 5cm/2in lengths
boiled rice, to serve

Cook's Tip

Traditionally, duck eggs are included, but these can be expensive or difficult to find, so quail's eggs are used instead.

1 Cut the chicken into six to eight pieces. Cut the belly pork and ham joint into large chunks. Bring a large pan of water to the boil, add the ham and cook it for 10 minutes, then drain.

2 Heat the oil in a wok over medium-high heat. Fry the ginger slices, turning often, until lightly browned. Add the pork and stir-fry for 2 minutes.

3 Add the chicken, ham and all the other ingredients, except the quail's eggs and spring onions, to the wok. Bring to a simmer, then cover and braise for 45 minutes.

4 Check the meats for tenderness, and continue to simmer for a further 10–20 minutes, if necessary. The broth should be thick and rich-tasting. Meanwhile, boil the quail's eggs for 5 minutes. Drain and cool in cold water, then remove the shells.

5 Add the quail's eggs and spring onions to the wok, and simmer for 1 minute more. Serve hot, with boiled rice.

STIR-FRIED DICED CHICKEN

This recipe comes from Jiangxi province, which borders Fujian to the east. Jiangxi cuisine borrows freely from that neighbour as well as from that of Hunan province, as they share a common border. This dish is an aromatic union, marrying the subtle cuisine of Fujian, which rarely features chillies, with the fiery flavours of Hunan styles. It is all at once hot, sweet and tart, and utterly divine.

1 Heat the oil in a wok over medium-high heat and fry the garlic for 20 seconds. Add the chillies and fry for 30 seconds.

3 Add the chicken pieces and stir-fry vigorously for 2–3 minutes, until they turn opaque. Add the hoisin sauce, rice wine, yellow bean sauce and sugar and stir well for 40 seconds.

3 Blend the cornflour with 100ml/7 tbsp water and add it to the pan. Stir until the sauce bubbles, thickens and coats the chicken pieces. Toss in the spring onion and stir for 10 seconds. Serve immediately, with boiled rice.

SERVES 4

30ml/2 tbsp vegetable oil
2 garlic cloves, chopped
3 dried chillies, soaked in water for 20 minutes, then drained, seeded and cut into small pieces
450g/1lb boneless chicken breast fillet, cut into 2cm/¾in cubes
15ml/1 tbsp hoisin sauce
15ml/1 tbsp rice wine
15ml/1 tbsp yellow bean sauce
2.5ml/½ tsp sugar
5ml/1 tsp cornflour/cornstarch
1 spring onion/scallion, chopped
boiled rice, to serve

Variation

For more fire and a lovely red sheen, use 15ml/1 tbsp each of vegetable oil and chilli oil instead of just vegetable oil.

SERVES 4

15 dried chestnuts, soaked overnight, or 15 peeled cooked chestnuts
30ml/2 tbsp vegetable oil
3 garlic cloves, crushed
30ml/2 tbsp preserved red beancurd (tofu ru), mashed with a fork until smooth
5ml/1 tsp sugar
15ml/1 tbsp light soy sauce
2.5ml/½ tsp ground white or black pepper
4 chicken breast fillets, cut into 2cm/¾in cubes
7.5ml/1½ tsp cornflour/cornstarch
chopped Chinese celery leaves, to garnish
boiled rice, to serve

CHICKEN WITH CHESTNUTS

Chestnuts really come into their own in Chinese cooking; their rustic looks belie a husky sweetness and deliciously crumbly texture. Chinese stores sell them shelled and dried. They have to be soaked or boiled until soft, but the brown membrane can be fiddly to remove, so you may prefer to use vacuum-packed cooked chestnuts.

1 If using dried chestnuts, drain them and remove any pieces of brown membrane. Discard any chestnut that is brown or cracked. Place them in a pan, cover with water and simmer, partially covered, for 25 minutes, until cooked through. Drain and set aside.

2 Heat the oil in a wok over high heat. Fry the garlic for 20 seconds, then add the mashed beancurd and fry for 15 seconds. Add the sugar, soy sauce and pepper and fry for 20 seconds, then add the chicken. Stir-fry for 1–2 minutes, until the chicken is almost cooked.

3 Blend the cornflour with 120ml/4fl oz/½ cup water. Add the chestnuts to the wok, followed by the cornflour mixture, and cook for 1–2 minutes more, until the sauce bubbles and thickens. Serve with rice, garnished with Chinese celery leaves.

SNOW FLOWER CHICKEN

Like many Chinese recipe names, the origin of the name of this dish from Fujian province is a mystery, though there are many theories. According to the late Kenneth Lo, owner of the London restaurant Memories of China, one theory has it that when the chicken is steamed, the glutinous rice coating almost resembles snowflakes. Whatever the meaning of the name, it is a very pretty dish that is also extremely tasty.

SERVES 4–6

15ml/1 tbsp light soy sauce
5ml/1 tsp sesame oil
2.5ml/½ tsp ground white pepper
45ml/3 tbsp rice wine
4 chicken breast fillets, about 600g/1lb 5oz total weight
250g/9oz white glutinous rice, soaked overnight
1 egg white
30ml/2 tbsp cornflour/cornstarch

1 Mix together the soy sauce, sesame oil, pepper, rice wine and 45ml/3 tbsp water in a shallow bowl. Cut the chicken breast fillets into large cubes and marinate in the mixture for 20 minutes.

2 Drain the rice well and spread thinly over a large plate.

3 Whisk the egg white and 15ml/1 tbsp water until frothy, then add the cornflour and beat well to make a light paste.

4 Drain the chicken pieces from the marinade, reserving the marinade. Dip each piece in the paste to coat thoroughly, then roll in the glutinous rice until completely and evenly coated.

5 Arrange the chicken pieces in a single layer in a large, wide heatproof dish that will fit into your steamer, and steam over medium-high heat for 45 minutes.

6 Put the marinade in a pan and bring to the boil over low heat. Simmer for several seconds, then pour over the steamed chicken before serving.

Cook's Tip

Minced pork, shaped into balls, can also be cooked in the same way, in which case omit the water from the marinade and do not drain the marinated pork.

BRAISED CHICKEN WITH TARO

Taro is widely used across the world but its versatility is most manifest in Chinese cookery, where it is a particular favourite of Fuzhou chefs, turning up in many dishes either mashed and wrapped or added as a starchy staple to stews and stir-fries. Taros can be as large as papayas or as small as plums, their white flesh stippled with brown or purple.

SERVES 4

- 3 taros, peeled and chopped into large chunks, or 6 baby taros, peeled and halved
- 1 chicken, about 1.2kg/2½lb
- 15ml/1 tbsp vegetable oil
- 2 garlic cloves, crushed
- 30ml/2 tbsp oyster sauce
- 5ml/1 tsp sesame oil
- 2.5ml/½ tsp ground black pepper
- 2.5ml/½ tsp salt
- 3 spring onions/scallions, chopped
- boiled rice or Chinese steamed bread, to serve

1 Steam the taros for 10 minutes over medium heat, until just tender.

2 Trim the chicken of any excess fat, skin and gristle, and chop into bitesize pieces. Rinse with boiling water and drain thoroughly.

3 Heat the oil in a wok over high heat, add the garlic and fry for 20 seconds. Add the chicken and stir-fry for 2 minutes, until golden.

4 Add the oyster sauce, sesame oil, pepper and salt, and stir for 30 seconds. Add 750ml/1¼ pints/3 cups water, then cover and simmer for 20 minutes.

5 Add the taro and simmer, uncovered, for 5–8 minutes, until tender and the sauce is thick. Add the spring onions and cook for 30 seconds more. Serve hot with plain boiled rice or steamed bread.

SERVES 4

4 chicken breast fillets, with skin
5ml/1 tsp rice wine
2.5ml/½ tsp salt
2.5ml/½ tsp ground white pepper
2 spring onions/scallions, cut into 10cm/4in lengths
4 thin slices of fresh root ginger, cut into strips

FOR THE SAUCE
45ml/3 tbsp cooked oil (see Cook's Tip)
10ml/2 tsp sesame oil
2 spring onions/scallions, minced
25g/1oz fresh root ginger, grated
3 garlic cloves, crushed
2.5ml/½ tsp salt

Cook's Tip

Cooked oil is oil that has been brought to just under smoking point, then allowed to cool, or oil that has been previously used to fry items such as crispy shallots.

CHICKEN IN SCALLION SAUCE

The wonderful flavour of this dish belies the simplicity of its cooking method. Shanghai chefs have the knack for transforming common, basic ingredients into ambrosial sauces, which exalt everyday chicken, meat or fish to the highest levels. For this dish, it is very important to use chicken with the skin on, as the true texture and taste of the chicken rely on the alchemy of skin and meat.

1 Cut the chicken into slices about 2cm/¾in thick, each containing both meat and skin. Rub the slices with rice wine, salt and pepper, and arrange them on a wide plate that will fit into your steamer.

2 Quickly blanch the spring onions in a pan of simmering water for 5 seconds to soften. Drape these and the ginger over the chicken. Steam over medium-high heat for 10 minutes. Remove from the heat and leave the chicken in the steamer, tightly covered, for 10 minutes more.

3 To make the sauce, combine the cooked and sesame oils in a small pan and warm over medium heat until hot. Stir in all the other sauce ingredients, which should sizzle when added.

4 Remove from the heat, stir the sauce well and pour it over the chicken. Serve hot or cold.

CHICKEN WITH CLOUD EARS

This much-loved fungus – not quite a mushroom in the familiar visual sense – is ubiquitous throughout China and especially in Fujian province. It has a smoky and woody flavour, keeps its crunch even after simmering, and is touted for its medicinal properties as a blood purifier. Its flavour complements succulent meats like pork and chicken. Sold in dried form it has an almost limitless shelf life, if kept in an airtight container.

SERVES 4

- 2 boneless chicken breast fillets, about 150g/5oz each
- 40g/1½oz cloud ear/wood ear mushrooms
- 30ml/2 tbsp vegetable oil
- 2 garlic cloves, finely chopped
- 10 water chestnuts, drained and coarsely diced
- 15ml/1 tbsp oyster sauce
- 15ml/1 tbsp hoisin sauce
- 2.5ml/½ tsp ground black pepper
- ¼ tsp salt
- 3 spring onions/scallions, roughly chopped
- noodles, to serve

1 Slice the chicken into thin strips. Soak the cloud ears in cold water for 20 minutes, or until they swell up and acquire a slippery texture. Using scissors, trim off and discard any hard woody parts from the cloud ears, then cut them into fine strips.

2 Heat the oil in a wok over high heat. Add the garlic and fry for 10 seconds, then add the chicken and cloud ears. Stir for 1 minute, then add 120ml/4fl oz/½ cup water.

3 Cook vigorously for 1 minute, then add the water chestnuts, oyster sauce, hoisin sauce, pepper and salt. Stir until there is just a hint of sauce left.

4 Add the spring onions and stir to mix, then serve with noodles.

MARINATED DUCK

With increasing tourism throughout eastern China, many visitors will no doubt fall in love with the incredible ambience and beauty of Zhejiang. Although one of China's smallest provinces, it is full of natural beauty, especially Hangzhou, which is known for its topography, Dragon Well tea and exquisite cuisine. Purists would insist that the duck for this classic Zhejiang dish should be marinated and hung for two days, drained and re-marinated and then hung again for another two days – but this is a bit much for the home cook! As long as you marinate it overnight, the flavours will certainly impress your guests.

SERVES 4

- 1 oven-ready duck, about 2kg/4½lb in weight
- 2.5ml/½ tsp salt
- 1.5ml/¼ tsp Chinese five-spice powder
- 15ml/1 tbsp Shaoxing wine or dry sherry
- 5ml/1 tsp sugar
- 3 spring onions/scallions, chopped, plus extra to garnish
- 25g/1oz fresh root ginger, peeled and shredded
- 200ml/7fl oz/scant 1 cup light soy sauce
- a sweet or spicy dip, to serve

1 Rub the duck all over with salt and Chinese five-spice powder. Put it on a rack in a tray, and leave it in a cool place for 3–4 hours. Alternatively, chill it, uncovered, overnight. This will dry it out sufficiently.

2 Cut down either side of the backbone and remove it, then open the duck out like a spatchcock, pressing it down until flat. Rub both sides with wine or sherry and sugar, and sprinkle with chopped spring onions and ginger. Set aside for 1 hour in a cool place.

3 Bring the soy sauce to a simmer in a wok over low heat. Brush the flavourings off the duck back into the marinade and reserve, then pierce the duck neck with a metal S-hook. Hold the duck by the hook over the wok and ladle the sauce over the duck, until the skin is dark.

4 Place the duck in a deep heatproof dish that will fit in your steamer, and top with the spring onions and ginger from the marinade. Steam over high heat for 1½–2 hours, or until the meat is tender.

5 Chop the duck into pieces and serve, garnished with spring onion, and with a dip.

Cook's Tip

For speed, use duck breasts, if you like, which are easier to cook and take half the time.

EASTERN CHINA
MEAT

FRAGRANT STIR-FRIES & SUCCULENT RIBS

The range of pork dishes from the eastern provinces is awe-inspiring. Each is given a special fillip with the appropriate seasonings and herbs, and is usually combined with vegetables and soya bean products, such as tofu and various pungent pastes and sauces.

Tofu in the form of preserved beancurd gives a tremendous lift to many an eastern Chinese meat dish, such as Pork in Preserved Beancurd – a deeply satisfying dish when served with fluffy white rice.

Lychee Pork takes on a delicious sweet edge with the addition of these fragrant fruits. The Hangzhou dish of Tung-Po Pork has earned its global cachet as a dish that was inspired by a Song dynasty poet, Su Tung-Po. Today, it is an eminent staple in Chinese restaurants around the world, as is Sweet-and-Sour Spare Ribs, another eastern Chinese classic.

Belly pork is commonly used in China, but it is important to buy it with the correct ratio of lean meat to fat. A Chinese butcher will be able to provide you with a piece of meat that is suitable for your recipe. For quick-cooking stir-fries, lean pork tends to be used.

There are some more unusual offerings. In this region, offal is regarded with much respect, and these 'spare parts' are combined with local rice wine or one of the pungent sauces to create sumptuous results such as the Stir-fried Kidneys. The appearance of frog's legs on the menu here may seem curious, but they have, in fact, been used in Shanghai cuisine for hundreds of years.

FROG'S LEGS IN BEAN SAUCE

Frog's legs have been a star item in Shanghai cooking for centuries. When properly cooked, they taste like young chicken but have a milder flavour and chewy texture. Farmed frogs are common in the swamps and wetlands of eastern China. Frozen frog's legs are available in Chinese stores and are sold skinned and cleaned as attached pairs.

SERVES 4

- about 60ml/4 tbsp vegetable oil
- 16 pairs prepared frog's legs
- 30ml/2 tbsp thinly sliced fresh root ginger
- 3 garlic cloves, thinly sliced
- 15ml/1 tbsp yellow bean sauce
- 5ml/1 tsp black bean sauce
- 5ml/1 tsp sugar
- 2.5ml/½tsp ground white pepper
- 5ml/1 tsp sesame oil
- shredded spring onions/scallions or fresh coriander/cilantro, to garnish

1 Heat 45ml/3 tbsp oil in a wok over high heat. Fry the frog's legs in batches for 3–4 minutes, until partially cooked and lightly browned. Add more oil if necessary. Drain on a rack as each batch is cooked.

2 Wipe out the wok and add 15ml/1 tbsp oil. Fry the ginger and garlic for 1 minute, until fragrant and browned, then add the yellow and black bean sauces, sugar, pepper and sesame oil. Stir to blend.

3 Add the frog's legs and stir-fry for 1 minute, being careful not to scorch them, then add 120ml/4fl oz/¼ cup water and cook for several seconds more, until the legs are thickly glazed with sauce. Serve hot, garnished with shredded spring onions or fresh coriander.

Variation

For a crisper finish, dust the prepared frog's legs with cornflour/cornstarch and deep-fry them until golden, instead of stir-frying them.

SERVES 4

450g/1lb boneless pork shoulder, cut into 1cm/½in cubes
2 cubes red or white preserved beancurd (tofu ru)
3 garlic cloves, finely chopped
30ml/2 tbsp vegetable oil
15ml/1 tbsp finely shredded fresh root ginger
5ml/1 tsp sugar
1 leek, white part only, thinly sliced
boiled rice or congee, to serve

Variation

Any kind of firm vegetables can be added to this dish, if you like. Celery and white radish, cut into matchsticks, are ideal since they have a fairly mild flavour but robust texture.

PORK IN PRESERVED BEANCURD

Preserved beancurd comes in two forms: a peachy white type with a pungent sharpness, and a red type fermented with crushed red rice (a special rice inoculated with a red fungus), which has a heady aroma and an intense rosy hue. Both are potent seasonings. The red variety is preferred in the cuisine of eastern China, especially that of Shanghai. In Jiangxi province, pork is often cooked with preserved beancurd for a hearty dish to be eaten with rice.

1 Combine the pork with the beancurd and half the garlic and leave to marinate, tightly covered, for at least 15 minutes.

2 Heat the oil in a wok over high heat. Add the ginger and remaining garlic, and fry for 40 seconds until lightly browned. Add the pork with all its marinade and stir-fry for 2 minutes.

3 Add the sugar and leek. Fry for 1 minute, then add 200ml/7fl oz/ scant 1 cup water. Bring to the boil and simmer for 2 minutes, until the sauce is thick and the pork is cooked. Serve with rice or congee.

LYCHEE PORK

Nubby-skinned lychees are iconic Chinese fruits that have become popular all over the world. Sweet, succulent and dripping with juice, they are more than a dessert fruit and are put to good use in many stir-fried and sweet-and-sour dishes. Fresh lychees can usually only be bought in season, but canned ones are universally available and make a good substitute. Indigenous to sub-tropical China and Thailand, they can grow to the size of small plums. Interestingly, some restaurants offer a similarly named dish that does not actually contain the fruit but has the meat cut into floral shapes that resemble lychees. This dish, however, does contain the delicious fruit.

1 Tenderize the pork a little with the blunt edge of a cleaver or a meat mallet. Cut the slices into cubes, then dredge with cornflour and shake off the excess.

2 Heat the oil for deep-frying in a wok or deep-fryer over medium heat and deep-fry the pork, in batches, until crisp and golden brown, about 2–3 minutes per batch. Drain on kitchen paper.

3 Combine 30ml/2 tbsp of the lychee juice with the vinegar, soy sauce, water, rice wine and salt.

4 Heat the vegetable oil in a wok over high heat. Add the spring onions and fry for 20 seconds, then add the lychee sauce mixture and bring to the boil.

5 Add the pork and lychees, and stir-fry for 1 minute, or until the sauce is thick.

6 Serve immediately with rice, and garnished with the reserved green parts of the spring onions, sliced in thin strips.

SERVES 4

300g/11oz lean pork, cut into 2.5cm/1in thick slices
50g/2oz/½ cup cornflour/cornstarch
vegetable oil, for deep-frying
12 fresh or canned lychees, drained and pitted, and halved if liked, juice reserved
15ml/1 tbsp rice vinegar
15ml/1 tbsp light soy sauce
15ml/1 tbsp water
10ml/2 tsp rice wine
2.5ml/½ tsp salt
15ml/1 tbsp vegetable oil
2 spring onions/scallions, white parts only, chopped (reserve the green parts for the garnish)
boiled rice, to serve

PORK, CABBAGE & MUSHROOMS

The stir-frying technique is used at all levels of Chinese cuisine, from rural home kitchens to imperial-style fine-dining restaurants. The goal is the same in every case, to bring out the very best flavour of the ingredients, using the precise and brief application of heat.

SERVES 4

8 dried shiitake mushrooms
400g/14oz lean pork, cut into strips 5mm/¼in wide
10ml/2 tsp rice wine
2.5ml/½ tsp sugar
2.5ml/½ tsp ground white pepper
115g/4oz crisp white or green cabbage
30ml/2 tbsp vegetable oil
2 garlic cloves, sliced
30ml/2 tbsp dark soy sauce
shredded spring onions/scallions, to garnish

1 Soak the mushrooms in warm water for 1 hour, until softened. Strain and reserve the soaking water. Snip off and discard the mushroom stems and cut the caps into quarters.

2 Combine the pork with the wine, sugar and pepper in a bowl and set aside.

3 Shred the cabbage coarsely but evenly and blanch in a pan of boiling water for 20 seconds. Drain well.

4 Heat the oil in a wok over high heat. Fry the garlic for 20 seconds, then add the pork and stir-fry for 1 minute.

5 Add the mushrooms and cabbage and fry for 1 minute more, then add the soy sauce along with 150ml/¼ pint/⅔ cup of the mushroom soaking liquid. Stir for 1–2 minutes more, until the liquid has almost all evaporated.

6 Serve immediately, garnished with shredded spring onions.

Variation

The large white cabbage-like Chinese leaves or Napa cabbage can be used in place of round cabbage if you prefer, as it has a similar taste. It will not need blanching as it is tender and cooks quickly.

PORK WITH CHINESE CHIVES

Chives are found in three forms throughout China: flat, slim-bladed green chives, which are usually stir-fried or chopped to enliven fillings for dumplings and spring rolls; yellow chives, grown under cloches to keep them pale and silky; and a different vegetable altogether, the thick-stemmed flowering garlic chives, which are tipped with pointed green buds. Green or yellow chives are used here.

SERVES 4

- 250g/9oz lean pork
- 15ml/1 tbsp rice wine
- 5ml/1 tsp sesame oil
- 2.5ml/½ tsp salt
- 2.5ml/½ tsp ground white pepper
- 30ml/2 tbsp vegetable oil
- 2 garlic cloves, finely chopped
- 200g/7oz Chinese green or yellow chives, cut into 5cm/2in lengths
- boiled rice or Chinese steamed bread, to serve

1 Cut the pork into thin matchsticks across the grain and combine with the rice wine, sesame oil, salt and pepper. Leave to marinate, covered, for 10 minutes.

2 Heat the vegetable oil in a wok over high heat. Stir-fry the garlic for 30 seconds until golden brown.

3 Add the pork with its marinade and fry for 1 minute, then add the chives and stir-fry vigorously for 1–2 minutes more, until the chives are deep green or yellow and just tender. Serve immediately with rice or Chinese steamed bread.

SERVES 4

75g/3oz dried cole vegetables or dried lily buds
30ml/2 tbsp vegetable oil
3 garlic cloves, halved
400g/14oz belly pork, skin removed and cut into 2.5cm/1in cubes
45ml/3 tbsp light soy sauce
5ml/1 tsp sugar
5ml/1 tsp sesame oil
salt, to taste
chopped spring onions/scallions, to garnish
congee or boiled rice, to serve

Variation

You can also add other dried ingredients such as soaked dried scallops and dried oysters for a more intensely savoury dish.

STEWED PORK & VEGETABLES

This dish comes from Hangzhou, where it is much loved as warming sustenance. Dried cole vegetables – sturdy-leaved members of the brassica family that resemble pak choi when fresh, and olive-green rags when dried – are most often used. Lily buds can be bought in Asian stores.

1 Soak the dried vegetables or lily buds in tepid water for 20 minutes, or until softened. Cut off and discard any hard tips or roots, then wash and drain, and cut the vegetables into short lengths.

2 Heat the oil in a wok or flameproof casserole over medium-high heat until very hot. Add the garlic and fry for 20 seconds. Add the pork and fry for 2 minutes, until lightly browned, then add the soy sauce, sugar and 750ml/1¼ pints/3 cups water and bring to the boil.

3 Add the dried vegetables or lily buds and partially cover. Simmer for 1–1¼ hours, until the pork is tender.

4 Stir in sesame oil and salt to taste, garnish with spring onions and serve with congee or rice.

TUNG-PO PORK

A Hangzhou dish, this has a genuine pedigree, because Su Tung-Po, a famous poet and gourmet of the Song Dynasty (960–1279), actually lived in this city and was its governor for a few years. The recipe has become popular all over the world, and is now a featured dish in many restaurants both in China and elsewhere. Traditionally, belly pork is used, but if you deem this too fatty, use a leaner cut streaked with some fat instead. True Tung-Po pork always has the skin on. Traditionally, the belly pork skin is first browned in hot fat before the whole piece is boiled. This version omits the frying step.

SERVES 4

- 400g/14oz belly pork
- 40g/1½oz/scant ¼ cup rock or crystallized sugar, crushed
- 30ml/2 tbsp Shaoxing wine or dry sherry
- 30ml/2 tbsp soy sauce
- 25g/1oz fresh root ginger, finely shredded
- 4 spring onions/scallions cut into 5cm/2in lengths
- boiled rice and stir-fried vegetables, to serve

Variation

A different version of this dish uses gammon (smoked or cured ham) or fresh bacon, which has to be soaked in cold water overnight and then drained and rinsed before boiling. This will create a saltier dish.

1 Cut the belly pork into three or four large chunks. Bring a large pan of water to a simmer over medium-high heat, add the pork belly and blanch for 10 minutes. (This tenderizes and plumps up the pork.) Drain the pork and reserve the stock for use in another recipe.

2 Put the crushed sugar and wine in a deep heatproof dish that will fit into your steamer and lay the pork pieces on top. Drizzle evenly with soy sauce and top with ginger and spring onions.

3 Put the dish in a steamer with a tight-fitting lid and steam over high heat for at least 1 hour, or until the pork is fork-tender. Uncover and baste the pork with the juices a few times during steaming.

4 Allow the pork to cool slightly, then slice it into thin pieces. Serve with the steaming juices poured over (strained, if you like), with plain rice and a side dish of stir-fried vegetables.

FUZHOU PORK

A blindingly crimson paste made from the lees of red rice wine is used to season many Fuzhou meat and poultry dishes. Although it is occasionally sold in Chinese stores, it is usually very difficult to find outside of China. Instead, I've suggested using the more common, similarly flavoured fermented red beancurd, which is coloured with red yeast rice. This is the kind of dish that takes pride of place when guests are invited to dinner.

SERVES 4

350g/12oz belly pork
150g/5oz taro, peeled and cut into 2.5cm/1in cubes
15ml/1 tbsp vegetable oil
3 garlic cloves, finely chopped
25ml/1½ tbsp mashed preserved red beancurd (tofu ru)
15ml/1 tbsp hoisin sauce
2.5ml/½ tsp sugar
2 spring onions/scallions, roughly chopped, plus sliced spring onion, to garnish
boiled rice or Chinese steamed bread, to serve

1 Remove the skin from the belly pork. Cut into strips and cut each strip into bitesize pieces.

2 Combine the pork and taro in a wide heatproof dish that will fit into your steamer and steam over hot water at high heat for 15 minutes.

3 Heat the oil in a wok over high heat. Add the garlic and stir-fry for 20 seconds, then add the preserved beancurd and stir-fry for 15 seconds, making sure that it does not scorch. Add the hoisin sauce and sugar and stir for 15 seconds more.

4 Add the steamed pork and taro to the wok and stir-fry vigorously for 1 minute. Add 120ml/4fl oz/½ cup water, stir well and cover. Reduce the heat to medium and cook for 1 minute, then uncover and cook for 1 minute more.

5 Add the spring onions and mix well, then serve immediately with rice or Chinese steamed bread, garnished with sliced spring onion.

PORK CHOPS IN BROWN SAUCE

The eponymous brown sauce has nothing to do with the British table sauce, but is merely a description of its colour. It is a typical Fuzhou blend of soy sauce, oyster sauce, wine, pepper and the aromatics garlic, onion and cloves. This dish has crossed borders and been copied by Cantonese chefs, but it is really a Fuzhou classic. The recipe uses pork chops, which are not traditionally used in Chinese cooking. Normally, a rib cut would be used, but chops are universally available and work well in this dish so I've used these instead. Seek out ones that have a thin rind of fat, as it will impart flavour.

SERVES 4

4 boneless pork chops, about 175g/6oz each
1 egg, lightly beaten
50g/2oz/½ cup cornflour/cornstarch, plus 5ml/1 tsp blended with 15ml/1 tbsp water
vegetable oil, for deep-frying, plus 15ml/1 tbsp
2 garlic cloves, finely chopped
1 large onion, halved and sliced
4 cloves
steamed pak choi/bok choy, to serve (optional)

FOR THE SAUCE

300ml/½ pint/1¼ cups water
30ml/2 tbsp dark soy sauce
15ml/1 tbsp oyster sauce
15ml/1 tbsp Shaoxing wine or dry sherry
2.5ml/½ tsp ground black pepper

1 Sandwich the pork chops between sheets of clear film/plastic wrap and beat with a meat mallet until they are about 5mm/¼in thick. Dip the chops in beaten egg to coat, then dredge with cornflour.

2 Heat the oil for deep-frying over medium heat. Deep-fry the chops until golden brown, then drain on kitchen paper and set aside.

3 Whisk all the sauce ingredients together to blend.

4 Heat the 15ml/1 tbsp oil in a clean wok over high heat and fry the garlic for 30 seconds, until golden brown. Add the onion and cloves and fry for 1–2 minutes more, until softened but not browned.

5 Add the sauce mixture and bring to the boil. Cook for 2 minutes or until reduced by about half, then add the cornflour mixture and stir for 30 seconds more, until the sauce bubbles and thickens.

6 Slice each pork chop into three to four pieces, then add to the sauce and toss well. Serve with steamed pak choi, if you like.

LION'S HEAD PORK BALLS

This noble-sounding Shanghai dish is every bit as grand-tasting as its name implies. The lion reference is simply because the pork dumplings are supposed to look like a lion's head, with the Chinese leaves representing the mane. This is a famous dish throughout eastern China, most particularly in Shanghai. The ratio of fat to lean meat is important for flavour and succulence, so use a cut of leg meat that is marbled with fat.

SERVES 4

- 450g/1lb slightly fatty pork leg meat, well chilled
- 1 spring onion/scallion, finely chopped
- 15ml/1 tbsp finely grated fresh root ginger
- 30ml/2 tbsp Shaoxing wine or dry sherry
- 15ml/1 tbsp light soy sauce
- 15ml/1 tbsp iced water
- 5ml/1 tsp sesame oil
- 2.5ml/½ tsp sugar
- 6 water chestnuts, fresh if possible, peeled and finely diced
- 45ml/3 tbsp cornflour/cornstarch
- 600ml/1 pint/2½ cups light pork or chicken stock
- 15ml/1 tbsp vegetable oil
- 200g/7oz Chinese leaves/Chinese cabbage, cut into 5cm/2in pieces

1 Cut the pork into very thin slices, then into very thin strips. With a repetitive chopping motion, mince or grind the pork on a chopping board using a heavy knife or cleaver for about 1 minute; halfway through, scrape up the pork into a ball and spread it out again. The minced/ground pork should not be completely smooth, but should hold together well.

2 Scrape the minced pork into a bowl, and add the spring onion, ginger, wine or sherry, soy sauce, iced water, sesame oil, sugar, water chestnuts and 15ml/1 tbsp of the cornflour. Stir in one direction until the mixture clings loosely together.

3 Shape the mixture into balls the size of small plums and dust lightly with the remaining cornflour.

4 Bring the stock to a gentle boil in a pan. Gently lower the meatballs into the pan; they should be spread out in a single layer. Turn the heat to very low, cover and cook for 45 minutes. The liquid should barely bubble.

5 Heat the oil in a clean pan over high heat. Fry the Chinese leaves for 30 seconds, until softened.

6 Carefully scoop the meatballs out of their pan and place on top of the Chinese leaves. Bring the cooking liquid to a full boil over high heat, then gently pour over the meatballs and leaves. Reduce the heat and simmer gently for 20 minutes more.

7 Ladle into a serving dish, with the 'lion's heads' on top, and serve.

SWEET-AND-SOUR SPARE RIBS

So typically Chinese as to be ubiquitous, you inevitably come across sweet-and-sour dishes in whichever Chinese province you happen to be dining. They may not always be named as such, however, even though they have the famous blend of sweet and sour flavours. You can use a number of sweetening agents, including plum sauce, honey, sugar and pineapple juice, and you can adjust the amount of these to taste. Vinegar or lemon juice provides the sour balance. Plum sauce, pineapple and rice vinegar give contrasting tastes in this classic dish, which showcases succulent ribs.

SERVES 4

600g/1lb 5oz pork ribs, chopped into 5cm/2in pieces (ask your butcher to do this for you)
1 egg, lightly beaten
45g/1½oz/⅓ cup cornflour/cornstarch
vegetable oil, for deep-frying
2 small tomatoes, cut into six wedges each
10 pineapple chunks
30ml/2 tbsp plum sauce
15ml/1 tbsp pineapple juice
15ml/1 tbsp light soy sauce
15ml/1 tbsp rice vinegar
120ml/4fl oz/½ cup water

1 Toss the ribs in beaten egg, then dredge with cornflour and shake off the excess.

2 Heat the vegetable oil for frying in a wok or deep-fryer and deep-fry the pork ribs until they are a rich golden brown; 2–3 minutes per batch. Remove them with a slotted spoon and drain them well on kitchen paper.

3 Combine the tomatoes, pineapple chunks, plum sauce, pineapple juice, soy sauce, vinegar and water in a wok. Bring to the boil over medium heat, stirring constantly.

4 Add the pork ribs and stir until well blended and the pork is glossy with sauce. Serve immediately, with finger bowls, if you like.

Cook's Tip

Making great-tasting sweet-and-sour sauce should hold no mystery. Do note, however, that a little bit of a salty element – the soy sauce – is necessary to keep the sweet and sour tastes in balance, or else the contrast may become too sharp.

SALT & PEPPER SPARE RIBS

This Fujian dish is a regular part of family meals, especially on festive occasions, and is particularly tasty when made with really thick, meaty ribs. When cooked with salt and pepper, as here, pork ribs are ambrosial.

SERVES 4

- 800g/1¾lb meaty pork ribs, chopped into 7.5cm/3in lengths (ask your butcher to do it for you, if you like)
- 30ml/2 tbsp cornflour/cornstarch
- 15ml/1 tbsp groundnut/peanut oil
- 10ml/2 tsp sesame oil
- 15ml/1 tbsp finely grated fresh root ginger
- 5ml/1 tsp salt
- 5ml/1 tsp sugar
- 5ml/1 tsp ground black or white pepper
- Chinese celery leaves, to garnish

1 Blanch the pork ribs in a pan of simmering water for 20 minutes. Lift them out with a large mesh strainer. While they are still warm, dust them all over with cornflour, patting it on to help it to adhere.

2 Bring the pan of water back to a simmer and blanch the ribs for 45 seconds, then transfer to a plate.

3 Heat the groundnut and sesame oils in a wok over high heat. Add the ginger and fry for 15 seconds.

4 Add the ribs, salt, sugar and pepper and stir-fry vigorously for 2–3 minutes, or until the ribs are lightly browned. For a moister texture, drizzle a tablespoon or two of the cooking liquid into the wok as you fry. Serve hot, garnished with Chinese celery leaves.

Cook's Tip

The ribs' cooked cornflour coating helps the seasonings to cling on to the meat.

SERVES 4

450g/1lb beef sirloin, loin or fillet/tenderloin
15ml/1 tbsp light soy sauce
15ml/1 tbsp rice wine
10ml/2 tsp oyster sauce
2.5ml/½ tsp ground white pepper
45ml/3 tbsp vegetable oil
150g/5oz Chinese celery sticks, with leaves
1 large onion, halved and thinly sliced
10ml/2 tsp lightly toasted sesame seeds, to garnish
boiled rice, to serve

Cook's Tip

This dish does not wait around for anybody – serve it immediately or else the freshness of its flavours will dissipate.

SHREDDED BEEF WITH CELERY

In Chinese cuisine, shredded beef requires a piece of sirloin or loin to be first sliced and then shredded with a sharp knife, or even a fine-edged metal spoon or ladle. This method yields exceptionally tender beef, which can then be used for quick stir-frying over high heat.

1 Cut the beef into thin slices then cut the slices across with a half-cutting, half-scraping motion to make thin, fragile julienne strips.

2 Combine the soy sauce, rice wine, oyster sauce, pepper and 15ml/1 tbsp of the oil. Add the beef and gently mix to coat. Cover and leave to marinate in the refrigerator for 15 minutes.

3 Cut the celery sticks into 2cm/¾in pieces and then chop some of the celery leaves to make about 30ml/2 tbsp.

4 Heat the remaining oil in a wok over high heat. Add the onion and fry, stirring, for 2 minutes, until softened and golden. Push to one side and add the beef and its marinade. Stir-fry for 1 minute, then mix the onion into the beef and fry for 30 seconds more.

5 Add the celery sticks and leaves, and fry for a further 15 seconds. Sprinkle with sesame seeds and serve immediately, with rice.

LAMB IN HOT BEAN SAUCE

When the Shanghai winter chill really begins to bite, citizens turn to hearty meats and sizzling dishes to warm them. Lamb is especially warming when cooked in a rich blend of bean sauce and chillies, wine and aromatics. Better still, serve it on a preheated cast-iron hot plate like those used in Chinese restaurants, to provide an attractive talking point. Chinese stores sell these cast-iron plates, which you simply heat over a gas flame or in the oven and then place on a wooden base for safe handling.

SERVES 4

- 450g/1lb lean lamb or best end of neck fillet
- 30ml/2 tbsp Shaoxing wine or dry sherry
- 2.5ml/½ tsp salt
- 15ml/1 tbsp garlic paste
- 30ml/2 tbsp vegetable oil
- 15ml/1 tbsp sesame oil
- 25g/1oz fresh root ginger, shredded
- 30ml/2 tbsp chilli bean paste (dou banjiang)
- 2.5ml/½ tsp sugar
- 2 spring onions/scallions, cut into 5cm/2in lengths
- 1 red or green bell pepper, halved, cored and thinly sliced
- shredded spring onions, to garnish
- boiled rice, to serve

1 Slice the lamb thinly with a cleaver and tenderize it by beating with the cleaver's blunt edge or using a meat mallet. Cut the slices across the grain into very thin strips.

2 Mix the lamb strips with the wine or sherry, salt and garlic paste, then cover and leave to marinate for 10 minutes.

3 Heat the vegetable and sesame oils in a wok over high heat. Fry the ginger for 1 minute, or until browned, then add the chilli bean paste and sugar and stir for 30 seconds, being careful not to scorch the paste.

4 Add the lamb and its marinade and stir-fry for 1 minute. Add the spring onions and pepper and stir-fry for 1 minute more.

5 Add 100ml/3½fl oz/scant ½ cup water and cook vigorously until the juices become a thick sauce glazing the ingredients.

6 Transfer to a hot plate (see Cook's Tip) or warmed serving bowls, and garnish with shredded spring onions. Serve with rice.

Cook's Tip

The best way to serve the lamb is on a hot plate, which creates an appealing sizzle when the lamb is put on to it. It also maintains the piping-hot serving temperature.

STIR-FRIED KIDNEYS

In China, offal meats and innards aren't regarded as secondary to main meats, and are thus accorded a status rarely granted to them in the West. The skilled cooking of liver, kidneys, tripe and brain can reach great culinary heights. This dish hails from Fujian and would have formed part of an imperial banquet. Mei kuei lu chiew – literally 'rose essence liquor' – is derived from kaoliang wine made in north China from sorghum and millet, by distilling it with rock sugar and a particular species of rose.

SERVES 4

2 pig's kidneys
30ml/2 tbsp rose-flavoured wine (mei kuei lu chiew) or dry sherry
2.5ml/½ tsp salt
2 Chinese celery sticks, with leaves
30ml/2 tbsp vegetable oil
25g/1oz fresh root ginger, shredded
3 garlic cloves, finely chopped
10ml/2 tsp sesame oil
2.5ml/½ tsp sugar
5ml/1 tsp cornflour/cornstarch, blended with 30ml/2 tbsp water
noodles, to serve

1 Halve the kidneys and open them out, then remove the white core from all halves. Rinse very well, pat dry with kitchen paper, then soak the kidney halves in fresh cold water for 30 minutes.

2 Cut each kidney half into three or four pieces. With a sharp knife, make deep cross cuts on the outer side, but only halfway through. (When cooked, the kidneys will shrink slightly, making each piece curl and exposing the cross cuts that will look like short studs. The finer and closer the cross cuts, the more the studs resemble the fat petals of an opened flower.)

3 Rinse the kidney pieces again, pat dry on kitchen paper and combine with the wine and salt in a bowl. Cover and leave to marinate for 10 minutes.

4 Cut the celery sticks on the diagonal into 1cm/½in pieces. Roughly chop a few of the celery leaves.

5 Heat the oil in a wok over high heat. Fry the ginger and garlic for 20 seconds, then add the kidney pieces with their marinade, and the celery sticks. Fry vigorously for 40 seconds. The kidneys will curl up and shrink a little.

6 Add the sesame oil, sugar and the cornflour mixture, and fry for 20 seconds. Add the celery leaves, stir once and serve immediately.

EASTERN CHINA
RICE & NOODLES

HEARTY FILLERS & ICONIC DISHES

The Yangtze River delta is a lush rice-growing landscape that produces some of the world's best grains. These range from fragrant jasmine rice to sticky glutinous rice from which comes not only rice wine but also rice noodles. Although wheat noodles are sometimes eaten here, it is rice and rice noodles that form the basis of most meals. Boiled or steamed rice is served several times a day, sometimes as a side but often in the form of fried rice dishes, such as the gloriously tasty Yangzhou Fried Rice or the Shanghai classic, Fried Rice with Mixed Meats.

Rural families often prefer gruel-like porridge, such as Fish & Salt Egg Congee, and glutinous or sticky rice is a favourite staple among these same countryside communities due to the sustaining nature of its starchy content.

Shanghai's Jia Jiang Noodles, with the rich flavours of pork, rice wine, garlic, ginger and yellow bean paste, has become nothing less than iconic. Whether eaten for its symbolism or satisfying sustenance, it is a real Shanghai classic.

A special variety of extremely fine rice noodles, which originated in Fujian but are now used throughout the region, are called mee sua. They are put to use in the quintessential Shanghai dish, Liver & Kidney in Fine Noodles. They are used on special occasions and can be recognized by the red string that holds the delicate bundles together. Mee sua may be difficult to find outside of China, so you just can substitute other fine rice noodles instead.

FISH & SALT EGG CONGEE

A real comfort food, congee is of peasant origin and is eaten in practically every province, city, town and family. This dish is the kind of supper congee that needs no accompaniments, and it is a favourite in Suzhou and throughout eastern China. The fish used could be any type, but the best are the thick-filleted varieties such as cod, halibut, monkfish and salmon. Salted duck eggs are a Chinese delicacy, cured in brine or salted charcoal.

SERVES 4

150g/5oz/¾ cup jasmine rice, washed and drained
275g/10oz meaty fish fillet, such as halibut, monkfish, cod or salmon
5ml/1 tsp ground white pepper
10ml/2 tsp sesame oil
2 salted duck eggs
30ml/2 tbsp light soy sauce or fish sauce

TO GARNISH
15ml/1 tbsp preserved winter vegetable, shredded
fresh root ginger, sliced
fresh coriander/cilantro

Cook's Tip

Traditionally, a broken medium-grain rice is used, which yields a smooth-textured porridge. You can simulate this by breaking up some of the raw rice with a mortar and pestle. Alternatively, replace 20g/¾oz of the rice with a short-grain variety, such as arborio.

1 Bring the rice and 1.5 litres/2½ pints/6¼ cups water to the boil in a large, heavy pan. Reduce the heat to maintain a slow simmer, then partially cover and cook for 30 minutes, stirring occasionally. Depending on the type of rice, you may have to top up the pan with more hot water if the congee thickens too quickly; it needs to become like a smooth porridge.

2 Slice the fish on a diagonal into 5mm/¼in thick slices, or alternatively into 2.5cm/1in cubes, removing any bones. Toss the fish with half the pepper and half the sesame oil and set aside.

3 Boil the salted duck eggs over medium heat for 10 minutes, then drain and rinse well with cold water. Shell and cut each egg into four to six pieces.

4 When the congee is soft and smooth, add the fish. Cook gently for another 3–4 minutes, or until the fish is just cooked through.

5 Add the egg pieces, soy or fish sauce and the remaining pepper and sesame oil and lightly stir through.

6 Serve immediately, topped with shredded preserved vegetable, sliced ginger and fresh coriander.

FRIED RICE WITH BEANSPROUTS

The appearance of beansprouts in fried rice is a Hangzhou speciality, the vegetable being more usually stir-fried and served just as it is. The crunchiness of the beansprouts uprovide a lively contrast to the rice, along with the ham. Jinhua ham is on the dry side so, to make it more succulent, you can slice it thinly then blanch it for a minute in boiling water before adding.

SERVES 4

- 450g/1lb cold, cooked rice (225g/8oz/generous 1 cup raw weight)
- 30ml/2 tbsp vegetable oil
- 2 spring onions/scallions, chopped
- 200g/7oz Jinhua ham, diced (see Cook's Tip)
- 15ml/1 tbsp oyster sauce
- 15ml/1 tbsp light soy sauce
- 2.5ml/½ tsp ground black pepper
- 90g/3½oz beansprouts

1 Your cooked rice should be completely cold. If it is in clumps, rake it through with a large fork to separate the grains. Heat the oil in a wok over high heat.

2 Fry the spring onions for 45 seconds, until softened, then add the ham and stir for 20 seconds. Add the rice and stir-fry for 1 minute.

3 Add the oyster sauce, soy sauce and pepper, and stir for 30 seconds more, then add the beansprouts and fry for 1–2 minutes, or until they are crisp but tender. Serve immediately.

Cook's Tip

Jinhua ham is dry-cured and has an intense flavour. If this is not available, use any dry-cured ham.

SERVES 4

30ml/2 tbsp groundnut or peanut oil
3 garlic cloves, crushed and finely chopped
2 eggs
450g/1lb cold, cooked basmati or jasmine rice (225g/8oz/ generous 1 cup raw weight), forked through
150g/5oz roast pork (cha shao), cut into 5mm/¼in dice
12 large prawns/shrimp, peeled and deveined
15ml/1 tbsp light soy sauce
4ml/¾ tsp ground white pepper
2.5ml/½ tsp salt, or to taste
30g/1¼oz/generous ¼ cup peas, thawed if frozen
2 spring onions/scallions, chopped
pickled green chillies, to serve

YANGZHOU FRIED RICE

This recipe was born in the town of Yangzhou on the Yangtze River delta but has been so copied, especially by Cantonese restaurateurs, that its origin is often forgotten. In its home town it is no more than family fare, but the ingredients are classic, ranging from roast pork to prawns, eggs and peas, and maybe ham and mushrooms.

1 Heat the oil in a wok over high heat. Add the garlic and fry for 20 seconds, then push it to one side of the wok and add the eggs. Break up the yolks and then scramble the eggs until half-set. Chop the eggs roughly with the wok ladle.

2 Add the rice, roast pork, prawns, soy sauce, pepper and salt, and stir-fry for 2–3 minutes. Stir vigorously with a to-and-fro motion, scraping the wok base and sides, so that all the ingredients are tossed and mixed well and the rice is thoroughly heated through.

3 Add the peas and spring onions and stir for 45 seconds. Serve immediately with pickled green chillies on the side.

FRIED RICE WITH MIXED MEATS

Egg-fried rice is very popular in Chinese restaurants outside China, but you will not find it anywhere in China. If rice is to be fried, it will always be enriched with a selection of meat, seafood or vegetables. Given that the dish evolved from the need to recycle leftover cooked rice, you can add anything you want to it. In Shanghai, fried rice is a complete meal in itself, and restaurant versions are studded with choice ingredients such as prawns or shrimp, scallops, lobster or chicken.

SERVES 4

- 450g/1lb cold, cooked rice (225g/8oz/generous 1 cup raw weight)
- 2 Chinese sausages, thinly sliced
- 30ml/2 tbsp vegetable oil
- 1 onion, finely chopped
- 3 eggs
- 75g/3oz/½ cup finely diced cooked ham
- 75g/3oz/generous ½ cup finely diced cooked chicken
- 30ml/2 tbsp light soy sauce
- 15ml/1 tbsp oyster sauce
- 2.5ml/½ tsp ground white pepper
- 2.5ml/½ tsp sesame oil
- 25g/1oz/¼ cup peas, thawed if frozen

1 Your cooked rice should be completely cold. If it is clumpy, rake it through with a large fork to separate the grains.

2 Combine the Chinese sausage with 200ml/7fl oz/scant 1 cup water in a small pan and simmer over medium heat for 2 minutes, or until slightly softened. (Alternatively, sauté them in a few drops of oil.) Drain on kitchen paper.

3 Heat the oil in a wok over high heat. Fry the onion for 1 minute, until softened, then push it to one side of the wok and add the eggs. Break up the yolks and then scramble the eggs until half-set. Chop the scrambled eggs roughly with the wok ladle.

4 Add all the remaining ingredients except the rice and peas and stir for 30 seconds. Add the rice and stir vigorously with a to-and-fro motion, scraping the wok base and sides, so that all the ingredients are tossed and mixed thoroughly.

5 When the rice is fully heated through, add the peas and stir for 30 seconds. Serve immediately.

TAOIST VEGETARIAN RICE NOODLES

On certain days during the Lunar New Year celebrations (which actually last for two weeks), Taoist temples are packed with devotees praying to their ancestors and the different deities within the Taoist pantheon. Temple priests stir up huge woks of vegetarian noodles on the third day of the Lunar New Year, as this is deemed a universal vegetarian day. Beancurd wafers are thin brown pieces of dried tofu, about 7.5 x 5cm/3 x 2in.

SERVES 4

- 12 dried shiitake mushrooms
- 40g/1$\frac{1}{2}$oz dried lily buds
- 6 pieces sweet beancurd wafers
- vegetable oil, for deep-frying, plus 30ml/2 tbsp and extra for drizzling
- 200g/7oz rice vermicelli
- 3 garlic cloves, finely chopped
- 175g/6oz Chinese leaves/Chinese cabbage, sliced thinly
- 15ml/1 tbsp dark soy sauce
- 2.5ml/$\frac{1}{2}$ tsp salt, or to taste

Cook's Tip

This is not an overly seasoned dish and is intended to be rather bland. Within Taoist vegetarian beliefs, even eggs are not supposed to be used. If you do not need to be so strict, make a thin omelette from 2 or 3 eggs, cut into strips, and use them as a garnish.

1 Soak the shiitake mushrooms in warm water for 1 hour, until softened. Strain and reserve the soaking water and top it up to make 300ml/$\frac{1}{2}$ pint/1$\frac{1}{4}$ cups. Snip off and discard the mushroom stems and slice the caps thinly.

2 Soak the dried lily buds in tepid water for 20 minutes, or until softened, then drain well. Snip off any hard tips. Wipe the beancurd wafers with a clean damp cloth. Cut them into 1cm/$\frac{1}{2}$in-wide strips with kitchen scissors.

3 Heat the oil for deep-frying in a wok over medium heat or in a deep fryer, and deep-fry the beancurd wafers until crisp. Drain on kitchen paper and set aside.

4 Soak the vermicelli in hot water for about 20 minutes or until they are soft and not brittle. Drain thoroughly and drizzle a little oil all over to prevent sticking.

5 Heat the 30ml/2 tbsp oil in a wok over high heat. Add the garlic and fry for 20 seconds, until fragrant, then add the mushrooms and lily buds. Fry for 1 minute, then add the Chinese leaves and fry 1 minute more.

6 Add the vermicelli and stir-fry for 1 minute, then add two-thirds of the reserved mushroom liquor, the soy sauce and salt.

7 Fry vigorously until the noodles are tender, sprinkling over the remaining mushroom water if they get too dry before they are cooked. Serve, sprinkled with the fried beancurd wafer strips.

DUMPLING NOODLES

Soupy noodles with wonton dumplings make a very satisfying breakfast or lunch choice. This Cantonese-style dish probably came by way of Hong Kong, where it is a street food item. Fujian chefs will enrich their wontons with crab meat for a more robust flavour. As a soupy noodle dish, it is a complete meal in itself. You can use a light pork, chicken or fish stock: a traditional one is made with dried anchovies (known as ikan bilis in South-east Asia).

SERVES 4

100g/3¾oz prawns/shrimp, minced or ground
100g/3¾oz white crab meat, minced or ground
15ml/1 tbsp light soy sauce
5ml/1 tsp cornflour/cornstarch
5ml/1 tsp sesame oil
2.5ml/½ tsp ground white pepper
16–20 round wonton wrappers
1.2 litres/2 pints/5 cups light stock
15ml/1 tbsp light soy sauce
115g/4oz Chinese leaves/ Chinese cabbage, sliced into 1cm/½in pieces
200g/7oz dry wheat noodles

TO GARNISH
ground white pepper
chopped spring onions/scallions
fresh coriander/cilantro leaves

1 Put the minced prawn, crab meat, soy sauce, cornflour, sesame oil and pepper in a bowl and mix thoroughly, stirring in one direction to compact the filling.

2 Take 1 heaped teaspoon of filling and wrap in a wonton skin. Run a wet finger around the rim of the skin, fold in half and press the edges well to seal, making a half-moon-shaped dumpling. Repeat with the remaining filling.

3 Bring a pan of water to a gentle but steady boil over medium-high heat. Simmer the dumplings for 2 minutes, or until cooked through, then drain and set aside on a plate.

4 Bring the stock to the boil and add the soy sauce and Chinese leaves. Simmer for 1 minute.

5 Blanch or boil the noodles according to the packet instructions, then drain.

6 Divide the noodles and dumplings between the serving bowls, and ladle the hot stock and vegetables over. Garnish with pepper, spring onions and fresh coriander leaves and serve immediately.

Cook's Tip

Never cook dumplings directly in soup broth, as they will make it murky. Always cook them separately in boiling water and drain well before adding them to the soup.

HANGZHOU PORK NOODLES

There are not enough words to do justice to the beauty of Hangzhou today, with its famous West Lake. Marco Polo was said to have likened Hangzhou to Venice, and some claim he took Hangzhou noodles west, though Italian culinary academics refute this. There are many brands of dry wheat noodles; choose one that is close to spaghetti in thickness for an authentic dish. Follow the packet instructions on how to rehydrate them.

SERVES 4

200g/7oz dry wheat noodles
5ml/1 tsp sesame oil
150g/5oz lean pork
10ml/2 tsp rice wine
10ml/2 tsp cornflour/cornstarch
5ml/1 tsp light soy sauce
15ml/1 tbsp vegetable oil
2 garlic cloves, finely chopped
2.5ml/½ tsp ground white pepper
90g/3½oz pak choi/bok choy, thinly sliced
2 shredded spring onions/scallions, to garnish

1 Cook the wheat noodles in boiling water according to the packet instructions, then drain well. Toss the noodles in the sesame oil until thoroughly coated, then cover and set aside.

2 Slice the pork into thin matchsticks, then mix with the rice wine, cornflour and soy sauce. Set aside to marinate for 10 minutes.

3 Heat the vegetable oil in a wok over medium-high heat. Add the garlic and fry for 20 seconds, then add the pork and fry for 1 minute.

4 Add the pepper and 90ml/6 tbsp water to the wok and stir-fry for 1 minute more.

5 Add the noodles and pak choi to the wok. Stir-fry vigorously for 1–2 minutes until the vegetables are crisp-tender and the noodles are heated through.

6 Serve immediately, garnished with shredded spring onions.

Cook's Tip

Stir-fried noodles are often cooked with a minimal amount of liquid. The finished dish should not be awash with stock but have just enough to moisten the noodles.

BRAISED NOODLES

When noodles are braised, it simply means that they are cooked slowly over a low heat. This treatment is usually reserved for a type of noodle called yi mien or yi fu. These are quite fine egg noodles, shaped like angel-hair pasta or thin linguine, but characterized by a golden colour. They have a slightly chewy texture due to the soda water used in making the dough. This simple dish from Fuzhou includes dried shrimps and onions. As dried shrimps are richly flavoured, the only seasoning needed is light soy sauce and a little pepper.

SERVES 4

- 130g/4½oz dried shrimps, soaked in hot water for 15 minutes
- 200g/7oz yi fu egg noodles
- 30ml/2 tbsp vegetable oil
- 1 large onion, quartered and thinly sliced
- 30ml/2 tbsp light soy sauce
- 600ml/1 pint/2½ cups water or light chicken stock
- 4ml/¾ tsp ground white pepper
- 2.5ml/½ tsp salt, or to taste
- chopped fresh coriander/cilantro or Chinese celery leaves, to garnish

1 Drain the soaked shrimps, then mince or grind them finely with a cleaver or heavy knife.

2 Blanch the noodles in a large pan of simmering water until they are half-cooked; they should be flexible but firm to the bite. (Cooking times vary, so it is best to check the packet instructions and judge by tasting rather than timing.) Drain the noodles thoroughly and set aside.

3 Heat the oil in a wok over high heat. Add the onion and stir-fry for 1 minute, until softened and lightly golden.

4 Add the dried shrimps, soy sauce and water or stock, then bring to the boil. Add the noodles and simmer for 2–3 minutes or until they are just tender, have absorbed most of the stock, and the remaining liquid has become a lightly thickened gravy.

5 Season with pepper and salt and serve immediately, garnished with fresh coriander or Chinese celery leaves.

JIA JIANG NOODLES

Although the spiritual home of this dish is Beijing, it was so popular that it crossed many borders over the centuries and is today as much a part of the eastern regional cooking school as the northern one. It is particularly entrenched in Shanghai; in fact some locals even claim that it originated here and was taken to the north when dynastic rulers combed the country for top chefs and the best dishes. Whatever its evolution, it is delicious.

SERVES 4

225g/8oz/1 cup minced/ground pork
30ml/2 tbsp rice wine
30ml/2 tbsp light soy sauce
15ml/1 tbsp cornflour/cornstarch
5ml/1 tsp sugar
1 cucumber, peeled and cored
4 spring onions/scallions
30ml/2 tbsp vegetable oil
½ large onion, finely chopped
3 garlic cloves, finely chopped
25g/1oz fresh root ginger, shredded
15ml/1 tbsp yellow bean paste
200g/7oz dry wheat noodles
salt, to taste

Cook's Tip

In other regions, lamb or beef would be used instead of pork, but the vegetables remain the same.

1 Mix the pork with the rice wine, soy sauce, cornflour and sugar, then cover and set aside to marinate for 15 minutes.

2 Slice the cucumber into fine julienne strips. Cut the spring onions on a sharp diagonal into similarly thin strips. Set aside, covered with dampened kitchen paper so that the strips keep their crispness.

3 Heat the oil in a wok over high heat. Add the onion, garlic and ginger, and fry vigorously for 45 seconds–1 minute, or until fragrant. Add the yellow bean paste and fry for 20 seconds, then add the pork and stir-fry for 2 minutes.

4 Add 200ml/7fl oz/1 cup water and cook for 1 minute more, or until the liquid thickens into a light sauce. Season with salt to taste.

5 Cook the noodles in boiling water according to the packet instructions. Drain well and divide between serving bowls.

6 Reheat the sauce if necessary and pour it over the noodles. Arrange the sliced spring onions and cucumber in small mounds next to the noodles and serve immediately.

LIVER & KIDNEY IN FINE NOODLES

Rites of passage and birthdays are invariably celebrated with the serving of noodles (mien) to symbolize longevity. This quintessential Shanghai dish is a favourite for such celebrations. The noodles used are always a special variety: fine, almost bone-white, and extremely delicate. These are normally sold in boxes containing skeins of the noodles, each wrapped with a red string and intended for special occasions. They are believed to have originated in Fujian and are called mee sua in the dialect. If these are not available, use the thinnest rice or wheat noodles you can find.

SERVES 4

200g/7oz pig's liver
1 whole pig's kidney
30ml/2 tbsp Shaoxing wine or dry sherry
1 litre/1$\frac{3}{4}$ pints/4 cups boiling water
100g/3$\frac{3}{4}$oz/$\frac{1}{2}$ cup minced/ground pork
15ml/1 tbsp sesame oil
2 garlic cloves, finely crushed
30ml/2 tbsp light soy sauce
225g/8oz mee sua noodles
chopped Chinese celery leaves and 5ml/1 tsp ground white pepper, to garnish

1 Wash the pig's liver and pat it dry with kitchen paper, then slice it thinly.

2 Halve the kidney and open it out, then remove the white core from both halves. Rinse well, pat dry, then slice it thinly.

3 Combine the liver, kidney and wine or sherry in a bowl and leave to marinate, covered, for 10 minutes.

4 Put the water in a large pan and return to a gentle simmer. Add the pork, stirring to break it up. Cook for 4–5 minutes.

5 Meanwhile, heat the sesame oil in a small pan over low heat and fry the garlic for 20 seconds. Add this and the oil to the pork stock with the soy sauce.

6 Add the liver and kidney with their marinade to the pan and cook for 1–2 minutes on high heat until the liver is just tender.

7 Immediately before serving, gently lower the noodles into the pan and cook for barely 1 minute, until just tender.

8 Ladle everything into individual serving bowls, garnish with celery leaves and pepper and serve immediately.

Cook's Tip

Unlike more robust noodles, mee sua do not need to be soaked or cooked separately, as they are so fine. Do not overcook them; they turn mushy very quickly.

EASTERN CHINA

VEGETABLES, EGGS & TOFU

FRESH, CRUNCHY & NUTRITIOUS

Many vegetables are grown in China, especially around the fertile Yangtze delta, that rarely, if ever, make it out of the country. Most local people shop for vegetables on a daily basis due to the cultural insistence upon fresh produce. The simplest of ingredients, such as mangetouts or snow peas, baby corn, pak choi, kai lan, mushrooms, spring onions, scallions and bamboo shoots are tossed with aromatic seasonings to create many tasty dishes.

Mushrooms are extremely versatile, a fact that is put to excellent use in wok-fried recipes such as Bamboo Shoots with Mushrooms, or Jade Button Mushrooms, as well as wonderful parcels of shiitake mushrooms wrapped in delicate bean curd skins.

Tofu features prominently alongside vegetables, as it has a chameleon quality that allows it to blend beautifully with just about every green; it can be used in any vegetable dish to add protein. Gluten products, such as the 'sausages' that appear in the recipe Bamboo Shoots with Sausages, can play a similar role to tofu, providing protein and substance.

The recipes in this chapter are not all vegetarian, though some certainly are. Be aware that oyster sauce is not a vegetarian product; if you are cooking a vegetable dish for vegetarians, you can substitute a mushroom-based version instead. Buddha's Vegetarian Stew is a simple and nourishing meat-free dish. Most of the vegetables used here are readily available in supermarkets and Chinese stores.

STIR-FRIED MIXED VEGETABLES

This Fujian stir-fry recipe is a template, and you can improvise by adding any Chinese vegetable, the fresher and greener the better. The important part of the process is the stir-frying over intense heat.

SERVES 4

30ml/2 tbsp vegetable oil
2 garlic cloves, finely chopped
12 baby corn, halved
12 mangetouts/snow peas
2 celery sticks, thinly sliced
200g/7oz green vegetables, such as kai lan, pak choi/bok choy, flowering cabbage or choy sum, cut into 5cm/2in lengths
30ml/2 tbsp oyster sauce
5ml/1 tsp sesame oil
100ml/3½fl oz/scant ½ cup water (optional)

1 Heat the oil in a wok over high heat until smoking, then fry the garlic for 30–40 seconds, until pale gold. Toss in all the vegetables and stir-fry vigorously for 1 minute.

2 Add the oyster sauce and sesame oil, and stir for 30 seconds, or until the juices thicken slightly. (The salt in the oyster sauce will draw out some liquid from the vegetables but, if necessary, add a little water should you need more sauce.) Serve hot.

SERVES 4

300g/11oz runner/green beans, cut diagonally into pieces 1cm/½in wide
15ml/1 tbsp vegetable oil
5ml/1 tsp ginger paste
15ml/1 tbsp chilli bean paste (dou banjiang)
2.5ml/½ tsp sugar
5 fat spring onions/scallions, cut into 5cm/2in lengths
5ml/1 tsp sesame oil
100ml/3½fl oz/scant ½ cup water

STIR-FRIED BEANS & ONIONS

In Chinese cooking, although specific types of vegetables are used for their intrinsic taste and texture, there are also many dishes that are generic. In almost all stir-fried dishes, such as this one from Shanghai, a blend of seasonings is used. It is rare to see a dish without aromatics, as individual flavours are not a part of the culinary heritage.

1 Blanch the beans in a pan of boiling water for 20 seconds, then drain, rinse with cold running water, and drain again.

2 Heat the oil in a wok over high heat, then add the ginger and fry for 20 seconds. Add the chilli bean paste and sugar and fry for 20 seconds.

3 Add the beans, spring onions and sesame oil and stir-fry vigorously for 1–2 minutes, then sprinkle in the water. Fry for 1 minute, or until the beans are just tender. Serve immediately.

BAMBOO SHOOTS WITH 'SAUSAGES'

This is a vegetarian dish, so it may seem surprising to find sausages in the title, but there is an explanation. Within the realm of Chinese vegetarian cooking there are many mock-meat products made chiefly from gluten. Some are so skilfully made that they actually look like chicken, duck, roast pork or sausage. These gluten sausages are now available in cans and vacuum packs in Chinese stores.

SERVES 4

300g/11oz canned bamboo shoots
150g/5oz gluten sausages or other shapes
100g/3¾oz cabbage, cut into thin strips
30ml/2 tbsp vegetable oil
3 garlic cloves, crushed
15ml/1 tbsp sesame oil
30ml/2 tbsp yellow bean sauce
2.5ml/½ tsp sugar
crisp-fried garlic or shallots, to garnish

1 If you have bought your bamboo shoots as whole pieces, slice them into 1cm/½in thick pieces. If they are already sliced, leave them as they are. Soak in plenty of cold water for 20 minutes to reduce the taste of the canning brine. Drain thoroughly.

2 Thoroughly drain the gluten sausages or pieces, then gently squeeze out the excess moisture. Slice into pieces of similar size to the bamboo shoots.

3 Boil a large pan of water over high heat. Blanch the bamboo shoots for 20 seconds, then lift out with a slotted spoon and drain well.

4 Blanch the gluten sausages for 1 minute and drain as before, then blanch the cabbage for 10 seconds and drain.

5 Heat the vegetable oil in a wok and fry the garlic for 30 seconds, until golden brown, then add the sesame oil, yellow bean sauce and sugar. Stir for 30 seconds, then add the blanched ingredients. Stir-fry for 1 minute.

6 Add 120ml/4fl oz/½ cup water and bring to the boil. Simmer over high heat until only a small amount of liquid remains. Serve immediately, garnished with fried garlic or shallots.

Variation

Firm or dried tofu cubes can be substituted for the gluten sausage. Rather than the normal soft tofu, these are fried cubes or squares that are sold in Chinese stores.

BAMBOO SHOOTS & MUSHROOMS

In summer, many Chinese will resort to dishes that have cooling properties, as dictated by traditional Chinese herbalism. Every Chinese ingredient is deemed either yin or yang, the former associated with coolness and the latter with heat. Then again, it can also depend on the method of cooking, as a yin product can become yang if ingredients like pepper and chillies are added. It's a minefield of near-mystical theories, but suffice to know that when a dish tastes good, one is left with a feeling of equanimity. This recipe is believed to have cool, yin, properties.

SERVES 4

- 300g/11oz canned bamboo shoots
- 30ml/2 tbsp vegetable oil
- 2 garlic cloves, crushed
- 2 spring onions/scallions, white part only, chopped
- 200g/7oz/3 cups straw mushrooms, halved
- 15ml/1 tbsp dark soy sauce
- 2.5ml/½ tsp sugar
- 5ml/1 tsp cornflour/cornstarch
- salt, to taste

1 Slice the bamboo shoots into thin strips. Heat the oil in a wok over high heat. Add the garlic and fry it for 30 seconds, then add the spring onions and fry for 30 seconds more.

2 Add the bamboo shoots and mushrooms and stir for 2 minutes. Add the soy sauce and sugar, then stir over high heat for 2 minutes.

3 Blend the cornflour with 120ml/4fl oz/½ cup water and add to the wok, stirring. When the sauce thickens, season. Serve immediately.

Variation

This is a basic stir-fry to which a plethora of vegetables, such as leeks, spinach and water chestnuts, can be added.

SERVES 4

200g/7oz mustard greens (sian chai), cut into 4cm/1½in squares
30ml/2 tbsp vegetable oil
2 garlic cloves, crushed
200g/7oz/3 cups fresh button/white mushrooms, thinly sliced
200g/7oz/3 cups fresh straw mushrooms
30ml/2 tbsp light soy sauce
2.5ml/½ tsp ground white pepper
30ml/2 tbsp Shaoxing wine or dry sherry
5ml/1 tsp cornflour/cornstarch
salt, to taste

Variation

Any green vegetable – mangetouts or snow peas, broad or fava beans and spinach – can symbolize jade in the dish.

JADE BUTTON MUSHROOMS

Within Chinese symbolism, there are endless references to acquiring wealth, wisdom and longevity – the three most desired objectives in the culture. For instance, noodles are eaten for the promise of longevity. Wisdom? Well, it can only come with longevity! Green vegetables are often likened to jade, which symbolizes wealth.

1 Blanch the greens in a pan of boiling water for 20 seconds, then drain, rinse with cold running water and drain again. (This helps to preserve their green colour.)

2 Heat the oil in a wok and fry the garlic for 20 seconds. Add the greens and mushrooms and stir-fry over high heat for 2 minutes. Add the soy sauce, pepper and wine or sherry and stir for 1 minute.

3 Blend the cornflour with 150ml/¼ pint/⅔ cup water and add to the wok. Stir until the sauce bubbles and thickens, then season with salt to taste. When serving, arrange the mustard greens so that they are prominent, as they are the 'jade' of the recipe name.

MUSHROOMS & BEANCURD SKIN

The shiitake mushrooms used in this recipe, known as black mushrooms, are the premium variety with large fissures in their caps. These are called 'winter mushrooms' in Fujian Province, and are eaten for their symbolism of longevity as well as for their husky taste and meaty texture.

SERVES 4

16 dried shiitake mushrooms, soaked for 1 hour in hot water
15ml/1 tbsp dark soy sauce
5ml/1 tsp garlic paste
5ml/1 tsp ginger paste
2.5ml/½ tsp salt
2.5ml/½ tsp ground white pepper
2.5ml/½ tsp sugar
5ml/1 tsp cornflour/cornstarch
1 or 2 sheets of beancurd skin
chilli and garlic sauce, to serve

1 Drain the mushrooms, snip off and discard the stems and slice the caps as thinly as you can. Marinate the slices with the soy sauce, garlic, ginger, salt, pepper, sugar and cornflour for 10 minutes.

2 Lay a sheet of beancurd skin on a flat surface and wipe over gently with a damp cloth. (This is to prevent it from cracking and splitting.) Cut into pieces 13cm/5in square.

3 Put 15ml/1 tbsp of mushroom mixture on the edge of each square and roll up like a spring roll, tucking in the sides to seal as you go.

4 Put the rolls on a flat plate that will fit inside your steamer and steam for 10–15 minutes. Serve with a chilli and garlic sauce.

Cook's Tip

These parcels can be brushed with a little lightly thickened stock after steaming, to give them a glossy, juicy finish. They can also be deep-fried, if they are first sealed with a cornflour and water paste.

SERVES 4

75g/3oz dried vegetable (may be called Sichuan cai or mui choy)
15ml/1 tsp vegetable oil
25g/1oz fresh root ginger, pounded to a paste
1 cube preserved red beancurd (tofu ru), mashed until smooth
12 pieces of fried tofu puffs, halved (see Cook's Tip)
8 pieces of dried tofu wafers, halved
2.5ml/½ tsp sugar
15ml/1 tbsp sesame oil
30ml/2 tbsp Shaoxing wine or dry sherry
2.5ml/½ tsp ground black pepper
Chinese celery leaves, to garnish

Cook's Tip

Buy ready-fried tofu puffs, or cut firm fresh tofu into cubes and deep-fry them slowly until golden.

TOFU & PRESERVED BEANCURD

Many vegetarian dishes in China feature tofu, making the most of the different types available such as soft, firm, fried or pickled tofu, all of which have a high protein content. Typical of Hangzhou cooking, this dish is highly flavoured and on the salty side, and is intended to be eaten alongside a bowl of congee. It is a comfort food from peasant origins. In this recipe preserved beancurd seasons the sauce which is a base for two other kinds of beancurd or tofu – fried golden brown tofu puffs, and dry tofu wafers.

1 Soak the dried vegetable according to the packet instructions until it swells up. Rinse and drain, then cut into small pieces.

2 Heat the oil in a wok and fry the ginger for 45 seconds over medium heat. Add the red beancurd and stir-fry for 20 seconds. Add both types of tofu, the sugar, sesame oil, wine or sherry and pepper. Stir for 1 minute, then add 250ml/8fl oz/1 cup water.

3 Braise for 20 minutes over medium heat until the barest hint of sauce is left. Serve garnished with celery leaves.

BUDDHA'S VEGETARIAN STEW

This is one dish that is especially rife with Buddhist symbolism. It originally used 18 different ingredients, representing each one of the sage's disciples. The noble name for it is 18 Lohan, this being the Sanskrit name of the Buddha. Most families in China will cook a modified version of this dish, as it is very time-consuming to stir up 18 ingredients; however, you should have no fewer than half a dozen if the food is going to taste any good. This is a truly glorious panful, a quintessential vegetarian dish that would surely please the Lord Buddha himself. It is traditionally prepared during the Lunar New Year and on festive occasions. It also keeps and freezes well.

SERVES 4

- 8 large dried shiitake mushrooms
- 40g/1½oz dried cloud ear/wood ear mushrooms
- 45ml/3 tbsp vegetable oil
- 6 garlic cloves, crushed to a paste
- 40g/1½oz fresh root ginger, grated
- 2 cubes preserved red beancurd, mashed until smooth
- 15ml/1 tbsp yellow bean sauce
- 30ml/2 tbsp hoisin sauce
- 5ml/1 tsp sugar
- 5ml/1 tsp salt
- 100g/3¾oz canned straw mushrooms, rinsed and drained
- 20 ginkgo nuts (vacuum-packed or canned), drained
- 20 canned lotus seeds, drained
- 10 mangetouts/snow peas
- 200g/7oz pak choi/bok choy, cut into 45cm/2in lengths
- 10ml/2 tsp sesame oil

1 Soak the dried shiitake mushrooms in warm water for 45 minutes, or until softened. Snip off and discard the stems and slice the caps in half.

2 Soak the cloud ear mushrooms in tepid water for 20–30 minutes, or until softened but not limp. Using scissors, trim off and discard any hard woody parts from the cloud ears, then cut into large bitesize pieces.

3 Arrange all the ingredients in plates near to hand, as they have to be added to the wok in sequence. Heat the oil in a wok over medium heat and fry the garlic and ginger for 1–2 minutes, or until golden brown and fragrant.

4 Add the preserved beancurd and yellow bean sauce to the wok. Stir-fry for 40 seconds, then add the hoisin sauce, sugar and salt and fry for 20 seconds more.

5 Add the vegetables in this order, stirring for 10 seconds between additions: shiitake mushrooms, straw mushrooms, ginkgo nuts, lotus seeds, cloud ears, mangetouts and pak choi.

6 Transfer the contents of the wok to a pan and add the sesame oil and 800ml/1.4 pints/3½ cups water. Partially cover and simmer for 30 minutes until all the flavours are well blended, then serve.

STEAMED EGGS WITH MUSHROOMS

This is a delicate dish that is generally cooked during the long, hot summer months in Shanghai when temperatures can be sweltering and appetites rendered sluggish. The lightness comes from the unusual addition of milk to the egg mixture. Traditionally, unsweetened soya milk would be used, but cow's milk makes only a slight difference to the taste, so use whatever you have. You could also use vegetable stock, if you prefer.

SERVES 4

- 30ml/2 tbsp vegetable oil
- 3 garlic cloves, chopped
- 3 eggs
- 150ml/¼ pint/generous ½ cup unsweetened soya milk or whole milk
- 200ml/7fl oz/scant 1 cup light chicken or vegetable stock
- a pinch of ground cloves
- 15ml/1 tbsp light soy sauce
- 2.5ml/½ tsp ground white pepper
- 4ml/¾ tsp salt
- 4 fresh shiitake mushrooms, very thinly sliced
- 1 spring onion/scallion, sliced, to garnish

1 Heat the oil in a small pan over medium-low heat and fry the garlic gently for 2 minutes or until golden. Drain and set aside, reserving the oil.

2 Lightly beat the eggs with the milk, stock, ground cloves, soy sauce, pepper and salt, then strain through a fine sieve/strainer into a bowl.

3 Divide the sliced mushrooms between individual small heatproof bowls, or one large, shallow bowl that will fit inside your steamer. Slowly pour in the eggs – the mixture should not be more than 4cm/1½in deep.

4 Steam the eggs over gently simmering water for 25–30 minutes, or until the custard is only just softly set.

5 Serve immediately, garnished with the fried garlic and oil and sliced spring onion.

Variations

10ml/2 tsp of chopped Chinese preserved vegetables (tung chai) can be added to this steamed dish for a smoky flavour. Chopped salted mustard greens (sian chai) will also give it a robust lift.

OYSTER OMELETTE

An iconic Fujian dish, this has been elevated to global status and is now a star item in many Chinese and South-east Asian restaurants overseas. Plump, good-quality oysters should be used, but street food vendors, ever ingenious, will sometimes use the meat of other similar bivalves. The secret of the dish is in the use of water chestnut flour for the batter. Purists will insist on lard or white cooking fat as the cooking medium, but vegetable oil can be used instead, as here. The finished dish should be fully set but with juicy curds of egg, crispy shards of batter and lightly cooked oysters.

SERVES 4

60g/4 tbsp water chestnut flour
45ml/3 tbsp vegetable oil
6 eggs, beaten roughly
12 large fresh oysters, cleaned
15ml/1 tbsp light soy sauce
5ml/1 tsp fish sauce
2.5ml/½ tsp ground white pepper
1.5ml/¼ tsp salt
2 spring onions/scallions, chopped
15ml/1 tbsp hot chilli sauce or paste (optional)
chopped fresh coriander/cilantro, to garnish

1 Mix the water chestnut flour with 250ml/8fl oz/1 cup water to make a thin mixture, the consistency of milk. (If the flour feels very coarse, crush it with a mortar and pestle; however, a little grittiness is normal.)

2 Heat 15ml/1 tbsp of the oil over medium-high heat in a large frying pan (a wok is not suitable) until smoking hot. Pour in the batter and swirl it to form a paper-thin crêpe. Cook until nearly set.

3 Add the eggs gradually, and spread them around to cover the crêpe. Turn the heat up to high and fry, adding the remaining oil a little at a time during this process. This will make it very crisp.

4 Stir the eggs on the surface to break it up a little, then add the oysters. Cook for 30 seconds, then add the soy sauce, fish sauce, pepper, salt, chopped spring onions, and chilli sauce or paste, if using.

5 Cook for 30 seconds more, then serve immediately, garnished with fresh coriander.

EASTERN CHINA SWEET SNACKS

SWEET SOUPS & BEAN FEASTS

Wheat flour and butter rarely feature in Chinese desserts, but the range of sweet buns or dumplings can be extensive on special occasions. On festive days, anything sugary is symbolically regarded as a 'honeyed bribe' for departing deities on their way to their celestial homes.

Symbolism plays a large part in the sweet menu of eastern China. The dish Five-flavoured Soup, for example, is based on the theories of numerology, and is believed to treat the ills of the five vital organs of the human body.

The most common ingredients in the region's sweet dishes are ginkgo nuts, lotus seeds, dates, sugared winter melon slices and sweet potatoes. These are all widely cultivated in eastern China and are relatively inexpensive locally. Today, even lotus seeds and ginkgo nuts are available in Chinese stores around the world.

Red beans play an important role in Shanghai's sweet dishes. They are often cooked, mashed and sweetened as a filling, but are also cooked with palm sugar in the typical dish Red Beans in Syrup. Mung beans are also good in desserts. In Fujian, they are simmered with sugar to make a porridge that is thickened with wheat flour.

The preferred sweetening agent in these provinces is rock sugar, with its large crystals that impart a subtle perfume along with its taste. Palm sugar or jaggery is also common, and both of these types of sugar are generally available, although you can also use muscovado sugar if that's what you have in stock.

FIVE-FLAVOURED SOUP

Numerology plays a significant role within Chinese culture and in traditional herbal preparations. The idea of the correct balance between all parts of the human body is based on the theory of the Five Elements: Water feeds vegetation to produce Wood that fuels Fire that produces ashes on Earth, which yields Metal. This same number is symbolic when applied to ingredients. Here, water and sugar do not count among the five.

SERVES 4

- 50g/2oz dried longan meat
- 1 litre/1¾ pints/4 cups boiling water
- 8 pieces preserved sweet winter melon slices
- 100g/3¾oz/½ cup rock sugar
- 20 canned lotus seeds, rinsed and drained
- 20 gingko nuts (vacuum-packed or canned), rinsed and drained
- 20 Chinese red dates, pitted

1 Wash and soak the dried longan meat for 25 minutes to rehydrate it, then drain.

2 Put the water in a pan and return to the boil. Add the melon and half the sugar. Simmer for 10 minutes or until the sugar has dissolved. Add all the remaining ingredients and simmer for 10 minutes.

3 Taste for sweetness and add the remaining rock sugar if you find it is not sweet enough for your taste (longan meat and winter melon slices contain a fair amount of sugar already).

Cook's Tip

It is time-consuming to prepare lotus seeds and ginkgo nuts from their dry state, as they require soaking for several hours, and then boiling to tenderize them. Canned or vacuum-packed versions are much more convenient.

SERVES 4

300g/11oz sweet potatoes
115g/4oz/generous ½ cup sugar
26 ginkgo nuts (vacuum-packed or canned), rinsed and drained
15ml/1 tbsp sweet potato flour (optional)

Variation

You could also use canned lotus seeds instead of ginkgo nuts, if you prefer.

SWEET POTATO & GINKGO NUTS

Those from eastern China tend to favour extraordinarily sweet dishes, and many of their desserts, especially this one from Shanghai, are laden with sugar. If you do not like such intensity, use less sugar, as it will not alter the intrinsic taste too greatly. Sweet potato is already naturally sweet. Look for varieties with orange or yellow flesh, as they tend to have the best flavour for this dish.

1 Cut the sweet potatoes into 1cm/½in-thick slices and then into 5cm/2in squares.

2 Bring 800ml/1.4 pints/3¼ cups water to the boil with the sugar and cook the sweet potatoes for 10 minutes.

3 Add the ginkgo nuts and simmer for 5 minutes. Blend the sweet potato flour (if using) with enough water to make a thin paste, and add to the pan. Stir until slightly thickened. If you prefer to have a thin sauce, omit the sweet potato flour. Serve hot or cold.

MUNG BEANS IN SYRUP

As a late-night snack or for breakfast, this sweet porridge is very popular in Fujian. There are two distinct versions of this dish – one using beans with the green skins still on, and the other using hulled beans in a thick sugar syrup. This recipe is for the former version, which is preferred in South-east Asia, having been introduced by the Chaozhou people from Shantou.

SERVES 4

- 1.2 litres/2 pints/5 cups boiling water
- 300g/11oz/1¾ cups mung beans, skin on, soaked overnight and drained
- 250g/9oz/1¼ cups palm sugar, jaggery or demerara/raw sugar
- 50g/2oz/½ cup sweet potato flour

1 Put the water in a large pan and return to the boil, then add the mung beans. Simmer for 15 minutes, then add the sugar. Continue to simmer until the beans are very soft and are almost breaking up.

2 Blend the sweet potato flour with enough water to make a slightly thickened liquid and add to the mung beans. Stir until thick. You may need to add more hot water if the mixture is too thick. (It should not be so thick that you see no liquid.)

3 Leave to cool slightly before serving the mixture warm.

Cook's Tip

Using more or less sugar is a matter of taste, and if palm sugar is not available, you can use demerara/raw sugar instead. Taste and adjust accordingly as you add the sugar.

SERVES 4

300g/11oz/1¾ cups Chinese red beans or red kidney beans, soaked overnight, rinsed and drained
115g/4oz/½ cup palm sugar/ jaggery
800ml/1.4 pints/3¼ cups boiling water
2–3 pieces of tangerine peel

Variation

You can use orange peel in place of tangerine peel.

RED BEANS IN SYRUP

This recipe hails from Shanghai and is a peasant staple, dating back centuries. Traditionally, tangerine peel is added for a citrus tang. Like most pulses, red beans have to be soaked for several hours or overnight before use. They swell up considerably when soaked and cooked.

1 Put the beans in a pan, add plenty of water and bring to the boil. Boil rapidly for 10 minutes, then cook for 30 minutes, or until very tender. Drain.

2 If using the solid palm sugar, grate with a sharp knife into a small pan with a little water and boil to dissolve the shavings. Once dissolved, strain the syrup through a fine sieve/strainer to remove any grit.

3 Put the boiling water in a pan and add the beans, the strained, dissolved sugar or the liquefied sugar, and tangerine peel. Simmer for 10 minutes, or until almost mushy. Serve either hot or warm.

SOUTHERN CHINA

Cantonese, Shantou, Hakka and Island cuisine

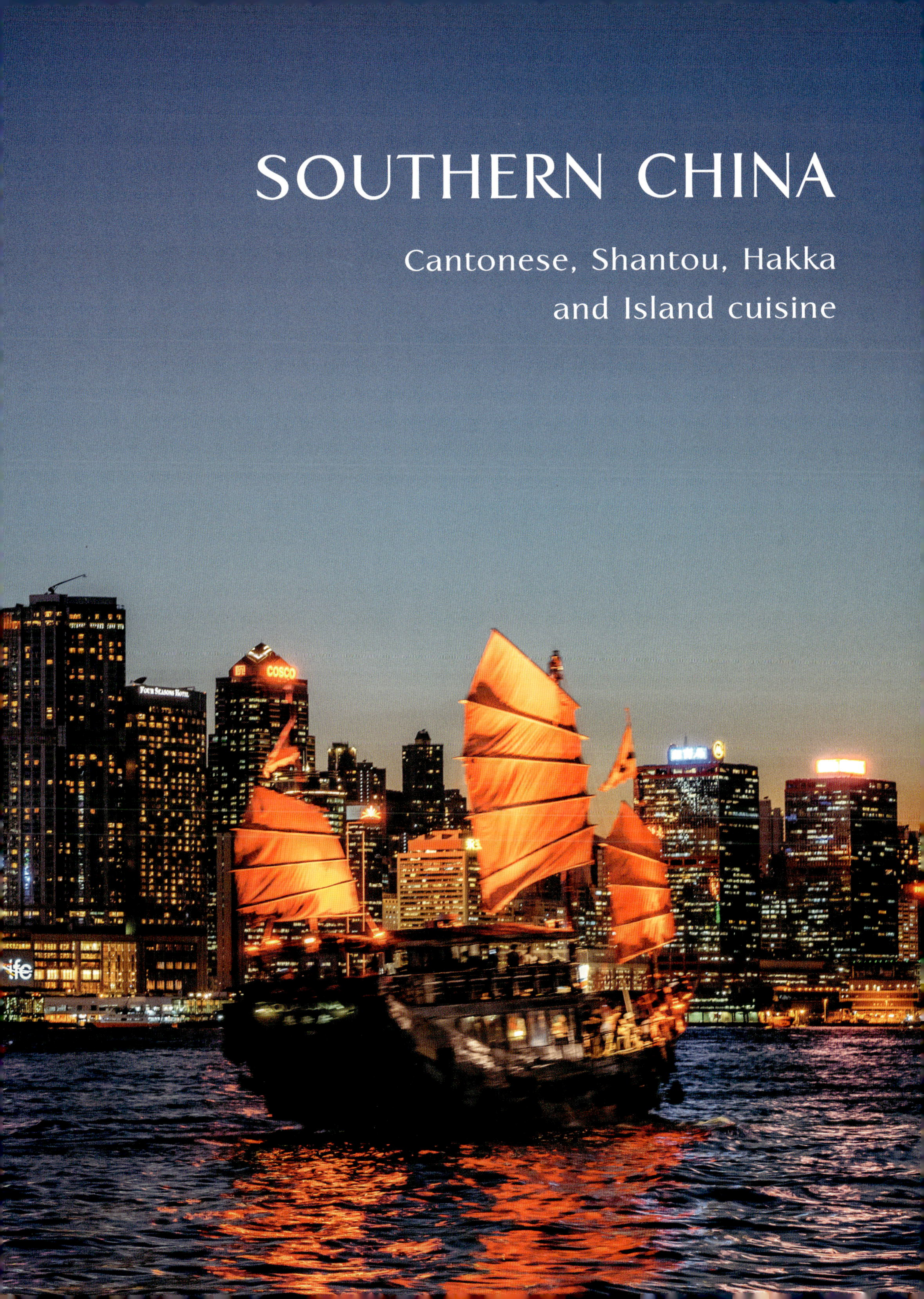

WARM & FERTILE WETLANDS

From the bustling market stalls of Hong Kong to rural kitchens in the outlying villages of the province, the people of southern China share a passion for their food. Differentiated from the rest of the country by its maritime climate and close trading links with the outside world, the area is divided into four gastronomic subdivisions: Hainan Island, Hong Kong, Guangdong, and Shantou, a town within Guangdong Province. Each of these has signature dishes, which reflect the cooking techniques and ingredients particular to that place.

A land of waterways, the south of China comprises the province of Guangdong, Hainan Island and Hong Kong. It is trisected by three rivers, the Xi Jiang (West River), Bei Jiang (North River) and Dong Jiang (East River). Their confluence forms the Zhu Jiang (Pearl River) and its delta runs into the South China Sea.

With such ready access to fresh water and the sea, it is perhaps little surprise that local dishes often feature seafood, whether as the star turn or as an additional flavour. From prawns, shrimp and lobster to carp and snapper, everything is used to create a wide and delectable range of regional culinary treats.

The terrain surrounding the rivers and coast varies: the north of Guangdong province is quite mountainous, while in the south the land tends to be lower and flatter, with fertile delta wetlands. These lower-lying parts are ideal for growing crops, especially rice, and for raising livestock such as poultry and pigs, making the region fairly self-sufficient. Isolated from the rest of the country by the mountains, locals have an outward-looking attitude, and are for the most part known to be receptive to new ideas and influences.

Below *With a benign maritime climate, rivers and long coastline, south China is abundant in natural produce.*

A warm, wet climate

The yearly average temperature in the south of the country is a tolerable 26°C/79°F, but this does not reflect the heat and humidity of the long summer, which can stretch from April to October. There are also frequent typhoons ('great wind' in Cantonese) between May and November, which can lash the region with great ferocity, disrupting transport and other local amenities. With frequent precipitation and long hours of sunshine, however, the region has ideal year-round growing conditions.

The delta wetlands and the low-lying Luizhou coastal plain, including Hainan Island, are especially fertile and support abundant rice crops as well as other staple foods such as corn and peanuts. The sub-tropical climate, regular rainfall and sunshine found here also allow crops such as tea, tobacco, sugar cane, bananas, pineapples, oranges, tangerines, longans and lychees to grow in profusion. Some of these fruits are incorporated into local dishes, adding a sweet note.

Hainan Island is the only truly tropical region in China, and produces important crops such as coffee and rubber. Scorching hot for most of the year, the months from late January to March offer the most comfortable temperatures, and the clement winter months are nowhere near as harsh as those in the north of the country.

Different influences

Famous for its magnificent local Cantonese cuisine, south China has always attracted migrants from both abroad and other regions of the country. Some indigenous tribes have survived, though, and there are thought to be about 39 minority tribes. Of these, the Li are the most numerous, with more than one million people. Believed to have migrated to the area from Fujian some 3,000 years ago, this hardy race have for centuries struggled to scratch a subsistence. Their livelihood today, however, depends largely on tourism and hospitality.

Contact with other cultures over the centuries has resulted in the introduction of new ingredients and cooking techniques to the local pool of culinary knowledge. This is particularly evident in Macau, where many Portuguese influences, including Egg Tarts, can be seen on the menu, and in Hong Kong, famous for its culinary innovation.

Above *Many different crops, including fruits such as lychees, grow in abundance in the delta wetlands.*

Guangdong and Shantou

The southernmost province of China, Guangdong is a natural conduit between the coast and the rest of inland China. Heavily urbanized compared to much of China there are still many traditional villages in the rolling hills and fertile river deltas.

Situated where it is, it is little surprise that the ancient maritime traditions have greatly influenced the life and culture of the southern regions. As the Chinese sea gateways to the world, the ports of Fujian and Guangdong gave easy access to trade routes leading both east and west, as well as enabling foreign powers such as the British and the Portuguese to colonize Hong Kong and Macau.

Hong Kong

The bustling island of Hong Kong is often considered to be something of a maverick, both because it was a Sino-British colony until its handover to China in 1997 and because it has always had an independent soul that is receptive to external influences. The 426sq mile/1,103sq km territory is divided into four main areas: Hong Kong Island, Kowloon, the New Territories and the relatively underpopulated Outlying Islands. In gourmet terms, Hong Kong Island and Kowloon have been the most influential as their forward-thinking people are cut from a feisty fabric, ever inventive in their culinary endeavours, which are recognized the world over.

Hainan Island

Formerly administered as part of Guangdong, Hainan Island is now a separate province. Blessed with superb beaches on the southern coast, the island has wild, thickly forested mountains at its heart, and its small villages are peopled by hill tribes.

Lying on the same latitude as Hawaii and Hanoi in Vietnam, the region is often called China's Hawaii and is an irresistible winter holiday destination for mainlanders from the north and west seeking to escape the bitter cold of their home provinces. Tourism is, therefore, big business here, and many hedonistic resorts have sprung up on the south coast. Hainan Island is one of China's principal rice-growing areas, and fish and shellfish are plentiful as you'd expect.

TRADE, TRAVEL & TRADITION

The region that now comprises southern China was for many years relatively untouched by the activities of more northern peoples, and it wasn't until the 6th century that Guangdong officially became part of China. Populated by indigenous tribes, the rural region slowly changed as people migrated further north, and traders from abroad introduced both new ingredients and the new religion of Islam. Subsequent changes came as large numbers of intrepid Cantonese people emigrated overseas, while Portuguese and British traders arrived to capitalize on the trading potential at the ports.

With easy access to the South China Sea, the southern provinces have always been a lure for foreigners, and it is thought that the region was visited by outsiders as early as the 2nd century CE, when the Romans passed by.

The development of south China

In the early first centuries AD, when the rest of China was busy carving out a civilization on the Yangtze River, south China was very much a rural backwater peopled by native tribes, the last survivors of which form the minority groups scattered throughout the region today.

Although Chinese administration in the region began with the Qin Dynasty (221–206BCE), which established the first unified Chinese empire, it was not until the era of the Three Kingdoms in the late 3rd century CE that Guangdong earned its provincial status as part of China.

From 221BCE until the end of the 3rd century, the demographics of what is now Guangdong slowly shifted, and there were several periods of nomadic immigration from the north of China, particularly at times of political turmoil. In addition, traders from as far afield as the Middle East arrived in the region in the 7th century, lured by the promise of silk, porcelain and tea, and leaving in their wake the heritage of Islam as well as an awareness of new ingredients and cooking techniques.

Around this time, the province of Guangdong enjoyed a degree of autonomy. The Tang Dynasty (CE618–907) was one of the most progressive periods in Chinese history and the imperial leaders set up a special residential quarter south of the Pearl River especially for foreigners who chose to stay in China for reasons of trade. As a result, Guangzhou became a rich and prosperous port, frequented by Arab, Persian, Malaysian and Western merchants, making the fertile region even more attractive to Chinese people from the north, who flocked to the area in droves, hoping to make their fortunes. Today, Guangzhou remains an important city.

China meets the world

In addition to making connections within China, the Cantonese looked beyond the boundaries of their own country and ventured further afield. This intrepid spirit was encouraged by early Ming emperors, and resulted in a number of renowned explorers, the most famous of whom was Admiral Cheng Ho, a Muslim eunuch who was the first Chinese person to

Left *The Portuguese influence in Macau is evident both in the architecture and the local cuisine.*

set foot in Malacca, off the west coast of Malaysia, between 1409 and 1411. This contact with the outside world was further enhanced by the arrival of European settlers, the Portuguese, in 1557. They established the first European settlement in the country in Macau, on the southern coast of Guangdong, where they had a great degree of autonomy, administering the region until the hand-over in 1997.

The British arrived in the 17th century and by the early 1700s Guangzhou, already a busy trading port, had become even more wealthy. This was helped in no small part by an imperial edict that created a merchant's guild, giving the port a monopoly on China's trade with foreign countries. The province of Guangdong as a whole benefited and, with easy access to the outer world, it became a staging post for emigrants leaving the increasingly overpopulated region to seek work abroad.

In 1842, the British influence strengthened further when Hong Kong was ceded to them. Although it was originally thought of as a far-flung Chinese outpost, by the middle of the 20th century it had developed into a buzzing trading and financial centre with an exceedingly vibrant social climate. Despite fears about what would happen after the 1997 handover, Hong Kong still retains a free-market economy and its own legal and social system. Mainland political observers describe the current situation as 'One country, two systems'.

Above *Ancient architecture and Buddhist temples can still be found in towns and cities, such as Foshan, here.*

The Cantonese abroad

Although people had been leaving the southern region for centuries, it wasn't until the early 19th century that the first large-scale instance of emigration occurred. At this time, many people of Cantonese, Hakka or Fujian stock left China to seek their fortunes in such distant places as South-east Asia, Britain, Australia, Canada, the USA and the Philippines. They took with them their culinary knowledge, and established the innumerable Cantonese restaurants and Chinese food stores that can be now found all over the world.

A MELTING POT OF CULINARY DELIGHTS

When considering Chinese regional cooking, one must bear in mind that despite the vastness of the country and the diversity of climates and resources, many dishes are eaten everywhere, with only slight regional takes on the classics. Having said this, the food of southern China is notable for the abundance of seafood on the menu and for its simple preparation, allowing natural flavours and textures to carry the dish. Dim sum also plays a crucial role, and this tradition of eating many small morsels, now so popular elsewhere in China and, indeed, the rest of the world, originated in Guangdong in the 10th century.

Across the regions, daily meals are prepared on the ancient premise of fan cai principles. This is literally translated as 'rice and dishes'. Put simply, it means the combination of the staple dishes of rice, grains and various forms of dumplings (fan) and a variety of cooked vegetables, meat or seafood (cai). The ultimate objective is a perfect synergy between the two basic ingredients, plus a harmonious balance of the four fundamental elements of colour, aroma, flavour and shape. This is a tenet that applies to every individual dish as well as to the whole meal.

Centuries of exposure to foreign elements have enriched Cantonese cuisine hugely, and adventurous chefs have refined and developed their remarkable styles of cooking throughout the world, wherever they have settled.

Taste and texture

The key feature of Cantonese cooking is an emphasis on different textures. Natural flavours are not altered and preparation is kept to a minimum; what is aimed for is the control of crispness and smoothness, leading to a subtle and complex overall texture.

One example of how this quest for texture is manifested is barbecue or 'hung' roasting. This highly developed art involves parboiling the meat to melt some of the fat, inflating the meat with air and hanging it up to dry, which promotes a crispy skin, and finally slathering it with a sweet glaze and roasting to produce a glossy, crunchy finish.

After texture, the second most distinctive aspect of the cuisine is its savoury quality, and how flavours are combined to maximize this preference. Seafood, for instance, is mixed with meat in many dishes, in its natural form or as sauces. Salted black beans are also used to impart a savoury taste, while shredded ginger or chopped fresh coriander is used to counteract any overpowering fishiness.

Soy sauces are often used in artful ways to bring out the flavours of meat and poultry, married with aromatics such as leeks, ginger and onions. Fruit is likewise often incorporated in Cantonese cooking, and citrus fruits like lemons, plums, tangerines and oranges are key ingredients in the tangy, sweet and sour sauces.

Three regional styles

As a result of centuries of immigration, the province of Guangzhou features many subdialects within its borders. This diversity is reflected in Cantonese cuisine, which embraces three distinct schools, each based around its own individual dialect group: Canton; Swatow (Chaozhou) from the city of Shandou; and the Hakkas from the region known as Dong Jiang.

The Canton school offers by far the largest spread of dishes; some, such as stinky tofu, an odorous delicacy from Hong Kong in which tofu is marinated in fermented vegetables for several months, so exotic that they have earned the cuisine its great reputation for adventurousness. Swatow or Shandou cuisine, on the other hand, is notable for its clear flavours and seafood dishes.

Hakka or Dong Jiang food is somewhat different; it has a distinct regional character, with many more rustic dishes that reflect the peasant culture. There is a trend towards thrift among Hakka cooks, who are loath to waste anything, from the tiniest bits of meat to any offcuts of ingredients they can get. As a result of this parsimonious approach, Hakka cuisine resembles more closely the food of the neighbouring province of Fujian, with its simpler culinary traditions. Unlike many others in south China, Hakka people eat beef, since they do not regard the cow as a sacred animal.

One factor that links all three schools is the close relationship between the food and eating habits and the history and culture of the region. For instance, cooks love wrapping food in leaves, as in Glutinous Rice in a Lotus Leaf, because this style of cooking reflects the largely pastoral nature of the area – a connection that is treasured even today.

Hong Kong and Macau

Universally recognized as the supreme pinnacle of Cantonese cuisine, the food of Hong Kong is renowned throughout the country and the world. Its style is related both to ancient classical tradition and to contemporary mores. Classic dishes have evolved over time as a result of the island's long exposure to foreign cooking methods and ingredients, as well as being driven by high levels of competition and innovation in restaurant kitchens. On a cosmopolitan island populated by wealthy business people, this cutting edge is essential if an eatery is to survive. In a bid to attract customers, many Chinese restaurants take pride in promoting dishes as being 'Hong Kong style', which really means 'Cantonese with attitude'.

The town of Macau is a former Portuguese colony that follows the same inventive approach as Hong Kong when it comes to cooking. Hence, Lobster Noodles, Portuguese Egg Tarts and other fusion dishes are typical of the menus in this area, making them stand out from the dishes that are eaten elsewhere in the south.

Below *Dim sum – a mouthwatering array of little dishes – originated in Guangdong before spreading worldwide.*

FESTIVALS & CELEBRATIONS

In China, the western or Gregorian calendar is followed for all practical purposes, but it is the lunar calendar that governs the cultural, festive, religious and spiritual life. Most of the major celebrations, such as the Lunar New Year, Moon Cake Festival and Dumpling Festival, have evolved over thousands of years and are important annual events everywhere.

Although many festivals are celebrated throughout the country, there are some major regional differences in how they are marked. These lie in the preparation of food as offerings and for family meals, with each regional variation reflecting indigenous ingredients and local customs. There are also different, smaller festivals tied to local history and traditions.

Whatever the occasion, Cantonese people pull out all the stops when it comes to preparing food. Edible treats form the delicious basis of every celebration, and what is going to be eaten is the topic of constant conversation in every Cantonese community in the lead-up to the event, from Shantou to Sydney and from Hong Kong to Hungary.

Below *The Dragon Boat Festival is a major annual event and is celebrated with the eating of dumplings.*

Lunar New Year

Falling on the first day of the first lunar month in the Chinese calendar (between 20 January and 21 February), Lunar New Year or Chinese New Year is a major holiday for Chinese people everywhere.

In the lead-up to the new year, homes are given a good clean and new clothes and hairstyles are worn, symbolizing renewal. On the eve of the event, there is usually a special family meal featuring a fish dish and, in the south, a special cake called niangao is made and pieces distributed to relatives and friends.

The day itself is marked with communal feasts and visits to family elders, as well as street parties and firework displays. Red, the colour of luck, can be seen everywhere, from decorations and the costumes worn by people in parades, to the red packet containing money that unmarried people receive.

Food containing symbolic ingredients plays an important role throughout the holiday, and there are various regional specialities, including the Cantonese chicken soup called 'broth of prosperity'. This contains shredded hen's eggs and pigeon or quail eggs, symbolizing gold and silver ingots, while the chicken symbolizes the phoenix rising from the ashes, meaning rebirth and rejuvenation.

Another favourite dish is braised, seasoned pork shoulder, which goes by the delightful name 'mist of harmony'. Almost all the major ingredients are imbued with meaning: transparent vermicelli (fun si) are referred to as 'silvery threads of longevity'; platters of chicken wings represent 'soaring one thousand miles'; and bamboo shoots are eaten because they grow so tall, meaning 'year after year, ascend to great heights'.

Flowers and fruits also play significant roles. Lotus blossoms are the symbol of womanhood, and the Goddess of Mercy (Kuan Yin), patron of seafarers, is always portrayed standing on a lotus leaf and carrying a lotus stem. Oranges and kumquats are a symbolic gift and during the New Year Cantonese people will never visit anyone without a pair of these fruits. Pomegranates, studded with jewel-like seeds, are also important as they symbolize fertility and good fortune.

Above *As well as being of symbolic importance, the lotus – in the form of its root – is also eaten in China.*

Tin Hau or T'ien Hou

This Hong Kong festival on the 23rd day of the third lunar month (late April/early May) is in homage to Tin Hau, the Goddess of the Sky, who is said to safeguard fishermen against storms and keep them from drowning. In southern coastal regions dominated by fishing communities there are numerous holy shrines constructed in her honour. The festival itself is also known as the Festival of Bun Hills in the south of China, after the spectacular bun towers that are created – large bamboo structures several storeys high heaped with special sweet buns that are reputed to bring good luck. People climb up the towers, picking up as many buns as they can possibly hold.

In addition to the bun towers there are magnificent processions and parades, with people dressed in costumes reflecting the imperial past, riding on flowered floats and walking on stilts. The young play a major role in the processions, with children perched above the crowd on vertiginous stilts. There is food of all kinds to be had, although the collecting and eating of sweet buns is the main focus.

Dumpling or Dragon Boat Festival

This is celebrated on the fifth day of the fifth lunar month (June/July) and is marked with the eating of rice and meat dumplings. The 'dragon boat' refers to the time when a court official, Qu Yuan, was drowned in a river. In an attempt to rescue him, his comrades are said to have rowed up and down the river looking for him. This incident has since mutated into a colourful festival with teams of rowers competing in races (to represent the quest to find Qu Yuan), many of their boats decorated with a heraldic symbol of a dragon or a phoenix to boost their competitive spirit.

SOUTHERN CHINA
SOUPS

ROBUST BOWLS & PALATE CLEANSERS

There is one fundamental difference between the Chinese meal structure and that of other cuisines: soups are rarely, if ever, served as stand-alone appetizers at the start of a meal. They are, however, nonetheless very important in Cantonese food philosophy and according to a traditional saying they are thought to 'smoothen the soul'.

There are various types of soup on offer in the region. Light ones, such as clear Egg Drop & Ginger Soup, with a hint of Chinese wine, are often served as an accompaniment and are designed to refresh the palate between helpings of other, perhaps richer, dishes. Other, more robust brews, such as Beef Ball Soup, and Liver & Matrimony Vine Soup, contain substantial ingredients such as fish and meat. These make good meal-in-one options when circumstances or lack of time demand less kitchen work and, therefore, uncomplicated, quick meals that deliver on flavour, substance and nutritional completeness.

Seafood and meat dumplings often feature in soups that are served specifically to complement particular rice or noodle dishes. Prawn Wonton Soup is a case in point, and is served whenever Chilli Noodles (see page 437) are on the menu, making for a well-balanced meal. That said, these types of soup could be served on their own, too, as a lighter meal – though perhaps not when you are in a rush, since making the wontons or dumplings inevitably requires a little time and effort, though no great labour.

EGG DROP & GINGER SOUP

The name of this dish is a literal one, as you physically drop the egg into the boiling stock where it forms long strands. The soup is very easy to make, nutritious and beautifully light; the sort of thing that would be served at home to refresh the palate between more elaborate dishes.

SERVES 4

750ml/1¼ pints/3 cups fresh vegetable stock
30ml/2 tbsp fresh root ginger, finely shredded
2 eggs
30ml/2 tbsp Chinese rice wine
chopped spring onions/scallions or fresh coriander/cilantro, to garnish

1 Bring the stock to the boil in a medium pan. Add the finely shredded ginger and cook for 3 minutes.

2 Meanwhile, beat the eggs in a bowl or jug or pitcher. Pour them into the boiling soup in a steady stream, using a fork or some chopsticks to stir the surface at the same time. As it cooks, the egg will set, forming long shreds or strands.

3 Stir in the rice wine. Ladle into bowls, garnish with the spring onions or fresh coriander, and serve hot.

Variation

For more substance, soak a handful of cellophane noodles in boiling water for 5 minutes. Drain and add to the soup just before dropping in the egg.

SERVES 4

200g/7oz pig's liver
4–6 stalks of matrimony vine
750ml/1¼ pints/3 cups fresh vegetable stock
30ml/2 tbsp fresh root ginger, finely shredded
30ml/2 tbsp light soy sauce
2.5ml/½ tsp ground black pepper
30ml/2 tbsp sesame oil

Variation

If you can't locate matrimony vine, use young spinach leaves instead.

Cook's Tip

Matrimony vine is called gow gei in Cantonese. The plant yields wolf or goji berries, which are claimed to have rejuvenating powers.

LIVER & MATRIMONY VINE SOUP

Matrimony vine also goes by the name of boxthorn on account of the sharp thorns at the base of each leaf stalk. Legend has it that if it is planted close to a house, marital discord will follow – hence the name 'matrimony vine'. Only the spinach-like leaves are eaten.

1 Put the liver in the freezer for about 10 minutes, until it is firm enough to slice very finely with a sharp knife.

2 Meanwhile, prepare the matrimony vine. Pull the leaves away from the stems, taking care to avoid the thorns. Wash the leaves thoroughly under cold running water and drain them in a colander.

3 Pour the stock into a large pan and bring to the boil. Add the ginger, soy sauce, pepper and sesame oil.

4 Add the matrimony vine leaves to the pan, simmer for 2 minutes, then add the sliced liver. Cook for 2 minutes more, until the liver is just cooked. Ladle the soup into warm bowls and serve immediately.

PRAWN WONTON SOUP

The light stock for this wonton soup derives its richness from dried fish like sprats or anchovies. While Chinese stores sell instant wonton soup stock, it is easier – and more satisfying – to make your own, not to mention tastier and likely to be of better quality. Extra flavour comes from the wontons, which are filled with a delicious seafood mixture.

SERVES 4

60g/2oz dried sprats or anchovies
750ml/1¼ pints/3 cups water
15ml/1 tbsp light soy sauce
shredded spring onions/scallions, to garnish

FOR THE WONTONS
300g/11oz raw prawns/shrimp, peeled and deveined
15ml/1 tbsp light soy sauce
15ml/1 tbsp sesame oil
2.5ml/½ tsp ground black pepper
15ml/1 tbsp cornflour/cornstarch
16 wonton wrappers

Variation

For a vegetarian version, use chopped mushrooms instead of prawns/shrimp in the wonton filling, and make the stock using some dried mushrooms instead of dried fish.

1 Start by preparing the wonton filling. Chop the prawns finely to make a coarse paste. This can be done in a food processor rather than using a sharp knife, but make sure you use the pulse button, or the prawns will become rubbery.

2 Scrape the chopped prawns into a bowl and add the soy sauce, sesame oil, pepper and cornflour. Mix well. Place about 5ml/1 tsp of the mixture in the centre of a wonton wrapper, bring the edges together so that they meet at the top and pinch the neck to seal. Fill the remaining wontons in the same way.

3 Bring a small pan of water to the boil. Add the wontons and cook them for 5 minutes. Drain in a colander, transfer to a bowl and toss with a light dribble of oil to prevent them from sticking together.

4 Put the dried sprats or anchovies in a large pan. Pour in the water, add the soy sauce and bring to the boil. Cook for 5 minutes, then taste and add more soy sauce if needed. Strain the soup, return it to the pan and heat through.

5 Place four wontons in each warmed soup bowl. Ladle the soup over, garnish with the spring onions and serve.

STUFFED SQUID SOUP

Squid enjoys an honourable position in the Cantonese kitchen. Chefs have innumerable ways of preparing it: in stir-fried and deep-fried dishes, as a major ingredient in noodle dishes and in a range of soups. This dish typifies the Cantonese genius for combining seafood and meat.

SERVES 4

50g/2oz cellophane noodles
8 medium squid
150g/5oz/⅔ cup minced/ground pork
5ml/1 tsp cornflour/cornstarch
15ml/1 tbsp sesame oil
15ml/1 tbsp finely chopped spring onions/scallions
5ml/1 tsp ground black pepper, plus extra, to garnish
15ml/1 tbsp fish sauce
750ml/1¼ pints/3 cups fish stock
15ml/1 tbsp preserved turnip (see Cook's Tip)

Cook's Tips

- Cellophane noodles go by various other names, including mung bean noodles, transparent noodles, bean thread noodles and glass noodles.
- Preserved turnip (tung chye) is sold in Chinese food stores. It is crunchy and slightly sweet, and goes very well with fish.

1 Put the noodles in a bowl and pour over just-boiled water to cover. Soak for 20 minutes, or until the noodles have softened.

2 Prepare each squid by cutting off the tentacles just below the eye. Remove the transparent 'quill' from inside the body and rub off the skin on the outside. Wash the squid thoroughly in cold water, drain and set aside on a plate.

3 Put the pork in a bowl. Add the cornflour, sesame oil, spring onions, pepper and fish sauce. Mix well.

4 Stuff each squid three-quarters full with the pork mixture. Do not use more, as the squid will shrink when cooked, and the filling may pop out.

5 Pour the stock into a pan that will hold the squid comfortably and bring to the boil. Add the squid and cook for 5 minutes.

6 Drain the softened noodles and add them to the pan. Cook for 2 minutes more.

7 Serve in warmed bowls, garnished with the preserved turnip and a grinding of black pepper.

CHICKEN BROTH OF PROSPERITY

The origin of this popular dish is rather obscure. Like many dishes that grace the family table in China, especially during celebrations such as Chinese New Year, the ingredients are imbued with symbolic meaning. Ham and quail's eggs suggest the wealth and prosperity alluded to in the title, while the chicken represents the legendary phoenix, a symbol of rebirth that is particularly appropriate at the start of a new year. This tasty soup is very substantial and nutritious, and is sometimes so thick that it can be served on plates rather than in bowls – you can adjust the consistency to your preference.

SERVES 4

- 4 quail's eggs
- 750ml/1¼ pints/3 cups fresh chicken stock
- 2 skinless chicken breasts
- 150g/5oz Chinese or Serrano ham, finely diced
- 30ml/2 tbsp sesame oil
- 30ml/2 tbsp light soy sauce
- 2.5ml/½ tsp ground black pepper
- 2 eggs, lightly beaten
- 30ml/2 tbsp cornflour/cornstarch blended to a paste with 60ml/4 tbsp cold water

1 Cook the quail's eggs in a pan of boiling water for 8 minutes. Drain, refresh under cold water and remove the shells while still slightly warm. Set the eggs aside.

2 Pour the chicken stock into a large pan and bring to the boil. Add the chicken breasts, lower the heat slightly and simmer for about 10 minutes or until cooked through. Using tongs, lift them out of the pan and leave to cool.

3 Add the ham to the pan of stock and simmer for 15 minutes. Meanwhile, cut the chicken into shreds.

4 Add the sesame oil, soy sauce and pepper to the ham and stock mixture. Simmer gently for 2 minutes, then add the shredded chicken and beaten eggs, stirring all the time so that the eggs form strands. Simmer for 2 minutes.

5 Stir in the cornflour paste. Continue to stir until the soup thickens, then add the shelled quail's eggs and heat through for 1–2 minutes. Ladle into warm bowls and serve.

BEEF BALL SOUP

Many southern Chinese do not eat beef as they regard the cow as a sacred animal, without which they would not be able to till the soil on their farms. The Hakka people, being seafarers by tradition, do not subscribe to this belief and happily cook this sustaining beef soup, with its richly perfumed and flavoursome stock.

SERVES 4

400g/14oz beef sirloin
15ml/1 tbsp cornflour/cornstarch
15ml/3 tsp salt
5ml/1 tsp ground black pepper
1 litre/1¾ pints/4 cups fresh beef stock
1 large onion, sliced
2 star anise
6 cloves
10cm/4in cinnamon stick
5ml/1 tsp black peppercorns
chopped coriander/cilantro, to serve

1 Chop the beef into small cubes and process in a blender or food processor until smooth. Add the cornflour, 5ml/1 tsp salt and ground black pepper and continue to blend the mixture until it has the consistency of smooth pâté.

2 Scrape the meat mixture into a bowl and shape it into small balls, each the size of a large cherry tomato. When you process meat for a long time, it takes on a springy texture that is a little chewy when it is cooked.

3 Pour the beef stock into a large pan. Bring to the boil and add the onion, star anise, cloves, cinnamon stick, peppercorns and remaining salt. Lower the heat and simmer for 20 minutes.

4 Using a slotted spoon, remove the onion and whole spices. Bring the stock to the boil again. Add the beef balls and cook them for 5 minutes.

5 Ladle the soup into four warm bowls and give each portion an equal number of the beef balls. Garnish with fresh coriander and serve immediately.

SOUTHERN CHINA
DIM SUM

MOIST MORSELS & CRUNCHY BITES

Literally meaning 'food to touch the heart', dim sum are very popular throughout China and the rest of the world. The evolution of this Cantonese way of eating since its ancient beginnings in Guangdong is closely connected with the Chinese penchant for consuming light snacks with tea. This led to a huge increase in demand and, over the centuries since 200BCE, chefs from all over China have been challenged to be ever more inventive in preparing bitesize morsels, dumplings, snacks and assorted finger food.

Dim sum were never meant to provide a full meal, and favourites such as char siew bau (Roast Pork Dumplings), shao mai (Pork & Prawn Dumplings) and savoury cakes made from root vegetables, were originally served much like Spanish tapas – as a light snack. Over time, however, the range has grown and today eating dim sum invariably means consuming an eclectic variety of small dishes that can comprise a full meal.

Each region of China makes use of local ingredients, resulting in dishes like Crystal Dumplings, made with special translucent skins. Seasonings, on the other hand, remain within the classic Cantonese canon of black bean sauce, hoisin sauce, sesame oil, garlic, and spring onions or scallions.

Fried or steamed, wrapped with rice or batters, there is a growing cornucopia of new types of dim sum joining the tried-and-tested repertoire. As a meal for one or ten, the most appealing element is that you eat what you like from the trolley and are not dictated to by a rigid menu.

YAM CAKE

The vegetable upon which this Cantonese classic is based inevitably causes confusion. In America it is called taro, whereas yam can refer to an orange-fleshed sweet potato. To muddy the waters still further, there is a Chinese vegetable called yam bean, but that is different again. What you want for this classic recipe is the large barrel-shaped vegetable with a hairy brown skin and purple-flecked flesh. Alternatively, you could use pumpkin.

SERVES 6–8

- 50g/2oz dried shrimp
- 75ml/5 tbsp vegetable oil
- 15 shallots, thinly sliced
- 2 Chinese sausages, diced finely
- 1kg/2¼lb yam
- 300g/11oz/2½ cups rice flour
- 115g/4oz/1 cup tapioca flour or 115g/4oz/1 cup cornflour/ cornstarch
- 750ml/1¼ pints/3 cups water
- 5ml/1 tsp salt
- 2 spring onions/scallions, plus extra, chopped, to garnish
- 30ml/2 tbsp light soy sauce
- 30ml/2 tbsp sesame oil
- 2.5ml/½ tsp ground black pepper
- chilli dipping sauce, for serving

1 Put the dried shrimp in a bowl and pour over water to cover. Soak for 1 hour, until soft.

2 Heat the oil in a frying pan and fry the shallots for 4–5 minutes, until brown and crisp. Lift out with a slotted spoon and set aside.

3 Drain the soaked shrimp and chop them roughly. Reheat the oil remaining in the pan and fry the shrimp with the diced sausage for 3 minutes. Transfer the shrimp and sausage to a bowl and set aside.

4 Peel the yam and remove the fibrous stalk. Cut the flesh into large chunks and put it in a steamer placed over simmering water. Steam for 20 minutes, until the flesh is soft.

5 Put the yam into a large bowl and mash until smooth with a potato masher. Stir in the rice flour and the tapioca or cornflour, then add the water and salt. Mix well.

6 Set aside 30ml/2 tbsp of the fried shallots. Add the remainder to the shrimp mixture. Stir in the spring onions, soy sauce, sesame oil and pepper, then fry gently in a hot wok for 2 minutes so that the flavours combine.

7 Add the mixture to the mashed yams. Mix well, then press into a lightly oiled tray suitable for steaming. Steam over rapidly boiling water for 15 minutes.

8 Cool, then cut into wedges, garnish with the reserved fried shallots and spring onions, and serve with the chilli dipping sauce.

Cook's Tip

Dried shrimp are sold in most Chinese food stores. They have a very strong smell, but this dissipates when they are cooked.

RADISH CAKE

Closely related to Yam Cake, this recipe makes innovative use of the large white radish that is also known as mooli or daikon. As a vegetable, white radish is bland, although it is useful for making soup stock. Process it to a paste and mix it with rice flour, however, and it is magically transformed.

SERVES 6–8

50g/2oz dried shrimp
1kg/2¼lb white radish (also called mooli or daikon)
300g/11oz/2½ cups rice flour
115g/4oz/1 cup tapioca flour or 115g/4oz/1 cup cornflour/cornstarch
750ml/1¼ pints/3 cups water
5ml/1 tsp salt
30ml/2 tbsp vegetable oil
30ml/2 tbsp light soy sauce
30ml/2 tbsp sesame oil
2.5ml/½ tsp ground black pepper
dipping sauce, optional, to serve

1 Put the dried shrimp in a bowl and pour over water to cover. Soak for 1 hour, until soft.

2 Meanwhile, peel the radish and chop it roughly. Process it in batches in a blender or food processor to a soft white purée. Scrape into a strainer and press down with a spoon to extract as much liquid as possible.

3 Tip the purée into a bowl and stir in the rice flour and the tapioca or cornflour. Add the water and salt and mix well.

4 Drain the soaked shrimp and chop them roughly. Spoon the radish purée into a non-stick pan and cook over low heat, stirring frequently, for 5 minutes.

5 Heat the vegetable oil in a frying pan or wok. Add the chopped shrimp and fry for 2 minutes, then add the radish purée. Stir well, then add the soy sauce, sesame oil and ground black pepper. Mix thoroughly to combine.

6 Press the mixture into a lightly oiled steaming tray. Steam over a pan of rapidly boiling water for 20 minutes. Set aside.

7 When cold, slice into bitesize pieces and serve plain or with a dipping sauce of your choice.

Cook's Tips

- White radishes are much larger than the more common red variety and can weigh up to 1kg/2¼lb. Choose ones that are pearly white and firm, as old radishes become fibrous.
- Radish cake can be frozen and thawed without losing any of its flavour.

BRAISED BEANCURD SKIN PARCELS

Beancurd skins are a healthier option than wheat-flour-based spring roll wrappers and taste much better, especially when they have a delicious chicken, mushroom and bean sauce filling. These little parcels are easy to make and do not take long to steam, and make an excellent addition to a selection of dim sum.

SERVES 4

4 dried Chinese black mushrooms
300g/11oz skinless chicken breast
30ml/2 tbsp vegetable oil
30ml/2 tbsp black bean sauce
2.5ml/½ tsp ground black pepper
2.5ml/½ tsp sugar
30ml/2 tbsp sesame oil
100ml/3½fl oz/scant ½ cup water
1–2 sheets of beancurd skins

1 Soak the mushrooms in a bowl of boiling water for 20–30 minutes, until soft. Drain and slice into thin strips, discarding the stems. Slice the chicken into 1cm/½in-thick strips.

2 Heat the vegetable oil in a wok or frying pan. Add the chicken and mushroom strips and stir-fry for 3 minutes. Add the black bean sauce, pepper, sugar and sesame oil and stir-fry for 2 minutes more.

3 Pour in the water. Cook over high heat until most of it has been driven off and the mixture is thick and almost dry. Transfer to a bowl and leave to cool.

4 Place a beancurd skin on a clean, flat surface or chopping board and cut into pieces about 10cm/4in wide. Top with two or three pieces each of chicken and mushroom, tuck in the edges and roll up to make a parcel about 6cm/2½in long. Fill the other skins in the same way.

5 Place the beancurd skin parcels on a large plate and steam over a wok of rapidly boiling water for 10 minutes. Serve hot.

Cook's Tips

• Dried beancurd skins are usually sold in large sheets. Check that they are not brittle or cracked, which would suggest they had been sitting too long on the grocer's shelf. Good beancurd skins should be soft and pliable. If the beancurd skins are a little brittle, dampen a clean dish towel and place it over them for 5 minutes.

• Any unused skins should be packed flat in plastic bags and sealed tightly. Keep in a dry larder but do not put in the refrigerator as dry, cold air makes them brittle.

Variations

• Add a few pieces of finely shredded fresh root ginger to the filling for a spicy touch.

• The mushroom soaking liquid can be strained and used in place of some or all of the water for the filling.

CRYSTAL DUMPLINGS

A much-loved street food, these dumplings are often sold by vendors carrying their wares in two baskets slung either side of a long bamboo pole. Called chui kuay (water dumplings) by the Swatow-speaking Shantou people on account of their translucent skins, they are especially delicious with a sweet soy sauce and chilli dip.

MAKES ABOUT 12 DUMPLINGS

- 200g/7oz/1¾ cups sweet potato flour
- 400ml/14fl oz/1⅔ cups water
- 30ml/2 tbsp vegetable oil
- 115g/4oz/1 cup tapioca flour

FOR THE FILLING

- 400g/14oz can bamboo shoots, drained
- 45ml/3 tbsp vegetable oil
- 3 garlic cloves, crushed
- 30ml/2 tbsp dark soy sauce
- 30ml/2 tbsp oyster sauce
- 5ml/1 tsp ground black pepper
- 200ml/7fl oz/scant 1 cup water

SWEET SOY SAUCE & CHILLI DIP

- 45ml/3 tbsp dark soy sauce
- 15ml/1 tbsp ginger purée
- 15ml/1 tbsp rice vinegar
- 15ml/1 tbsp sesame oil
- 5ml/1 tsp sugar
- 5ml/1 tsp chilli bean paste

Variation

If you do not have bamboo shoots, use swedes/rutabagas or turnips.

1 Put the sweet potato flour in a non-stick pan. Add the water and oil and cook over low heat, stirring occasionally, until thick. Remove from the heat and leave to cool for 15 minutes.

2 Meanwhile, shred the bamboo shoots for the filling until they are more or less the shape and size of beansprouts. Put them in a colander, rinse thoroughly and drain.

3 Heat the oil in a wok and fry the crushed garlic over low heat for 40 seconds. Do not let it burn. Add the bamboo shoots, soy sauce, oyster sauce, pepper and water. Cook over medium heat for 10 minutes, until the mixture is almost dry. Remove from the heat and leave to cool.

4 Stir the tapioca flour into the cool sweet potato flour mixture. Mix well, then transfer to a floured board. Knead the dough for at least 5 minutes, punching the dough as you roll and fold. This makes it very light. Shape the dough into a long roll, about 5cm/2in in diameter. Slice off pieces 9mm/⅜in thick and flatten each with a rolling pin to form very thin, unbroken circles.

5 Place about 30ml/2 tbsp bamboo shoots on each circle, fold over into a half-moon shape and seal the edges. Trim off any excess dough and fold and pinch until you get a serrated edge on each one.

6 Place the dumplings on an oiled plate and steam over a wok of boiling water for 30 minutes, topping up the water as necessary.

7 Meanwhile, mix together all the ingredients for the sweet soy sauce and chilli dip in a small bowl. Transfer to a serving bowl. Serve the dumplings warm with the dip.

CHIVE DUMPLINGS

These dumplings are lovely and light, thanks to the wheat starch flour used for the wrappers. Although there is an art to making them, the end result is well worth the effort. Some versions feature a filling of bamboo shoots or sweet Chinese turnips, but the Chinese chives used here add crunch and flavour. These are different from regular chives, being flatter and broader and with a fresh aroma.

MAKES 12 DUMPLINGS

150g/5oz/1¼ cups wheat starch
200ml/7fl oz/scant 1 cup water
15ml/1 tbsp vegetable oil
50g/2oz/½ cup tapioca flour
pinch of salt
sesame oil, for brushing the dumplings
chilli sauce, for dipping

FOR THE FILLING
200g/7oz Chinese chives
30ml/2 tbsp light soy sauce
15ml/1 tbsp sesame oil
2.5ml/½ tsp ground black pepper
15ml/1 tbsp cornflour/cornstarch
1 egg, lightly beaten

1 Put the wheat starch in a non-stick pan. Add the water and oil and cook over low heat, stirring occasionally, until very thick. Remove from the heat and leave to cool for 15 minutes.

2 Meanwhile, prepare the filling. Chop the chives finely, then put them in a bowl and stir in the soy sauce, sesame oil, pepper and cornflour until well combined.

3 Heat a wok, then add the chive mixture and toss over low heat for 5 minutes. Stir in the lightly beaten egg to bind the mixture, then set it aside.

4 Stir the tapioca flour and salt into the cool wheat starch mixture. Mix well, then transfer to a floured board. Knead the dough for at least 5 minutes, until smooth. Roll out the dough and stamp it out into 12 circles, 7.5cm/3in in diameter.

5 Place 1 heaped tablespoon of the filling on each dough circle and fold to make half-moon shapes. Seal the edges with a little water. Brush each dumpling with a little sesame oil to prevent them from sticking together when being steamed.

6 Place the dumplings on a plate and steam over rapidly boiling water for 10 minutes. Serve immediately, with a chilli sauce dip.

PORK & PRAWN DUMPLINGS

While dim sum are generally attributed to southern China, these bitesize morsels, called shao mai, are enjoyed throughout the entire country. Pork is the main ingredient in the filling used here, but there are also seafood versions.

MAKES 16 DUMPLINGS

- 100g/3¾oz raw prawns/shrimp, peeled and deveined
- 2 spring onions/scallions
- 225g/8oz/1 cup minced/ground pork
- 30ml/2 tbsp light soy sauce
- 15ml/1 tbsp sesame oil
- 2.5ml/½ tsp ground black pepper
- 15ml/1 tbsp cornflour/cornstarch
- 16 round wonton wrappers
- 16 large garden peas, thawed if frozen
- chilli sauce, for dipping

1 Chop the prawns finely to make a coarse paste. This can be done using a sharp knife or in a food processor, but if you use a food processor use the pulse button, or the prawns will become rubbery. Scrape into a bowl.

2 Chop the spring onions very finely. Add them to the prawns, with the pork, soy sauce, sesame oil, pepper and cornflour. Mix well.

3 Holding a wonton wrapper on the palm of one hand, spoon a heaped teaspoon of the filling into the centre. Cup your hand so that the wrapper enfolds the filling to make the classic dumpling shape. Leave the top slightly open. Top each gap with a pea. Fill the remaining wonton wrappers in the same way.

4 Place the dumplings on an oiled plate and steam over a wok of rapidly boiling water for 10 minutes. Serve with a chilli sauce dip.

Cook's Tip

If you can only find square wonton wrappers, trim off the corners to make a rough circle before filling them.

MAKES 16 WONTONS

300g/11oz/1½ cups minced/ground pork
15ml/1 tbsp light soy sauce
15ml/1 tbsp sesame oil
2.5ml/½ tsp ground black pepper
15ml/1 tbsp cornflour/cornstarch
16 wonton wrappers
vegetable oil for deep-frying
chilli dipping sauce or plum sauce, to serve

Cook's Tips

- If the wonton skins are brittle, wipe them with a damp towel or they will be difficult to shape without cracking.
- Filled wontons take very little time to cook. Make sure your oil is not too hot as they scorch quickly.

DEEP-FRIED WONTONS

These are a close cousin of shao mai (pork dumplings). They have much the same ingredients but are fried rather than steamed. Crisp on the outside, with a tender filling, it may be an idea to make double the quantity.

1 Put the pork in a bowl. Add the soy sauce, sesame oil, ground black pepper and cornflour. Mix well.

2 Place about 5ml/1 tsp of the mixture in the centre of a wonton wrapper, bring the corners together so that they meet at the top, and pinch the neck to seal. Fill the remaining wontons in the same way.

3 Heat the oil in a wok or deep-fryer. Carefully add the filled wontons, about four or five at a time, and deep-fry until they are golden brown.

4 Carefully lift out the cooked wontons with a slotted spoon, drain on kitchen paper and keep hot while frying successive batches. Serve the wontons hot with chilli dipping sauce or plum sauce.

PORK & NUT DUMPLINGS

These dainty little bites use basically the same dough as for chive dumplings, but their taste and texture is totally different. This is thanks to the unusual filling, with its interplay of succulent pork, crunchy nuts and aromatics. These are a typical Shantou dim sum.

MAKES 12 DUMPLINGS

150g/5oz/1¼ cups wheat starch
200ml/7fl oz/scant 1 cup water
15ml/1 tbsp vegetable oil
50g/2oz/½ cup tapioca flour or cornflour/cornstarch
pinch of salt

FOR THE FILLING
30ml/2 tbsp vegetable oil
200g/7oz/scant 1 cup minced/ground pork
90ml/6 tbsp water
50g/2oz/½ cup peanuts, chopped
30ml/2 tbsp light soy sauce
15ml/1 tbsp sesame oil
2.5ml/½ tsp ground black pepper

BLACK VINEGAR & GINGER DIP
45ml/3 tbsp black vinegar
15ml/1 tbsp finely shredded fresh root ginger
small pinch of salt

1 Put the wheat starch in a non-stick pan. Add the water and oil and cook over low heat, stirring occasionally, until very thick. Remove from the heat and leave to cool for 15 minutes.

2 Meanwhile, make the filling. Heat the vegetable oil in a pan and fry the pork for 2 minutes. Add the water, peanuts, soy sauce, sesame oil and ground black pepper. Stir for 3 minutes until the pork is cooked through and there is the barest hint of sauce. Set aside to cool.

3 Stir the tapioca flour and salt into the cool wheat starch mixture. Mix well, then transfer to a floured board. Knead the dough for at least 5 minutes. Divide into 12 portions, then flatten each piece of dough and roll them into 7.5cm/3in circles.

4 Place a heaped tablespoonful of the filling on each dough circle and fold to make half-moon shapes. Seal the edges with a little water. Brush each dumpling with a little sesame oil to prevent them from sticking together when being steamed.

5 Place the dumplings on a large plate and steam over a wok of rapidly boiling water for 10 minutes.

6 Meanwhile, mix together all the ingredients for the Black Vinegar & Ginger Dip in a small bowl. Transfer to a serving bowl. Serve the dumplings hot, with the dipping sauce.

ROAST PORK DUMPLINGS

Known as char siew bau in Cantonese, these quintessential dim sum delicacies owe their excellence to a trade secret that has long eluded the common cook. The secret lies in the special low-gluten flour that makes these dumplings light, white and fluffy, which is called dai garn fun in Cantonese and is available in Chinese food stores.

MAKES 12 DUMPLINGS

200g/7oz/1¾ cups low-gluten flour (dai garn fun)
pinch of salt
5ml/1 tsp easy-blend/rapid-rise dried yeast
120ml/4fl oz/½ cup warm water
5ml/1 tsp vinegar

FOR THE FILLING

115g/4oz cold roast pork, finely diced
30ml/2 tbsp hoisin sauce
1 spring onion/scallion, finely chopped

1 Put the flour and salt in a large mixing bowl and sprinkle in the yeast. Make a well in the centre and pour in the warm water and vinegar. Mix to a dough.

2 Place the dough on a floured board and knead for 10 minutes. Return it to the bowl, cover and set aside in a warm place to rise for 20 minutes or until it has doubled in bulk.

3 Knock back/punch down the dough, knead it again, return it to the bowl and set aside in a warm place for 15 minutes.

4 Meanwhile, make the filling. Put the diced pork in a bowl. Stir in the hoisin sauce to moisten it, then add the spring onion.

5 Roll out the dough on a floured board and shape it into a 30cm/12in-long roll, about 5cm/2in in diameter. Cut the roll into 2.5cm/1in slices and flatten each of these with a rolling pin to a thin round, about 9cm/3½in across.

6 Holding a pastry round on the palm of one hand, spoon a heaped teaspoon of the filling into the centre. Cup your hand so that the dough enfolds the filling, pleating and pinching it where necessary. Pinch off the excess dough at the top and seal with a twisting action. Fill the remaining dumplings in the same way.

7 Cut 12 5cm/2in squares of baking parchment. Stand a dumpling on each piece of paper in a steamer and steam for 15 minutes. Serve immediately.

Cook's Tip

Don't throw away the bits of pastry you pinch off the top of the dumplings. Rolled together, they will yield enough dough for two more dumplings.

SOUTHERN CHINA FISH & SHELLFISH

SIMPLE FLAVOURS & TENDER FLESH

The preparation of fish and shellfish in southern Chinese cooking is governed by the sauces and seasonings that will be used with it. Sweet-and-Sour Snapper and Braised Carp in Ginger Sauce are perfect examples of this, as great care is taken both to cook the fish and create the aromatic sauces that accompany them so that everything works together in perfect harmony. Delicate freshwater fish is steamed in Shantou or Fujian style, with just a hint of ginger and sour plums to add background notes without drowning out the subtle fish flavour. More robust seafood, such as prawns or large shrimp, are often served with rich tomato or oyster sauces, resulting in dishes such as Red Prawns on the Shell.

Shellfish are plentiful on the shores off Hainan Island and the signature dish here is called Wenchang Steamed Crab, whose simple preparation casts the spotlight on the exquisite richness of this crustacean. Even when left raw, as in Chilled Pickled Crab, the flavours are delectable. Much of the seafood, such as tiny shrimps, squid and anchovies, are also dried as seasoning bases, which can then be combined with meat or poultry to create distinctively southern Chinese combinations of meat and fish.

What's more, in addition to being enjoyed for their flavour and because of their ready availability, shellfish are eaten for symbolic reasons. Prawns, for instance, signify happiness, and lobster represents the dragon and nobility. As ever, try to buy the freshest seafood you can.

FISH-STUFFED VEGETABLES

This complex dish of aubergines and bitter gourd stuffed with seafood paste and served with a squid and tofu broth is Hakka in origin. It is a popular street food in Singapore and Malaysia, where there are sizeable Cantonese and Hakka communities, as well as in China. It takes a little time to prepare, but is so delicious it is worth the effort.

SERVES 4

75g/3oz/½ cup dried soya beans
1 litre/1¾ pints/4 cups water
300g/11oz skinless, boneless fish, cubed
15ml/1 tbsp cornflour/cornstarch
5ml/1 tsp salt
1 whole aubergine/eggplant
1 whole bitter gourd
1 reconstituted dried squid
250g/9oz pack fresh tofu
1 seafood or fish stock cube
chilli sauce and hoisin sauce, to serve

Variations

- For an even richer dish, add fish balls and water convolvulus.
- For a more substantial dish, add boiled noodles.

1 Put the soya beans in a large, heavy pan. Pour in the water. Bring to the boil, then lower the heat and simmer for 45 minutes. Strain the stock into a large, shallow pan. Discard the soya beans, reserving a few for the garnish.

2 Put the cubes of fish into a food processor. Process until finely chopped, then add the cornflour and salt. Process in short bursts for about 15 minutes, adding up to 30ml/2 tbsp water, until the mixture has a slightly springy texture. Scrape into a bowl.

3 Slice the aubergine diagonally into 2cm/¾in thick rounds. Slice the bitter gourd into rounds of similar size, also on the diagonal. This will help to keep the filling in place.

4 Make a deep slit in each aubergine piece three quarters down to make a cavity. Remove the pith and seeds from the bitter gourd pieces. Stuff each piece of vegetable with the fish mixture and smooth on both sides with a butter knife.

5 Slice the reconstituted squid into bitesize pieces. Cut the tofu into bite-size chunks. Bring the soya bean stock to a simmer and crumble in the stock cube. Add the squid, tofu and stuffed vegetables and cook for 10 minutes.

6 Serve in bowls, garnished with the reserved soya beans, and with dips of chilli sauce and hoisin sauce on the side.

Cook's Tip

Don't skimp on the processing time for the fish; it needs to be springy, and the longer you process it the springier it becomes.

STEAMED FISH WITH SOUR PLUM

Shantou restaurants take great pride in steamed fish dishes such as this one. The addition of sour plums is a particularly inspired touch, especially when salmon, pomfret or sea bass is used, as the tartness of the plums really cuts the rich oils in the fish and perfectly balances the dish, as well as bringing a different texture to the plate.

1 Cut deep slashes on either side of the fish, where the flesh is thickest. Put the fish on a plate that will fit in your steamer. If the fish is too large, cut it in half.

2 Drain the sour plums and put them in a bowl. Mash to a rough purée and spread over the fish. Dribble over the fish sauce and scatter with the ginger and spring onions. Lay the bacon on top.

3 Put the plate in the steamer. Steam the fish over rapidly boiling water for about 15 minutes or until it is cooked through. Transfer to a warm platter, garnish with the fresh coriander and serve immediately.

SERVES 4

- 1 whole fish, about 500g/1¼lb, cleaned and scaled
- 4 canned sour plums
- 15ml/1 tbsp fish sauce
- 15ml/1 tbsp finely shredded root ginger
- 2 spring onions/scallions, finely shredded
- 3–4 strips of streaky/fatty bacon
- chopped fresh coriander/cilantro, to serve

Variation

Add a few strips of fresh chilli with the spring onions/scallions for a spicy highlight.

SERVES 4

1 large carp, about 1kg/2¼lb, cleaned and scaled
400ml/14fl oz/1⅔ cups water
15ml/1 tbsp grated fresh root ginger
45ml/3 tbsp dark soy sauce
30ml/2 tbsp sesame oil
5ml/1 tsp sugar
4 cloves
salt and ground black pepper
15ml/1 tbsp cornflour/cornstarch mixed with 30ml/2 tbsp water
shredded spring onions, to garnish
boiled rice, to serve (optional)

Variation

Tilapia or any firm-fleshed fish like salmon and halibut can be used.

BRAISED CARP IN GINGER SAUCE

Braising fish in water and aromatics is a method that is typical of both Fujian cooking and of the neighbouring province of Guangzhou. The recipe is very easy to make – the fish is simply braised in a tasty stock – but the combination of flavours works extremely well.

1 Make deep cuts diagonally across both sides of the carpfish. If the fish is too large for your wok, cut it into two pieces.

2 Pour the water into the wok and add the ginger, soy sauce, sesame oil, sugar, cloves, and a pinch of salt and pepper. Bring to the boil. Lower the fish into the liquid, reduce the heat and braise for 15 minutes, until cooked. Transfer to a serving dish and keep hot.

3 Stir the cornflour mixture into the liquid remaining in the wok. Bring to the boil and cook, stirring, for 2 minutes, until the sauce thickens. Spoon the sauce over the fish, garnish with spring onions, and serve immediately, with rice if you like.

SWEET-AND-SOUR SNAPPER

Originating in the northern region of Shandong, this dish turns up on most regional menus and is a popular dish in Cantonese cooking. Comprising simply a whole deep-fried fish served with a medley of vegetables, it is distinguished by the sauce. This is based on Kao Liang wine vinegar, which is made from sorghum and millet grains.

SERVES 4

4 dried Chinese black mushrooms
1 whole snapper or similar fish, about 800g/ 1¾lb, cleaned and scaled
15ml/1 tbsp salt
45ml/3 tbsp cornflour/cornstarch
oil for deep- and shallow-frying
15ml/1 tbsp thinly sliced root ginger
15ml/1 tbsp crushed garlic
1 spring onion, cut into 2.5cm/1in lengths, plus extra, to garnish
30ml/2 tbsp thinly sliced bamboo shoots
½ red bell pepper, thinly sliced

FOR THE SAUCE

60ml/4 tbsp Kao Liang wine vinegar
15ml/1 tbsp sugar
15ml/1 tbsp light soy sauce
10ml/2 tsp cornflour/cornstarch mixed with 45ml/3 tbsp water
200ml/7fl oz/scant 1 cup water or stock

1 Soak the mushrooms in a bowl of boiling water for 20–30 minutes, until soft.

2 Meanwhile, rinse the fish inside and out, then pat dry with kitchen paper. Make deep cuts diagonally across both sides of the fish. Rub with the salt, rinse again and pat dry. Dust the fish all over with the cornflour.

3 Heat the oil in a wok that is large enough to hold the fish comfortably. Carefully lower the fish into the oil and fry over medium heat for 7–8 minutes, until the skin is crisp and golden brown and the fish is cooked through.

4 Remove the fish from the wok and drain on kitchen paper. Place the fish on a serving platter with a decent lip to hold the sauce, and keep hot.

5 Drain the mushrooms and slice them thinly, discarding the stems. In a clean wok, heat 30ml/2 tbsp oil and stir-fry the ginger and garlic for 1 minute. Add the spring onion, bamboo shoots and pepper, with the sliced mushrooms. Stir-fry for 2 minutes more.

6 Mix all the sauce ingredients together in a bowl. Add to the wok, bring rapidly to the boil and simmer for 1 minute, until the sauce thickens and bubbles.

7 Pour the sauce over the fish and garnish with more sliced spring onions. Serve immediately.

Variations

• Kao Liang wine vinegar is recommended for its robust flavour, but if you cannot locate it, any wine vinegar can be used.

• The snapper can be substituted with any firm-fleshed fish, such as cod, grouper or halibut. If you find the sight of a whole fish a little off-putting, use fish fillets.

RED PRAWNS ON THE SHELL

Known as ha loke in Cantonese, this has become a staple dish in Chinese restaurants throughout South-east Asia. For aesthetic reasons, and to maximize the flavour, the prawns are not shelled, although you can remove the heads without compromising the flavour too much.

1 Clean the prawns and cut off 1cm/½in from the head end of each, then slice each in half down its length, leaving the shells on.

2 Heat a wok. Dribble the oil around the rim so that it flows down to coat the surface. Once hot, stir-fry the ginger and garlic.

3 Add the onion and stir-fry for 2 minutes. Toss the prawns into the wok and stir-fry over high heat for 2–3 minutes or until they have turned pink. Using a slotted spoon, transfer the prawns to a bowl.

4 Pour the tomato sauce and oyster sauce into the wok, add the water and quickly bring to the boil, stirring all the time.

5 Arrange the lettuce on a platter or on individual plates. Divide the prawns among them and spoon the sauce over. Serve immediately.

SERVES 4

450g/1lb tiger prawns/jumbo shrimp
30ml/2 tbsp vegetable oil
30ml/2 tbsp chopped root ginger
30ml/2 tbsp chopped garlic
1 large onion, sliced
30ml/2 tbsp tomato sauce/ketchup
30ml/2 tbsp oyster sauce
100ml/3½fl oz/scant ½ cup water
whole lettuce leaves, to serve

Cook's Tips

- Use the largest prawns you can find – ones with fat bodies and large heads.
- Do not let the garlic burn or it will taste bitter.

SERVES 4

16 large tiger prawns/jumbo shrimp
45ml/3 tbsp vegetable oil
15ml/1 tbsp chopped garlic
15ml/1 tbsp ground black pepper
10ml/2 tsp salt

Cook's Tip

To appreciate the flavours at their magnificent best, this dish should always be served piping hot.

SALT & PEPPER PRAWNS

This is the simplest way of preparing prawns in their shells and Cantonese chefs have the technique down to a fine art. Chefs in Hong Kong are particularly skilled, employing the flash stir-frying method by which they coax flames to catch in the wok. It is pure theatre.

1 Clean the prawns thoroughly and cut off 1cm/½in from the head end of each. Remove the whiskers. If the prawns are particularly large, use a sharp knife to split each one in half down its length.

2 Heat a dry wok. Add the prawns to the hot pan and flash fry over high heat for 2 minutes or until they turn pink, shivering the wok to keep them on the move at all times. Tip the prawns into a bowl.

3 Add the oil to the wok and heat it. When it is very hot, add the garlic and fry for 1 minute, stirring constantly. Add the prawns, with the pepper and salt and stir rapidly over high heat for 2–3 minutes. Cover the wok with a lid and cook for 1 minute more.

4 Transfer the prawns to a dish and serve immediately.

BUTTERFLY PRAWNS

A classic Cantonese restaurant dish, this takes its name from the way each prawn is slit and opened out so that it looks like a butterfly. The prawns are dipped in a very light batter, almost like tempura, and then quickly cooked in very hot oil until golden and crispy.

SERVES 4

16 large prawns/shrimp
30ml/2 tbsp plain/all-purpose flour
15ml/1 tbsp self-raising/self-rising flour
pinch of bicarbonate of soda/ baking soda
15ml/1 tbsp sesame oil
120ml/4fl oz/½ cup cold water
vegetable oil for deep-frying
chilli and garlic dipping sauce, to serve

1 Clean the prawns and shell them, but leave the tails intact. Using a sharp knife, slit each prawn halfway through the back, then spread them flat so that they resemble butterflies.

2 Mix the plain flour and self-raising flour in a bowl. Add the bicarbonate of soda, then the sesame oil and cold water. Stir to make a smooth batter.

3 Heat the oil in a wok or deep-fryer to 190°C/375°F. Dip each prawn in turn in the batter, gently shaking off the excess, and add to the hot oil. Repeat with more prawns, but do not overcrowd the wok or fryer.

4 After 2–3 minutes, when the prawns are golden brown, lift them out with a slotted spoon and drain on kitchen paper. Keep warm while cooking successive batches. Serve hot, with the chilli and garlic dipping sauce.

Cook's Tips

- For a crisp batter, always use very cold water or iced water.
- If you don't have time to butterfly the prawns, simply shell them, dip them in batter and fry as above. They won't looks as good but will still taste delicious.
- Serve the deep-fried prawns immediately after frying, when the batter is still very hot.

WENCHANG STEAMED CRAB

A small county town on the east coast of Hainan Island, Wenchang has two major claims to fame. The first is its excellent seafood, and the second is as the ancestral home of two sisters, Song Qingling and Song Meiling, the wives of Generals Sun Yat Sen and Chiang Kai Shek respectively.

SERVES 4

4 whole crabs, about 250g/9oz each
15ml/1 tbsp chopped root ginger
30ml/2 tbsp Chinese wine
15ml/1 tbsp light soy sauce
5ml/1 tsp ground black pepper
chilli and garlic sauce, for dipping

1 Clean the crabs and remove the belly flap from each, together with any fibrous tissue attached to it. Prise the shell away from the body and cut each crab into four pieces. Crack the large claws for easy removal of the meat after the crabs are cooked.

2 Mix the chopped ginger, wine, soy sauce and pepper in a shallow heatproof bowl that will both accommodate all the crabs and fit in your steamer.

3 Put the bowl in the steamer and cook the crabs over boiling water for 15 minutes or until they turn pink all over. Serve hot or cold, with chilli and garlic sauce on the side for dipping.

Cook's Tip

The liquor that collects at the bottom of the plate or bowl in any steamed shellfish dish is delicious when mixed with rice.

SERVES 4–6

- 4 fresh mottled crabs or any small crabs, about
- 100–150g/3¾–5oz each 600ml/ 1 pint/2½ cups rice wine vinegar
- 6 garlic cloves, crushed
- 25g/1oz root ginger, peeled and crushed
- 25g/1oz/4 tsp rock salt
- 4 fresh red chillies (optional)

Cook's Tips

- Be sure to use rice wine vinegar – other types of vinegar will not do, as they do not have the right flavour.
- The pickled crab tastes wonderful served with plain congee.

CHILLED PICKLED CRAB

Shantou chefs are adept at pickling crustaceans, especially the small mottled crabs that live on coastal beaches and in tropical mangrove swamps. When pickled, the crabs keep for weeks in the refrigerator.

1 Clean the crabs and remove any fibrous matter. Prise the shell away from the body and cut each crab into four pieces. Trim off the ends of the smaller legs. Remove and discard any coral. Wash the crabs thoroughly, drain and dry with kitchen paper.

2 Put the vinegar in a non-reactive pan and add the garlic, ginger and salt, together with the whole chillies, if using. Bring to the boil. Remove the pan of liquid from the heat and leave until cold.

3 Pack the crabs in one or more sterilized jars and pour over the pickling liquid so that the crabs are completely submerged. If using more than one jar, divide the chillies among them.

4 Close the jars, making sure they are airtight. Store the jars in the refrigerator, stirring once every day with a clean dry spoon. The pickled crabs will be ready for eating after the third day.

STEAMED SCALLOPS WITH BLACK BEAN SAUCE

When scallops are fresh, they taste exquisite when simply steamed in their shells. Here, they are served with a little flavoursome sauce made from Chinese wine, black bean sauce and fresh ginger, which perfectly complements the sweet, tender flesh of the scallops.

SERVES 4

- 8 scallops, preferably in the shell
- 30ml/2 tbsp Chinese Hsiao Hsing wine
- 15ml/1 tbsp fermented black beans
- 15ml/1 tbsp chopped root ginger
- 2.5ml/½ tsp sugar
- 15ml/1 tbsp spring onions/scallions

Cook's Tips

- Frozen scallops are sold in most Chinese food stores.
- Save the scallop shells. They can be used as decorative containers in the future.
- When black beans are used in any dish, they provide plenty of salt, so there is no need to add any more.

1 Preheat the oven to 160°C/325°F/Gas 3. Spread the scallops in a single layer on a baking sheet. Heat them for a few moments until they gape, then remove them from the oven.

2 Hold a scallop in a clean dish towel, flat side up. Using a long, flexible knife, run the blade along the inner surface of the flat shell to cut through the muscle that holds the shells together. Ease the shells apart completely.

3 Lift off the top shell. Pull out and discard the black intestinal sac and the yellowish frilly membrane. Cut the white scallop and orange coral from the bottom shell and rinse briefly under cold water. Remove and discard the white ligament attached to the scallop flesh.

4 Mix the wine, black beans, ginger and sugar in a shallow dish. Add the scallops and marinate for 30 minutes.

5 Return the scallops and marinade to the half shells and place them in a steamer. If you have bought shelled scallops, divide them – and the marinade – among four ramekins. Steam for 10 minutes.

6 Meanwhile, slice the spring onions and use to garnish the scallops. Serve immediately.

STIR-FRY SQUID & MANGETOUT

Like many people who live near the sea, the Cantonese have a passion for all shellfish. Squid and octopus are especially popular, both at home and as premium restaurant dishes. They demand skilful cooking as they rapidly become rubbery and unpalatable if overdone.

SERVES 4

175g/6oz squid tubes, cleaned
15ml/1 tbsp vegetable oil
30ml/2 tbsp garlic, crushed
175g/6oz mangetouts/snow peas, trimmed
30m/2 tbsp oyster sauce
2.5ml/½ tsp ground black pepper
30ml/2 tbsp sesame oil
10ml/2 tsp cornflour/cornstarch
105ml/7 tbsp water

1 Using a sharp knife or kitchen scissors, slice through the side of each squid tube and open them out so that they lie flat.

2 Cross-hatch the surface of each piece of squid by making deep cuts at 1cm/½in intervals, first in one direction and then in the other. Cut each piece of squid in half lengthways.

3 Heat the oil in a wok and fry the garlic for 30 seconds. Toss in the mangetouts and squid and stir-fry over high heat for 2 minutes. Add the oyster sauce, pepper and sesame oil and stir for 1 minute.

4 Blend the cornflour with the water, then add to the wok and stir until the sauce thickens. Spoon into a serving bowl and serve.

Cook's Tip

If you rub squid with bicarbonate of soda or baking soda the flesh becomes more tender and succulent. You do not need much – a scant teaspoon will be plenty.

SERVES 4

450g/1lb live green-lipped or standard mussels, scrubbed and bearded
30ml/2 tbsp vegetable oil
15ml/1 tbsp chopped root ginger
3 garlic cloves, chopped
30ml/2 tbsp Chinese wine or sherry
150ml/¼ pint/⅔ cup water
2.5ml/½ tsp salt
2.5ml/½ tsp ground black pepper

Cook's Tip

Drizzle a little sesame oil on top of the mussels just before serving them for a nutty fragrance and added flavour.

STIR-FRY MUSSELS WITH GINGER

Any kind of edible bivalve can be used, but green-lipped mussels are ideal for this dish. Mussels have a great affinity with aromatics such as ginger and garlic and, when steeped in a wine sauce, echo the French dish moules marinière. Hong Kong chefs sometimes use large clams instead.

1 Carefully check over the mussels, discarding any that have cracked shells, as well as any that are open and that do not snap shut when tapped on a firm surface.

2 Heat the oil in a wok and fry the ginger and garlic for 40 seconds, until light brown. Add the mussels and stir rapidly over high heat for 2 minutes, shaking the pan to move the mussels around.

3 Pour in the Chinese wine or sherry and the water. Season and toss the mussels over the heat for a further 2–3 minutes, until all of them have opened. Discard any that remain closed. Pile the mussels into a warm serving bowl and serve immediately.

SOUTHERN CHINA
POULTRY

LIGHT BITES & FAMILY FEASTS

Chinese cooks have a high regard for poultry and will coax maximum flavour out of every bird. Fried, boiled, steamed or roasted, many iconic Chinese poultry dishes like Cantonese Roast Duck are so delicious they are now global favourites.

The cuisine did not evolve on the basis of roasting or baking, as fuel is scarce and expensive, and poultry is rarely served whole. Instead, it is usually cooked and served in juicy bitesize pieces that can be easily eaten with chopsticks. Even if the bird is cooked whole, as in the Hainan classic Chicken with Ginger Wine, it will arrive at the table carved and jointed. Knives are frowned on as table cutlery, as it is deemed that this is a job for the cook.

However poultry is cooked, there is almost always a marinade. Even the simplest steamed chicken or braised duck dish will have many seasonings and aromatics to help bring out the flavours and cut the fat. Ginger, garlic, spring onions or scallions and soy sauce make up the classic flavourings, while wine gives a heady lift to gamey dishes such as Crispy Quail. Sweet sauces made from fruit such as plums are also popular.

The balance of flavours and textures is, as ever, all-important, and one star dish in this regard is Duck Stuffed with Glutinous Rice, with its compendium of fillings, including lotus seeds, ginkgo nuts and mushrooms. Other dishes, such as Chicken with Cashew Nuts from Hong Kong, are simpler, but still display a splendid interplay of flavours and textures. Tuck in!

CHICKEN WITH CASHEW NUTS

This classic, must-have restaurant dish has an intriguing, universal appeal, which can perhaps be explained by the pleasing contrast of the succulent chicken and crunchy cashews, and similar interplay between the sweetness of the carrots and the saltiness of the soy sauce.

SERVES 4

1 carrot, about 115g/4oz, cubed
30ml/2 tbsp vegetable oil
2 garlic cloves, crushed
2 skinless chicken breasts, diced
150g/5oz/1¼ cups cashew nuts
15ml/1 tbsp light soy sauce
15ml/1 tbsp sesame oil
5ml/1 tsp cornflour/cornstarch
150ml/¼ pint/⅔ cup water
boiled rice, to serve (optional)

1 Bring a small pan of water to the boil. Add the cubed carrot. Blanch for 1 minute, then drain and set aside.

2 Heat the oil in a wok and fry the garlic over medium heat until light brown. Do not let it burn or it will taste bitter.

3 Add the chicken cubes and stir-fry for 2 minutes until almost cooked. Add the carrot, with the cashew nuts, soy sauce and sesame oil. Stir-fry for 1 minute.

4 Blend the cornflour with the water to make a paste. Add to the wok and stir over the heat until the sauce simmers and thickens. Transfer to a heated dish and serve immediately, with rice if liked.

Cook's Tip

If you prefer, par-cook the chicken breasts whole by poaching them in water for 10 minutes before cutting them into cubes. Use some of the poaching liquid instead of the water that is mixed with the cornflour.

SERVES 4

2 skinless chicken breasts
1 egg, beaten
6 crackers, finely crushed (about ⅔ cup cracker crumbs)
vegetable oil for deep-frying
45ml/3 tbsp plum sauce
15ml/1 tbsp hoisin sauce
100ml/3½fl oz/scant ½ cup water
cucumber sticks, to garnish

Variation

- If you cannot find Chinese plum sauce, use apricot jam instead. Add a squeeze of lemon juice if it is too sweet.
- To make the dish a little more substantial, you could add some quartered tomatoes.

PLUM SAUCE CHICKEN

The fruity sweetness of plum sauce is the perfect foil for meat and poultry, either on its own or as an ingredient in a sweet-and-sour sauce. Here, it partners tender chicken that is coated with cracker crumbs and quickly deep-fried to give a flavoursome and crisp crust.

1 Cut each chicken breast into four pieces. Put the egg in one shallow bowl and the cracker crumbs in another. Heat the oil in a wok or deep-fryer.

2 Dip each piece of chicken in egg and then in cracker crumbs, patting the crumbs on firmly to coat. Discard any excess crumbs. Deep-fry, in batches if necessary, for 3–4 minutes, until golden brown and cooked. Using a slotted spoon, transfer to a board.

3 Put the plum sauce and hoisin sauce in a pan and stir in the water. Heat until bubbling.

4 Meanwhile cut the chicken into bitesize pieces and pile on a platter. Pour over the sauce, garnish with the cucumber and serve.

CHICKEN WITH SHRIMP PASTE

This new dish is an innovation that draws on Singaporean cooking elements in its use of shrimp paste, ground coriander and turmeric. These ingredients are generally unknown in southern Chinese cooking but have been adopted with enthusiasm in recent years as they add an extra savoury note to a simple dish.

SERVES 4

450g/1lb boneless chicken thighs
20g/¾oz shrimp paste
30ml/2 tbsp water
30ml/2 tbsp ground coriander
5ml/1 tsp ground turmeric
5ml/1 tsp ground black pepper
10ml/2 tsp sugar
115g/4oz/1 cup cornflour/ cornstarch
vegetable oil for deep-frying
shredded spring onion and chopped fresh red chilli, to garnish
chilli dipping sauce, to serve

Cook's Tip

Known as belacan in Malay and ha cheong in Cantonese, shrimp paste has a sharp pungency that is tempered and subtly muted when cooked.

1 Rinse the chicken thighs under cold running water and pad dry with kithcen paper. Cut each into 2–3 pieces.

2 Put the shrimp paste in a small bowl and add the water. Mash well to mix, then add the ground coriander and turmeric along with the pepper and sugar. Mix to a smooth paste.

3 Spread out the cornflour in a shallow bowl.

4 Rub the paste all over the chicken, pressing it in well, then transfer the pieces to the bowl of cornflour and coat them on all sides.

5 Heat the vegetable oil in a wok or deep-fryer to 190ºC/375ºF. Carefully add the coated chicken pieces and deep-fry, in batches if necessary, for 3–4 minutes, until golden brown and cooked through.

6 Lift out the pieces using a slotted spoon and keep hot while you cook the remaining pieces in the same way.

7 Drain on kitchen paper to absorb any excess oil and serve immediately, garnished with chilli and spring onion, and with a chilli dipping sauce alongside.

Variation

To give this dish some extra fire, add 2.5ml/½ tsp chilli powder to the seasoning, if you like.

CHICKEN & BANANA ROLLS

Bananas do not often turn up in savoury cooking, but in Hong Kong and Hainan Island, the fruit has a special place in the kitchen. In this unique dish, sweet chunks of banana are wrapped in succulent chicken and deep-fried, making an unusual but delicious snack.

SERVES 4

2 skinless chicken breasts
1 egg, lightly beaten
150g/5oz/1 ¼ cups cornflour/cornstarch
2 ripe bananas
vegetable oil, for deep-frying

1 Slice the chicken breasts diagonally into 3–4 thin escalopes. Put these between pieces of clear film/plastic wrap and pound lightly with a meat mallet to tenderize.

2 Put the beaten egg in one shallow bowl and spread out the cornflour in another.

3 Slice each banana into 3–4 lengths. Dip each piece in a little egg and place on an escalope. Fold up and over to make a secure roll. Coat the roll with cornflour, patting the coating on firmly. Set aside.

4 Heat the vegetable oil in a wok or deep-fryer to 190°C/375°F. Fry the rolls, in batches if necessary, for 3–4 minutes, until crisp and golden brown. Drain on kitchen paper, then slice each chicken and banana roll diagonally, pile the pieces on a plate and serve.

Variation

If bananas are not to your taste, slices of mango or melon work equally well.

SERVES 6

- 1 whole chicken, about 1.6kg/ 3½lb
- 30ml/2 tbsp finely grated fresh root ginger
- 5ml/1 tsp salt
- 60ml/4 tbsp ginger wine, Chinese wine or sherry
- 5 spring onions/scallions, cut into 5cm/2in lengths and then into fine strips
- 2 fresh red chillies, seeded and sliced into long, thin strips
- dipping sauce, to serve (optional)

CHICKEN WITH GINGER WINE

The rub for this recipe isn't based on a Chinese product, but rather on a ginger wine that has been made in England since the 18th century. It is widely available, but gingered Chinese wine or sherry can be substituted. Steaming the chicken makes it tender, and the ginger gives it flavour.

1 Place the chicken on a deep plate that will fit in your wok or steamer. Put the ginger in a bowl and add the salt. Stir in the wine or sherry. Spread the mixture over the chicken and rub it in well.

2 Sprinkle the spring onion and chilli strips evenly over the chicken, then place the plate containing the chicken in the steamer or wok. Cover and steam for 1 hour or until it is cooked through, topping up the water in the steamer as necessary.

3 Carve the chicken and arrange the pieces on a platter. Serve hot or cold, with reduced cooking juices or a dipping sauce.

SOY-BRAISED CHICKEN

The local name for this Cantonese classic is see yau gai and it has as many variations as a chicken has feathers. Guangzhou Cantonese do not use galangal, but the Cantonese in Singapore and Malaysia insist on it and I like it so I've included it here. Omit it if you prefer. Caramelizing the chicken gives it a delicious bittersweet flavour.

SERVES 4–6

30ml/2 tbsp vegetable oil
15ml/1 tbsp sugar
1 chicken, about 1.6kg/3½lb
150ml/¼ pint/⅔ cup dark soy sauce
8 garlic cloves, peeled and bruised
1 large knob of galangal, bruised
1.5 litres/2½ pints/6¼ cups water
30ml/2 tbsp cornflour/cornstarch blended with 30ml/2 tbsp water
sliced cucumber, to garnish
chilli sauce, to serve (optional)

1 Heat the oil in a wok large enough to hold the chicken. Sprinkle in the sugar and cook over medium to high heat until the mixture froths and caramelizes. When it is pale brown in colour, add the chicken and turn it several times to coat the skin.

2 Add the soy sauce to the wok. Using two spatulas or large forks, turn the chicken several times to coat it thoroughly and let it steep in the sauce.

3 Add the garlic, galangal and water. Bring to the boil, reduce the heat, cover and simmer for 50 minutes. Turn off the heat, leaving the wok covered with the lid, and leave for a further 10 minutes, during which time the chicken will continue to cook.

4 Check that the chicken is fully cooked, then transfer it to a board. Cover with foil and leave to stand. Strain the cooking liquid into a pan. Discard the solids in the strainer.

5 Bring the liquid in the pan to the boil, add the cornflour mixture and stir until the sauce is thick and glossy.

6 Carve the chicken and arrange the slices on a platter. Garnish with the cucumber. Serve the thick, slightly reduced, sauce on the side with a side dip of chilli sauce, if you like.

Variation

For a sauce with a more intense garlic flavour, do not throw away the garlic cloves with the knob of galangal after straining. Instead, crush them to a purée and return them to the sauce.

Cook's Tip

Galangal is a rhizome, like ginger. There are two types: greater galangal, which comes from Indonesia, while lesser galangal is a native of southern China. The latter, used here, has a pungent flavour, like a cross between ginger and black pepper.

JADE & SILVER CHICKEN

The name of this dish stems from the use of broccoli and chicken, which symbolize jade and silver. Pretty, tasty and nutritious, it is a star item in most Chinese restaurants around the world. Traditionally, Chinese Jinhua ham is used but this is rarely found outside China and any smoked or honey-cured ham can be used to good effect.

SERVES 4

2 skinless chicken breasts
250ml/8fl oz/1 cup water
2 slices honey-cured or smoked ham
150g/5oz Chinese broccoli (kai lan) or tenderstem broccoli
15ml/1 tbsp cornflour/cornstarch
½ chicken stock/bouillon cube
30ml/2 tbsp Chinese wine
30ml/2 tbsp sesame oil
5ml/1 tsp ground black pepper

Variation

Use prosciutto or Chinese ham instead of the honey-cured or smoked ham, if you like.

1 Put the chicken breasts in a pan and pour over the water. Bring to the boil, lower the heat and simmer for 10 minutes or until cooked through. Lift out the chicken portions with tongs and put them on a board. Reserve the cooking liquid in the pan.

2 Slice the ham into 2.5cm/1in-wide strips and cut the spears of broccoli into strips of similar length. Slice each piece of chicken in half lengthways and then in 2.5cm/1in strips.

3 Layer the broccoli, ham and chicken strips in a deep plate that will fit inside a wok or steamer. Steam the mixture over rapidly boiling water for 5 minutes.

4 Meanwhile, in a small bowl, blend the cornflour to a paste with a little of the water used for cooking the chicken.

5 Crumble the chicken stock cube into the remaining water in the pan and add the cornflour paste, Chinese wine, sesame oil and black pepper. Bring to the boil, stirring, until the sauce has the consistency of pouring cream.

6 Remove the steamed broccoli, ham and chicken from the steamer and pour the sauce over the top. Serve immediately.

Variation

You can give a lift to the dish by adding 30ml/2 tbsp Shaoxing wine or dry sherry in the last 5 minutes of cooking time, if you like.

HAINAN CHICKEN RICE

This dish originated from Hainan Island, where it evolved into a classic street food but has now been elevated to five-star status in hotels and upmarket restaurants. Comprising tender pieces of poached chicken mixed with rice and aromatics, it is always served with a classic combination of seasonings – dark soy sauce, finely chopped fresh chilli, fresh root ginger, and garlic – and with a bowl of soup stock on the side.

SERVES 4

1 chicken, about 1.6kg/3½lb
about 1.2 litres/2 pints/5 cups water
½ large onion, sliced
4 garlic cloves, peeled and left whole
10 black peppercorns
1 large knob of fresh root ginger, bruised
15ml/1 tbsp soy sauce
30ml/2 tbsp sesame oil
200g/7oz/1 cup long grain white rice or jasmine rice

TO SERVE

shredded spring onions/scallions, to garnish the soup
30ml/2 tbsp finely chopped fresh red and green chilli
60ml/4 tbsp vinegar
30ml/2 tbsp finely chopped garlic
30ml/2 tbsp finely chopped fresh root ginger
30ml/2 tbsp dark soy sauce
sliced cucumber and tomatoes, to garnish the plate (optional)

1 Trim off and discard any excess fat from the chicken, then place it in a large pan. Pour in the water. It should just cover the chicken, so top up if necessary.

2 Add the onion, garlic, peppercorns, ginger, soy sauce and sesame oil to the pan. Bring to the boil, lower the heat and simmer, uncovered, for 40 minutes.

3 Turn off the heat, cover the pan and leave to stand for about 15 minutes, during which time it will continue to cook by means of residual heat.

4 Check that the chicken is fully cooked. Lift it out of the stock, put it on a platter and keep it hot. Strain the stock into a clean pan.

5 Put the rice in a colander and rinse it well. Drain, then tip the rice into a pan. Add enough of the chicken stock to cover the rice by 2.5cm/1in. Bring to the boil, cover the pan and reduce the heat to medium. Cook for 15 minutes.

6 Meanwhile, heat the stock remaining in the pan. Taste and adjust the seasoning. When the rice is dry and fluffy, spoon it into a heated bowl. Put the soup in a separate bowl and garnish it with the shredded spring onions.

7 Slice the chicken and arrange it on a large platter. Garnish with the slices of cucumber and tomato. Mix together the finely chopped chilli and the vinegar to make a sour sauce.

8 Serve the chicken with the rice, the soup, the chilli and vinegar sauce, and side bowls of mixed chopped garlic, chopped ginger and soy sauce.

DUCK STUFFED WITH GLUTINOUS RICE

If you have a helpful butcher, ask him to debone the duck for you. Otherwise, stuff it on the bone. This version has similarities with the classic Shanghai recipe Eight Treasure Duck but has been tweaked to suit Cantonese tastes. Start preparations the day before serving.

SERVES 6–8

75g/3oz/½ cup raw glutinous rice
6 dried black Chinese mushrooms
6 Chinese sweet red dates or Medjool dates, pitted and chopped
20 canned ginkgo nuts, drained
2.5ml/½ tsp ground black pepper
45ml/3 tbsp oyster sauce
1 oven-ready duck, about 2.5kg/5½lb
60ml/4 tbsp dark soy sauce
150ml/¼ pint/⅔ cup oil
2 litres/3½ pints/8 cups water
30ml/2 tbsp sesame oil
2 spring onions/scallions, shredded, plus extra to garnish
6 garlic cloves, peeled and left whole
2.5ml/½ tsp ground black pepper

Cook's Tip

Don't waste the stock used for cooking the duck. Strain it into a clean pan and boil it for 30 minutes until it has reduced. Pour into a jug or pitcher, cool quickly, then chill in the refrigerator until the fat solidifies on the top and can be removed and discarded. The stock can then be heated and served as a sauce on the side or tossed with stir-fried noodles.

1 Rinse the glutinous rice in several changes of cold water, then leave it to soak overnight in a bowl of fresh cold water. Next day, drain the rice and spread it evenly in a steamer lined with muslin or cheesecloth. Cover and steam over simmering water for 25 minutes or until tender and fluffy.

2 Meanwhile, soak the Chinese mushrooms in boiling water for 20–30 minutes, until soft. Drain, remove the hard stalks and dice the caps finely.

3 Put the mushrooms in a bowl and add the rice, dates, ginkgo nuts, pepper and oyster sauce. Mix well.

4 Remove the excess fat from the duck and enlarge the entrance to the cavity slightly. Stuff it with the rice mixture. Using a poultry needle and fairly strong thread, sew up the slit. Rub the duck all over with half the soy sauce.

5 Heat the oil in a large wok and add the duck. Fry, turning frequently, until the skin is well sealed and brown.

6 Place the duck in a deep pan. Pour in the water and add the sesame oil, spring onions, garlic cloves, remaining soy sauce and black pepper. Bring to the boil. Cover, lower the heat and simmer for 2–2¼ hours, turning several times and topping up the water when necessary.

7 When the duck is cooked, lift it on to a platter. Carve it in the kitchen or serve it at the table, to be carved with a flourish. Garnish with spring onion and accompany it with a flavourful reduced sauce (see Cook's Tip).

Variation

Chinese sweet red dates are called mat cho. Look for them in Chinese food stores, or use Medjools or other Middle Eastern dates instead.

CANTONESE ROAST DUCK

You see this vermilion-coloured bird hanging in every Chinese restaurant window, usually with the head still on. There is a reason for this: Chinese-Taoist belief holds that no living creature should go into the afterlife with parts missing. Few take this superstition seriously, but the tradition persists simply because there is a lot of flavour in the head and neck.

SERVES 8

1 duck, about 2.5kg/5½lb
15ml/1 tbsp maltose or honey
15ml/1 tbsp hoisin sauce
30ml/2 tbsp Chinese wine
15ml/1 tbsp red cochineal food colouring (optional)
sliced cucumber and chilli sauce, to serve

1 Clean the duck inside and out and pat it dry with kitchen paper. Tie kitchen string/twine firmly around the legs of the bird and suspend it from a butcher's hook from a shelf in the kitchen or garage, whichever is the coolest. Place a bowl underneath to catch the drips and leave to dry overnight.

2 Next day, bring a large pan of water to the boil. Add the duck and blanch it for 3–4 minutes. This will remove excess fat and also shrink the skin, promoting crispness when cooked. Lift the duck out of the pan, drain it thoroughly and dry it well with kitchen paper.

3 Put the maltose or honey in a bowl and stir in the hoisin sauce and wine, with the colouring, if using. Generously brush the mixture all over the duck skin. Leave to dry for 1–1½ hours.

4 Preheat the oven to the highest setting: 240–250°C/475–500°F/Gas 9–10. Put the duck on a rack over a roasting pan and roast in the oven for 20 minutes.

5 Reduce the oven temperature to 200°C/400°F/Gas 6 and roast for 30 minutes. Remove the duck from the oven and pierce the thickest part of the thigh with a sharp knife. If the juice runs out clear, turn off the oven, return the duck to it and leave it to continue cooking in residual heat for another 20 minutes. If the duck juices are still a little bloody, leave the oven on and check the bird again after 10–15 minutes.

6 Let the duck cool a little, then chop it up or slice it off the bone into serving pieces. Pile on a platter and serve with sliced cucumber and a chilli sauce for dipping.

Cook's Tip

If you take the duck off the bone for serving, use the bones to make a flavoursome stock. To make, sauté 1 chopped onion, 2 chopped celery stalks and 1 chopped carrot in 15ml/1 tbsp vegetable oil for 5 minutes, until softened slightly. Add the bones and enough water to cover. Add a bay leaf and a few black peppercorns, cover and bring to a simmer. Simmer for about an hour, then strain the liquid into a clean pan. Bring to the boil and reduce by half. Cool quickly and skim off any fat.

SOY-BRAISED DUCK

A traditional Cantonese dish, this takes time to prepare but is worth the effort. It is served – usually cold – for festive occasions, along with brandy.

1 Heat the oil in a wok large enough to hold the duck. Sprinkle in the sugar and cook over medium to high heat until caramelized. Add the duck and turn it several times to coat the skin.

2 Add the soy sauce to the wok. Using two spatulas or large forks, turn the duck several times to coat it thoroughly.

3 Add the galangal or ginger, garlic, star anise and cinnamon. Pour in the water and bring to the boil. Lower the heat, cover and simmer for $1\frac{1}{2}$ hours, until the meat starts to come off the bones.

4 Lift the duck on to a board and set it aside while you make the gravy. Strain the cooking liquid into a clean pan, skim the fat and boil over high heat until reduced to the consistency of gravy.

5 Carve the duck and arrange on a platter. Garnish with cucumber slices and serve with the gravy.

SERVES 8

30ml/2 tbsp vegetable oil
30ml/2 tbsp sugar
1 oven-ready duck, about 2.5kg/$5\frac{1}{2}$lb
150ml/$\frac{1}{4}$ pint/$\frac{2}{3}$ cup dark soy sauce
1 large knob galangal or fresh root ginger
6 garlic cloves, peeled and bruised
4 star anise
5cm/2in piece of cinnamon stick
2 litres/$3\frac{1}{2}$ pints/8 cups water
sliced cucumber, to garnish

Cook's Tip

If you are short of time, the gravy can be thickened by whisking in a paste made by blending 15ml/1 tbsp cornflour with water, but the taste will not be as intense.

SERVES 2

4 quail
5ml/1 tsp salt
2.5ml/½ tsp five-spice powder
30ml/2 tbsp Chinese wine
vegetable oil for deep frying
lemon wedges, to serve

Variation

Five-spice powder is a pungent spice, so use it judiciously. It isn't to everyone's taste, so if you do not like it, use 5ml/1 tsp ground coriander instead.

CRISPY QUAIL

Quail is not as popular in China as some other types of poultry, but when you can get them, these birds make delicious eating. In supermarkets, the birds are usually sold in packs of two or four as they are very small, and two are cooked and served per person.

1 Pat the the quail all over with kitchen paper. The drier the skin before cooking, the crispier it will be after cooking.

2 Mix the salt, five-spice powder and wine in a small bowl. Rub the quail all over with the mixture. Set aside for 30 minutes.

3 Heat the vegetable oil in a wok or deep-fryer to 190°C/375°F. Add the quail, in batches if necessary, and deep-fry for 4–6 minutes, turning once or twice, until crisp and golden brown. Lift out and drain on kitchen paper.

4 Put the quail on a serving platter or individual plates and serve hot, with the lemon wedges for squeezing over the crispy skin.

SOUTHERN CHINA
MEAT

STICKY SNACKS & FLAVOUR FUSIONS

Although all kinds of meat are eaten in China, the favoured animal protein is pork. In Cantonese cooking especially, it rules the culinary realm, turning up in a hundred different guises. The dish it is intended for dictates the way pork is cut, rather than the cut of meat determining what dish is cooked, as is the case in the Western world. Whatever animal is eaten, the southern Chinese make good use of every part, from the kidneys and innards to the ribs and loin, combining them with carefully selected ingredients and cooking techniques in a manner that will maximize the flavour.

Among the many favourite rib dishes are Spare Ribs in Black Bean Sauce, unctuous in their meatiness, and Cantonese Roast Pork, made from a rib cut that is streaked with fat and cut as a long strip. Marinated in a rich blend of honey, hoisin sauce and preserved red beancurd, it has won fans around the world. Minced pork makes an appearance in dishes like Minced Pork Rolls in Beancurd Skin and various dumplings. When pork is needed for slow-cooking, the hock or leg cut or belly meat is used, as in Mist of Harmony.

Offal or variety meats like liver and kidney are treated with respect and used in many dishes, which use seasonings to temper their intense flavours. Beef is regarded as a luxury meat and is inevitably imported since there is a very small cattle industry in China. Expensive and hard to come by, it is generally served in restaurants; Sautéed Beef in Oyster Sauce is a signature Hong Kong dish.

天津特产
GOLDEN STAR
金星 商標
【中華老字號】
玫瑰露酒
MEI KUEI LU CHIEW
500ml
天津食品進出口股份有限公司監制
PACKED BY
FOODSTUFFS IMPORT & EXPORT CO.,LTD.

SPARE RIBS IN BLACK BEAN SAUCE

Spare ribs are popular throughout China. Recipes from the south tend to be less rich than those from the north, where marinades contain considerably more wine. The best way to ensure the ribs are really succulent is to braise them, as deep-fried ribs tend to be dry.

SERVES 4

500g/1¼lb pork spare ribs, cut into 5cm/2in lengths

FOR THE MARINADE

30ml/2 tbsp light soy sauce
5ml/1 tsp sugar
30ml/2 tbsp black bean sauce
30ml/2 tbsp Chinese wine
30ml/2 tbsp oyster sauce
30ml/2 tbsp hoisin sauce
750ml/1¼ pints/3 cups water
shredded spring onions/scallions, to garnish

1 Combine all the ingredients for the marinade in a large, shallow dish. Add the ribs, making sure they are completely submerged. Cover and marinate for 30 minutes, turning the ribs once or twice.

2 Transfer the ribs and marinade to a deep pan. Cover with a tight-fitting lid and bring to the boil. Cook over high heat for 15 minutes.

3 Lower the heat to medium and continue to cook the ribs for a further 40 minutes, until the pork is cooked and the sauce is thick.

4 Pile the ribs on to a platter, pour the sauce over, garnish with spring onions and serve. The best way to eat ribs is with the fingers, so be sure to have wipes handy.

Cook's Tip

For braising the ribs, use a deep pan that is not too wide, so that they remain submerged in the sauce. A tight-fitting lid will help to reduce evaporation.

SERVES 4

250g/9oz pork rib-eye steak
30ml/2 tbsp sesame oil
30ml/2 tbsp vegetable oil
15ml/1 tbsp sliced garlic
40g/1½oz fresh young root ginger, sliced into very fine strips
2 spring onions/scallions, shredded
30ml/2 tbsp oyster sauce
5–10ml/1–2 tsp ground black pepper
30ml/2 tbsp Chinese rice wine
30ml/2 tbsp water

Cook's Tips

- The best cut of pork for this is rib-eye steak.
- Make sure that the ginger is young, fresh and juicy.

STIR-FRIED PORK WITH GINGER

Pork marries well with ginger, garlic and onions – three ingredients that are regarded as the essential basis of Chinese seasoning. This is a good Cantonese standby for those occasions when you fancy a simple meal. Be lavish with the ginger as it is the hallmark of this dish.

1 Cut the pork into thin strips. Place these on a board and tenderize them slightly, using a meat mallet or the blunt edge of a cleaver. Rub the strips with sesame oil and set them aside for 15 minutes.

2 Heat the vegetable oil in a wok. Add the garlic and ginger and fry for 1 minute, until pale brown.

3 Add the pork and spring onions. Stir-fry for 2 minutes, then add the oyster sauce and black pepper. Stir over the heat for 2 minutes until the seasonings have been thoroughly absorbed by the pork.

4 Pour in the rice wine and water. Continue to cook, stirring, for 2 minutes, until the liquid bubbles and the pork is fully cooked. Spoon into a heated bowl and serve.

CANTONESE ROAST PORK

This classic dish is based on a pork rib cut that is a mixture of fat and lean meat. Traditionally, chefs use a special clay oven inside which the pork is hung on a metal hook. However, a convection oven will work if you use a rack set in a roasting tin. Some restaurants add red food colouring to the marinade, but this is unnecessary as the hoisin sauce and beancurd provide plenty of colour without the e-numbers.

1 If the piece of steak is 7.5cm/3in thick or more, cut it in half horizontally. Using a sharp knife, score the surface at regular intervals to a depth of about 1cm/½in.

2 In a shallow dish that is large enough to allow the piece or pieces of meat to lie flat, mix the honey or maltose with the hoisin sauce. Add the preserved red beancurd, mashing it so that it combines with the other ingredients. Stir in the wine.

3 Add the pork and rub it all over with the marinade, making sure to penetrate the scored cuts. Cover the dish and marinate the pork for 1 hour or overnight.

4 Preheat the oven to 220°C/425°F/Gas 7. Place the piece or pieces of pork on a rack set in a roasting pan and roast for 20 minutes, then reduce the oven temperature to 180°C/350°F/Gas 4 and roast for 20 minutes more.

5 Preheat the grill or broiler. Place the pan containing the pork under the heat until the surface chars lightly in places. Let the pork cool.

6 Serve in slices, with sliced cucumber and a hot chilli sauce dip. Rice and greens are a good accompaniment.

SERVES 8

- 900g/2lb pork rib-eye steak, in one piece
- 30ml/2 tbsp honey or maltose
- 30ml/2 tbsp hoisin sauce
- 15ml/1 tbsp preserved red beancurd
- 30ml/2 tbsp Chinese wine
- sliced cucumber and a hot chilli sauce dip, to serve
- steamed greens and rice, to serve (optional)

Cook's Tip

Pork roasted this way freezes well, especially if you slice it before freezing. Slices thaw quickly, which is useful because this type of roast pork is not only valued as a dish in its own right, but is also the basis of several composite Chinese dishes.

SWEET-AND-SOUR PORK

The sweet and sour flavours of this iconic dish reflect the yin-yang principle of universal harmony that is at the heart of Chinese cooking. Although it originated in Shanghai, every province has its own version. The sweetening agent is plum sauce and the sourness is vinegar or pineapple juice.

SERVES 4

- 1 egg, beaten
- 75g/3oz/¾ cup cornflour/cornstarch
- 300g/11oz leg of pork, cut into 1cm/½in cibes
- oil for deep-frying
- 1 small carrot, cubed
- 1 large onion, quartered
- 1 tomato, quartered
- 30ml/2 tbsp plum sauce
- 30ml/2 tbsp hoisin sauce
- 45ml/3 tbsp pineapple juice or 15ml/1 tbsp vinegar
- 200ml/7fl oz/scant 1 cup water

1 Put the egg in a dish and the cornflour in a clean, strong plastic bag. Dip the pork in the egg, then shake them in the bag of flour.

2 Heat the oil in a wok to 190°C/375°F. Fry the pork, in batches if necessary, until cooked and golden. Drain on kitchen paper.

3 Drain off all but 15ml/1 tbsp of the oil from the wok. Add the carrot; fry for 2 minutes. Add the onion and tomato and stir-fry for 1 minute.

4 Combine the plum sauce, hoisin sauce, pineapple juice, vinegar and water. Add to the wok and cook, stirring, for 1 minute.

5 Add the cubes of fried pork to the wok and stir quickly until the ingredients are thoroughly mixed. Serve immediately.

Variations

Try cucumber batons or celery sticks instead of carrots, and drained canned lychees or pineapple chunks.

SERVES 4

15ml/1 tbsp cornflour/cornstarch
450g/1lb pork rib-eye steak streaked with a little fat, cut into thin slices
30ml/2 tbsp oil
½ large onion, finely sliced
2 garlic cloves, finely sliced
30ml/2 tbsp preserved red beancurd
5ml/1 tsp sugar
120ml/4fl oz/½ cup water
rice, to serve

Cook's Tip

Check that the pork is fully cooked by cutting a piece in half before serving. If necessary, cook it for a minute or two longer.

PORK IN PRESERVED BEANCURD

Cantonese chefs use two main types of preserved beancurd: the more common white variety known as fu yee in Cantonese, and a red one, known as lam yee. The latter not only has a more intense flavour, but it also gives the dish a very attractive bright red colour.

1 Put the cornflour in a bowl or strong plastic bag, add the pork and toss lightly to coat.

2 Heat the oil in a wok and fry the onion for 2 minutes. Add the garlic and fry for 1 minute. Push the onion and garlic to the sides of the wok and add the pork to the middle. Stir-fry for 2–3 minutes, until the pork is well sealed. Bring the onion mixture back to the centre and mix it with the pork.

3 Add the beancurd and mash well. Continue to stir-fry the mixture until the pork is thoroughly coated in the beancurd mixture.

4 Add the sugar and water and bring to a boil. When the sauce has reduced by half, the pork should be done. Serve hot with rice.

MIST OF HARMONY

This charming name describes a classic Shantou-style dish consisting of braised pork in soy sauce. Rice is the usual accompaniment, although the northern Chinese have a version that is served with steamed breads. The dark soy sauce specified here is a very thick variety, usually available in Chinese stores. It has a sweet edge to it that serves the dish well.

SERVES 6

30ml/2 tbsp oil
15ml/1 tbsp sugar
900g/2lb belly pork, in one piece
60ml/4 tbsp dark soy sauce
15ml/1 tbsp five-spice powder
1 litre/1¾ pints/4 cups water
2 thumb-size knobs of fresh root ginger, bruised
pickled ginger, sliced cucumber, sliced carrot and rice, to serve

Cook's Tips

- If preferred, the pork can be braised in a deep pan. Cover with a lid and cook it for an hour.
- With this, or any other long-braised dish, it may be necessary to top up the liquid after a while. Make sure any water added is boiling or hot. Check the taste and add more soy sauce if required.

1 Heat the oil in a wok large enough to hold the piece of pork. Sprinkle in the sugar and cook over medium to high heat until the mixture froths and caramelizes. When it is golden brown in colour, add the pork and turn it on all sides so that it is coated all over with caramel.

2 Add the soy sauce, five-spice powder, water and fresh ginger to the wok. Braise the pork over medium heat for 1 hour or until the pork is tender and the sauce is fairly thick. If the liquid seems to be evaporating too rapidly, lower the heat and cover the wok, or add more water (see Cook's Tip).

3 Lift the pork on to a plate and set aside to cool.

4 Slice the pork and arrange on a platter, with the cucumber, carrot and strips of pickled ginger. Reheat the sauce in the wok to serve with the pork, accompanied by rice.

Variation

This can be cooked in a pressure cooker. Use a wok for the first stage, to caramelize the meat, then transfer it to the pressure cooker. Add the remaining ingredients, but use only two-thirds of the amount of water. Check timings by consulting a similar recipe in your handbook; the meat will probably be cooked in less than 30 minutes.

MINCED PORK ROLLS IN BEANCURD SKINS

This classic dish of the Swatow people from Shantou is so sublime that it is often cooked as a festive offering during Taoist festivals. It is nothing like the ubiquitous spring roll and is unique in that it uses crinkly beancurd skins as wrappers. The filling is a rich amalgam of ingredients with delightful, contrasting textures. Unlike many regional Chinese dishes, this is a local dish and seldom appears on menus elsewhere.

SERVES 4

400g/14oz/1¾ cups minced/ground pork
1 small carrot, thinly shredded
10ml/2 tsp light soy sauce
5m/1 tsp ground black pepper
50g/2oz/⅓ cup finely chopped drained canned water chestnuts
8 spring onions/scallions, finely chopped
1 egg
25g/1oz/¼ cup cornflour/cornstarch
1 package beancurd skins
vegetable oil, for deep-frying
sliced cucumber and chilli dipping sauce, to serve

1 Put the pork in a bowl and add the shredded carrot. Stir in the soy sauce, pepper, water chestnuts and spring onions.

2 Lightly beat the egg in a small bowl and add it to the mixture. Stir to combine, then stir in the cornflour and mix well.

3 Bring a small pan of water to the boil. Pinch off a small lump of the pork mixture, add it to the boiling water and cook for 2 minutes. Scoop it out, let it cool slightly, then taste and adjust the seasoning if necessary. This step is just done in order to assess the seasoning of the pork mixture, using a sample. The meat can be added back to the bowl.

4 Keeping the remaining beancurd sheets covered under a damp dish towel, place one sheet on a flat surface. Spread about 30ml/2 tbsp of the pork mixture along one edge. Roll over one and a half times, fold in the sides, then roll again to make a firm roll. Cut through the bean curd to separate the roll from the sheet. Repeat the action, using more sheets when required, until all the filling has been used.

5 Heat the oil in a wok or deep-fryer to 190°C/375°F. Add the rolls and fry for 3–4 minutes until golden brown and crisp.

6 Drain on kitchen paper and leave to cool. Slice into diagonal pieces and serve with sliced cucumber and a chilli dipping sauce.

Cook's Tip

Beancurd skins are sold in Chinese stores, and are folded flat inside the packaging. Storage sometimes makes them brittle and liable to cracking, so wipe each sheet over with a damp kitchen towel before use.

CANTONESE BEEFSTEAK

This is a typical Hong Kong restaurant dish, which echoes Western-style steak but which is cooked by the traditional Cantonese stir-fried method. The unusual ingredient here is Worcestershire sauce, very likely a British colonial touch. This imparts a subtle vinegar and pepper flavour to the dish.

SERVES 4

- 600g/1lb 5oz sirloin or rump/round steak
- 15ml/1 tbsp cornflour/cornstarch
- 30ml/2 tbsp Chinese Mui Kwai Lo wine or sweet sherry
- 15ml/1 tbsp Worcestershire sauce
- 30ml/2 tbsp oyster sauce
- 45ml/3 tbsp oil
- 15ml/1 tbsp grated root ginger
- 2.5ml/½ tsp sugar
- lettuce leaves, to serve

1 Slice the steak thinly into medallions. Put the cornflour in a bowl or strong plastic bag. Add the steak and toss to coat.

2 In a small bowl, mix the wine or sherry, Worcestershire sauce and oyster sauce. Stir, then set aside.

3 Heat the oil in a wok or frying pan. Add the grated ginger and fry for 30 seconds. Add the beef. Stir-fry over high heat for 1 minute, then pour in the wine and sauce mixture. Stir-fry for 1 minute more, then sprinkle over the sugar.

4 Continue to stir for 2 minutes more for medium-rare, or 3 minutes for well-done beef. Serve on a bed of lettuce leaves.

Variation

Mui Kwai Lo (or Mei Kuei Lu), the recommended wine to use in this dish, is rose-flavoured and very aromatic. Sweet sherry is a good substitute.

SERVES 4

- 350g/12oz sirloin or rump/round steak
- 5ml/1 tsp bicarbonate of soda/ baking soda
- 10g/¼oz dried tangerine peel
- 15ml/1 tbsp vegetable oil
- 2 garlic cloves, crushed
- 30ml/2 tbsp sesame oil
- 5ml/1 tsp sugar
- 8 spring onions/scallions, cut in 5cm/2in pieces
- 30ml/2 tbsp water

Cook's Tip

To dry tangerine peel, remove only the coloured skin and not the bitter pith underneath. Dry the peel by placing it on sheets of kitchen paper and leaving it in a warm room overnight.

TANGERINE PEEL BEEF

The tangerine, like the orange, is a fruit with auspicious meaning. The Cantonese name for tangerine, kum, sounds like the word for gold, which symbolizes prosperity. It is one of the most widely used flavourings and is particularly popular in Cantonese and Sichuan cooking.

1 Slice the steak into thin strips. Put the bicarbonate of soda into a dish, moisten it with a little water, then add the beef strips and rub the bicarbonate of soda into the meat. Set aside for 10 minutes.

2 Meanwhile, soak the tangerine peel in a bowl of water. When it is soft, drain it and slice it into thin strips.

3 Heat the oil in a wok and fry the garlic for 40 seconds, until light brown. Do not let it burn. Add the beef. Stir-fry over high heat for 1 minute, then stir in the tangerine peel.

4 Add the sesame oil, sugar, spring onions and water. Stir-fry for about 2 minutes or until the beef is cooked the way you like it. Spoon into a dish or individual bowls and serve, with rice if like.

SAUTÉED BEEF IN OYSTER SAUCE

Featured on Chinese restaurant menus the world over, this southern dish is one of the easiest to recreate at home. Bicarbonate of soda helps to tenderize beef without altering its flavour. It is important to cut meat and peppers to the same size so that they cook in the same time.

SERVES 4

- 450g/1lb sirloin steak
- 1 large green bell pepper
- 5ml/1 tsp bicarbonate of soda/ baking soda
- 30ml/2 tbsp oil
- 2 garlic cloves, crushed
- 15ml/1 tbsp grated fresh root ginger
- 30ml/2 tbsp oyster sauce
- 5ml/1 tsp ground black pepper
- 30ml/2 tbsp cornflour/cornstarch mixed with 45ml/3 tbsp water

Cook's Tip

To intensify the colour of the green bell pepper and keep it crisp, blanch the strips in a pan of boiling water for 30 seconds, then drain and plunge them straight into iced water.

1 Using a sharp knife or cleaver, cut the steak into thin strips. Cut the green pepper into strips of similar width and length. Put the pepper strips in a bowl and set them aside.

2 Put the bicarbonate of soda into a shallow dish, moisten it with a little water, then add the beef strips. Using clean hands, rub the bicarbonate into the meat. Cover and set aside for 10 minutes.

3 Heat the oil in a wok and fry the garlic and ginger for 40 seconds, until light brown. Drain the beef strips, add them to the wok and stir-fry for 1 minute over high heat. Add the pepper strips and stir-fry for 1 minute.

4 Stir in the oyster sauce and pepper, then the cornflour mixture. Continue to stir-fry over high heat for 2 minutes until the meat is well-done. Spoon into a heated bowl and serve immediately.

MUTTON AND BEANCURD STICKS

This slow-cooked mutton dish is typical of Hainan cooking. Dry beancurd sticks, called fu choke in Cantonese, are pale yellow in colour. They have a bland taste, but are rich in protein and are believed to be cooling; notwithstanding, this is ideal for keeping out the cold in the winter.

SERVES 4

- 350g/12oz lean mutton or lamb, cut into bitesize chunks
- 15ml/1 tbsp oil
- 3 garlic cloves, sliced
- 5ml/1 tsp sugar
- 45ml/3 tbsp dark soy sauce
- pinch of five-spice powder
- 600ml/1 pint/2½ cups water
- 2.5ml/½ tsp ground black pepper
- 100g/3¼oz beancurd sticks, soaked in a bowl of hot water for 30 minutes, until soft

1 Place the mutton or lamb on a board and tenderize slightly, using a meat mallet or the blunt edge of a cleaver.

2 Heat the oil in a wok and fry the garlic until golden brown. Add the meat and fry for 2 minutes to seal in the flavour.

3 Sprinkle the sugar over the meat, then stir in the soy sauce, five-spice powder, water and pepper. Transfer to a pan, cover with a tight-fitting lid and cook over medium heat for 30 minutes.

4 Drain the beancurd sticks and cut them into 5cm/2in lengths. Stir them into the stew, then replace the lid and simmer for 20 minutes Remove the lid, increase the heat to high and reduce the sauce for a further 10 minutes. Serve immediately.

Cook's Tip

If the stew is too oily for your taste, cool it quickly, then put it in the refrigerator. On chilling, the fat will solidify on top and can easily be lifted off. Reheat the stew to serve.

SERVES 4

- 1 pig's kidney
- 30ml/2 tbsp vegetable oil
- 15ml/1 tbsp chopped garlic
- 15ml/1 tbsp chopped fresh root ginger
- 8 spring onions/scallions, cut in short lengths
- 30ml/2 tbsp oyster sauce
- 7.5ml/1½ tsp ground black pepper
- 30ml/2 tbsp Chinese rice wine
- 10ml/2 tsp cornflour/cornstarch mixed with 120ml/4fl oz/½ cup cold water

Cook's Tip

If the kidneys have a very strong smell, soak them in milk instead of water, or simply soak them in water for twice as long as recommended in the recipe.

FLOWER KIDNEYS WITH GINGER

Kidneys are revered in China for their nutritional properties and symbolism. Sliced artfully, they open up like flowers when cooked. Seasonings for kidneys tend to be robust to counteract their strong aroma and flavour. Use a strong cooking wine like Hsiao Hsing or Hua Teow.

1 Wash the kidney thoroughly and slice each in half lengthways to reveal the white membrane in each. Remove these completely, then soak the kidney halves in plenty of cold water for 10 minutes.

2 Cut each kidney half into 5cm/2in squares, then score the squares deeply in a criss-cross pattern. Put them on a plate and set them aside.

3 Heat the oil in a wok and fry the garlic and ginger for 40 seconds. Add the spring onions and stir-fry for 30 seconds. Add the kidney and stir-fry over high heat for 1 minute, until they curl up to resemble flowers.

4 Add the oyster sauce, pepper and wine and bring rapidly to the boil. Add the cornflour mixture and stir over the heat until the sauce thickens. Spoon into a heated dish and serve.

SOUTHERN CHINA

RICE & NOODLES

SMOOTHLY SIMPLE & STICKILY SAVOURY

As the world's most populous country, China would not have been able to sustain its one-and-a-half billion people were it not for rice. Grown throughout most of the country, apart from the far north, it is the single most important element in the diet. No southerner would dream of sitting down to a meal without a bowl of fluffy rice, providing the perfect foil for savoury dishes. Noodles made from rice or wheat are also popular. Very versatile, they are used in many dishes, from simple stir-fries to luxurious treats.

The Guangdong Delta and Hainan Island are among China's principal rice-growing areas. Rather than being a bland staple, the grain is regarded as a blank canvas on which many culinary portraits can be painted. In Shantou, rice soup is a favourite supper dish and cold, cooked rice is the basis of many ingenious fried creations. Clay Pot Rice with Dried Oysters is one such dish, redolent of the smoky flavour of dried oysters.

Rice is also transformed into noodles in the south, although northern noodles made from wheat are used too. Tossed in oyster sauce or spicy chilli paste, they are consumed with relish. There can be marked differences in the tastes of noodle dishes, as more robust wheat noodles lend themselves to frying and boiling, while rice noodles, with a more silken nature, are treated with care, usually in soupy dishes and the occasional stir-fry. Whatever noodle or rice dish is on order, the accompanying ingredients should provide the essential balance of flavours.

RICE WITH MIXED VEGETABLES

A Cantonese staple, this originally called for 10 different greens to be cooked with the rice. The tradition doesn't have to be followed to the letter for it to taste scrumptious, but it is a good idea to use several types of vegetable, plus a little meat for extra flavour.

SERVES 4

- 4 dried Chinese black mushrooms, soaked in 150ml/1¼ pint/⅔ cup boiling water for 30 minutes
- 30ml/2 tbsp vegetable oil
- 2 garlic cloves, chopped
- 150g/5oz lean pork, finely sliced
- 150g/5oz pak choi/bok choy, finely sliced
- 30ml/2 tbsp peas, thawed if frozen
- 30ml/2 tbsp light soy sauce
- 5ml/1 tsp ground black pepper
- 5ml/1 tsp cornflour/cornstarch blended to a paste with 15ml/1 tbsp cold water
- 800g/1¾lb/7 cups cooked rice

1 Using a slotted spoon, transfer the mushrooms to a board. Cut off and discard the stems. Chop the caps finely. Strain the soaking liquid into a jug or cup and set aside.

2 Heat the oil in a wok, add the garlic and fry over medium heat for 40 seconds, until light brown. Add the pork and fry for 2 minutes.

3 Add the pak choi, peas and mushrooms. Stir, then add the soy sauce, pepper and the soaking liquid. Cook, stirring, for 4 minutes.

4 Add the cornflour paste and stir until the mixture thickens slightly. Finally stir in the cooked rice. As soon as it is piping hot, spoon the mixture into a heated bowl and serve.

SERVES 4

200g/7oz white fish fillets
1.2 litres/2 pints/5 cups fresh fish stock
350g/12oz/1⅔ cups jasmine rice or long grain rice
5ml/1 tsp ground black pepper
leaves from 1 stalk Chinese celery, finely chopped
30ml/2 tbsp fried shallots or garlic, to garnish

Variation

Crisp bread croûtons can be used as a garnish instead of fried shallots or garlic.

RICE SOUP FROM SHANTOU

Although this dish contains many of the same ingredients as the rice congee cooked by the peoples of both Shantou and Guangzhou, it is actually very different: the rice stays relatively firm and every mouthful offers the contrasting textures of smooth soup and crunchy grain.

1 Using a sharp cook's knife, skin the fish, then cut it into small, thin pieces, removing any stray bones in the process. Pour the fish stock into a pan and bring it to the boil.

2 Put the rice in a colander and rinse it under cold running water. Drain well, then add to the fish stock. Simmer for 8–10 minutes or until the rice is just cooked; it should retain plenty of texture.

3 Add the pieces of fish, with the ground black pepper, and simmer for 2 minutes. Stir in the finely chopped Chinese celery, spoon into heated soup bowls and garnish with the fried shallots or garlic. Serve immediately.

CLAY POT RICE WITH DRIED OYSTERS

Dried oysters are a prime ingredient in Cantonese cooking. They are prized for their rich, smoky flavour, which is quite different to that of the fresh mollusc. When they are used in a recipe, there is no need for additional seasoning. They are also surprisingly meaty and add bulk to the dish. Here, they are combined with rice and tender chunks of Chinese sausage, and cooked in a pan before being served in a clay pot.

SERVES 4

350g/12oz/1⅔ cups jasmine rice
600ml/1 pint/2½ cups water
30ml/2 tbsp vegetable oil
30ml/2 tbsp chopped onions
4 slices fresh root ginger
2 Chinese sausages, thinly sliced
100g/3¾oz salt fish, fried and flaked
10 dried oysters
30ml/2 tbsp sesame oil
5ml/1 tsp black pepper
30ml/2 tbsp dark soy sauce
15ml/1 tbsp oyster sauce
slices of spring onion/scallion, to garnish

1 Put the rice in a large pan and pour over the water. Bring to the boil, then lower the heat and simmer for 8 minutes.

2 Meanwhile, heat the oil in a wok and fry the chopped onions for 2 minutes. Add the root ginger, Chinese sausages, salt fish, dried oysters, sesame oil and pepper. Stir over the heat for 2 minutes, then stir in the soy sauce and oyster sauce.

3 When the rice is almost dry, but still bubbly on the top, stir in the onion mixture. Cover with a lid and cook for 8 minutes more.

4 Spoon the mixture into a preheated clay pot, if you have one (see Cook's Tip), or on to a warmed serving platter if you don't. Serve immediately, garnished with spring onion.

Cook's Tip

The clay pot isn't essential, but it does add a rustic touch. Clay pots are ideal for serving, but are not meant to be used for long cooking over a direct flame as they crack easily. Before spooning in the rice mixture, warm the pot briefly over a direct flame or in a preheated oven.

SEAFOOD FRIED RICE

This is one of those dishes that is found throughout China, although the ingredients will vary depending on the location. This version allows the flavour of the seafood to take centre stage. For festive occasions, luxury ingredients such as lobster and scallops are often added.

SERVES 4

30ml/2 tbsp vegetable oil
2 garlic cloves, crushed
2 eggs, lightly beaten
100g/3¾oz raw or cooked prawns/shrimps, peeled
800g/1¾lb/7 cups cold cooked rice
30ml/2 tbsp light soy sauce
2.5ml/½ tsp ground black pepper
2 spring onions/scallions, chopped
spring onion curls (see Cook's Tip), to serve

1 Heat the oil in a wok and fry the garlic until golden brown. Do not let it burn or it will become bitter. Push the garlic aside to leave a clear space in the middle of the wok. Add the eggs and cook until they set to form an omelette.

2 Cut the omelette up roughly in the wok, and push it aside. Add the prawns and rice and stir rapidly for 5 minutes or until the shrimps are cooked and the rice is piping hot.

3 Sprinkle over the soy sauce. Add the black pepper and chopped spring onions. Toss to mix, then spoon into a bowl and serve garnished with the spring onion curls.

Cook's Tip

Spring onion/scallion curls make a dramatic garnish. Trim 4 spring onions, removing the roots and bulbs. Using a sharp knife, finely shred the spring onions to within 2.5cm/1in of the root end. Place the shredded spring onions in a bowl of iced water and chill for at least 30 minutes or until the shredded ends have curled. Drain on kitchen paper.

CLASSIC CANTONESE FRIED RICE

One of the most widely travelled Chinese dishes, this is a Cantonese invention, deriving from the pragmatic need to recycle leftovers. Some luxurious versions are packed with premium ingredients such as crab meat and lobster. Others are really simple. What follows is a basic recipe that can easily be adapted to suit the ingredients available.

SERVES 4

2 spring onions/scallions, chopped
30ml/2 tbsp vegetable oil
3 eggs, lightly beaten
800g/1¾lb/7 cups cold cooked rice
150g/5oz roast pork or cooked ham, cut into 1cm/½in cubes
100g/3¾oz raw tiger prawns/jumbo shrimp, peeled
30ml/2 tbsp frozen green peas
30ml/2 tbsp light soy sauce
5ml/1 tsp ground black pepper
1 chicken stock/bouillon cube
rice, to serve

1 Set aside about one-fifth of the spring onions for the garnish. Heat the oil in a wok and fry the remaining spring onions for 30 seconds. Push them aside to leave a clear space in the middle of the wok. Add the eggs and cook until they set to form an omelette.

2 Cut the omelette up roughly in the wok, then add the rice, pork or ham, and prawns or shrimp. Stir vigorously for 3 minutes, then add the peas. Stir in the soy sauce and black pepper and crumble the stock cube over the surface.

3 Toss over the heat for 3 minutes more, or until the rice is piping hot all the way through. Spoon into a bowl and garnish with the reserved spring onions. Serve immediately.

Variations

- If you can only locate cooked prawn or shrimp, add them with the peas.
- For a vegetarian option, leave out the meat and seafood and substitute with diced mushrooms and green beans.

GLUTINOUS RICE IN A LOTUS LEAF

Serving food in a leaf reveals the enduring connection the southern Chinese have with the land. For maximum impact, serve this piping hot and open it at the table with a dramatic flourish. The aromatic steam released at the critical moment will delight guests and whet their appetites for the delicious rice mixture hidden within the rice parcel.

SERVES 4

400g/14oz/2 cups glutinous rice
4 dried Chinese black mushrooms
15ml/1 tbsp salt
1 large lotus leaf, about 50cm/20in in diameter
30ml/2 tbsp vegetable oil
2 garlic cloves, crushed
200g/7oz skinless boneless chicken, diced
1 Chinese sausage, finely sliced
8 drained canned Chinese chestnuts
30ml/2 tbsp light soy sauce
15ml/1 tbsp dark soy sauce
30ml/2 tbsp oyster sauce
30ml/2 tbsp sesame oil
30ml/2 tbsp chopped spring onions/scallions
5ml/1 tsp ground black pepper
chilli sauce, to serve

1 Rinse the glutinous rice under running water until the water runs clear, then soak it in a bowl of water for 2 hours. Meanwhile, soak the mushrooms in a separate bowl of boiling water for 30 minutes.

2 Drain the rice, tip it into a bowl and stir in the salt. Line a large steamer with clean muslin or cheesecloth and spoon in the rice. Cover and steam over a wok of boiling water for 15 minutes. Remove and set aside.

3 Soak the lotus leaf in warm water for 15 minutes. Meanwhile, drain the mushrooms, cut off and discard the stems, then chop the caps finely.

4 Heat the oil in a wok and fry the garlic for 40 seconds. Add the chicken and Chinese sausage and stir-fry for 2 minutes.

5 Add the mushrooms, chestnuts, light and dark soy sauce, oyster sauce, sesame oil, spring onions and black pepper and stir-fry for 2 minutes. Sprinkle over 15ml/1 tbsp water, add the rice and cook for 2–3 minutes more.

6 Drain the lotus leaf. Lay it on a flat surface and pile the fried ingredients in the middle. Gather up the sides of the leaf and fold into a large bundle. Tuck the sides in firmly.

7 Prepare a steamer. Place the filled lotus leaf, seam side down, on a plate that will fit inside the steamer. Steam for 10 minutes.

8 Serve the parcels whole, so you can open it at the table, with chilli sauce.

Cook's Tip

The longer you soak glutinous rice, the softer and more succulent it becomes. Give it a minimum of 1 hour, but to render it really soft, 2 hours is the optimum time.

OYSTER SAUCE NOODLES

Noodles are usually cooked with other ingredients and eaten as snacks or light meals. This recipe is a basic one for rice noodles and can be adapted to include other types of meat, seafood or vegetables, as you prefer.

SERVES 4

250g/9oz skinless chicken breasts
400g/14oz fresh hor fun (flat rice noodles) or dried rice noodle sticks
30ml/2 tbsp vegetable oil
15ml/1 tbsp crushed garlic
2 spring onions/scallions, cut in 2.5cm/1in strips, plus extra to garnish
200ml/7fl oz/scant 1 cup water
30ml/2 tbsp oyster sauce
5ml/1 tsp ground black pepper
30ml/2 tbsp sesame oil

1 Slice the chicken breast into thin strips. If using fresh hor fun, separate the noodles. If they stick together, steam them lightly first. If using dried rice noodle sticks, soak them in boiling water until soft, then drain well.

2 Heat the oil in a wok and fry the crushed garlic over medium heat until golden brown. Do not let it burn.

3 Add the chicken strips and stir-fry over high heat for 3 minutes. Add the noodles, spring onions, water, oyster sauce, pepper and sesame oil. Toss over high heat for 2 minutes.

4 Tip into a heated bowl or individual bowls, garnish with more shredded spring onions and serve immediately.

Variation

Rice noodles, preferably fresh hor fun, are preferred in Cantonese cooking but you can use egg or wheat noodles, too.

SERVES 4

- 400g/14oz dry wheat flour noodles
- 200g/7oz choi sum
- 250g/9oz roast pork, thinly sliced
- 60ml/4 tbsp chilli and garlic sauce
- 30ml/2 tbsp vegetable and sesame oil
- 30ml/2 tbsp light soy sauce
- 30ml/2 tbsp tomato sauce or ketchup
- Prawn Wonton Soup (see page 333), optional

CHILLI NOODLES

Street stalls and tea houses all over Hong Kong almost always have this on their menus, each establishment having a slightly different version from the next, depending on the class of diner. Humble places offer basic noodles tossed in chilli sauce with slices of roast pork. More upmarket eateries add lavish accents like oyster sauce and sesame oil and even offer wonton soup on the side. This recipe is one of the more luxurious versions.

1 Cook the noodles in boiling water until tender, following the packet directions. Drain the noodles and put them in a bowl.

2 Bring a pan of water to the boil, add the choi sum and blanch for 1 minute. Drain and mix with the noodles.

3 Halve the roast pork slices if necessary; the aim is to have about 32 pieces of pork in all. Set aside.

4 Mix the chilli and garlic sauce with the oil, soy sauce and tomato sauce. Add to the noodles and greens and toss to coat. Top with the pork. Serve with Prawn Wonton Soup on the side, if you like.

BUDDHIST VEGETARIAN NOODLES

During Buddhist festivals, this dish takes centre stage as temple chefs cook huge cauldrons of it to serve to devotees, free of charge. It is a simple dish, redolent with flavour and with a lovely crunchy texture that balances the silky substance of the noodles.

SERVES 4

- 10 dried Chinese black mushrooms
- 4 pieces sweet dried beancurd wafers
- 300g/11oz rice vermicelli
- 45ml/3 tbsp vegetable oil
- 30ml/2 tbsp crushed garlic
- 1 large onion, thinly sliced
- 100g/3¾oz/½ cup beansprouts
- 115g/4oz drained canned bamboo shoots, sliced into thin strips
- 115g/4oz Chinese long beans or green beans, sliced into thin strips
- 30ml/2 tbsp hoisin sauce
- 30ml/2 tbsp oyster sauce
- 30ml/2 tbsp dark soy sauce
- 45ml/3 tbsp sesame oil
- 400ml/14fl oz/1⅔ cups water

1 Soak the dried Chinese black mushrooms in a bowl of boiling water for 20–30 minutes until soft. Meanwhile soak the beancurd wafers and rice vermicelli until soft, following the directions on the packets.

2 Drain the mushrooms thoroughly, then cut off and discard the stems and slice the caps into thin strips. Drain the beancurd wafers and slice them thinly. Drain the noodles and set them aside.

3 Heat the oil in a wok and fry the garlic for 40 seconds, until light brown. Add the onion and stir-fry for 2 minutes, then add the beansprouts, bamboo shoots, beans and mushrooms. Stir-fry for 1 minute, then stir in the hoisin sauce, oyster sauce, soy sauce and sesame oil.

4 Add the beancurd wafers to the wok and stir-fry for 2 minutes more. Add the noodles and pour in the water. Toss over the heat for about 4 minutes, until all the ingredients are cooked and the mixture is well blended. Spoon into a bowl and serve.

Cook's Tips

- The mushroom soaking water can be substituted for some of the water added at the end of cooking. Strain it first, to remove any pieces of grit.
- Sweet beancurd wafers are crisp, brown slices, sold in small packets. Each measures about 12.5 x 5cm/5 x 2in. They are called tim choke in Cantonese. If you deep-fry them without soaking them first, they can be crumbled on to the cooked dish as a garnish.

SILVER THREADS OF LONGEVITY

The 'silver threads' of the recipe title are cellophane noodles. In China these symbolize longevity and are often served at birthdays and other special occasions.

SERVES 4

50g/2oz dried lily buds
150g/5oz cellophane noodles
45ml/3 tbsp vegetable oil
30ml/2 tbsp crushed garlic
100g/3¾oz/½ cup beansprouts
30ml/2 tbsp oyster sauce
30ml/2 tbsp light soy sauce
45ml/3 tbsp sesame oil
200ml/7fl oz/scant 1 cup water
chopped fresh coriander/cilantro, to garnish

1 Soak the lily buds in a bowl of warm water for 30 minutes or until soft. Meanwhile, soak the cellophane noodles in a separate bowl of warm water for 15 minutes.

2 Drain the lily buds, rinse under water and drain again. Snip off the hard ends. Drain the noodles. Using a pair of scissors or a sharp knife, chop the strands into shorter lengths for easier handling.

3 Heat the oil in a wok and fry the garlic for 40 seconds. Add the beansprouts and stir-fry vigorously for 1 minute. Add the lily buds and the noodles and toss over the heat for 2 minutes.

4 Add the oyster sauce, soy sauce, sesame oil and water. Continue to toss until the liquid is hot and everything is combined.

5 Transfer to a serving dish, garnish with fresh coriander and serve.

Variation

Dried wood ears can be used in place of lily buds. Soak them in water for 30 minutes, drain, rinse and drain again. Discard any hard roots and sandy bits, then separate the clump into individual 'ears'.

SERVES 4

- 1 large live or freshly cooked lobster, about 1kg/2¼lb
- 400g/14oz dried egg noodles
- 30ml/2 tbsp vegetable oil
- 15ml/1 tbsp crushed garlic
- 100g/3¾oz/½ cup beansprouts
- 200ml/7fl oz/scant 1 cup water
- 30ml/2 tbsp oyster sauce
- 5ml/1 tsp ground black pepper
- 30ml/2 tbsp sesame oil

Variation

Any kind of firm vegetables can be added to this dish, if you like. Celery and white radish, cut into matchsticks, are ideal since they have a fairly mild flavour but robust texture.

LOBSTER NOODLES

Hong Kong chefs constantly invent and innovate, striving to create dishes at the cutting edge to impress gourmet taste buds. This one is in the luxury league.

1 If the lobster is live, place it in a plastic bag and put it in the freezer for 5 hours. Bring a large pan of water to the boil, add the lobster and cook for 10 minutes or until the shell has turned scarlet. Remove and set aside to cool. Heat a separate pan of water and cook the noodles according to the packet instructions. Drain and set aside.

2 Cut off the lobster's head and the tip of the tail. Rinse and set aside for the garnish. Twist off the claws and set aside Using a pair of scissors, cut down the shell from the top to the tail. Remove the meat, and slice into rounds. Remove the meat from the claws and legs.

3 Heat the oil in a wok and fry the garlic for 40 seconds. Add the beansprouts and toss for 2 minutes. Add the noodles, water, oyster sauce, pepper and sesame oil and cook, stirring, for 2 minutes. Add the lobster slices and toss lightly. Arrange on a plate, ensuring the lobster pieces are prominent. Decorate with the head and tail.

SOUTHERN CHINA
VEGETABLES

FLASH-FRIED & FRESH-FLAVOURED

The fertile fields of southern China produce a wonderful array of fresh indigenous ingredients, including a wide range of vegetables. Mixed with aromatics and often fish or meat (vegetable dishes aren't usually vegetarian!), they encapsulate the balance of taste and texture that regional cooks strive to attain.

Chinese people are not given to eating vegetables raw, and most are usually fried. Stir-fried lettuce, for instance, is given a briny fillip with conpoy (scallop) sauce, while more robust greens, such as kai lan – a green vegetable related to kale – are also enjoyed and, served Hong-Kong style with oyster sauce, make a star appearance at restaurants around the world.

Beansprouts grow like weeds and show up in numerous dishes. Stir-fried and flavoured with salt fish and sesame oil, they are highly revered. Bitter melon or gourd, a marrow of acquired taste, features in the Guangzhou dish of Stir-Fried Bitter Gourd. Root vegetables like yam or taro are played with at will, and Hakka cooks are adept at bringing out the texture and flavour with inventive dishes like Abacus Beads, in which the vegetable is cooked, mashed and shaped into large discs or beads that represent the abacus.

Water convolvulus, while indigenous to South-east Asia, has been incorporated into the southern Chinese repertoire. Grown in swampy areas, it has hollow stalks and delicate leaves that demand quick cooking. It goes by several names, including water spinach, swamp cabbage and morning glory.

BRAISED CHINESE LEAVES

Chinese leaves, also known as Chinese or Napa cabbage, taste delicious in a salad or stir-fry and need little seasoning apart from soy sauce, as they have a natural sweet flavour. This dish is somewhat soupy, since the leaves contribute extra liquid. It is often served with rice porridge or congee, and keeps well for a few days in the refrigerator.

SERVES 4–6

1 head Chinese leaves/Chinese cabbage
30ml/2 tbsp sesame oil
300ml/½ pint/1¼ cups water
5ml/1 tsp ground black pepper
30ml/2 tbsp light soy sauce

1 Slice the Chinese leaves lengthways and remove the hard tip and core. Cut in 2.5cm/1in slices and place in a colander. Rinse under cold water, then drain thoroughly.

2 Mix the oil, water, pepper and soy sauce in a wok. Bring to simmering point, add the Chinese leaves and braise for 15 minutes over medium heat. Spoon into a heated dish and serve immediately.

Cook's Tip

Don't confuse Chinese leaves with pak choi/bok choy, which has thick white stems topped by glossy green leaves.

SERVES 4

500g/1¼lb mustard greens
30ml/2 tbsp vegetable oil
30ml/2 tbsp crushed garlic
30ml/2 tbsp oyster sauce
200ml/7fl oz/scant 1 cup water
cooked rice or congee, to serve

Cook's Tip

Mustard greens are widely grown and are especially popular with home gardeners and allotment holders. Look for them at farmers' markets or Chinese food stores.

GREENS WITH OYSTER SAUCE

Also known as mustard cabbage (gai choy in Cantonese) mustard greens have thick, curved, ribbed stalks and ruffled bright green leaves. Shantou people are inordinately fond of this vegetable and usually serve it with congee for breakfast or lunch. In China, the bulk of the crop is salted and preserved.

1 Cut off any fibrous bits from the stalks of the mustard greens, then cut the stalks and leaves into bite-size pieces. Rinse and drain.

2 Bring a pan of water to the boil. Add the greens and blanch for 2 minutes, then drain and pat dry with kitchen paper.

3 Heat the oil in a wok. Add the garlic and fry until golden brown. Do not let the garlic burn or it will become bitter.

4 Add the blanched greens to the wok. Sprinkle over the oyster sauce, then add the water. Cook over high heat for 2–3 minutes, tossing constantly with two spoons or spatulas, so that they cook evenly. Spoon into a heated dish and serve immediately with rice.

STIR-FRIED KAI LAN

There was a time when this popular Chinese vegetable was practically unobtainable outside its country of origin, but airfreight has changed all that and most Chinese food stores now stock it. Known as Chinese broccoli – kai lan in Cantonese – it actually bears no resemblance to broccoli, being more closely related to kale.

SERVES 4

350g/12oz kai lan (Chinese broccoli)
30ml/2 tbsp vegetable oil
30ml/2 tbsp shredded fresh root ginger
30ml/2 tbsp crushed garlic
30ml/2 tbsp oyster sauce
30ml/2 tbsp Chinese wine

1 Separate the kai lan leaves from the stalks. Cut each leaf in half. Trim the stalks, then peel them thinly, removing any tough portions of outer skin. Slice each stalk diagonally in half.

2 Bring a pan of water to the boil and blanch the kai lan leaves for 1 minute. Drain immediately and refresh under cold water, then drain again. Repeat the process with the kai lan stalks, keeping leaves and stalks separate.

3 Heat the oil in a wok and fry the ginger and garlic until the latter is golden brown. Add the kai lan stalks and stir-fry for 1 minute. Add the leaves, stir well, then add the oyster sauce and wine. Stir rapidly over the heat for 2 minutes. Serve immediately.

Variation

Tenderstem broccoli, now available in most supermarkets, comes close to kai lan in flavour and texture. Purple sprouting broccoli or chard can be used as a substitute.

SERVES 4

4 pieces conpoy
200ml/7fl oz/scant 1 cup warm water
2 heads cos or romaine lettuce
15ml/1 tbsp vegetable oil
15ml/1 tbsp chopped fresh root ginger
2 garlic cloves, chopped
30ml/2 tbsp Chinese wine
shredded spring onion/scallion, to garnish

Variation

Any type of firm lettuce can be used instead of Cos or romaine. This is also excellent with chicory or Belgian endive.

LETTUCE WITH CONPOY SAUCE

Chinese cooks rarely eat vegetables raw, even when using the most tender salad-type greens. Stir-frying them with conpoy (a Cantonese dried scallop, pictured on page 444) and aromatics such as garlic and ginger is popular, and a liquid is often added toward the end of cooking to soften the ingredients slightly and provide a tasty sauce.

1 Soak the conpoy in warm water for 2–3 hours until soft. Then, shred the lettuce, put in a colander and rinse it under cold water. Drain well, then dry the lettuce thoroughly in a clean dish towel.

2 Drain the conpoy, reserving the soaking liquid. Shred finely.

3 Heat the oil in a wok and fry the ginger and garlic for 40 seconds, until golden. Add the lettuce and stir-fry over high heat for 1 minute.

4 Add the conpoy, with the reserved soaking liquid. Bring to a quick simmer, stirring constantly, for 2 minutes. Serve immediately.

STIR-FRIED BITTER GOURD

Also known as bitter melon, this pale green vegetable has a distinctive, warty skin. It has a sweet and fragrant smell, but a rather bitter flavour. Look for the large Chinese gourds, around 30cm/12in long, rather than the smaller ones often found in Indian and Caribbean stores. Salting the raw vegetable helps to remove some of the bitterness and promotes a crunchy texture. Cooking it with hoisin and oyster sauces and a little sugar also helps to offset any astringency. Prawns are often added to this stir-fry to make it more substantial, but this is optional.

SERVES 4

1 bitter gourd, about 300g/11oz
5ml/1 tsp salt
30ml/2 tbsp vegetable oil
15ml/1 tbsp crushed garlic
30ml/2 tbsp hoisin sauce
30ml/2 tbsp oyster sauce
2.5ml/½ tsp sugar
5oz/150g peeled prawns or shrimp (optional)

1 Slice off about 1cm/½in from either end of the bitter gourd. Cut it in half lengthways and scoop out the white pith and soft pink seeds.

2 Cut the gourd diagonally into 1cm/½in slices. Spread these out in a colander, sprinkle with the salt and place the colander in a sink. Leave to stand for 30 minutes.

3 Rinse under cold water to remove the excess salt, then drain. Take handfuls of the now slightly softened bitter gourd and squeeze out as much moisture as possible.

4 Heat the oil in a wok and fry the garlic until golden brown. Do not let it burn or it will taste bitter. Add the pieces of gourd to the pan and stir-fry for 1 minute.

5 Stir in the hoisin and oyster sauces, then add the sugar and about 200ml/7fl oz or a scant cup of water. Add the prawns, if using.

6 Bring to the boil over high heat, simmer for 3–5 minutes until the prawns are cooked through and the sauce has reduced slightly, then spoon into a bowl and serve.

Variation

Cooked crab meat is also good, instead or as well as prawns; the tender meat will contrast well with the crisp, slightly bitter vegetable. Add just before serving.

Cook's Tip

Traditional Chinese Medicine (TCM) regards bitter gourd as a yin, or cooling, vegetable and values it for its curative properties.

WATER CONVOLVULUS STIR-FRY

Water convolvulus is an all-year-round tropical vegetable that appears in many South-east Asian cuisines. It is a favourite with the people of southern China, who usually stir-fry it with chopped garlic. Cantonese cooks also sometimes add preserved beancurd, while in Hakka cuisine yellow bean paste or whole preserved yellow beans is added, as here.

SERVES 4

- 400g/14oz water convolvulus/ swamp cabbage
- 30ml/2 tbsp vegetable oil
- 30ml/2 tbsp chopped garlic
- 200g/7oz raw prawns/shrimp, heads peeled
- 30ml/2 tbsp whole preserved yellow beans
- 2 fresh red chillies, seeded and sliced
- 90ml/6 tbsp water

1 Slice the water convolvulus stalks thinly and pluck off the leaves. Wash in plenty of water as the vegetable is grown in brackish water and mud is sometimes trapped in crevices in the stalks. Drain well and leave to air dry or pat dry with kitchen paper.

2 Heat the oil in a wok and fry the garlic for 40 seconds, until golden brown. Add the prawns, yellow beans and chillies and toss together over the heat for 1 minute.

3 Add the water. Cover the wok with a lid, or improvise and make one from foil. Cook for 3 minutes until the leaves and stalks of the water convolvulus shrink and turn dark green. Tip into a heated bowl and serve immediately.

Variations

- Substitute spinach if you can't locate water convolvulus. This vegetable is seldom found in Western supermarkets, but may be available from Chinese food stores.
- For a hotter and spicier result, leave the seeds in the chillies.

SERVES 4

100g/3¾oz salt fish fillet
60ml/4 tbsp vegetable oil
600g/1lb 5oz/2⅓ cups beansprouts
2 spring onions/scallions
30ml/2 tbsp crushed garlic
15ml/1 tbsp light soy sauce

Cook's Tip

Sprout your own soya beans, if possible. If you do buy the sprouts, however, look for ones with large heads, as these are the healthiest option.

BEANSPROUTS WITH SALT FISH

This simple peasant dish has been elevated to gourmet status. The important thing is to use the best salt fish available, ideally salted fillets of snapper or an expensive tropical fish called threadfin (ma yeow yu in Cantonese). If this is not obtainable, the closest substitute is salt cod.

1 Cut the salt fish into small chunks. Heat the oil in a wok and fry the pieces of salt fish until fragrant and slightly brittle. With a slotted spoon, transfer them to a board. Let them cool slightly, then shred them roughly.

2 Wash the beansprouts, drain them thoroughly and remove any green husks. Cut the spring onions into 5cm/2in lengths.

3 Pour off all but 30ml/2 tbsp of the oil from the wok. Heat the remaining oil and fry the garlic until golden brown. Add the beansprouts and salt fish and stir rapidly for 2 minutes.

4 Add the spring onions and stir-fry for 1 minute. Drizzle over the soy sauce, stir for 1 minute more and serve immediately.

ABACUS BEADS

Most people are familiar with the abacus, the ancient Chinese counting instrument consisting of a wire-strung frame on which beads are threaded. Many Chinese storekeepers still prefer the abacus to the calculator and use one with great dexterity. In a cultural context, the abacus, and this dish, symbolizes prosperity. Hakka people traditionally serve it at Lunar New Year celebrations to bring good fortune for the year ahead. The abacus beads are represented by large discs of boiled yam or taro paste.

SERVES 4–6

30ml/2 tbsp vegetable oil
4 garlic cloves, sliced
200g/7oz raw prawns/shrimp, peeled
1 Chinese leafy celery stick, roughly chopped
5ml/1 tsp ground black pepper
30ml/2 tbsp light soy sauce
5ml/1 tsp sugar
30ml/2 tbsp sesame oil
90ml/6 tbsp water
rice, to serve

FOR THE YAM BEADS

300g/11oz yam or taro
75ml/5 tbsp water
2.5ml/½ tsp salt
50g/2oz/½ cup rice flour
15ml/1 tbsp cornflour/cornstarch or tapioca flour

1 Make the beads. Peel the yam or taro and cut it into small chunks. Place in a steamer and cook over simmering water for 30 minutes or until very soft. Cool, then place in a food processor. Add the water and salt. Process until very smooth.

2 Add the rice flour and cornflour or tapioca flour to the yam paste. Continue to process the mixture until all the ingredients combine to form a smooth dough. Transfer to a lightly floured board.

3 Pinch off pieces of dough, each the size of a walnut, and roll and shape into little discs. Press each disc in the middle on both sides to make small dimples. Place on a lightly oiled plate and steam for 10 minutes.

4 Meanwhile, heat the oil in a wok and fry the garlic for 40 seconds, until light brown.

5 Add the prawns and stir-fry for 2 minutes. Add the celery, black pepper, soy sauce, sugar, sesame oil and water. Stir for 1 minute, then add the steamed yam beads. Stir until well mixed, spoon into a bowl and serve hot, accompanied by rice.

Cook's Tip

Chinese celery is sold in specialist stores and is quite different from regular celery, having more leaves than stalk. If you can't locate it, just use celery.

Variation

Thin strips of chicken or pork can be used instead of prawns, or for a vegan version, strips of mushroom.

SOUTHERN CHINA
SWEET THINGS

SILKLY SMOOTH & CRISPLY CRUNCHY

The sweet foods in this chapter are not necessarily served at the end of a meal in south China, or indeed anywhere in the country. The communal Chinese meal has never been structured to embrace desserts as a final flourish. More often than not, only Chinese tea and perhaps some fresh fruit are served as a palate cleanser. Sweet things are generally regarded as between-meal snacks, or for special and festive occasions like the Lunar New Year, when sweet buns and dumplings of every hue and shape make a splendid show as offerings to deities.

Although the range of sweet foods that are eaten in south China is quite wide, they have not had much impact outside the country, possibly because these items are so different from the wheat flour and butter-based products that are more typical of the Western genre.

Instead, most Chinese desserts are made from rice flour or another type of flour, such as water chestnut flour. Even sweet buns based on wheat flour doughs invariably include a distinctively Chinese substance like sweet bean paste, almond paste or sesame paste.

Dairy products are rarely, if ever, used, either in the dough or the filling. The famous Egg Tarts from Macau, which use Cheddar cheese, are a Portuguese creation dating from when the island was a Portuguese enclave in the 16th century.

Other popular desserts include jellies made from a seaweed extract called agar agar, and fruits, nuts and seeds in a simple sugar syrup, as in Lotus Seeds in Syrup.

LOTUS SEEDS IN SYRUP

Within the pantheon of Chinese herbal remedies, lotus seeds are believed to aid blood circulation and stimulate sluggish appetites, while ginkgo nuts have for thousands of years been famed for their curative properties. Both turn up in herbal soups and sweet drinks like this one.

SERVES 4

750ml/1¼ pints/3 cups water
100g/3¾oz rock sugar
40 drained canned lotus seeds
40 drained canned ginkgo nuts
6 pieces preserved sweet winter melon

1 Put the water in a pan. Bring to the boil and add the rock sugar. Stir over the heat until it has dissolved.

2 Taste the syrup for sweetness and add more sugar if necessary. Stir in the lotus seeds and nuts with the preserved sweet winter melon. Simmer for 20 minutes. Serve hot or cold.

Cook's Tip

Chinese rock sugar comes in large opaque crystal lumps (pictured on the previous page); it is slightly less sweet than granulated sugar.

SERVES 4

750ml/1¼ pints/3 cups cold water
25g/1oz agar agar strips
15ml/1 tbsp powdered gelatine
300g/11oz/1½ cups sugar
150ml/¼ pint/⅔ cup evaporated milk
15ml/1 tbsp almond extract
fruit cocktail or lychees, to serve

Variations

- The flavour of almond is not to everyone's taste. Use vanilla as a substitute if you prefer.
- Evaporated milk gives the jelly its opaque appearance; you can use water alone if you prefer a translucent jelly.

ALMOND JELLY

This dish from Hong Kong is traditionally made using soaked, ground whole almonds. This simplified version, using almond extract, requires less effort and gives results that are just as good. The jelly has a subtle, sweet flavour that is popular with children and adults alike.

1 Pour the cold water into a medium pan and add the agar agar strips. Sprinkle the gelatine on the surface. Heat gently, stirring until all the agar agar and gelatine has dissolved.

2 Add the sugar. Simmer, stirring constantly, until the sugar has dissolved, then stir in the evaporated milk and almond extract.

3 Rinse a jelly mould with cold water and stand it upside down to drain. Stir the almond mixture well, then pour it into the jelly mould. Leave to cool, then chill until set.

4 Loosen the sides of the jelly with a knife, then unmould it on to a serving plate. If it is reluctant to leave the mould, dip it briefly in warm water before trying again. Serve with fruit cocktail or lychees.

EGG TARTS

These simple yet delectable little egg tarts clearly demonstrate the hybrid Portuguese-Chinese nature of the food from Macau, which was a Portuguese enclave for more than 400 years. Over the centuries, this sweet snack has become a favourite throughout the region and abroad and is probably the only Chinese dessert that contains cheese. The ingredients used outside China can vary, however, with the cheese often being omitted and a dash of ground cinnamon being sprinkled over the top.

MAKES 24 TARTS

150ml/¼ pint/⅔ cup single/light cream or whipping cream
75ml/5 tbsp sugar
45g/1½oz mild Cheddar cheese, grated
3 large eggs, lightly beaten
pinch of salt
2.5ml/½ tsp vanilla extract
175ml/6fl oz/¾ cup milk
450g/1lb shortcrust pastry, thawed if frozen

1 Pour the cream into a large, heavy pan and stir in the sugar. Heat gently, stirring continuously, until the sugar dissolves, then bring to the boil. Be careful not to let the mixture stick on the bottom or it will burn.

2 Add the cheese to the cream mixture and cook over low heat until the cheese melts and the mixture is smooth. Remove the pan from the heat and set aside until the mixture has cooled a little.

3 In a bowl, beat the eggs lightly with the salt. Add to the cream mixture with the vanilla extract and milk. Strain through a fine sieve or strainer into a clean bowl.

4 Preheat the oven to 200°C/400°F/Gas 6. On a lightly floured surface, roll out the pastry to a thickness of around 3mm/⅛in, and cut out 24 rounds with a pastry cutter. Fit these into two 12-hole tartlet tins/muffin pans, pressing them down gently.

5 Pour the filling into the pastry cases, filling them almost to the top. Bake for 20 minutes or until the filling has just set and is golden brown.

6 Remove from the pans and cool on wire racks. Serve warm.

Cook's Tips

- Beat the eggs lightly. If they are over-beaten the filling will rise too much while baking.
- If not eaten immediately, the tarts can be kept in an airtight container for a day or two. Reheat them in an oven preheated to 180°C/350°F/Gas 4 for 10 minutes to refresh them.

BEAN PASTE BUNS

There are scores of different dumplings in the dim sum repertoire, many of them varying only in the fillings. Bun flour, also called Hong Kong or waterlily flour, is bleached which partially breaks down the gluten and makes the results softer. The filling is a sweet bean paste called tau sa, which is available in cans in most Chinese stores.

MAKES ABOUT 12 BUNS

200g/7oz/1¾ cups bun flour or waterlily flour
or self-raising/self-rising flour
5ml/1 tsp sugar
pinch of salt
15g/½oz easy-blend/rapid-rise dried yeast
120ml/4fl oz/½ cup warm water
1 can sweet bean paste (about 300g/11oz)
lychees, to serve (optional)

1 Put the flour, sugar and salt in a large mixing bowl and sprinkle in the yeast. Make a well in the middle and pour in the warm water. Mix to a dough.

2 Place the dough on a floured board and knead for 10 minutes. Return it to the bowl, cover and set aside in a warm place to rise for 20 minutes or until it has doubled in bulk.

3 Knock back/punch down the dough, knead it again, return it to the bowl and set aside in a warm place for 15 minutes.

4 Roll out the dough on a floured board and shape it into a 30cm/12in long roll about 5cm/2in in diameter. Cut the roll into 2.5cm/1in slices and flatten each of these with a rolling pin to a thin round, about 10cm/4in across.

5 Holding a pastry round on the palm of one hand, spoon a tablespoon of the filling into the centre. Cup your hand so that the dough enfolds the filling, pleating and pinching it where necessary. Pinch off the excess dough at the top and seal with a twisting action. Sealing is important or the buns will gape when steamed. Fill the remaining dumplings in the same way.

6 Cut 5cm/2in squares of baking parchment. Stand a dumpling on each piece of paper in a steamer. Steam for 15 minutes, then serve immediately. Canned lychees are a delicious accompaniment!

Variation

Canned chestnut purée can also be used to good effect in these simple steamed buns.

WATER CHESTNUT CAKE

That this has become a quintessential Cantonese dessert says a lot for the free exchange of culinary ideas in China, since it originated in the north of the country. Water chestnuts give the cake a delightful crunchy texture. It is sometimes fried after being steamed, but is just as delicious cold. The unusual sweet-savoury flavour makes it equally suitable for serving as a dessert or a snack, perhaps with a cup of tea.

SERVES 6

- 150g/5oz/1¼ cups water chestnut flour
- 200ml/7fl oz/scant 1 cup milk
- 200g/7oz can water chestnuts, drained
- 60ml/4 tbsp corn or vegetable oil
- 150g/5oz/¾ cup caster/superfine sugar
- 400ml/14fl oz/1⅔ cups water

1 Put the water chestnut flour in a bowl and stir in the milk with a wooden spoon to make a smooth paste. Set aside.

2 In a food processor, grind the water chestnuts to a fine pulp. Add the oil, sugar and water and process until well mixed. Scrape into a pan and bring to the boil.

3 Add half the water chestnut flour paste to the pan. Simmer, stirring, for 5 minutes. Remove from the heat and leave to cool for 10 minutes.

4 Add the remaining paste, a little at a time, stirring constantly. Return to the heat and cook, stirring, for 3 minutes, until it has the consistency of thick cream.

5 Spoon the mixture into a tray or pan that will fit in a steamer, then smooth the top with a moistened knife. Steam for 30 minutes.

6 Remove and leave to cool and set; it will be quite firm. Cut into squares and serve cold or fry lightly in oil to serve warm.

Cook's Tip

Water chestnuts are widely available. Fresh ones are fiddly to prepare when raw, so save time by buying them in cans. The texture will be just the same. Water chestnut flour is available at most Chinese food stores.

WESTERN CHINA

Sichuan, Hunan, Hubei, Yunnan, Guizhou and Shaanxi cuisine

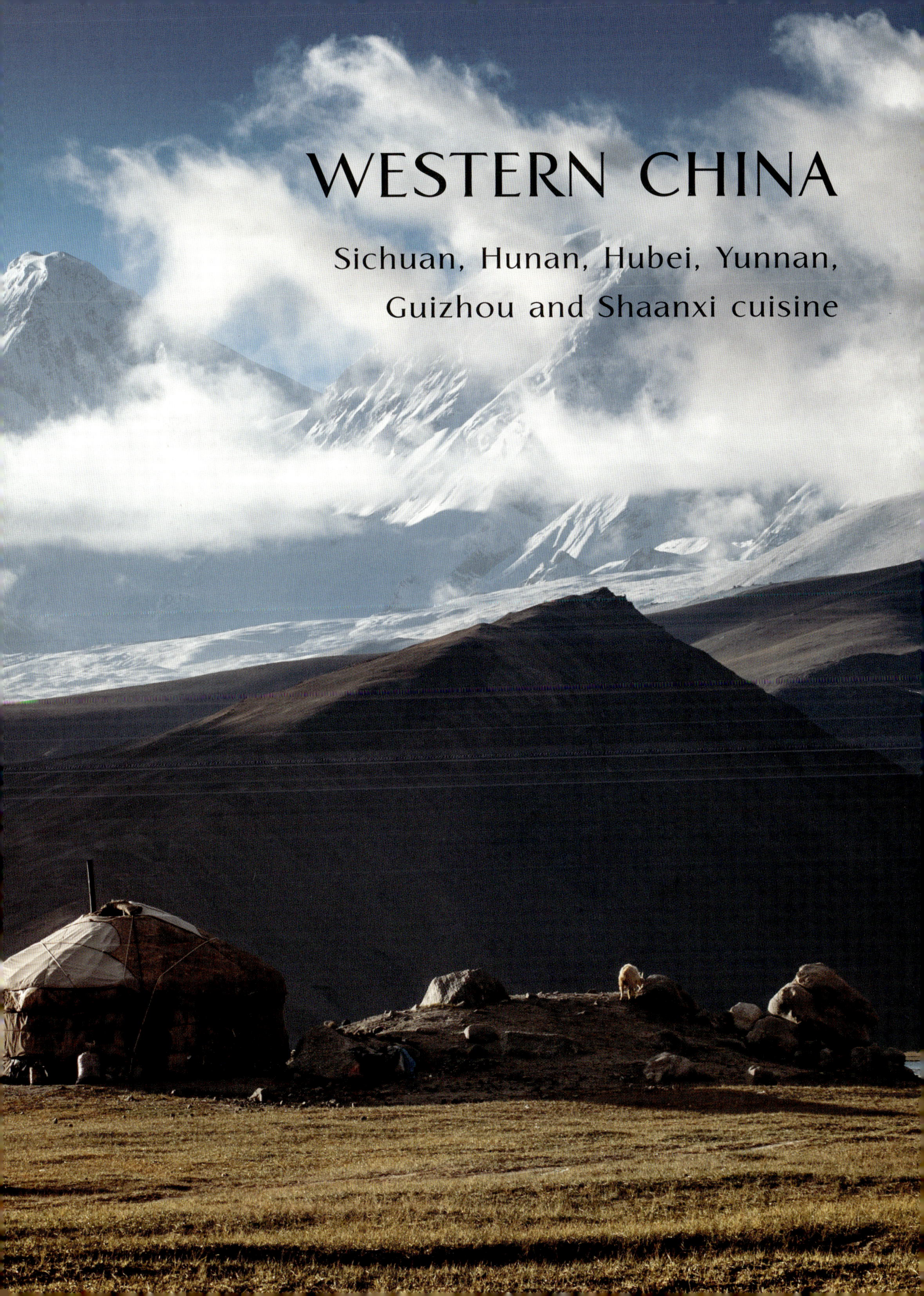

A MYSTERIOUS LAND OF FIRE & MIST

The landscapes of western China are both sublime and bewitching. This vast area is humid and fertile, defined by expansive green rainforests, epic meandering rivers and majestic lakes, surrounded by verdant plains and foreboding mountain ranges to the west and south. The region embraces the large province of Sichuan, world-famous for its sizzling cuisine, as well as the municipality of Chongqing and the smaller provinces of Shaanxi, Hunan, Hubei, Guizhou and Yunnan, where traditional ways of life still persist.

West China is a landlocked area, hundreds of miles from the sea, where agriculture has been practised for centuries in a traditional style that sometimes seems untouched by the modern day. The region has a large population of livestock, with pigs and chickens being the most common animals, as well as cattle, water buffalo, horses, mules and donkeys. In most rural areas, sheep, goats and camels are still raised in the traditional way by nomadic herders, moving around the country to find the best grazing.

The province of Sichuan also contains the Wolong Nature Reserve, home to the giant panda. The panda's diet is exclusively bamboo leaves, while the shoots are a main part of the human population's food.

Below *Western China encompasses the vibrant metropolises of Chengdu and Xi'an and the verdant rice terraces of the Yangtze river basin.*

The influence of the Yangtze River

West China's heartland is the fertile Red Basin of Sichuan, which is surrounded by fields and mountains. Here, the rainfall is predictably heavy and the climate humid, with a dampness that cloaks the air for most of the year. During the summer months, ocean-going vessels make their way up the Yangtze River as far inland as Wuhan, and flat-bottomed barges can be taken upstream as far as Chongqing, bringing with them the produce from other provinces to augment the kitchens of the area. The climate is relatively mild, with fertile soil, making the Red Basin one of the most productive, intensely cultivated and densely populated regions in the whole of China.

Most of China's rice is grown south of the Huai River, in the Yangtze valley, the Zhu Jiang delta, and in Yunnan, Guizhou, and Sichuan provinces. Rice fields, arranged in spectacular terraces, some of which date back centuries, dominate the verdant landscape. Other crops include potatoes, sweet potatoes, citrus fruits, as well as other fruits and vegetables, sugar cane, sugar beets, and green, black and jasmine teas.

Hubei and Hunan provinces are also dominated by the Yangtze River, and these fertile farmlands have been cultivated since at least the 11th century. The region was an important grain producer during the Ming and Qing dynasties. Today, Hubei is one of the largest pig-rearing provinces in China, and pork is predictably an important ingredient. Hunan is the birthplace of Mao Zedong, and boasts not only an exquisite cuisine but also the geographical splendour of China's second-largest lake, Dongting Hu, and the soaring mountain scenery of Wulingyuan in the north-west.

Above *Terraced rice fields, such as this one in YuanYang in western China, are submerged during water season.*

On the western fringes

Yunnan, in the far south-west of the area, has an incredible diversity of landscapes and climates. The province is framed by the Tibetan highlands at its north-western edge, and there is a mix of tropical rainforests and volcanic plains to the south, with the centre criss-crossed by hills and valleys. It is home to a third of China's ethnic minorities and, in culinary terms, has much in common with neighbouring Myanmar, Laos and Vietnam. The Dai people occupy the lush lands of the Xishuangbanna region and have been cultivating rice, sugar cane and bananas here for centuries. Their diet features esoteric ingredients such as ants' eggs and wild moss, and rice is often steamed inside hollowed bamboo stalks.

Ancient heartlands of China

Shaanxi province (not to be confused with its neighbour, the northern province of Shanxi) lies on the Loess Plateau, and is rich in natural resources, particularly coal and oil. The south of this province is a comparatively lush, mountainous area with a mild climate, whereas the north is a harsh landscape of ravines and near-vertical cliff faces where the soft soil has been eroded over the years. The Great Wall of China starts its march to Beijing in the far northern corner of this province.

Guizhou province, sandwiched between Yunnan and Hunan, is a mountainous landscape of weathered limestone pinnacles that hide many of China's largest natural caverns. Despite the poor soil and over-abundant rainfall, the indigenous ethnic tribes of Miao and Dong people have managed to retain their unique lifestyle, customs and cuisine.

The red-silted Chisui River – the name means 'Red Water' – runs through waterfalls and thick bamboo groves. Bamboo symbolizes the Confucian values of devotion and righteousness, and is extolled in poems and paintings for its promise of enlightenment. Local people harvest the mature stems of bamboo to make all sorts of mats and cooking utensils, and use the young shoots for cooking. Bamboo shoots in every guise – boiled, pickled, fried and steamed – therefore unsurprisingly pop up in many dishes. The region is also famous for its fiery alcoholic beverage, called Maotai, which adds its kick to many delicious local recipes, as well as being drunk by itself.

POLITICS, POWER & GLOBAL PROMINENCE

The six provinces and one municipality that make up western China are some of the first areas known to be settled in historical China. This culinary history of this land dates back to at least the 5th century BCE, since when the land has been inhabited and farmed. It is a fertile part of the country, making it ideal for agriculture, with abundant rain and warm weather. People initially gathered in the most hospitable valleys of the area, and some of these early village settlements became the flourishing imperial cities of later dynasties.

The name Sichuan means 'four rivers', paying tribute to the important element of water as dictated by feng shui (wind and water geomancy). It was established as a province in 1644 and was a base for the Chinese navy, which could use the Yangtze River to control other provinces. Today, Sichuan has an enviable reputation as the foremost culinary centre of the area, with many dishes now famous all over the world, especially for their use of tangy, hot spices.

Early Chinese culture in Shaanxi

Shaanxi province has evidence of human civilization dating back to prehistory. It remained the political heart of China until the 9th century CE. Its capital, Xi'an, enjoyed a reputation akin to that of Rome and Constantinople as one of the greatest cities in the world. It was here that China reached the zenith of imperial power during the Tang Dynasty, established in 618. This period was truly China's Golden Age, with economic success, territorial acquisitions and political stability.

Today the city of Xi'an is chiefly known for the machinations of China's infamous Qing Qin Shi Huangdi, the Yellow Emperor. He was especially noted for commissioning gigantic building projects, most notably an early version of the current Great Wall of China and the city-sized mausoleum guarded by his terracotta soldiers.

The breakaway province of Yunnan

Yunnan was the seat of the pastoral Dian Kingdom, founded in the 3rd century CE, but the province remained isolated from the rest of China for centuries afterward, resisting Han influences and maintaining its local traditions. Even today, the province is home to a third of China's ethnic minorities.

Above *The magnificent terracotta warriors of Xi'an have become famous throughout the world.*

The capital city of Kunming is blessed with clement weather and in ancient times was dubbed the City of Eternal Spring. It was already a thriving cosmopolitan centre by the 13th century. Within the different tribal communities are rich and unique food cultures, reflecting the distinctive characteristics of each ethnic group. The Zhuang in Yunnan form the largest group among China's ethnic minorities, and are particularly skilful at preparing festive dishes using ingredients such as hare, rabbit, frogs and other wild meats.

Farming in Hunan and Hubei

During the political upheavals in northern China between the 8th and 11th centuries, the fertile fields of Hunan had begun to lure millions of people to the province in search of a more peaceful life, farming and developing the land. Hunan is famous for being the birthplace of Mao Zedong, as well as for its cuisine, which is as fiery as that of Sichuan.

As early as 770BCE, the province of Hubei was home to the powerful state of Chu, a culturally unique tributary state of the Zhou Dynasty. It claimed much of the middle and lower Yangtze River area, which was a rich agricultural region with an abundance of small farms on the land. Because of the landlocked topography of the region, its borders have remained relatively constant for the past 500 years. The construction of the Three Gorges Dam over the Yangtze River in 1993 brought the Hubei province into world prominence, with some controversy over the treatment of people who were displaced by the dam, as well as the environmental impact of this massive project.

Guizhou in the Qing Dynasty

The province of Guizhou was well known by the people of China for thousands of years, but did not come into world prominence until the 17th century, under the rule of the Qing Dynasty. The lush climate supports the growing of many tropical crops, including rice, maize, tobacco, tea and rapeseed. Much of Guizhou cuisine reflects the diverse but ancient culinary traditions of its 18 different ethnic minority tribes, although some of their tastes, such as the consumption of dog meat, are frowned upon today by people from other areas of China, as well as by the rest of the world.

West China in recent history

Following the Communist Party of China's victory in the Chinese Civil War (1927–50), control of the farmlands of western China was handed to the 300 million peasant farmers. In the following years, the government formally took control of the land, further structuring the agricultural areas into large government-operated collective farms. Emphasis shifted on to industrialization rather than agriculture, and today, as China continues to industrialize, huge expanses of agricultural land are being converted for industrial use, and factory work is becoming the source of income for many farmers. The political and economic landscape of China continues to evolve, but western China nonetheless remains one of the world's biggest food producers, and its ingredients are exported around the globe.

Below *Zhaoxing village in Guizhou is one of the largest traditional communities in south-west China, and is home to the Dong tribe.*

THE FIERY HEART OF CHINESE COOKING

The western area of China is known as the 'land of plenty': its agricultural fecundity is a result of the warm climate and abundant rain and river water. The great reputation of western Chinese regional cooking stems back 2,200 years, but became known to the outside world only in the second half of the 20th century. Now, Sichuan cuisine is renowned all over the globe for its depth of flavour, which centres around eye-wateringly spicy chillies, as well as piquant aromatics, sour pickles and perfectly cooked meat.

The humid climate of western China means the preservation of food takes top priority. Food may be easy to grow here, but it also deteriorates quickly unless it is preserved using a variety of techniques, from the ancient to the modern. Salting, drying, pickling, spicing and smoking all help to keep foodstuffs edible in the extreme moist heat.

Aromatics such as onions, garlic and ginger feature prominently in the cuisine, as do sesame seeds, peanuts, soy bean products and fermented black soy beans. Mixed together, they produce the characteristic piquant spiciness of the region's cuisine. Throughout the whole area, the cooking embraces a diverse medley of flavours, including hot, sweet, sour and salty, and often all at once.

Spicy Sichuan cooking

Sichuan, as well as being the most populous province in western China, leads the way in the region's cooking. The cuisine of this province is often described as being a baptism of gustatory fire, and Sichuan cooking is typified by bold combinations of flavours in a single dish.

Many Sichuan recipes certainly do live up to their fiery reputation, using large quantities of spicy chillies and other robust flavourings, but there are also dishes that are not touched by chillies or pungent Sichuan peppercorns. The sophistication and diversity of Sichuan cuisine is reflected in the vast range of traditional recipes, which local gourmets claim stretch to some 5,000 different dishes, with superlative examples of taste and texture.

Sichuan cooks are proud of their delicious dumplings, pickled vegetables, and meat and poultry dishes that are quite unlike any other regional equivalent. Up there among the Sichuan culinary stars are dishes that were originally from the neighbouring provinces of Shaanxi, Hubei, Hunan and Guizhou as well as from the southernmost province of Yunnan, with its intriguing mix of Han Chinese and ethnic minority tribes.

Below *Hanging bunches of chillies are an iconic sight in Sichuan, where they are dried to prevent rotting.*

The cuisine of Sichuan seems to successfully break all the culinary rules, mixing a whole host of pungent aromatics and intense spices. It is, however, not without logic: the careful balance of spices is not meant to burn the mouth, but to tempt the tastebuds, and to preserve foods in the hot and humid climate.

Delicacies of Hunan and Hubei

The two provinces of Hunan and Hubei share nearby Sichuan's liberal use of chillies in their cuisines. Although the cooking styles here are regarded as being of separate schools from that of Sichuan, they do share similar traits, especially when it comes to fiery flavours. The dishes are not always hot, but they are always complex in terms of ingredients. Hubei food has one unusual feature: the skilful blending of seafood flavours with meat and poultry, as in the unique dish Dragon Phoenix Eels.

Chefs from Hunan are masters of many ancient culinary techniques, which cover all aspects of food preparation. These include cutting meat and poultry in specific ways to suit each dish, which are judged by colour, texture and visual appeal as well as taste.

The pickles of Guizhou

Guizhou cuisine actually uses more chilli peppers than Sichuan, which many would find surprising. However, it is best known for the liberal use of vinegar to preserve vegetables, such as the famous Pickled Mustard Greens. There is a local folk saying:

Above *Colourful food crops in Yunnan include rice, wheat, corn, canola and many types of vegetable.*

'Without eating a sour dish for three days, people will stagger with weak legs.' Each family in Guizhou makes its own sour pickles, and these form a major part of the diet. Although it is landlocked, the province also offers some seafood dishes, including Clay-pot Fish Stew.

Meat and noodle dishes of Shaanxi

Shaanxi cuisine makes elaborate use of ordinary materials, particularly the staple meats, pork and mutton. Noodles take on extraordinary shapes, with some as wide as lasagne. The chief characteristics of Shaanxi cuisine are similar to those of Sichuan, but the flavours tend to be heavier and spicier. The mixture of chillies and vinegar is typical, and features in the hot-and-sour dishes of the area.

Foreign influences in Yunnan

Yunnan borders Myanmar, Laos and Vietnam and is relatively isolated from the rest of China, so the cuisine reflects many influences from the surrounding countries. This province is home to the Miao, Bai, Sami, Yi and Dai hill tribes, all of whom have their own typical methods and ingredients for favourite dishes. Rice, sugar cane, pineapples and bananas are cultivated in Yunnan province and figure prominently in the cooking.

HIGH DAYS & HOLIDAYS

Western China is a landlocked area far from the bustling, cosmopolitan centres of Beijing and Shanghai. Traditions founded here many centuries ago have therefore persisted over the years, and certain festivals with their attendant foods are celebrated today in much the same way as they always have been. From sweet almond cakes for the Moon Cake Festival to glacé or candied fruits for the Lunar New Year, the many delicate and tasty little snacks are a hugely important part of the rituals.

Festival traditions are vibrantly alive in western China, and many have great significance in the lives of its people, often for spiritual or social reasons.

Lunar New Year

Of all the festivals, Lunar New Year is the most important. Socially, it is a time of family reunions and harmony, the burial of old feuds, and tying up of loose ends. The festival is celebrated in every home, not merely as the start of a new calendar year but as a symbol of life's renewal: the old year disappears and everyone has a chance to start afresh. In the last month of the old lunar year, every home is alive with hectic preparations. Many auspicious foods are eaten, such as nuts, dates, melon seeds, glacé and candied fruits, sugared melon slices and other sweet confections. These are presented in an eight-sided tray called the 'tray of togetherness' (henian guanhe). Each food on the tray invokes good fortune, prosperity, luck and all of life's positive elements. Peaches are a favourite at this time, as they

Below *Lunar New Year is celebrated in Guizhou with traditional dancing.*

Right *Home-made moon cakes can be filled with a range of ingredients, from seeds to salted eggs.*

symbolize a long life. The Chinese icons of Fu Lu Shu (prosperity, happiness and longevity) are portrayed in china or carved wooden figurines, and the 'longevity' figure is always holding a peach.

Water Splashing Festival

In Yunnan province, in the middle of April, a special festival is celebrated by the Dai ethnic minority group, which involves some boisterous water fun. The festival has strong echoes of the similar Thai Water Festival of Songkran, as some of the ethnic minority groups in China have close cultural ties with those of Indo-China and enjoy the same ancient traditions. The festival can last for up to five days. Prayers are said in Buddhist temples, statues of the Lord Buddha are thoroughly cleaned, and people dress up as peacocks to perform traditional dances. Best of all there is a wealth of food, such as dan dan noodles, glutinous rice dumplings in bamboo leaves, red bean paste cakes and numerous chicken dishes.

Moon Cake Festival

Throughout China, people celebrate this mid-autumn festival on the 15th day of the eighth lunar month, but the Sichuanese, with their proud food traditions, try to go one better. On one occasion in 2006, a giant moon cake was baked by the citizens of Chengdu that weighed in at an enormous 400kg/ 882lb. It was cut up and distributed free to the local citizens. Moon cakes are heavy, round pastries stuffed with all manner of fillings, from meat to almond paste or even salted duck's eggs. In Sichuan the classic fillings are melon seed, lotus seed and almond paste. The crusts are decorated with symbols such as dragons or a phoenix. Traditionally, 13 moon cakes are piled in a pyramid to symbolize the 13 months of the lunar leap year.

Dumpling (Dragon Boat) Festival

This nationwide festival has been already described in other chapters, of course, but there are regional differences to be found in the celebrations. Legend tells us that Qu Yuan, a high-ranking official of the Zhou dynasty, was slandered by corrupt officials and threw himself into a river, but the people of his village, learning of this, searched the river in boats trying to find him, to no avail. They threw rice into the river so he would not go hungry in the next life, and to stop the rice being eaten by fish, they wrapped the food in leaves wound with silk thread.

This sad event evolved into the colourful festival of today. Teams of rowers compete in races, many of their boats painted with symbols such as dragons to boost their competitive spirit. As well as the racing and feasting, according to tradition, on this day, unmarried girls would stand at their windows and throw an embroidered ball out to a crowd of unmarried men below. The man who caught the ball had to marry her – at least that's how the legend goes.

As elsewhere in China, this festival is celebrated on the fifth day of the fifth lunar month. The main food is rice dumplings filled with an assortment of meats and sweet bean paste, which is much loved by the Sichuan people. In the run-up to the festival, families prepare a huge range of delicious snacks such as Sesame Seed Pastries, Crystal Dumplings and Sweet Potato Cakes to distribute to all the children.

WESTERN CHINA

SOUPS & DIM SUM

CLEANSING SOUPS & FIERY BITES

Soups in western China tend to be mild, giving a refreshing and cleansing break from the spicy flavours of Sichuan cuisine. One exception to this rule is the iconic Hot-and-Sour Soup, which is thick, intensely flavoured, and full of chicken and tofu chunks. Others are milder, such as Corn Soup, or they are delicately flavoured with pickled and salted vegetables. In Guizhou, cooks are adept at using fish to enhance their soups.

Dim sum, which translates as 'food to touch the heart', comprises a wide range of dumplings wrapped in a variety of different types of pastry. As the chief characteristics of this regional school of cooking lie in the frequent and lavish use of various soy bean pastes, these are invariably used in the seasonings for dim sum, making them richer than those of other regions. Soy sauces, sesame oil, peppercorns and oyster sauce are touched with wine and other alcoholic beverages for heady measure.

Snacks such as Sweet Potato Cakes are sold on the streets in Chengdu, and Glutinous Rice Balls with Sesame Paste appear unfailingly during the Lunar New Year as a festive must. In a culinary triumph, Jicama Dumplings have, over the past century, crossed not only regional borders but also oceans: they are now a favourite in restaurants throughout South-east Asia.

Whatever type of dim sum is served there will always be the requisite dipping sauces, such as black vinegar with ginger, garlic, salt and oil (and usually some fiery chilli paste added), to accompany it.

SPICY FISH SOUP

A Guizhou staple, this soup of monkfish or cod with crisp garlic makes a light but aromatic first course. Any type of firm-fleshed fish can be used, but monkfish is particularly good, as it has the texture of chicken and no tiny bones to worry about. The spicing comes from the famous Sichuan peppercorns, known for their liquorice flavour and subtle fire, as well as the liberal quantity of garlic.

SERVES 4

- 200g/7oz firm-fleshed fish fillet, such as monkfish or cod, membrane or skin removed
- 45ml/3 tbsp groundnut/peanut oil
- 4 garlic cloves, sliced
- 1 garlic clove, crushed
- 800ml/1½ pints/scant 3¼ cups boiling water
- 30ml/2 tbsp light soy sauce
- 2.5ml/½ tsp finely ground Sichuan peppercorns
- small bunch of watercress or shredded lettuce leaves

1 Cut the fish into 5mm/¼in-thick slices. Heat the oil in a large, heavy pan and fry the garlic slices until golden brown. Lift out the garlic using a slotted spoon and set aside. In the remaining oil, fry the crushed garlic for 30 seconds until golden brown.

2 Add the boiling water to the pan and then add the fish, soy sauce and Sichuan peppercorns. Return to the boil, then simmer for 2 minutes, then add the watercress or lettuce and simmer for 1 minute or until the fish is cooked. Serve garnished with the fried garlic.

Cook's Tip

This can be made with an equal quantity of shellfish, such as prawns, shrimp or scallops.

SERVES 4

800ml/1½ pints/scant 3¼ cups boiling water
1 skinless chicken breast, about 125g/4¼oz
50g/2oz silken or firm tofu, cut into 1cm/½in cubes
30ml/2 tbsp Xinkiang black vinegar, or a dark wine vinegar
2.5ml/½ tsp ground Sichuan peppercorns
2 fresh red chillies, finely chopped
1 spring onion/scallion, finely chopped
30ml/2 tbsp light soy sauce
2.5ml/½ tsp caster/superfine sugar
15ml/1 tbsp cornflour/cornstarch
salt and ground black pepper
fried onions or garlic slices, to garnish

HOT-AND-SOUR SOUP

This Sichuan soup has crossed more borders in China than the Great Wall and it has become a part of Hunan and even Cantonese cooking. The blend of black Xinkiang (or Sinkiang) vinegar, chopped chillies and pepper is aromatic and spicy, and it really catches the throat. Generally chicken is added, but a vegetarian version can feature just the diced tofu. Long-life tofu is available in two types – silken and firm; either are suitable.

1 Pour the boiling water into a pan and cook the chicken breast for 10 minutes. Lift out using a slotted spoon and dice into small 1cm/½in cubes.

2 Return the chicken cubes to the stock and add all the remaining ingredients except the cornflour and garnish. Bring to the boil, then reduce the heat to a simmer and cook for 5 minutes. Taste and adjust the seasoning if necessary.

3 Put the cornflour in a small bowl and blend with a little cold water. Stir into the soup and cook, stirring, until thickened. Serve topped with fried onions or garlic slices.

CORN SOUP

This well-loved recipe is believed to have originated in Hubei, but since there have been centuries of cuisines crossing borders, it is difficult to establish this with any historical accuracy. In a further complication, you can find this soup in just about every Chinese restaurant from Sydney to San Francisco. Whatever its origins, it makes a great dish. Chicken is used here, although pork is another favourite. This recipe uses fresh corn for authenticity as well as flavour and texture – it is so much tastier than canned corn, which is generally used to make the soup in takeaways.

SERVES 4

2 corn on the cob, as fresh as possible
15ml/1 tbsp cornflour/cornstarch
500ml/scant 1 pint/2 cups light chicken stock
1 skinless chicken breast
10ml/2 tsp sesame oil
2 eggs, lightly beaten
salt and ground white pepper
1 shredded or chopped spring onion/scallion, to garnish

1 Stand each cob on end and, using a sharp knife, slice the kernels off as close to the cob as possible, then scrape as much juice out of the cob as you can and pour it into a blender. Add the kernels, cornflour and half the stock, then blend for 1–2 minutes, or until almost smooth. Set aside.

2 Put the remaining stock into a large, heavy pan and add the chicken. Cook, covered, over a low heat for 15 minutes. Lift out the chicken using a slotted spoon and cut it into small dice or tear into small shreds.

3 Return the chicken to the pan and add the corn mixture. Bring to the boil, then reduce the heat and simmer, stirring frequently, for 6–8 minutes, or until slightly thickened and the cornflour has cooked. Season with sesame oil and salt to taste.

4 Using a wooden spoon, stir the simmering soup in circles with one hand while you pour in the lightly beaten eggs in a thin stream with the other. The egg will form thin threads.

5 Serve the soup immediately, garnished with shredded or chopped spring onion.

Cook's Tip

If you prefer your soup to be thickened without cornflour, simply leave it out – the corn's natural starches will provide some thickening.

PORK BALLS IN CLEAR SOUP

Minced or ground pork is used in many ways in Chinese cuisine. Here it is mixed with cloud ears and flavourings, then formed into tiny balls to be cooked in soup. Minced pork from the supermarket is not ideal, as it will not have the correct ratio of fat to lean meat that gives the best flavour and succulence. For an authentic soup, it is best to make your own mince for the pork balls, using one-third fatty pork belly and two-thirds shoulder meat.

SERVES 4

4 cloud ear/wood ear mushrooms, soaked in lukewarm water for 10–15 minutes
45ml/3 tbsp vegetable oil
3 shallots, very thinly sliced
1 spring onion/scallion, finely chopped
200g/7oz minced/ground pork
5ml/1 tsp cornflour/cornstarch
5ml/1 tsp light soy sauce
2.5ml/½ tsp ground black pepper
800ml/1½ pints/scant 3¼ cups meat stock
salt, to taste
coriander/cilantro leaves or chopped spring onion/scallion, to garnish

1 Rinse and drain the cloud ears, then snip off the tough parts with kitchen scissors and chop the remainder finely. Put into a large bowl.

2 Heat the oil in a small pan over a medium-low heat and fry the shallots, stirring frequently, until they are crisp and brown. Drain on kitchen paper and set aside.

3 Add the spring onion to the bowl with the cloud ears, then add the pork, cornflour, soy sauce and pepper. Mix well. Shape the mixture into small balls the size of large grapes.

4 Put the stock into a large pan and bring to the boil, then turn down to a vigorous simmer over a medium-low heat. Add the pork balls and simmer for 4–5 minutes, or until cooked through and risen to the surface.

5 Season the soup with salt to taste and serve hot, sprinkled with the fried shallots and some sprigs of fresh coriander or chopped spring onions.

Cook's Tip

Normally, 200ml/7fl oz/scant 1 cup of liquid will fill a typical Chinese rice bowl. When you add the other ingredients to the quantity of stock listed here, each person will receive about 250ml/8fl oz/1 cup soup – perfect for a first course.

CHICKEN & PICKLED GREEN SOUP

Pickled or salted mustard greens are eaten throughout most of China and are used not only as a vegetable, but as a salting agent as well. In Chinese wet markets, the rural predecessors to supermarkets, the greens are sold in large earthenware crocks; elsewhere, they are available vacuum-packed or canned in most Chinese stores.

SERVES 4

- 2 or 3 pickled mustard green pieces
- 30ml/2 tbsp groundnut/peanut oil
- 2 garlic cloves, crushed
- 800ml/1½ pints/scant 3¼ cups boiling water
- 1 skinless chicken breast, about 125g/4¼oz
- 15ml/1 tbsp sesame oil
- 15ml/1 tbsp rice wine or vinegar
- 2.5ml/½ tsp caster/superfine sugar
- 15ml/1 tbsp light soy sauce, or to taste

1 Cut the pickled greens into thin strips, wash in plenty of cold water and squeeze them dry. If you want to reduce the salt content, leave the greens to soak in cold water for an hour or so before use.

2 Heat the oil in a large, heavy pan and fry the garlic for 30 seconds. Add the water and chicken, boil for 10 minutes, then lift out the chicken using a slotted spoon and shred into thin strips.

3 Return the shredded chicken to the stock and add the sesame oil. Add the mustard greens to the soup with the rice wine or vinegar and sugar, and simmer for 4 minutes. Taste and add soy sauce if necessary. Serve hot.

Cook's Tip

The quality of canned and vacuum-packed mustard greens can vary. Generally speaking, the vacuum-packed greens are the best quality.

MAKES ABOUT 20 CAKES

500g/1¼lb orange-fleshed sweet potatoes, unpeeled
about 115g/4oz/1 cup glutinous rice flour or wheat starch
vegetable oil, for deep-frying
cornflour/cornstarch, for dusting
honey, to serve

Variations

- You can also roll the balls in sesame seeds before deep-frying, if you like.
- These are also delicious with ice cream and golden/light corn syrup or maple syrup drizzled over.

SWEET POTATO CAKES

In Chengdu, many versions of these cakes are popular as street food. Some are a simple blend of sweet potato and rice flour, as here, whereas others are filled with lotus seed or red bean paste. They are easy to make and you can eat them dipped in honey or even with ice cream.

1 Preheat the oven to 180°C/350°F/Gas 4. Place the sweet potatoes on a baking tray and bake for 45 minutes to 1 hour, or until soft.

2 Leave the potatoes to cool slightly, then halve and scoop the flesh into a bowl. While still warm, mash the flesh until smooth, then add the flour and mix to make a dough, adding more flour if necessary.

3 Heat the oil for deep-frying over a medium heat. Pinch off walnut-size pieces of dough and roll in cornflour to coat lightly. Deep-fry a few balls at a time, stirring so that they fry on all sides, until they bob to the top of the oil and turn golden brown.

4 Lift out with a slotted spoon or wire basket and drain on kitchen paper. Serve warm or cold, with honey.

SESAME SEED PASTRIES

These sweet pastries with their sesame seed filling are more like pancakes, with a slightly savoury flavour to balance out the sugar. In Mandarin they are called ping, which can often refer to any small pastry.

SERVES 4

115g/4oz/1 cup plain/all-purpose flour
1 egg
pinch of fine salt
60ml/4 tbsp vegetable oil

FOR THE FILLING
175g/6oz sesame seeds
15ml/1 tbsp lard or white cooking fat
40g/1½oz caster/superfine sugar

1 To make the filling, put the sesame seeds into a dry pan and stir over a medium heat for 8–9 minutes, or until pale golden. Grind the warm toasted seeds to a paste using a food processor, grinder or mortar and pestle, then add a few drops of water to make a stiff paste.

2 Heat the lard or white cooking fat in a wok over a medium heat, add the sugar and cook until it has dissolved. Add the sesame seed mixture and cook for 2 minutes over a low heat to obtain a smooth, thick paste. Transfer to a plate and leave to cool completely.

3 Sift the flour into a large bowl and make a hollow in the centre. Beat the egg and salt together in a small bowl and add to the well in the centre of the flour. Pour in 200ml/7fl oz/scant 1 cup water and whisk everything quickly together to make a thick but flowing batter.

4 Grease a non-stick frying pan with some of the oil and set it over a medium-low heat. Pour in 60–75ml/4–5 tbsp batter to make a thin pancake. Cook until set on top, then flip the pancake over and cook for 10 seconds. Transfer to a plate. Use the remaining batter to make more pancakes.

5 Spread 30ml/2 tbsp of the filling on to the centre of each pancake. Fold opposite sides into the centre, then the top and bottom, to make a parcel.

6 Heat the remaining oil in a large frying pan over a medium heat. Quickly fry the folded pancakes until crisp and golden on both sides. Cut into slices and serve warm or at room temperature.

GLUTINOUS RICE BALLS WITH SESAME PASTE

Known as tang yuan in Sichuan, Hubei and other parts of China, these light rice balls are integral to the Lunar New Year festival. In rural Sichuan and Hubei, they are still made in a time-honoured way, which involves soaking glutinous rice for several days and then grinding it in a granite grinder. Water is then squeezed out through layers of muslin or cheesecloth until a wet dough is left. These days, glutinous rice flour is a labour-saving option.

MAKES 20 BALLS

200g/7oz/1¾ cups glutinous rice flour
30ml/2 tbsp rice flour
90g/3½oz crystallized winter melon, sliced, to serve

FOR THE FILLING

20g/¾oz/1½ tbsp sesame seeds
20g/¾oz/1½ tbsp caster/superfine sugar
10ml/2 tsp lard or white cooking fat

Cook's Tips

- At step 1, instead of toasting and grinding the sesame seeds, you can use the equivalent amount of light sesame seed tahini. Depending on the type you buy, adjust with sugar to taste and heat to blend.
- Crystallized or candied winter melon is a popular sweet snack (pictured on page 481); it is beautifully translucent.
- You can also add a few drops of vanilla extract to the melon water, to add a subtle fragrance, if you like.

1 To make the filling, put the sesame seeds into a dry pan and stir over a medium heat for a few minutes until light golden. Grind the toasted sesame seeds until fine, using a mortar and pestle, then stir in the sugar.

2 Heat the lard or white cooking fat in a wok, add the sesame seeds and fry the mixture over a low heat until you get a creamy texture. Set aside, cool, then chill, covered, until needed.

3 Put the two rice flours into a large bowl and stir in 200ml/7fl oz/ scant 1 cup warm water to make a soft dough. Divide the dough into three pieces and roll each on a floured board into a sausage shape about 2.5cm/1in thick.

4 Pinch off small pieces of dough the size of large grapes: the dough should make 20 balls. Flatten each piece to make an indentation in the centre.

5 Place a teaspoonful of paste in each piece of dough and draw over the sides to make small balls. Shape and smooth the balls to make them neat.

6 Bring a large pan of water to the boil and cook the dough balls for about 15 minutes, or until they float to the surface.

7 Meanwhile, boil 1 litre/1¾ pints/4 cups water in a pan and add the winter melon slices. Cook for 5 minutes. Divide this sweetened water among serving bowls.

8 Using a slotted spoon, transfer the cooked rice balls to the serving bowls; there should be 5 per serving.

JICAMA DUMPLINGS

The filling for these dumplings is made with jicama, a root vegetable that resembles a large, sweet turnip with a thin brown skin. It tastes faintly of crunchy water chestnuts and goes well with prawns and soy sauce in these light, steamed dim sum.

MAKES 10 DUMPLINGS

75g/3oz wheat starch or glutinous rice flour, plus extra for dusting
90g/3½oz/generous ½ cup cornflour/cornstarch
about 250ml/8fl oz/1 cup boiling water
15ml/1 tbsp vegetable oil
sweet soy sauce, to serve

FOR THE FILLING

250g/9oz jicama, peeled and thinly sliced into rounds
25g/1oz/2 tbsp dried prawns/shrimp
45ml/3 tbsp groundnut/peanut oil
2 garlic cloves, crushed
30ml/2 tbsp light soy sauce
5ml/1 tsp ground black pepper

1 To make the filling, slice the jicama rounds into thin strips, then wash and drain well. Soak the dried prawns in warm water for 15 minutes, then crush with a mortar and pestle.

2 Heat the oil in a wok or heavy pan and fry the garlic for 30 seconds. Add the jicama, soy sauce, pepper, dried prawns and 200ml/7fl oz/scant 1 cup water. Cook over a medium heat for 20 minutes, or until almost dry – the jicama should be soft but not mushy. Drain off the excess juices if necessary. Remove from the heat and leave to cool.

3 Put the wheat starch or rice flour in a large pan (preferably non-stick) with 25g/1oz/¼ cup cornflour and gradually stir in the boiling water. Keep stirring over a low heat until the dough is smooth, then remove from the heat.

4 Add the remaining cornflour and the oil. Add a little more water, if necessary, as you work the dough, until it becomes slightly elastic and moist.

5 Once it is cool enough to handle, transfer the dough to a lightly floured board and knead well, punching it occasionally to make it very light.

6 Shape the dough into a long roll about 5cm/2in in diameter. Divide into 10 pieces about 2.5cm/1in thick and flatten each with a rolling pin until it is about 5mm/¼in thick.

7 Place 1 heaped tablespoonful of filling slightly off-centre on each dough circle. Fold over the dough to make a half-moon shape and moisten the edges. Pinch to seal the edges. Trim off the excess dough and crimp the edges with the tines of a fork.

8 Place the dumplings on a lightly oiled plate and transfer to a steamer placed over simmering water. Steam for 30 minutes.

9 Serve warm with a thick, sweet soy sauce.

Cook's Tips

- It's important that the filling is quite dry, as too much moisture can cause the dough skin to burst as they steam.
- Sweet soy sauce is a specific type of sauce sold widely and also known as kicap (or kecap) manis, which is widely used in Malaysian and Indonesian cooking.

PORK & CABBAGE DUMPLINGS

These dumplings are Hubei staples that are eaten as snacks. Unlike other dumplings, they are usually made with self-raising flour and dry yeast. The filling is a mild blend of fried minced pork and cabbage flavoured with pepper, garlic and soy sauce.

MAKES 12 DUMPLINGS

200g/7oz/1¾ cups self-raising/self-rising flour, plus extra for dusting
15g/½oz/1 tsp easy bake/rapid-rise yeast
pinch of salt
5ml/1 tsp caster/superfine sugar
120ml/4fl oz/½ cup warm water

FOR THE FILLING

75g/3oz white cabbage leaves
30ml/2 tbsp groundnut/peanut oil
2 garlic cloves, crushed
90g/3½oz/scant ½ cup minced/ground pork
30ml/2 tbsp dark soy sauce
2.5ml/½ tsp ground black pepper
2.5ml/½ tsp caster/superfine sugar
1.5ml/¼ tsp salt

1 Sift the flour into a bowl and stir in the yeast, salt and sugar. Make a well and pour in the water. Stir to form a dough, then knead for 10 minutes on a floured surface. Return to the bowl, cover and leave in a warm place to rise for 30–40 minutes, until doubled in bulk. Gently turn the dough over to deflate it, then cover and leave for a further 15 minutes.

2 Meanwhile, make the filling. Fill a pan with boiling water and plunge in the cabbage for 45 seconds–1 minute, until just limp. Drain, then squeeze to remove excess moisture. Finely chop the cabbage.

3 Heat the oil in a wok or pan over a high heat and fry the garlic for 30 seconds. Add the pork and cabbage, and fry for 1 minute. Add the soy sauce, pepper, sugar, salt and 100ml/3½fl oz/ scant ½ cup water, then cook for 3 minutes, or until the filling is nearly dry. Spread the filling on to a plate to cool completely.

4 Press out the dough into a rectangle on a floured surface. Roll it up tightly into a log about 5cm/2in in diameter, then cut into 12 slices. Dust a slice with flour and roll it out into a round 9cm/3½in in diameter, making the edges slightly thinner than the centre.

5 Place a heaped teaspoonful of filling in the centre of the round and bring up the sides to enclose the filling, ruching and gathering up the edge as you rotate the dumpling in your palm. Pinch the top tightly to seal, and pinch off the excess dough. Repeat.

6 Cut 12 5cm/2in squares of baking parchment. Place each dumpling on one, then transfer to a steamer over simmering water. Steam over a high heat for 15 minutes.

WESTERN CHINA

FISH & SHELLFISH

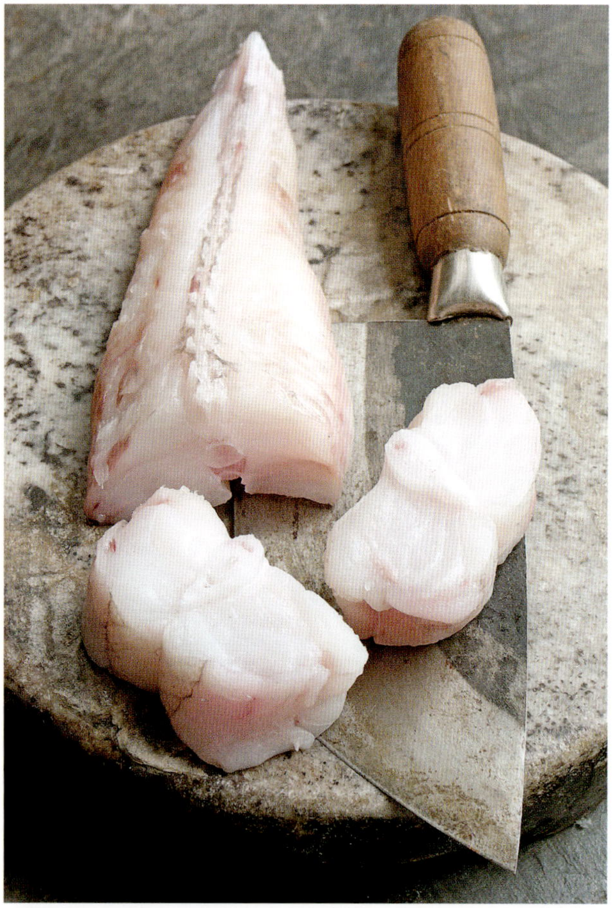

SPICY SQUID & BRAISED FISH

Western Chinese cooks are skilled at making the most of flavourful local fish. Although some farmed fish from inland lakes and paddy fields can be often tainted with the scent of mud, they are nevertheless used by adept chefs: the fish are simply left to swim in tanks of clean water before they are prepared.

The region's humidity affects many of the cooking styles, and the preservation of food takes top priority. Salted, dried and pickled aromatics and vegetables are used as seasonings for seafood. When combined with sesame oil and fermented soy bean sauces they achieve the piquant flavours for which the area is renowned.

Shellfish come into their own in the cooking of this region: prawns and shrimp are marinated in wine, braised, stir-fried or even wrapped in rice paper before being deep-fried; and squid and octopus are drenched in fiery chilli sauce. Regional cooks embrace a medley of flavours, including hot, sweet, sour and salty, and often all at once. The foods of Sichuan, Hunan and Hubei are well documented for their fiery promise.

Excess fish and shellfish are often processed into cakes and balls, and steamed or fried as main courses or snacks. Small fish like anchovies and whitebait are dried and stored for the winter months, and are used frequently as stock ingredients, due to their rich flavour. Chrysanthemum Fish Hot Pot is a rich mix of intoxicating flavours perfumed with chrysanthemum petals and leaves, and uses several varieties of fish and shellfish.

CHRYSANTHEMUM FISH HOT POT

Autumn-flowering chrysanthemum leaves are used to perfume this glorious, richly flavoured seafood dish, which is commonly served in that season throughout western China. The bitesize pieces of food are traditionally cooked in simmering stock at the table in a charcoal-heated fire pot (huo kuo). As burning charcoal is not suitable indoors, use an electric fire pot or steamboat instead, or a large fondue pan over a burner.

SERVES 8–10

- 90g/3½oz fish maw (dried fish bladder)
- 10 dried Chinese mushrooms, soaked in warm water for 30 minutes
- 200g/7oz cod or halibut fillet, thinly sliced
- 20 Chinese fish balls
- 2 large Chinese fish cakes, sliced
- 10 raw tiger prawns/jumbo shrimp, shelled
- 350g/12oz pack silken tofu
- 90g/3½oz chrysanthemum leaves (tong ho)
- 90g/3½oz mangetouts/snow peas
- 2 litres/3½ pints/8 cups meat stock
- 5ml/1 tsp ground Sichuan peppercorns
- 5ml/1 tsp salt

FOR THE DIPS

- 60ml/4 tbsp Xinkiang black vinegar
- 15ml/1 tbsp crushed garlic
- 15ml/1 tbsp finely grated ginger
- 5ml/1 tsp sesame oil
- chilli sauce
- soy sauce

1 Soak the fish maw in hot water for about 10 minutes, until it swells. Drain and cut into bitesize pieces. Thinly slice the softened mushrooms. Put all the raw fish ingredients and the mushrooms, tofu, chrysanthemum leaves and mangetouts on to small plates or in bowls and arrange around a fire pot or steamboat on the table.

2 To make the dips, mix the black vinegar with the garlic, ginger and sesame oil. Spoon into a small bowl. Put the chilli sauce and soy sauce into small bowls and place on the table. Heat the fire pot or steamboat at the table.

3 Pour the stock into a large pan and bring to the boil, then carefully transfer to the fire pot or steamboat and season with the Sichuan pepper and the salt. Keep the stock simmering at the table.

4 Each diner takes morsels of food from the plates or bowls and either spears them on to a long fork or puts them into a brass wire spoon. The food is then submerged in the boiling stock until cooked, then eaten with the accompanying dips.

5 When all the food has been cooked, serve the rich stock in bowls as a soup.

Cook's Tips

• You can use water instead of stock, if you like. This will give you a lighter stock, but it will still have a good flavour from the ingredients that have been cooked in it.

• Fish balls, fish cakes and fresh chrysanthemum leaves can be bought from Chinese stores. Chrysanthemum petals, due to their delicate nature, are rarely imported from China.

CLAY-POT FISH STEW

Monkfish, mushrooms, tofu and mangetouts are cooked in a sauce strongly flavoured with garlic, hoisin and oyster sauces and served in a traditional clay pot, which is used throughout China to keep the food beautifully hot. The dish will first be cooked in a pan and then transferred to the preheated clay pot, then covered with its lid. If you don't have a clay pot, you can use a flameproof casserole heated on the top of the stove or in the oven.

SERVES 4

350g/12oz monkfish (or other firm-fleshed fish), membrane removed
8 dried Chinese mushrooms, soaked for 30 minutes in warm water
30ml/2 tbsp vegetable oil
3 garlic cloves, crushed
8 pieces of fried tofu
30ml/2 tbsp Chinese wine
15ml/1 tbsp hoisin sauce
30ml/2 tbsp oyster sauce
16 mangetouts/snow peas
10ml/2 tsp cornflour/cornstarch
salt and ground white pepper, to taste
fresh coriander/cilantro sprigs, to garnish

Cook's Tip

Clay pots are simple cooking vessels that are not made to last a lifetime, so be careful not to overheat it or it might crack.

1 Preheat a clay pot or flameproof casserole on the stove for a few minutes or in the oven heated to 200°C/400°F/Gas 6 for 10 minutes. Cut the fish into 2.5cm/1in chunks and slice the mushrooms.

2 Heat the oil in a wok over a medium heat, then add the garlic and fry for 1 minute. Add the mushrooms and fried tofu, then stir-fry for 2 minutes.

3 Add the wine, hoisin sauce and oyster sauce and fry for 1 minute, then add 200ml/7fl oz/scant 1 cup water and bring to a simmer.

4 Add the fish and simmer gently, stirring frequently, for 2–3 minutes, or until it is just cooked. Add the mangetouts, stir and cook for 1 minute more.

5 Put the cornflour in a bowl and blend with 15ml/1 tbsp water, then add to the wok and cook for a few seconds until the sauce boils and thickens. Season with salt and white pepper.

6 Preheat a clay pot or flameproof casserole over a direct flame for a few minutes or in a hot oven for 10 minutes. Transfer to the clay pot and serve, garnished with fresh coriander.

BRAISED GROUPER IN CHILLI SAUCE

Grouper is highly prized for its exquisite flesh and crisp, flavourful skin when fried, as here. It belongs to a large family of fish found widely in warm waters, especially along coral reefs, but they also thrive in temperate climes, in deep oceans and river estuaries.

1 Using a sharp knife, score deep cuts across the thickest part of the fish, then dust with cornflour and shake off the excess. If you do not have a wok large enough to hold a whole fish, cut the fish into two pieces down the middle.

2 Heat the vegetable oil in a wok or deep-fryer, then add the fish in batches if necessary and deep-fry until golden brown. Set aside.

3 To make the sauce, heat the oil in a large wok or frying pan, then add the ginger and spring onion and fry for 1 minute. Add the chilli bean paste, sugar, chillies and soy sauce, then fry for 30 seconds.

4 Add the wine and 300ml/½ pint/1¼ cups water, then bring to the boil. Lower the fried fish into the sauce to simmer for 2 minutes. The initial coating of cornflour will fuse with the sauce to thicken it.

5 Transfer the cooked fish pieces to a serving platter, arranging them to make the whole fish, and sprinkle with shredded spring onions or fresh coriander before serving.

Variation

If you prefer not to deep-fry the fish it can instead be cooked in the sauce for 8 minutes, or until it is cooked through. This will give a different texture to the fish.

SERVES 4

2 whole grouper (675g/1½lb total weight), cleaned and fins removed
60ml/4 tbsp cornflour/cornstarch
vegetable oil, for deep-frying

FOR THE SAUCE
30ml/2 tbsp vegetable oil
30ml/2 tbsp grated fresh root ginger
1 spring onion/scallion, chopped
45ml/3 tbsp chilli bean paste (dou banjiang)
5ml/1 tsp caster/superfine sugar
2 fresh green chillies, seeded and sliced
15ml/1 tbsp light soy sauce
30ml/2 tbsp Chinese wine
shredded spring onion and mooli/daikon decorations (see Cook's Tip), to garnish

Cook's Tip

You can buy decorative Chinese vegetable cutters to make pretty mooli garnishes.

BRAISED FISH WITH GARLIC

Being closely affiliated with Sichuan, Hunan cooking has much in common with her sister province and is often even more fiery. The spiciest variety of chilli that grows here is a fingertip-sized pod called 'to the sky', as it grows facing upward. Shaoxing wine, Sichuan pepper, ginger and spring onions make up the classic marinade described as xian, which defies translation – it is indefinable and utterly intoxicating.

SERVES 4

- 2 whole snapper (675g/1½lb total weight), cleaned and fins removed
- 30ml/2 tbsp cornflour/cornstarch
- 120ml/4fl oz/½cup vegetable oil
- 8 garlic cloves, halved
- 25g/1oz fresh root ginger, thinly sliced
- 2.5ml/½ tsp Sichuan peppercorns
- 2 spring onions/scallions, cut into 5cm/2in lengths
- 30ml/2 tbsp Shaoxing wine or dry sherry
- 15ml/1 tbsp dark soy sauce
- 10ml/2 tsp rice wine or vinegar
- 5ml/1 tsp caster/superfine sugar
- 2 fresh red chillies, finely chopped
- salt, to taste
- shredded spring onions, to garnish

1 With a very sharp knife, make a few parallel slashes through the thickest part of the fish on both sides. Dust the snapper evenly with cornflour, shaking off the excess.

2 Heat the oil in a large wok or frying pan and shallow-fry the fish over a medium heat until well browned, turning once. (The fish will not be fully cooked on the inside.) Set aside.

3 Drain off all but 15ml/1 tbsp oil from the pan. Add the garlic, ginger and peppercorns to the oil in the pan, then increase the heat to high and fry for 1 minute.

4 Add the spring onions, wine or sherry, soy sauce, rice wine or vinegar, sugar and 400ml/14fl oz/1⅔ cups water. Bring to the boil and cook for 2–3 minutes to reduce the liquid and intensify the flavours.

5 Return the fried fish to the pan, and reduce the heat to medium. Partially cover the pan and braise the fish for 3 minutes. Turn the fish over, add the chillies and cook for a further 2 minutes, until the sauce has reduced and thickened and the fish are cooked through.

6 Season the sauce with salt to taste and serve immediately, garnished with shredded spring onions.

TOFU FISH IN A SPICY SAUCE

For the Chinese, texture is every bit as important as flavour and colour, and is often described as kou kan, which is loosely translated as 'mouth feel'. In this dish, kou kan is highlighted in the contrasting textures of soft tofu with the crispness of the fried fish combined in a hot chilli sauce.

SERVES 4

- 75ml/5 tbsp vegetable oil
- 200g/7oz firm tofu, cut into 2cm/¾in cubes
- 600g/1lb 5oz monkfish or any firm-fleshed fish, membrane or skin removed, cut into 2.5cm/1in cubes
- 2 garlic cloves, crushed
- 15ml/1 tbsp yellow bean sauce
- 15ml/1 tbsp dark soy sauce
- 3 fresh red chillies, seeded and sliced
- 5ml/1 tsp caster/superfine sugar
- 150ml/¼ pint/½ cup water
- 1 sliced spring onion/scallion, to garnish

1 Heat 60ml/4 tbsp oil in a wok over a high heat. When very hot, add the tofu cubes and fry, turning frequently, until well browned. Lift out using a slotted spoon and drain on kitchen paper.

2 Reduce the heat to medium and add the fish to the remaining oil. Fry for 4 minutes, gently turning the cubes a few times, until they are golden all over and almost cooked. Transfer to a plate and set aside.

3 Wipe the wok using kitchen paper and add the remaining oil. Add the garlic and fry for 1 minute, then add yellow bean sauce, soy sauce, chillies and sugar, and fry for 1 minute.

4 Add the water and simmer for 1 minute, then return the fish and tofu to the wok. Cover and cook for 1 minute more, until the fish is cooked through. Serve immediately, sprinkled with spring onion.

Cook's Tip

For an extra crunchy texture add a handful of mangetouts/snow peas or 30ml/2 tbsp shredded cooked bamboo shoots in step 4.

FIVE-SPICE CARP

SERVES 4

- 1 large carp (about 600g/1lb 5oz), cleaned and fins removed
- 30ml/2 tbsp cornflour/cornstarch
- 30ml/2 tbsp vegetable oil, plus extra for deep-frying
- 25g/1oz fresh root ginger, chopped
- 15ml/1 tbsp sesame oil
- 30ml/2 tbsp dark soy sauce
- 2.5ml/½ tsp caster/superfine sugar
- 30ml/2 tbsp Shaoxing wine or dry sherry
- 5ml/1 tsp rice wine or vinegar
- 2.5ml/½ tsp five-spice powder
- chopped spring onions/scallions and fresh coriander/cilantro leaves, to garnish

Carp is a favourite freshwater fish often used in Chinese cooking, and in this Sichuan dish it is imbued with ginger and the quintessential Chinese seasoning, five-spice powder, which gives the dish its pronounced flavour.

1 Coat the carp with cornflour and shake off the excess. Heat the oil for deep-frying in a wok or deep-fryer to 190°C/375°F and add the carp. Deep-fry until crisp. Lift out and drain on kitchen paper.

2 Heat a large frying pan or the cleaned wok with the 30ml/2 tbsp vegetable oil and fry the ginger for 1 minute. Add the sesame oil, soy sauce and sugar and stir for 30 seconds. Stir in the wine or sherry, rice wine or vinegar, five-spice powder and 75ml/5 tbsp water.

3 Put the fish into the pan, spooning the sauce over liberally. Simmer for 1–2 minutes, or until well heated through. Serve hot, garnished with chopped spring onions and whole fresh coriander leaves.

SWEET-AND-SOUR CARP

Such is its popularity, every province, town, and even family has its own version of sweet-and-sour sauce; this universal sauce of perfectly balanced contrasting flavours is quintessential to the culinary heritage of China and to many of its dishes. In Chengdu restaurants, sweet-and-sour sauce with carp is considered to be the masterpiece, using the Sichuan combination that includes Shaoxing wine (the more subtle Cantonese version uses a blend of fruity and sour flavours from plum and vinegar). This recipe is for a whole fish but tastes just as wonderful with fillets, if you prefer to use those.

SERVES 4

- 1 large carp (about 600g/1lb 5oz), cleaned, or same weight of fillets
- 75g/3oz/½ cup cornflour/cornstarch
- 3 garlic cloves, sliced
- 15ml/1 tbsp shredded fresh root ginger
- 2 spring onions/scallions, cut into 5cm/2in lengths
- vegetable oil, for deep-frying

FOR THE MARINADE

- 30ml/2 tbsp Shaoxing wine or dry sherry
- 2.5ml/½ tsp salt
- 1 garlic clove, crushed
- 5ml/1 tsp finely grated ginger

FOR THE SAUCE

- 15ml/1 tbsp light soy sauce
- 60ml/4 tbsp caster/superfine sugar
- 15ml/1 tbsp Shaoxing wine
- 30ml/2 tbsp Xinkiang black vinegar
- 15ml/1 tbsp sesame oil
- pinch of salt

1 Using a sharp knife, make deep gashes into the thickest part of the fish, then put the fish into a shallow dish. Put the marinade ingredients in a bowl and mix well together. Rub liberally over the outside and inside of the fish, then set aside for 20 minutes.

2 Lift the fish from the marinade and then coat it with the cornflour. Heat the vegetable oil for deep-frying in a wok or deep-fryer and fry the fish until the skin is golden brown and crisp. Lift out and drain on kitchen paper.

3 Fry the sliced garlic and shredded ginger in the remaining oil in the wok or deep fryer until golden brown, then drain.

4 Put the sweet-and-sour sauce ingredients in a bowl and mix well, then pour into a small pan and cook over a low heat until the sugar has dissolved.

5 Transfer the sauce to a clean wok and add the fried garlic, shredded ginger and spring onions. Add the fried fish and turn once or twice so that it is well coated in the sauce. The sauce will thicken from the cornflour coating.

6 Serve the fish with the sauce poured over.

Variation

To give the sauce a fruity flavour, use 30ml/2 tbsp plum sauce instead of the sugar.

FISH IN HOT SWEET-AND-SOUR SAUCE

Sweet-and-sour sauce is given some fire here with the addition of the rich red chilli bean paste, called dou banjiang, which is characteristic of many Sichuan dishes and found in every kitchen in the region. The best dou banjiang is said to come from the town of Pixian, outside Chengdu, but most grocery stores sell a variety of brands. It's salty and hot, and a little of it goes a long way – but it's just right with crispy cod or halibut.

SERVES 4

675g/1½lb cod, halibut or monkfish fillets, or other firm-fleshed white fish, skin or membrane removed
60ml/4 tbsp potato flour or any starchy flour
vegetable oil, for deep-frying
25g/1oz fresh root ginger, cut into fine strips

FOR THE SAUCE

30ml/2 tbsp chilli bean paste (dou banjiang)
10ml/2 tsp caster/superfine sugar
30ml/2 tbsp rice wine or vinegar
15ml/1 tbsp light soy sauce
1 leek, thinly sliced

1 Cut the fish into slices about 1cm/½in thick, then pat them dry with kitchen paper. Dust the slices lightly with potato flour.

2 Heat the vegetable oil in a wok over a medium heat or in a deep-fryer, then add the fish, in batches if necessary, and deep-fry until golden brown, about 2–3 minutes per batch. Lift out and drain on kitchen paper, then set aside.

3 In the same oil, deep-fry the ginger strips for several seconds, until light brown. Drain on kitchen paper and set aside.

4 To make the sauce, put the chilli bean paste in a small bowl and blend in the sugar, rice wine or vinegar, soy sauce and 250ml/8fl oz/1 cup water. Pour into a wok or frying pan and bring to a simmer over a medium heat.

5 Add the sliced leek and cook for 1–2 minutes, or until it is tender but still crisp.

6 Add the fish and stir gently to mix well. Garnish with the fried ginger and serve immediately.

Variation

Seed and slice 2 fresh red chillies and add to the sauce with the leeks for extra fire, if you like.

CRISPY HOT WHITEBAIT

Sichuan provincial towns and villages are criss-crossed with rivers, and the people who live there can often be seen with small nets catching whatever happens to be swimming by. Not surprisingly, then, freshwater fish of all kinds, usually small fish and shrimps, are commonly deep-fried and sold as snacks. Here, the fried fish are given a spicy seasoning using Sichuan peppercorns, chillies and ginger.

SERVES 4

600g/1lb 5oz whitebait
vegetable oil, for deep-frying
90g/3½oz plain/all-purpose flour
15ml/1 tbsp potato starch
finely chopped spring onions/ scallions, to garnish

FOR THE SEASONINGS
2.5ml/½ tsp Sichuan peppercorns
5ml/1 tsp coarsely ground dried chillies
2.5ml/½ tsp caster/superfine sugar
5ml/1 tsp sesame oil
2.5ml/½ tsp salt
15ml/1 tbsp fresh root ginger, grated and ground to a paste

Cook's Tip

In Europe, whitebait usually refers to young herring that are thumb-sized. Whitebait are tender and edible and the entire fish is eaten including head, fins and gut. You might also be able to find the Singaporean version, called ikan bilis, in some Asian stores.

1 If the whitebait are frozen, thaw and drain them thoroughly in a sieve or strainer. Pat very dry with kitchen paper – if they are at all damp they will not crisp up when fried.

2 Put the Sichuan peppercorns for the seasoning in a dry pan and toast for 1 minute. Grind to a powder using a mortar and pestle, then transfer to a small bowl. Coarsely grind the chillies and add to the peppercorns. Add the remaining seasonings and stir until well blended. Set aside.

3 Heat the vegetable oil for deep-frying in a wok over a medium heat or in a deep-fryer.

4 Put the flour and potato starch into a large plastic bag and shake to combine, then add the whitebait and shake well to coat the fish completely. Transfer the floured whitebait to a strainer and shake gently to remove the excess flour.

5 Deep-fry the whitebait in batches for about 1 minute, until crisp and golden brown. Drain on kitchen paper and keep warm.

6 Sprinkle the seasoning over the whitebait and toss well to coat. Garnish with spring onions and serve immediately.

DRAGON PHOENIX EELS

The phoenix and dragon are both rich with symbolism and are favourite metaphors for certain types of food. The phoenix, which represents the female, is likened to the chicken and symbolises rebirth, while prawns and fish represent the male and are symbolic of the dragon. In this Hubei dish of eels and chicken, these metaphors also serve to emphasise the Chinese gift for combining seafood and poultry in one creation. Eels are usually bought while still alive, as their flavour deteriorates rapidly once dead. They are difficult to prepare, so you can ask your fishmonger to do this for you.

SERVES 4

30ml/2 tbsp groundnut/ peanut oil
2 spring onions/scallions, white part only, chopped
20g/¾oz fresh root ginger, shredded
1 cube red fermented tofu (tofu ru)
450g/1lb brown eels, cut into thick strips
300g/11oz skinless chicken breast, sliced into thick strips
30ml/2 tbsp oyster sauce
5ml/1 tsp caster/superfine sugar
30ml/2 tbsp sesame oil
30ml/2 tbsp Shaoxing wine or dry sherry
12 mangetouts/snow peas
2 spring onions, chopped
fresh coriander/cilantro leaves, to garnish

1 Heat the oil in a wok and fry the spring onions and shredded ginger for 1 minute. Lightly crush the fermented tofu and add to the pan. Fry for 30 seconds.

2 Add the eel and chicken strips and stir-fry for 2 minutes, then add the oyster sauce, sugar, sesame oil, wine or sherry, and mangetouts. Stir-fry for a further 2 minutes.

3 Add 200ml/7fl oz/scant 1 cup water, bring quickly to the boil and cook for 5 minutes. Add the spring onions, then stir for 20 seconds.

4 Serve immediately, garnished with fresh coriander.

JADE PRAWNS CHENGDU-STYLE

In this Chengdu dish, fried bright pink prawns contrast with the brilliant green of peas – the jade of the title – cooked with Shaoxing wine and ham. Sichuan cooking reaches its peak in the provincial capital, Chengdu, the centre of the province's culture and cuisine with a history that goes back 2,500 years.

SERVES 4

1 egg white
2.5ml/½ tsp salt
450g/1lb raw large prawns/jumbo shrimp or tiger prawns, shelled
15ml/1 tbsp and 10ml/2 tsp cornflour/cornstarch
vegetable oil, for deep-frying
15ml/1 tbsp groundnut/peanut oil
2 garlic cloves, crushed
2 spring onions/scallions, cut into 2cm/¾in lengths
40g/1½oz Hunan or any dry-cured ham, finely diced
50g/2oz/½ cup peas, thawed if frozen
10ml/2 tsp Sichuan pepper
30ml/2 tbsp Shaoxing wine or dry sherry

1 In a large bowl, beat the egg white with salt until almost stiff, then add the prawns and sprinkle over the 15ml/1 tbsp cornflour. Mix well, then cover and set aside to marinate for 15 minutes.

2 Heat the vegetable oil in a wok over a medium heat or in a deep-fryer. Using a slotted spoon, plunge the prawns into the oil for 20 seconds – they should barely sizzle. Drain on kitchen paper.

3 In a clean wok, heat the groundnut oil over a high heat and fry the garlic for 15 seconds. Add the spring onions, ham, peas and prawns with the Sichuan pepper and Shaoxing wine or sherry, and stir-fry vigorously for 1 minute.

4 Blend the 10ml/2 tsp cornflour with 45ml/3 tbsp water, then add to the wok and continue to stir until the juices thicken. Serve.

SERVES 4

450g/1lb raw large prawns/jumbo shrimp
45ml/3 tbsp mei kuei lu wine
5ml/1 tsp caster/superfine sugar
15ml/1 tbsp groundnut/peanut oil
1 leek, white part only, thinly sliced
1 spring onion/scallion, chopped
1 green/bell pepper, chopped
1 small celery stick, thinly sliced
15ml/1 tbsp light soy sauce
5ml/1 tsp sesame oil

Cook's Tip

In Sichuan they don't cook the prawns; instead, the wine in the marinade pickles them, then they are tossed with the fried vegetables before serving.

WINE-MARINATED PRAWNS

Large prawns are marinated in wine and sugar then quickly fried with leek, green pepper and celery in this delicate dish. Of all the Chinese wines, the Sichuan-brewed wu liang ye (five-grained wine) is best to bring out the richness of the prawns. It is an intensely flavoured liquor made from sorghum grains, glutinous rice, barley, wheat and corn and is a heady 60 per cent proof. However, it is also expensive and not easy to find except in major Chinese supermarkets, so the next best thing is the rose-flavoured wine, mei kuei lu, from northern China.

1 Put the prawns in a bowl and add the wine and sugar. Cover, then leave to marinate in the refrigerator for 20 minutes.

2 Heat the oil in a wok over a high heat. Fry the leek, spring onion, green pepper and celery for 1 minute.

3 Add the prawns and their marinade to the wok and stir-fry vigorously for 1 minute, then add the soy sauce and sesame oil. Cook for 1 minute, stirring, then serve immediately.

PRAWNS IN SICHUAN PEPPER SAUCE

There is nothing quite like cooking prawns in their shells to retain their excellent flavour, and they go very well tossed in a sauce of Sichuan peppercorns. Although most people think of wok cooking as stir-frying, Sichuanese cooks use the wok for many other cooking techniques besides this. Dry-frying is the method used here, called gan pian, in which small pieces of food are stirred vigorously in very little oil until nearly dry.

1 Using kitchen scissors, trim the prawns by snipping off the feelers and the pointed top of the head just behind the eyes. Wash the prawns, drain well and pat very dry with kitchen paper.

2 Put the Sichuan peppercorns in a dry pan and toast for 1 minute. Grind to a powder using a mortar and pestle. Set aside.

3 Heat the oil in a wok over a high heat. When it starts to smoke, add the prawns and fry, stirring vigorously for 1–2 minutes, or until they are only just pink.

4 Add the garlic, ginger and Sichuan pepper, and cook, moving the ingredients backwards and forwards constantly, using a wooden spoon, for 1–2 minutes more, or until the prawns are well coated with the aromatics and cooked through.

5 Add the salt, sesame oil and sugar to the wok and toss together for 15 seconds. The finished prawns should be dry, slightly shiny with oil and speckled with the seasonings. Serve immediately.

SERVES 4

500g/1¼lb medium prawns/shrimp, in their shells
5ml/1 tsp Sichuan peppercorns
30ml/2 tbsp groundnut/peanut oil
2 garlic cloves, crushed
25g/1oz fresh root ginger, finely grated
4ml/¾ tsp salt
5ml/1 tsp sesame oil
2.5ml/½ tsp caster/superfine sugar

Variation

For a quick version of this dish, you can marinate the prawns or shrimp in the seasonings mixed with the sesame oil and sugar, then drain them thoroughly. Heat the wok with the groundnut oil and add the prawns. Cook for 4–5 minutes, or until pink.

PAPER-WRAPPED PRAWNS

Unlike the inedible paper used for a similar Cantonese dish, the paper used for these parcels is completely edible. Sold as 'wafer pastry' in Chinese supermarkets, it is very delicate and needs deft and quick handling. The prawns are first seasoned with lime juice and oyster sauce then wrapped in the pastry and immediately fried to make them superbly crisp and light. Sesame oil is added to the vegetable oil to give a nutty fragrance.

SERVES 4

16 tiger prawns/jumbo shrimp, peeled
15ml/1 tbsp oyster sauce
5ml/1 tsp lime juice
5ml/1 tsp caster/superfine sugar
5ml/1 tsp ground black pepper
15ml/1 tbsp cornflour/cornstarch
vegetable oil, for deep-frying
30ml/2 tbsp sesame oil
16 or more Chinese wafer pastry sheets

FOR THE CHILLI DIP
3–4 red chillies, finely chopped
60–75ml/4–5 tbsp Kao Liang vinegar or sherry
a pinch of salt

Variation

Instead of the pastry wrappers, coat the prawns liberally with cornflour or tapioca flour, then drop them into the hot oil. They will have a thin, crisp coating that bears a faint resemblance to the wrappers.

1 Make a shallow cut down the centre of the curved back of each prawn. Pull out the black vein with a cocktail stick, toothpick or your fingers, then rinse the prawn thoroughly and pat dry. Make a deep slit down the underside to open up the prawns and give them a better shape. Put them in a shallow dish.

2 Put the oyster sauce in a small bowl and mix in the lime juice, sugar, pepper and cornflour. Sprinkle this seasoning over the prawns and turn to coat.

3 To make the chilli sauce, grind the chillies in a mortar and pestle or coffee grinder until very fine. Add the vinegar and salt, then stir to mix.

4 Heat the vegetable oil in a wok or deep-fryer, then add the sesame oil.

5 Remove a pastry sheet carefully and place a prawn in the middle. Fold the pastry up, drawing all sides toward the centre and press the edges together to seal in the prawn. This is the same method used for making wontons. Occasionally, the moistness of the marinade might render the pastry a little mushy. When this happens, wrap both the prawn and the paper in an additional paper.

6 Drop the pastry-wrapped prawn into the oil. Remove with a slotted spoon as soon as it turns light brown. The pastry will firm up as it browns in the hot oil; be careful not to let the parcel become scorched. Wrap and cook the remaining prawn parcels as you make them; do not pre-wrap the prawns and leave them to fry in one go, as they will quickly become soggy.

7 Drain on kitchen paper and serve hot with the chilli dip.

Cook's Tip

So long as you work quickly and add the prawns to the hot oil immediately, the seasoning won't have a chance to seep through the pastry and make it soggy.

CHILLI SQUID

This member of the vast cephalopod family is an important seafood and is eaten widely in most of coastal China. Squid can range in size from 2.5cm/1in long to giants of enormous size, but the best size for eating are those about 7.5cm/3in long, which are available frozen in many Chinese and South-east Asian stores. Squid cooks in moments and is delicious stir-fried in a chilli, garlic and yellow bean sauce.

SERVES 4

200g/7oz squid
5ml/1 tsp cornflour/cornstarch
3 fresh red chillies, seeded and roughly chopped
2 garlic cloves, crushed
15ml/1 tbsp yellow bean sauce
5ml/1 tsp caster/superfine sugar
30ml/2 tbsp groundnut/peanut oil
½ leek, thinly sliced in rounds

1 To prepare the squid, pull the tentacles and head free of the body sac. Cut across the tentacles just below the eyes, and discard the eyes and everything above them. Pop out and discard the mouth from inside the tentacles. Cut any longer tentacles into smaller pieces. Slice down the back of the body sac and flatten out. Remove the transparent quill and any fatty, spongy matter. With a sharp knife, slice down the back of the body sac of the squid and flatten out. Score shallow parallel cuts in the flesh, cutting only halfway through. Turn the sac 90 degrees and make another series of cuts to form a grid pattern. Slice into large pieces about 4cm/1½in across. Wash all the cut squid, including the tentacles and wings, then drain.

2 Put the cornflour in a small bowl and gradually blend in 60ml/4 tbsp of cold water. Set aside.

3 Put the chillies and garlic in a mortar and grind to a fine paste using a pestle. Transfer to a small bowl and mix with the yellow bean sauce and sugar.

4 Heat the oil in a wok over a high heat and fry this paste for 45 seconds, or until fragrant.

5 Add the sliced leek and stir-fry for 1 minute, then add the squid and fry for 15 seconds. Stir in the cornflour mixture and cook for 1 minute, or until the squid begins to curl up and the sauce has thickened slightly. Serve.

Cook's Tips

• You can of course ask a fishmonger to prepare the squid for you, if you like.

• Do not overcook squid as it will become rubbery. As soon as it begins to curl up, it is ready.

WESTERN CHINA
POULTRY

SUCCULENT CHICKEN & CRISPY DUCK

The Chinese were among the earliest peoples to domesticate fowl and, in some rural farmhouses, you can see an exotic, black-skinned breed of chicken covered by wispy white feathers. Even today, people regard this breed as having special nutritional qualities for new mothers to regain their strength after childbirth.

Many chicken dishes achieve exquisite flavour from the aromatics, wine and chillies that are used in cooking. Spicy chicken dishes such as Kung Po Chicken and Chilli Chicken are perfect examples of supremely tasty western Chinese cooking. Kung Po is attributed to a governor of Sichuan in the late Qing dynasty, Gong Bao. Interestingly, its name had to be changed when it incurred the wrath of Cultural Revolution radicals, but today, you can find Kung Po sauce in supermarkets all over the world.

Another method of cooking chicken is to braise it in rice wine or vinegar. This makes a lovely winter warmer when it is teamed with typical local produce like cloud ears, bamboo pith and even tripe. Hubei chefs are famously fond of using garlic, which they do to an extent that elsewhere might send people scurrying. Shaanxi is known for its distinctive method of dry-frying, best manifest in dry-fried Hot-and-Sour chicken.

Duck is cooked with pride and a medley of flavourings in western China, and Sichuan is the birthplace of the world-famous and delicious Aromatic Crispy Duck, which has even nudged Peking duck into second place in popularity.

KUNG PO CHICKEN

This dish is derived from the name of a late Qing Dynasty official, Ding Baozhen (1820–86), who became Gong Bao, or palatial guardian, and was given the title Kung Pao, or Kung Po. The chicken is cooked with the authentic flavourings of Sichuan peppercorns and fresh, boiled peanuts. Purists would use authentic Sichuan chillies, which are small and fiery, but here we use chilli bean paste, dou banjiang, to give the dish its heat.

SERVES 4

- 300g/11oz skinless chicken breasts
- 15ml/1 tbsp cornflour/cornstarch
- 30ml/2 tbsp Shaoxing wine or dry sherry
- 15ml/1 tbsp light soy sauce
- 15ml/1 tbsp sesame oil
- 30ml/2 tbsp groundnut/peanut oil
- 2 garlic cloves, chopped
- 30ml/2 tbsp chopped fresh root ginger
- 15ml/1 tbsp Sichuan peppercorns, finely crushed
- 30ml/2 tbsp chilli bean paste (dou banjiang)
- 50g/2oz/⅓ cup boiled peanuts (see Cook's Tip)
- 30ml/2 tbsp soft dark brown sugar

1 Cut the chicken into 2.5cm/1in cubes. Put the cornflour in a bowl and blend with the wine or sherry, soy sauce and sesame oil. Add the chicken cubes to this mixture and toss to coat completely. Leave to marinate for 20 minutes.

2 Heat the oil in a wok and stir-fry the garlic and ginger for 40 seconds until golden brown. Add the peppercorns and chilli bean paste, and stir for 30 seconds until well mixed.

3 Add the chicken to the wok and continue to stir over a high heat for 3–4 minutes, or until the chicken is cooked and the sauce is reduced a little – the chicken should be fairly dry but succulent.

4 Stir in the boiled peanuts, sugar and 150ml/¼ pint/⅔ cup water, then continue to stir over a high heat until the mixture comes to the boil. Serve immediately.

Cook's Tips

- Although chilli bean paste (dou banjiang) is characteristic of Sichuan cooking, you can use normal chilli paste or sauce instead, if you like.
- Boiled peanuts are usually available in cans or jars in Chinese supermarkets. Alternatively, you can buy ordinary, shelled raw peanuts in their skins and boil them for 1 hour until soft.

GARLIC CHICKEN IN CHILLI OIL

This rich and fiery dish hails from Hubei and is strongly flavoured with fried garlic, against a backdrop of the intense chilli oil that is used throughout the western regions of China. It is hot and spicy, truly scrumptious. Use chicken thighs instead of breast meat for a more succulent flavour. Serve on a bed of rice.

1 Cut the chicken into small dice. Heat the oil in a wok over a medium heat and fry the garlic for 1–2 minutes, or until golden brown. Add the chicken pieces and stir-fry for 2 minutes, or until they turn opaque and are almost cooked through.

2 Add the chilli oil, sugar and soy sauce, then cook, stirring frequently, for 1–2 minutes, or until the chicken is cooked.

3 Add 100ml/3½fl oz/scant ½ cup water and the spring onions, then continue to stir-fry until the mixture is nearly dry. Serve with the boiled rice.

SERVES 4

450g/1lb boneless chicken thighs
45ml/3 tbsp groundnut/peanut oil
6 garlic cloves, sliced
15ml/1 tbsp chilli oil
5ml/1 tsp caster/superfine sugar
15ml/1 tbsp light soy sauce
2 spring onions/scallions, chopped
boiled rice, to serve

Variations

If you like your food hot, some Hunan versions also include a few large dried Sichuan chillies snipped into pieces and added at the same time as the chicken.

SERVES 4

200g/7oz bamboo shoot slices, drained and rinsed
450g/1lb skinless chicken breasts
30ml/2 tbsp groundnut/peanut oil
15ml/1 tbsp chopped Chinese celery leaves
15ml/1 tbsp sesame oil
15ml/1 tbsp yellow bean sauce
2.5ml/½ tsp caster/superfine sugar
15ml/1 tbsp light soy sauce, or to taste
5ml/1 tsp cornflour/cornstarch

Cook's Tip

Prepared bamboo shoots can be bought in vacuum packs. Because they never become mushy even when cooked for a long time, they can be added with the chicken.

CHICKEN WITH BAMBOO SHOOT

This classic dish from Yunnan, the southernmost province of western China, is simple to prepare and uses ingredients that are common throughout China: Chinese celery leaves, chicken, sesame oil and yellow bean sauce, which marry well with the strong flavour of bamboo shoots.

1 Soak the bamboo shoots in cold water for 10 minutes. Meanwhile, slice the chicken into strips about 2cm/¾in wide. Slice the soaked bamboo shoots into strips or leave as thin slices if they are small.

2 Heat the oil in a wok until you can see the barest hint of smoke curling up, then add the chicken and stir-fry for 1 minute.

3 Add the bamboo shoots and stir-fry for 1 minute. Add the celery leaves and cook, stirring, for 1 minute, then add the sesame oil, yellow bean sauce and sugar, and stir for 1 minute more. Taste and add soy sauce only if the dish requires further salting.

4 Blend the cornflour in 200ml/7fl oz/scant 1 cup water, then pour into the wok and cook, stirring, for 3 minutes, until the sauce is thick.

CHILLI CHICKEN

If Sichuan cooking comes in at 8 on the chilli scale of 1–10, Hunan dishes can top 11! This sister province, while leaning heavily on Sichuan culinary techniques, goes one better when adding the hot pod. Strangely though, this high-octane chicken dish does not scorch the tongue so much as tantalize it – the better to savour the flavour of the whole dish. Most diners do not eat the dried chilli pieces, but you can do so if you want an other-world experience.

SERVES 4

- 30ml/2 tbsp groundnut/peanut oil
- 5 large dried chillies, soaked and seeded (see Cook's Tip), then drained and snipped into two or three pieces
- 450g/1lb skinless chicken breasts, cut into 1cm/½in cubes
- ½ large onion, finely chopped
- 25g/1oz fresh root ginger, sliced
- 2 spring onions/scallions, cut into short lengths
- 2.5ml/½ tsp salt
- 30ml/2 tbsp Shaoxing wine or dry sherry
- 30ml/2 tbsp sesame oil

1 Heat the oil in a wok and fry the chillies for 30 seconds, or until the oil takes on an intense red colour. Remove the chillies using a slotted spoon and set aside. Fry the chicken pieces in the remaining oil for 2 minutes, then remove and drain on kitchen paper.

2 Add the onion and ginger to the wok and fry for 2 minutes, or until golden. Return the chicken to the pan with the spring onions, salt and wine or sherry. Stir-fry for 2 minutes.

3 Return the fried chillies to the pan and continue to stir-fry for 2 minutes. Pour in the sesame oil and stir to mix. Serve immediately.

Cook's Tip

The best dried chillies are the largest, each about 7.5cm/3in long and deep burgundy in colour.

SERVES 4

2 skinless chicken breasts
200ml/7fl oz/scant 1 cup boiling water
30ml/2 tbsp groundnut/peanut oil
2 garlic cloves, chopped
3 fresh red chillies, seeded and chopped, plus 1 fresh red chilli, seeded and sliced, to garnish
30ml/2 tbsp sesame oil
50g/2oz/⅓ cup boiled peanuts (see Cook's Tip, page 533)
5ml/1 tsp caster/superfine sugar
5ml/1 tsp cornflour/cornstarch
1 spring onion/scallion, chopped
boiled rice, to serve

Cook's Tip

Instead of peanuts, you can use cashew nuts or even some diced water chestnuts.

CHILLI CHICKEN WITH PEANUTS

At first glance this Guizhou dish might appear to be similar to the famous Sichuan Kung Po Chicken. However, this provincial variation has more fire due to its liberal use of fresh chillies, and contains fewer aromatics.

1 Cut the chicken into 1cm/½in cubes and put into a pan with the water. Bring to the boil and cook for 6–8 minutes. Lift out the chicken with a slotted spoon and set aside. Leave the stock to cool.

2 Heat the oil in a wok and fry the garlic for 40 seconds, or until golden brown. Add the chillies and fry for 1 minute, or until soft. Add the sesame oil, peanuts, chicken and sugar, then stir-fry quickly for 1 minute.

3 Put the cornflour in a bowl and blend with the cold stock. Add to the wok and cook for 1 minute, until the sauce thickens, then add the spring onion. Stir to mix, then immediately remove from the heat. (Alternatively, you can sprinkle over the spring onions as part of the garnish.) Serve with rice, garnished with the sliced chilli.

HOT-AND-SOUR CHICKEN

Shaanxi is perhaps less known for its culinary excellence than for the discovery of those spectacular terracotta soldiers from its capital Xi'an, which was China's former capital. It borrows many of its cooking concepts, such as the dry-frying used here, from its southern neighbour Sichuan and Hubei to the east. The technique of dry-frying uses very little oil or liquid, giving the chicken and vegetables a crisp, almost pickled flavour.

SERVES 4

- 450g/1lb boneless chicken thighs
- 15ml/1 tbsp groundnut/peanut oil
- 25g/1oz fresh root ginger, sliced into strips
- 2 Chinese or English celery sticks, sliced
- 2 spring onions/scallions, sliced into short lengths
- 30ml/2 tbsp chilli bean paste (dou banjiang)
- 2.5ml/½ tsp caster/superfine sugar
- 2.5ml/½ tsp Sichuan peppercorns, crushed
- 15ml/1 tbsp rice vinegar
- noodles, to serve

1 Cut the chicken into strips about 2cm/¾in wide. Heat the oil in a wok and fry the ginger for 1 minute, or until golden brown. Add the chicken, celery, spring onions and chilli bean paste. Stir-fry for 2 minutes over a medium heat.

2 Add the sugar to the wok, then the peppercorns and rice vinegar, and continue to stir-fry for a further 2 minutes, or until the chicken is nearly cooked through.

3 Sprinkle 30ml/2 tbsp water over the chicken and cook until the wok is nearly dry and the chicken is cooked through and has a darkish hue from the sauce. Serve with noodles.

CHICKEN & CLOUD EAR STIR-FRY

The contrasting textures of this dish make it especially attractive. Cloud ears have a pleasant crunchy texture and smoky flavour, and Chongqing cooks use them liberally. Chinese chives are thicker, coarser and more pungent than the Western kind, adding to the contrasts in the dish.

SERVES 4

- 450g/1lb skinless chicken breasts
- 5g/⅛oz cloud ear/wood ear mushrooms, soaked in warm water for 10–15 minutes
- 30ml/2 tbsp groundnut/peanut oil
- 2 stalks Chinese chives, chopped
- 20g/¾oz fresh root ginger, shredded
- 30ml/2 tbsp sesame oil
- 15ml/1 tbsp yellow bean sauce
- 2.5ml/½ tsp caster/superfine sugar
- 5ml/1 tsp cornflour/cornstarch
- boiled rice, to serve

1 Cut the chicken into cubes. Trim off any tough parts from the cloud ears, then rinse and drain them. Slice the larger pieces into two. Set aside.

2 Heat the oil in a wok and fry the chives and ginger for 2 minutes, or until light brown. Add the chicken and cloud ears to the wok and stir-fry for 3 minutes.

3 Add the sesame oil, yellow bean sauce and sugar, and stir-fry for 2 minutes. Put the cornflour in a bowl and gradually blend in 100ml/3½fl oz/scant ½ cup water. Pour into the sauce and stir until it thickens. Serve with boiled rice.

SERVES 4

1 chicken, about 1.6kg/3½lb, or 8 chicken portions
250g/9oz prepared tripe
30ml/2 tbsp groundnut/peanut oil
3 garlic cloves, crushed
25g/1oz fresh root ginger, sliced
½ large onion, sliced
30ml/2 tbsp Shaoxing wine or dry sherry
15ml/1 tbsp light soy sauce
30ml/2 tbsp oyster sauce
15ml/1 tbsp sesame oil
2.5ml/½ tsp ground black pepper
800ml/1.4 pints/3½ cups water
fresh coriander/cilantro leaves, to garnish

Variation

If you use skinless chicken breast, cook it for just 30 minutes.

BRAISED CHICKEN WITH TRIPE

Although tripe may seem like an unusual ingredient, chefs in Yunnan are adept at combining the most unlikely foods and making them work brilliantly. Tripe is included in their cuisine as much for its texture as for its taste, and here it is combined with chicken and aromatic seasonings and sauces. The dish is traditionally cooked with a whole chicken on the bone, but using joints reduces the cooking time.

1 If using a whole chicken, joint it into eight or more pieces. Removing any excess fat and gristle from the joints or chicken portions. Wash and slice the tripe into small pieces, each about 5cm/2in long x 2.5cm/1in wide.

2 Heat the oil in a wok and fry the garlic, ginger and onion for 1 minute. Add the chicken and tripe, and stir-fry for 2 minutes. Add the wine or sherry with the soy sauce, oyster sauce, sesame oil and pepper. Cook, stirring, for 2 minutes over a high heat.

3 Add the measured water, then bring to the boil and simmer, covered, for 40 minutes, or until all the meat is tender. Serve immediately, garnished with fresh coriander.

CHICKEN IN VINEGAR SAUCE

This tart and aromatic dish is steeped in a rich vinegar sauce, which has a great affinity with bamboo shoots. Chongqing, a municipality bordering Sichuan, has a cuisine that is generally regarded as being distinct from its famous neighbour, and certainly not representative of typical western Chinese cooking. This Chongqing dish, however, has fragrant echoes of the classic Sichuan style, especially in its use of spicy chillies.

SERVES 4

- 1 egg white
- 2 skinless chicken breasts, about 300g/11oz in total
- 5ml/1 tsp salt
- 30ml/2 tbsp Shaoxing wine or dry sherry
- 2 dried chillies, soaked until soft
- 15ml/1 tbsp groundnut/peanut oil
- 90g/3½oz bamboo shoot strips
- fresh coriander/cilantro, to garnish
- boiled rice, to serve

FOR THE VINEGAR SAUCE

- 5ml/1 tsp cornflour/cornstarch
- 15ml/1 tbsp rice vinegar
- 15ml/1 tbsp light soy sauce
- 5ml/1 tsp caster/superfine sugar
- 5ml/1 tsp finely grated ginger
- 1 garlic clove, crushed
- 1 spring onion/scallion white part only, very finely chopped

1 Put the egg white in a bowl and whisk until almost stiff. Cut the chicken into thin pieces, about 4cm/1½in square and 5mm/¼in thick. Put the salt and wine or sherry into the bowl with the egg white, then add the chicken and toss to coat evenly. Leave to marinate for 15 minutes.

2 Cut the chillies in half and remove the seeds, then cut them into small dice. Heat the oil in a wok and fry the chillies for 30 seconds – be careful not to scorch them.

3 Add the chicken and its marinade to the wok, then add the bamboo shoots. Stir-fry for 1 minute.

4 To make the vinegar sauce, put the cornflour in a small bowl and gradually blend in the remaining sauce ingredients and 45ml/3 tbsp water. When well combined, add to the wok.

5 Cook, stirring frequently, for 2–3 minutes, or until the sauce thickens and the chicken is cooked through. Serve with boiled rice, garnished with fresh coriander if you like.

Variation

The bamboo shoots can be replaced with sliced leeks for an even more pungent flavour, if you like.

WINE-BRAISED CHICKEN

Cantonese rice wine, or mi jiu, which is a pale, light alcohol, makes a good marinade for the chicken in this dish, combined with the flavours of celery, garlic and ginger.

1 Cut the chicken into 2.5cm/1in cubes. Put the rice wine in a bowl and blend in the garlic, ginger, pepper, sugar and salt. Stir in the chicken to coat evenly and leave to marinate for 15 minutes.

2 Heat the oil in a wok over a high heat. Fry the celery for 30 seconds, then reduce the heat slightly and add the chicken and its marinade. Stir-fry for 2 minutes, or until the chicken is barely cooked and the juices have reduced slightly.

3 Stir in the soy sauce and sesame oil. Put the cornflour in a bowl and gradually blend in 200ml/7fl oz/scant 1 cup water. Stir into the wok mixture, then simmer for 1 minute, or until the sauce bubbles and thickens. Garnish with celery leaves and serve with noodles.

SERVES 4

450g/1lb skinless chicken breasts
45ml/3 tbsp Chinese rice wine or medium-dry sherry
30ml/2 tbsp crushed garlic (4–5 cloves)
30ml/2 tbsp grated fresh root ginger
2.5ml/½ tsp white pepper
2.5ml/½ tsp caster/superfine sugar
2.5ml/½ tsp salt
30ml/2 tbsp groundnut/peanut oil
1 celery stick, sliced
15ml/1 tbsp light soy sauce
5ml/1 tsp sesame oil
5ml/1 tsp cornflour/cornstarch
200ml/7fl oz/scant 1 cup water
Chinese celery leaves, to garnish
egg noodles, to serve

SERVES 4

- 4 duck legs, deboned, or 2 duck breasts
- 30ml/2 tbsp groundnut/peanut oil
- 3 garlic cloves, crushed
- 25g/1oz fresh root ginger, chopped
- 30ml/2 tbsp dark soy sauce
- 15ml/1 tbsp yellow bean sauce
- 1 small piece of tangerine peel, about 5cm/2in square
- 10 Chinese dried sweet dates, pitted
- 5ml/1 tsp caster/superfine sugar
- 75g/3oz bamboo piths, soaked in warm water for 20 minutes, until soft
- noodles, to serve
- shredded spring onions/ scallions, to garnish

DUCK WITH BAMBOO PITHS

Bamboo piths (pictured on page 531) have a crunchy texture and robust taste, and are cooked in many dishes from Hubei and Sichuan. Here they are partnered with duck and Chinese dried sweet dates.

1 If you are using duck legs, debone and cut each leg into three or four pieces. If you are using duck breast fillets, remove the skin if you prefer, then slice each into three or four pieces.

2 Heat the oil in a wok and fry the garlic and ginger for 1 minute. Add the duck and stir-fry for 2 minutes, or until sealed. Add the soy sauce and yellow bean sauce, then cook, stirring often, for 2 minutes.

3 Add the tangerine peel, dates, sugar and 600ml/1 pint/2½ cups water, then cook, stirring occasionally, over a high heat for 3 minutes, or until the sauce is reduced by half and thickens. Cut the bamboo piths into small pieces and add to the wok.

4 Reduce the heat to low and simmer for 5–8 minutes, or until the duck is tender. Serve, garnished with shredded spring onions.

AROMATIC CRISPY DUCK

Of all Sichuan exports, this dish has earned its place in the global culinary hall of fame. Five-spice powder, Sichuan peppercorns, garlic and ginger give the duck its wonderful aroma. It is first steamed in the aromatics, then left to absorb all the flavours before being quickly fried. It is sometimes confused with Peking Duck, but is prepared in a completely different way. Although it requires more work than its Peking cousin, it is worth the effort.

SERVES 8–10

1 oven-ready duck, about 2.5kg/5½lb
5ml/1 tsp salt
4 garlic cloves, crushed
25g/1oz fresh root ginger, finely grated
3 spring onions/scallions, cut into 5cm/2in lengths
45ml/3 tbsp rice wine or vinegar
5ml/1 tsp five-spice powder
5ml/1 tsp Sichuan peppercorns, lightly crushed
30–45ml/2–3 tbsp cornflour/cornstarch or water chestnut flour
vegetable oil, for deep-frying

FOR THE ACCOMPANIMENTS
24–30 Mandarin pancakes (see page 127)
spring onions/scallions, sliced into thin strips
cucumber, sliced into thin batons
hoisin sauce

1 Clean the duck inside and out, then pat it dry with kitchen paper. Cut down the breastbone, then open the bird out and press it flat to spatchcock it. Remove any excess fat pads.

2 Put the salt in a small bowl and add the garlic, ginger and spring onions. Stir in the rice wine or vinegar, five-spice powder and peppercorns. Rub this all over the duck, pressing on the aromatics.

3 Put the duck on a tray or in a large bowl and place over a wok or steamer containing simmering water. Steam over a high heat for 1¼–2 hours, or until completely tender but not collapsed. Take the tray or bowl out of the wok and leave the duck to steep in its juices for 1 hour. Drain and place on a rack. (Save the juices for a soup or stock.)

4 Remove all the aromatics from the duck, and leave it to stand until the skin is dry.

5 Meanwhile, prepare the accompaniments: put the pancakes in a steamer, put the spring onions, cucumber and hoisin sauce in separate small dishes, and transfer to the table.

6 With a pastry brush, dust the duck lightly all over with cornflour or water chestnut flour.

7 Heat the vegetable oil in a wok over a medium heat or in a deep-fryer. Carefully lower the duck into the oil (a wide Chinese mesh strainer is perfect for this) and deep-fry until crisp and golden, turning and basting the duck with oil during frying. If your wok is too small, cut the duck into quarters and fry a piece at a time. Lift out the duck and drain on kitchen paper.

8 Transfer the duck to a serving plate and use a knife and fork to shred the crisp skin and meat into strips, removing the bones as you do so.

9 Steam the pancakes in a steamer set over simmering water for 3 minutes, until hot, then take to the table. Each diner spreads a little hoisin sauce on a pancake, then tops it with a few strips of spring onion and cucumber, and some shredded duck. Then simply roll up the pancake, and your sleeves, and eat.

Cook's Tips

- If you are not serving a large party, use 2 skinless duck breasts, but steam for 45 minutes and deep-fry as normal.
- The pancakes need only to be lightly steamed and can also be microwaved for 10 seconds per batch of 2 skins, but they tend to go brittle after a few minutes if not eaten immediately.

BRAISED DUCK WITH TOFU

As a winter warmer this dish is very comforting, with its wine sauce and blended seasonings that bring out the flavour of the duck. While fruity sauces like plum really cut the fat of duck, aromatics like garlic and ginger also do the same job. Tofu pieces with their firm outside and soft centre provide the perfect contrast. Although typical of Sichuan, it is by no means exclusive to this province – Hubei and Hunan have their own versions. If you can find French duck breasts, they are ideal for this dish as they have more lean meat in relation to fatty skin. However, in most Chinese dishes, poultry skin is an important part of the dish, providing flavour and succulence.

SERVES 6–8

2 duck breasts
250g/9oz packet firm tofu
75ml/5 tbsp groundnut/ peanut oil
25oz/1 oz fresh root ginger, finely grated
4 garlic cloves, crushed
1 large onion, sliced
30ml/2 tbsp hoisin sauce
15ml/1 tbsp oyster sauce
30ml/2 tbsp Chinese wine or dry sherry
pickled ginger, to serve

Cook's Tip

There is another type of tofu called tofu gan, or firm dried squares, which does not need to be fried as it already has a firm skin. Use this cut into cubes as above and add it for the last 5 minutes of cooking.

1 Cut the duck breasts into slices about 5mm/¼in thick. Cut the tofu into 2cm/¾in cubes.

2 Heat the oil in a wok until smoking hot and fry the tofu cubes until a brown skin forms on all sides. Remove with a slotted spoon and drain on kitchen paper. Set aside.

3 Add the duck pieces to the wok and fry in the remaining oil over a high heat for 2 minutes. Remove with a slotted spoon and drain on kitchen paper.

4 Pour out all but 15ml/1 tbsp of the oil and fry the ginger, garlic and onion for 1 minute, or until nearly brown. Add the hoisin sauce, oyster sauce, wine or sherry and 600ml/1 pint/2½ cups water, then bring to the boil.

5 Return the duck pieces to the wok and braise over a high heat for 2 minutes, or until the sauce is thick and slightly glossy. Add the tofu and cook for a further 3 minutes.

6 Serve with slices of pickled ginger to taste. These come in thin slices in jars or vacuum-packed.

WESTERN CHINA
MEAT

STICKY SNACKS & FLAVOUR FUSIONS

Pork, when it is on the menu, comes with particular requirements in western Chinese cooking. Roast pork has to be made from a rib cut that is streaked with the requisite amount of fat, as well as being cut in a wide, long strip. When pork is needed for long cooking or braising, usually the hock or leg cut is used.

There is a specific ratio of lean meat to fat and skin that is adhered to by local cooks. This works out at eight parts lean to two parts fat and skin, which results in superb flavour, succulence and texture. This is typified in Twice-Cooked Pork, where the skin is left on for extra texture, artfully cooked to a crunchy tenderness.

Beef is made into an imperial offering in the iconic Sichuan Crispy Chilli Beef, now a signature dish in restaurants across the world. It gets a fiery kick from chilli bean paste, as does Boiled Fiery Beef, which also benefits from the additional heat of dried chillies.

Some of these meat dishes are tongue-searingly hot from a blend of two of the region's most potent ingredients – chillies and Sichuan peppercorns. Red-cooked Beef (hong shau) is another piquant favourite, where beef is liberally soused with blends of fermented red beancurd and hoisin sauce.

Western Chinese cooking makes good use of offal, too, elevating it to great heights, such as in the tasty Hot-and-sour Kidneys. Although not very common, the odd game recipe, such as Rabbit in Hot Bean Sauce, demonstrates the exceptional skills of Sichuan chefs.

COLD GARLIC PORK

Pork and garlic go very well together, and are a tasty combination in this cold dish. This Sichuan classic is popular in summer, when the temperature and humidity in the province can be unyieldingly oppressive. Sichuan chefs use a special local soy sauce with nuances of sugar and spice, but this product is rare outside the region, so this recipe uses a light soy sauce tweaked with a little sugar and chilli oil to create a similar flavour.

SERVES 4

450g/1lb pork shoulder
25g/1oz fresh root ginger, bruised
2 spring onions/scallions
pickled ginger slices, to serve

FOR THE SAUCE
6–7 garlic cloves, grated
45ml/3 tbsp light soy sauce
5ml/1 tsp caster/superfine sugar
15ml/1 tbsp sesame oil
15ml/1 tbsp chilli oil

1 Put the pork in a large pan and add boiling water to cover. Boil over a high heat for 30 seconds, then remove the pork, put it into a colander and quickly cool with cold water.

2 Put the pork in a large pan and add 1.5 litres/2½ pints/6¼ cups water, the ginger and spring onions. Cover and bring to the boil, then reduce the heat to maintain a simmer and cook, partially covered, for 45–55 minutes, or until the pork is just cooked through.

3 Remove the pan from the heat and allow the pork to cool completely in the cooking liquid, then cover and transfer to the fridge. Leave to chill for at least 2 hours.

4 To make the sauce, put the garlic in a mortar and crush to a paste with a pestle. Transfer to a small bowl and stir in the remaining ingredients. Cover and leave to stand for 15 minutes.

5 When you are ready to serve, slice the pork thinly and arrange the slices on a serving platter, fanning them out and overlapping them slightly. Pour the sauce over and serve with pickled ginger.

Variation

If you like your meat to have a strong contrast between its texture and that of the fat and jelly-like skin, use pork belly instead of shoulder for the recipe.

PORK RIBS IN PEPPERCORN SAUCE

Ribs are given a hot and spicy marinade before being steamed in this dish from Hunan. In some local restaurants the recipe is also adapted to use carp as well as pork ribs. However, pork ribs on their own are wonderfully succulent and savoury. This dish is perfect served as an appetizer.

1 Bring a pan of water to the boil. Add the spring onions, peppercorns and ribs and bring back to the boil. Simmer for 30 minutes. Remove from the heat and leave to steep for 15 minutes.

2 Place a dish inside a steamer. Remove the ribs with a slotted spoon and put them into the dish. Mix together the ginger, chillies, sugar, ground peppercorns, sesame oil and wine or sherry, then pour over the pork and combine. Leave to marinate for 20 minutes.

3 Cover the steamer and transfer it to a wok filled with simmering water. Steam for 30 minutes, then serve.

SERVES 4

- 3 spring onions/scallions
- 5ml/1 tsp whole Sichuan peppercorns
- 450g/1lb pork ribs, cut into 2.5cm/1in lengths
- 25g/1oz ground ginger
- 3 fresh red chillies, seeded and sliced into strips
- 5ml/1 tsp caster/superfine sugar
- 2.5ml/½ tsp ground Sichuan peppercorns
- 30ml/2 tbsp sesame oil
- 30ml/2 tbsp Shaoxing wine or dry sherry

Variation

Add a chopped pickled lime or sliced red chillies before steaming.

SERVES 4

450g/1lb pork rib steak or leg of pork, cut into 2cm/¾in cubes
1 egg, lightly beaten
45ml/3 tbsp tapioca flour
vegetable oil, for deep-frying
lettuce leaves, to serve

FOR THE SAUCE
30ml/2 tbsp rice wine or vinegar
30ml/2 tbsp plum sauce
30ml/2 tbsp groundnut/peanut oil
1 medium onion, thinly sliced
3 garlic cloves, thinly sliced
3 fresh red chillies, seeded and chopped

Cook's Tip

Chinese chefs rarely, or never, use a wet batter on meats, as it tends to go soft very quickly.

PORK IN HOT-AND-SOUR SAUCE

This dish from Shaanxi is a spicy take on the well-known sweet-and-sour sauce, with a unique flavour from the blend of rice wine or vinegar, chillies and plum sauce, as well as depth from the onion and garlic.

1 Put the pork into a bowl. Pour over the egg and toss the pork to mix. Put the tapioca flour in a plastic food bag. Lift out the pork using a slotted spoon and allow the excess egg to drain off, then put the pork pieces into the bag. Hold the bag closed and shake it to coat the pork in the flour. Take out the pork and shake off the excess flour. Leave it on a plate for 15 minutes.

2 Heat the oil in a wok or deep-fryer and fry the pork, in batches if necessary, until golden. Drain on kitchen paper and keep warm.

3 To make the sauce, mix the rice wine or vinegar with the plum sauce and 45ml/3 tbsp water. Heat the oil in a wok and fry the onion and garlic for 2 minutes, or until light brown. Add the chillies and plum sauce mixture, then bring to a rapid boil.

4 Remove from the heat and toss the pork in the sauce. Serve on a bed of lettuce.

  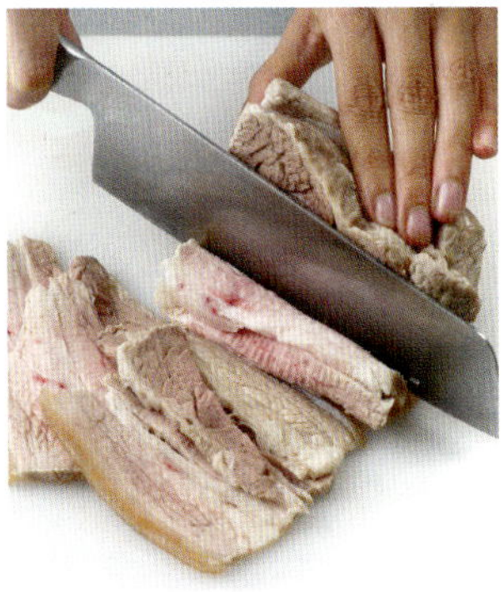 

TWICE-COOKED PORK

A Sichuan all-time favourite, the name of this dish is fairly self-explanatory. It is simply pork that is parboiled and then stir-fried with a blend of Sichuan seasonings. This is a very old method from when tougher meats, such as mutton and wild boar, were more common and had to be made tender by precooking.

SERVES 4

450g/1lb meaty pork belly, or pork leg with skin and fat
1 small leek
1 green/bell pepper
45ml/3 tbsp vegetable oil
10ml/2 tsp caster/superfine sugar
15ml/1 tbsp dark soy sauce
15ml/1 tbsp light soy sauce
2 garlic cloves, chopped
15ml/1 tbsp hoisin sauce
30ml/2 tbsp chilli bean paste (dou banjiang)
noodles, to serve (optional)

Cook's Tip

If you like, you can add 15ml/1 tbsp Chinese wine with the chilli bean paste for a richer flavour.

1 Cut the pork into two pieces, then put in a colander over the sink and rinse both sides with boiling water. Drain well. Put the pork in a large pan and cover completely with boiling water. Bring to the boil over a medium heat, then simmer for 30–40 minutes, or until cooked through.

2 Drain (reserve the cooking liquid for a soup or stock) and leave to cool completely, then wrap tightly in clear film or plastic wrap and chill for 2 hours, or until firm.

3 Using a sharp knife, thinly slice the pork crossways into strips as thin as a bacon rasher – each piece should be edged with some fat and skin. Cut the leek diagonally into 5mm/¼in-thick slices. Cut the pepper into 2.5cm/1in pieces.

4 Heat the oil in a wok over a high heat. Add the pork slices, sugar and soy sauces, and fry vigorously for about 2 minutes, or until the pork is lightly browned and caramelized.

5 Add the garlic, leek and pepper, and stir-fry for 30 seconds, then push all the ingredients to the edge of the wok. Add the hoisin sauce and chilli bean paste to the centre of the wok and fry for several seconds until fragrant, then mix everything together and fry for 1 minute more.

6 Serve immediately, on a bed of noodles, if you like.

COLD SPICY BEEF

Although cold food is not a great favourite among most Chinese, when summers dawn with unrelenting heat – especially in land-locked areas like Sichuan, Hunan and Hubei – this spicy beef dish makes a welcome change.

SERVES 4

450g/1lb rump/round or rib-eye beef, in one piece
15ml/1 tbsp rice wine or vinegar
15ml/1 tbsp red rice wine lees or red fermented tofu (tofu ru)
5ml/1 tsp Sichuan peppercorns
6 cloves
1 stick cinnamon, about 5cm/2in
1 star anise
30ml/2 tbsp light soy sauce
5ml/1 tsp caster/superfine sugar

FOR THE SAUCE
2 garlic cloves, crushed
15ml/1 tbsp finely grated ginger
15ml/1 tbsp sesame oil
5ml/1 tsp salt

1 Fill a pan with boiling water and add the beef. Boil for 30 seconds, transfer it to a colander, and rinse it quickly under cold water.

2 Put 1.5 litres/2½ pints/6¼ cups water in the clean pan and add the rice wine or vinegar, red wine lees or fermented tofu, spices, soy sauce and sugar. Add the beef. Cover and bring to the boil, then reduce to a simmer. Cook, partially covered, for 1½ hours, until the beef is tender. Remove from the heat and allow the beef to cool completely in its cooking liquid.

3 Lift out the beef, wrap tightly in clear film or plastic wrap, then chill for 15 minutes to firm it. Meanwhile, make the sauce by mixing all the ingredients together in a small jug or bowl.

4 Slice the beef very thinly and arrange the slices on a serving platter. Drizzle with the sauce and serve immediately.

Cook's Tip

This dish can be cooked a day before serving; chill the beef in its covered pan of cooking liquid.

SERVES 4

450g/1lb fillet steak/beef tenderloin
15ml/1 tbsp groundnut/peanut oil
2 garlic cloves, sliced
15ml/1 tbsp dark soy sauce
5ml/1 tsp caster/superfine sugar
pinch of ground cloves
2.5ml/½ tsp ground Sichuan peppercorns
15ml/1 tbsp sesame oil
15ml/1 tbsp sesame seeds
noodles, to serve

FOR THE MARINADE
15ml/1 tbsp finely grated ginger
1 spring onion/scallion, chopped
2.5ml/½ tsp salt
15ml/1 tbsp rice wine or vinegar

SESAME BEEF

This marinated beef dish originated from Hubei, although it is more usually cooked there using pork. However, there is a sizeable population of Muslims in western China, and this dish was tweaked to suit their religious requirements.

1 Cut the beef into thin slices, each measuring 2.5cm/1in wide by 7.5cm/3in long. Combine the marinade ingredients in a bowl, pour over the beef and toss to coat. Leave to marinate for 20 minutes.

2 Heat the oil in a wok and fry the garlic until crisp and light brown. Add the beef slices with their marinade and stir-fry for 1 minute, then add the soy sauce, sugar, ground cloves, Sichuan peppercorns and sesame oil, and stir-fry for 1 minute over a high heat.

3 Add 150ml/¼ pint/⅔ cup water and stir until the sauce is reduced by half and the beef is fairly dry and glossy. Serve with noodles, sprinkled with sesame seeds and extra shredded spring onion.

CRISPY CHILLI BEEF

A restaurant-starred dish, crispy chilli beef has earned legions of fans around the world. Although it is considered to be a Sichuan invention, it has nevertheless been adopted by other regional cuisines, and some Hong Kong chefs have even claimed that it came from their kitchens. It is actually possible that this dish originated from anywhere in China, as imperial courts were forever poaching ideas from other regions. Wherever it first originated, it is certainly a very delicious mouthful. Serve it with boiled rice, if you like.

1 Cut the beef into thin strips about 6cm/2½in long by 1cm/1½in wide. Put the strips into a shallow dish.

2 In a small bowl, mix together the marinade ingredients, then pour over the beef and stir to coat evenly. Cover and leave to marinate for 20 minutes (marinating will keep the steak juicy).

3 Heat the vegetable oil in a wok or deep-fryer. Sprinkle the cornflour over the beef and toss to coat, then deep-fry the meat in batches until golden and crispy, stirring with chopsticks to keep the strips separate.

4 Drain on kitchen paper and keep warm. Deep-fry the carrot strips for 15 seconds and drain well.

5 Heat the groundnut oil in a clean wok over a high heat, then fry the garlic for 10 seconds. Add the celery and fry for 20 seconds more.

6 Add the beef, carrot and chilli bean paste, with the hoisin sauce, sesame oil, sugar and salt. Sir-fry vigorously for 1 minute, or until everything is coated with a glossy glaze. Serve immediately, with rice, if you like.

SERVES 4

450g/1lb rump/round or rib-eye steak
vegetable oil, for deep-frying
45ml/3 tbsp cornflour/cornstarch
90g/3½oz carrot, cut into thin strips
30ml/2 tbsp groundnut/peanut oil
2 garlic cloves, finely chopped
1 celery stick, cut into thin strips
30ml/2 tbsp chilli bean paste (dou banjiang)
15ml/1 tbsp hoisin sauce
2.5ml/½ tsp sesame oil
10ml/2 tsp caster/superfine sugar
2.5ml/½ tsp salt
rice, to serve (optional)

FOR THE MARINADE
15ml/1 tbsp rice wine or vinegar
1.5ml/¼ tsp salt
1.5ml/¼ tsp caster/superfine sugar

RED-COOKED BEEF

The method of braising known as 'red cooking' is not exclusive to Sichuan. It is a technique used in many regions, and various ingredients are used to achieve the characteristic red colouring. Cantonese chefs invariably use a blend of fermented red tofu and hoisin sauce. In Shanghai and Suzhou in the eastern provinces, red wine lees gives the braise an intense colour and alcoholic flavour. Here, both chilli bean paste and hoisin give the dish a hot-sweet finish. Whichever ingredients are used, it is the method of slow braising that gives the meat its flavour and texture. This is typically served with plain rice.

SERVES 4

675g/1½lb stewing steak
30ml/2 tbsp vegetable oil
25g/1oz fresh root ginger, sliced
3 garlic cloves, sliced
30ml/2 tbsp chilli bean paste (dou banjiang)
30ml/2 tbsp hoisin sauce
5ml/1 tsp Sichuan peppercorns
75ml/5 tbsp rice wine or vinegar
1 mooli/daikon
salt and ground black pepper
fresh coriander/cilantro, to garnish

1 Cut the beef into large chunks, about 4cm/1½in. Bring a large pan of water to the boil, add the beef and boil it for 1 minute to blanch it. Lift it out with a slotted spoon and drain on kitchen paper. (Doing this helps to eliminate scum and debris in the braising pan later.)

2 Heat the oil in a large, heavy pan over a medium heat. Add the ginger and garlic and fry for 1–2 minutes or until fragrant.

3 Add the chilli bean paste and fry for 30 seconds, then add the hoisin sauce, Sichuan peppercorns, 1 litre/1¾ pints/4 cups water and the rice wine or vinegar.

4 Add the beef, then cover and simmer for 1½ hours, or until the beef is tender.

5 Peel the mooli and cut horizontally into slices about 2.5cm/1in thick. Quarter each slice, or halve smaller slices. Add to the pan and partially cover, then cook for 30 minutes more, or until the mooli is translucent and tender and the beef is very tender.

6 Adjust the seasoning to taste with salt or pepper to taste and serve immediately, garnished with fresh coriander.

FIVE-SPICE BEEF IN BEAN SAUCE

The famous blend of five spices is universally used in China, and Sichuan is no exception. When the pungent mix is combined with fiery chilli bean paste, the alchemy is nothing short of sensational.

SERVES 4

- 450g/1lb sirloin or rump/round steak, sliced into strips about 1cm/½in thick
- 5ml/1 tsp cornflour/cornstarch
- 30ml/2 tbsp sesame oil
- 15ml/1 tbsp dark soy sauce
- 30ml/2 tbsp groundnut/peanut oil
- 2 garlic cloves, crushed
- 25g/1oz fresh root ginger, chopped
- 2 spring onions/scallions, cut into 5cm/2in lengths
- 15ml/1 tbsp chilli bean paste (dou banjiang)
- 2.5ml/½ tsp five-spice powder
- 2.5ml/½ tsp caster/superfine sugar
- thick egg noodles or rice, to serve

1 Put the beef into a bowl. Put the cornflour into a different bowl and blend in the sesame oil and soy sauce. Sprinkle this mixture over the beef and toss to coat. Leave to marinate for 10 minutes.

2 Heat the groundnut oil in a wok and fry the garlic and ginger for 30 seconds, or until light brown. Toss in the beef and stir-fry over a high heat for 1 minute. Add the spring onions, chilli bean paste, five-spice powder, sugar and 45ml/3 tbsp water.

3 Stir the beef and sauce over a high heat for 2 minutes, or until the sauce is thick. Serve immediately, with thick egg noodles or rice, sprinkled with shredded spring onions.

SERVES 4

5ml/1 tsp cornflour/cornstarch
30ml/2 tbsp Shaoxing wine or dry sherry
2 garlic cloves, crushed
2.5ml/½ tsp salt
450g/1lb sirloin or rump/round steak, sliced into thin slices across the grain
100ml/3½fl oz/scant ½ cup sunflower oil
8 dried chillies, seeded if you like, crushed into coarse flakes
5ml/1 tsp crushed Sichuan peppercorns
30ml/2 tbsp chilli bean paste (dou banjiang)
15ml/1 tbsp light soy sauce

Variation

You can cook chicken or pork in the same way.

BOILED FIERY BEEF

The Chinese name shui zhu niu rou means 'beef boiled in water', which sounds mild, but in reality it is tongue-tinglingly hot from a blend of two of the region's most potent ingredients: Sichuan dried chillies and peppercorns.

1 Blend the cornflour, wine or sherry, garlic and salt, then add the beef and toss to coat. Set aside while you prepare the sauce.

2 Heat half the oil in a wok over medium-low heat. Add the dried chilli flakes and peppercorns and stir for 10 seconds, then pour the oil and spices into a heatproof bowl and leave to cool.

3 Heat the remaining oil in a clean wok and fry the bean paste for 30 seconds over a medium heat. Add 500ml/scant 1 pint/2 cups water and the soy sauce, then turn heat to high and bring to the boil. Add the beef and its marinade, stir and cook for 2–3 minutes, until the beef is just cooked, then transfer to a serving plate.

4 Heat 30–45ml/2–3 tbsp of the chilli oil mixture, depending on how spicy you want it, in a pan until very hot, then drizzle over the beef – the sauce should sizzle. Serve immediately.

MIXED SMOKED MEATS

Smoking foods is a particular Sichuan style of cuisine, where the meats absorb the flavour from tea leaves along with a variety of other smoking materials. In rural Sichuan, meats will be smoked over bamboo leaves, pine needles, rice straw or even peanut husks and sawdust from aromatic woods, but it is the type of tea that is added that will really determine the final flavour. Semi-fermented oolong tea from the Fujian province gives a delicious smokiness, or you can use jasmine tea for a much milder flavour. This is a fairly lengthy recipe, but the results are well worth the effort.

SERVES 4

225g/8oz duck breast
225g/8oz skinless chicken breast
225g/8oz pork rib steak
vegetable oil, for deep-frying
shredded spring onions/scallions, to garnish
pickled ginger, to serve

FOR THE MARINADE
5ml/1 tsp salt
5ml/1 tsp ground Sichuan peppercorns
30ml/2 tbsp Shaoxing wine or dry sherry
30ml/2 tbsp red fermented tofu (tofu ru), finely crumbled

SMOKING MATERIALS
50g/2oz tea leaves of your choice
3 dried bamboo leaves or 1 lotus leaf, roughly chopped

Cook's Tips

- Dried bamboo leaves are easily available. Camphor wood chips can be bought at health-food stores but you can substitute these with peanut husks if necessary.
- You can omit the steaming step and smoke the meats for twice as long if you want to reduce the cooking time for the recipe. However, the initial steaming gives them more succulence.

1 Cut each poultry breast and pork steak into two pieces. Put the marinade ingredients into a bowl and mix together, then rub all over the meats. Put into a deep heatproof dish, cover with clear film/plastic wrap and chill for at least 8 hours, turning once or twice during this time.

2 When you are ready to cook, allow the poultry and meat to come to room temperature, then put the dish in a wok or steamer placed over simmering water and steam over a high heat for 15 minutes. Remove the dish and take out the meats. Drain on kitchen paper and set aside.

3 Line a large wok with a double sheet of foil. Mix the smoking materials together and sprinkle them over the base of the wok in an even layer. Put several small Chinese teacups or heatproof eggcups among the smoking material, and put a small wire rack or piece of wire netting on top so that there is a space between the smoking material and the meat.

4 Put the marinated meats on the rack or wire mesh. Turn on the heat to the very lowest setting and cover the wok tightly. Twist and wind several pieces of kitchen paper around the lid so that all the smoke is trapped inside. Smoke for 20 minutes, checking occasionally. Turn off the heat and remove the smoked meats.

5 Heat the vegetable oil in a wok or deep-fryer, then deep-fry the smoked meats, a few pieces at a time. Cook until a crisp skin forms. Cool slightly, then slice thinly.

6 Serve garnished with shredded spring onions, and with some pickled ginger.

RABBIT IN HOT BEAN SAUCE

Although game doesn't appear very often on traditional western Chinese menus, when it does, it is cooked with tremendous skill and passion.

SERVES 4

800g/1¾lb rabbit
1 large onion, thinly sliced
5ml/1 tsp Sichuan peppercorns
15m/1 tbsp groundnut/peanut oil
30ml/2 tbsp grated fresh root ginger
30ml/2 tbsp chilli bean paste (dou banjiang)
30ml/2 tbsp light soy sauce
15ml/1 tbsp hoisin sauce
30ml/2 tbsp sesame oil
fresh coriander/cilantro leaves and chillies, to garnish

1 Cut the rabbit into bitesize pieces, removing as much bone as possible. Bring a large pan of water to the boil and add the onion, Sichuan peppercorns and rabbit pieces. Simmer for 10 minutes, then lift out the rabbit using a slotted spoon. Set aside.

2 Heat the oil in a wok and fry the ginger for 40 seconds until lightly browned. Add the chilli bean paste, soy sauce, hoisin sauce and sesame oil, then stir briefly for 20 seconds.

3 Add the rabbit and stir-fry over a medium heat for 3–4 minutes, or until it is thoroughly covered in the sauce. Garnish each portion with a coriander leaf and a decorative chilli, and serve.

Variation

You can also use a 1kg/2¼lb whole chicken or 4 chicken legs.

HOT-AND-SOUR KIDNEYS

SERVES 4

- 2 pig's kidneys
- 5ml/1 tsp cornflour/cornstarch
- 8 dried Chinese mushrooms, soaked for 30 minutes in warm water until soft
- 15ml/1 tbsp groundnut/peanut oil
- 3 fresh green chillies, seeded and sliced
- 5ml/1 tsp chilli paste
- 15ml/1 tbsp light soy sauce
- 30ml/2 tbsp rice wine or vinegar
- 15ml/1 tbsp sesame oil
- 1 green bell pepper, seeded and cut into chunks
- 75g/3oz bamboo shoot slices
- fresh coriander/cilantro leaves, to garnish

Variation

If you like, you can use half kidneys and half liver in this recipe, as the two taste good together.

In Chinese cooking, particularly in Chengdu, Sichuan's capital city, offal (or organ meat) is much revered for its robust flavour and nutritional value. The kidneys in this recipe are cooked in a hot-and-sour blend of flavourings, which is typical of the regional cuisine.

1 Cut the kidneys horizontally to make two halves, then trim off the white membrane. Soak in cold water for 15 minutes, then drain on kitchen paper. Blend the cornflour with 75ml/5 tbsp water. Set aside.

2 Make criss-cross cuts halfway down the outer side of each kidney half, but do not cut all the way through. Cut each half into three or four pieces. Quarter the softened mushrooms.

3 Heat the oil in a wok and fry the green chillies for 30 seconds, then add the chilli paste, soy sauce, wine or vinegar and sesame oil. Stir-fry for 1 minute, then add the mushrooms, green pepper and bamboo shoots. Stir for 1 minute and add the kidney pieces.

4 Stir over a high heat for 30 seconds, then add the cornflour mixture. Cook for 1 minute more, or until the sauce is thick and the kidneys are cooked through. Serve, garnished with fresh coriander.

WESTERN CHINA

RICE & NOODLES

SPEEDY STIR-FRIES & STICKY PARCELS

In western China, the majority of rice is grown in Yunnan, Guizhou and Sichuan provinces. When reference is made to 'sticky rice' it can refer to any rice that is high in starchy molecules, which form a gel enclosing the water within their strands.

Throughout China, when rice is cooked, there are two basic methods: boiling or steaming. Once rice is cooked, it can be used as the basis for the iconic fried rice. Starchier rice such as glutinous is best soaked for several hours and then steamed or boiled. Sichuan, Hubei and Hunan chefs use this to encase savoury or sweet fillings and then wrap the whole thing in lotus or bamboo leaves to create tempting parcels.

While rice is the fundamental staple in some Chinese regions, in the western provinces, noodles and other wheat flour products are equally popular carbohydrates. They are eaten at all hours of the day in Sichuan and Hunan, whether simply stir-fried with some vegetables or enriched with meat and fish for a more nourishing dish.

Noodles take on an extraordinary variety of shapes, some as wide as lasagne and others so thin they resemble silk thread. The range is endless: fresh or dried, round or flat, and made from wheat, mung beans or, less often, rice flour. In Chengdu, hand-made noodles are expertly made on the streets and in restaurants: noodle-makers can be seen kneading large lumps of dough, pulling and stretching every which way until, miraculously, they are transformed into fine or thick threads.

BLACK RICE PORRIDGE

SERVES 4

150g/5oz/generous ⅔ cup black glutinous rice, soaked overnight
90g/3½oz smoked ham, diced into 1cm/½in cubes
90g/3½oz skinless chicken breast, diced into 1cm/½in cubes
30ml/2 tbsp light soy sauce
15ml/1 tbsp sesame oil
salt and ground white pepper
fresh coriander/cilantro leaves or chopped spring onions/ scallions, to garnish

Grown throughout subtropical China, black rice is particularly common in Sichuan and Hunan. It is generally glutinous and has to be treated like normal glutinous rice, needing a long soak to soften the dense grains.

1 Drain the rice and place in a large pan with 2 litres/3½ pints/ 9 cups water. Bring to the boil, then reduce the heat to low and simmer for 45 minutes. Check occasionally that it doesn't become too thick, adding more hot water if necessary. The consistency should be like a creamy porridge.

2 Add the ham and chicken and cook for a further 5 minutes, then add the soy sauce, sesame oil, and the salt and pepper. Continue to simmer for 10 minutes more, then serve, garnished with fresh coriander leaves or chopped spring onions.

Cook's Tip

Soak glutinous rice overnight to achieve a creamy porridge.

SERVES 4

30ml/2 tbsp groundnut/peanut oil
3 garlic cloves, crushed
2 eggs, lightly beaten
200g/7oz/1 cup long grain or jasmine rice, cooked and left to become cold, or 400g/14oz/ 2 cups cold cooked rice
150g/5oz fresh pineapple, diced
75g/3oz dry-cured ham, diced into 5mm/¼in cubes
2 spring onions/scallions, chopped
25g/1oz/2 tbsp garden peas
2.5ml/½ tsp ground Sichuan peppercorns
15ml/1 tbsp sesame oil

PINEAPPLE RICE

This recipe of rice with pineapple and ham comes from Yunnan, which has a rugged terrain dissected by deep valleys and crossed by mountains. It has a subtropical, humid climate where rice, tea, peanuts, pineapples and other tropical fruits grow in abundance.

1 Heat the oil in a wok and fry the garlic for 30 seconds. Push it to one side and pour in the eggs. Cook until set, then cut up roughly with a wok ladle. Add the cold rice and stir for 2 minutes over a medium heat.

2 Add the pineapple, ham, spring onions, peas, pepper and sesame oil, then continue to stir-fry over a medium heat for 5 minutes. Serve hot, garnished with an extra sprinkling of ground Sichuan peppercorns, if you like.

GLUTINOUS RICE IN BAMBOO LEAVES

Blade-shaped bamboo leaves make versatile wrappers and also impart a pleasant flavour to whatever food you wrap in them. Although they are usually used to wrap individual dumplings – traditionally for the dumpling festival in China – they can be overlapped in a container to wrap a larger amount, such as the rice and stuffing in this recipe. When the leaves are opened at the table, the lovely aromas are released.

SERVES 4

400g/14oz/2 cups glutinous rice
5ml/1 tsp salt
6–8 dried bamboo leaves
hoisin or Xinkiang black vinegar, to serve

FOR THE STUFFING
4 dried shiitake mushrooms, soaked in hot water for 30 minutes
30ml/2 tbsp groundnut/peanut oil
2 garlic cloves, crushed
200g/7oz lean pork, diced
30ml/2 tbsp light soy sauce
30ml/2 tbsp oyster sauce
15ml/1 tbsp sesame oil
5ml/1 tsp ground black pepper
1 small spring onion/scallion, chopped

Cook's Tips

• It is important not to add salt to the rice before it is steamed, as it won't cook properly.

• You can use dried lotus leaves instead of bamboo, if you like.

1 Soak the glutinous rice in water for at least 6 hours or overnight. Drain well. Spread the rice in a steamer tray over simmering water. Steam over a high heat for 20 minutes – do not add salt. Fluff up the rice using a fork and then stir in the salt. Set aside.

2 To make the stuffing, drain the shiitake mushrooms and rinse well to remove any grit. Cut off and discard the stalks and cut the caps into small dice.

3 Heat the oil in a wok over a high heat. Fry the garlic for 30 seconds, then add the pork and mushrooms, and stir-fry for 5 minutes. Add the remaining ingredients with 100ml/3½fl oz/scant ½ cup water. Partially cover and cook for 5 minutes, stirring occasionally. Cover and set aside.

4 Plunge the bamboo leaves in a pan of simmering water for 1–2 minutes, to blanch them until softened and flexible. Place 3 or 4 leaves in a deep dish or casserole, fanning them out to cover the base and sides. Spread half the rice on top of leaves, then top with the pork mixture. Cover with the remaining rice and pat into a neat mound. Cover with the rest of the bamboo leaves, and tuck in the edges to seal. Put the dish into a steamer over simmering water.

5 Steam the parcel over a high heat for 20–25 minutes, or until fully heated through. Serve, with a hoisin or black vinegar dip.

Variation

Shelled roasted or boiled chestnuts make a great addition to the filling.

CLAY-POT RICE WITH SALT FISH

This Sichuan dish is real comfort food all over China, especially among rural folk. Cooked first in an ordinary pan and than served in a heated clay pot, it's like a casserole and is full of flavour. Seasonings vary from region to region, as do the meats and seafood. Look for salt fish made from meaty fish such as haddock or cod. If these are not available, Portuguese dried salt fish, bacalao, can be used but it requires soaking first.

SERVES 4

45ml/3 tbsp vegetable oil
90g/3½oz Chinese salt fish, cut into small dice
1 Chinese sausage, thinly sliced
400g/14oz/2 cups jasmine rice
2 garlic cloves, crushed
200g/7oz skinless chicken breast, diced
4 dried Chinese mushrooms, soaked and chopped
30ml/2 tbsp oyster sauce
30ml/2 tbsp sesame oil
5ml/1 tsp ground black pepper
15ml/1 tbsp light soy sauce

1 Heat the oil in a wok and fry the salt fish over a medium heat until fragrant and crisp. Remove the fish from the pan and leave to cool. Fry the sliced sausage for 2 minutes over a low heat and remove.

2 Put the rice in a pan and add water to come up to 2.5cm/1in above the level of the rice. Bring to the boil and simmer, covered, for 20–25 minutes, or until tender.

3 While the rice is cooking, heat the oil remaining in the pan, add the garlic and fry for 30 seconds.

4 Add the chicken, mushrooms, oyster sauce, sesame oil, ground black pepper and soy sauce, then stir-fry for 2 minutes. Add 75ml/5 tbsp water and stir for 2 minutes, or until thick.

5 Heap the chicken mixture on to the rice for the last 5 minutes of cooking and blend well. If you like, heat a clay pot in a hot oven for 10 minutes and transfer the rice to it for serving, although you can, of course, just serve from the pan.

DAN DAN NOODLES

Of all the Sichuan street foods, this dish has probably the highest profile and is also the most well-travelled. It was originally sold by itinerant hawkers in Chengdu, and the name is believed to derive from the bamboo pole, or dan, slung across the hawkers' shoulders. The dan held baskets at each end containing cooking paraphernalia such as a stove and other kitchen equipment. The hawkers announced their arrival by shouting 'Dan dan mien!'

SERVES 4

- 15ml/1 tbsp groundnut/peanut oil
- 45g/1¾oz/3 tbsp Sichuan pickled vegetables, chopped
- 4 spring onions/scallions, chopped
- 30ml/2 tbsp light soy sauce
- 30ml/2 tbsp fresh chilli paste or chilli oil
- 15ml/1 tbsp Xinkiang black vinegar
- 5ml/1 tsp Sichuan peppercorns, finely ground
- 350g/12oz thin fresh wheat noodles (see Cook's Tip)

FOR THE TOPPING

- 15ml/1 tbsp groundnut/peanut oil
- 115g/4oz/½ cup minced/ground pork or beef, not too lean
- 15ml/1 tbsp Chinese wine or dry sherry
- 15ml/1 tbsp dark soy sauce
- 10ml/2 tsp yellow bean paste

1 Heat the oil in a wok and fry the pickled vegetables briefly for 30 seconds. Remove from the pan and put in a bowl. Set aside.

2 To make the topping, heat the oil in a wok over a high heat and stir-fry the pork or beef for 1 minute. Add the wine or sherry, soy sauce and yellow bean paste. Stir-fry for 1 minute more, or until the meat is cooked through.

3 Add the spring onions to the pickled vegetables in the bowl and stir in the soy sauce, chilli paste or oil, vinegar and peppercorns.

4 Plunge the noodles into a pan of rapidly boiling water and cook them for 1–2 minutes, or until they are just tender but not limp. Drain the noodles thoroughly and transfer them to a serving bowl.

5 Toss the seasoned vegetables into the noodles, then top with the meat mixture. Mix well before serving.

Cook's Tip

There are several types of fresh wheat noodles available today, but for this recipe use one that is the thickness of spaghetti or even spaghettini.

COLD NOODLES

SERVES 4

25g/1oz/2 tbsp dried prawns/shrimp
30ml/2 tbsp light soy sauce, plus extra to serve
30ml/2 tbsp rice wine or vinegar
15ml/1 tbsp sesame oil, plus extra for drizzling
2 spring onions/scallions, chopped
450g/1lb fresh wheat or egg noodles, the thickness of spaghetti
½ cucumber, peeled, cored and sliced into fine shreds

TO SERVE
25g/1oz/2 tbsp Sichuan pickled vegetables, soaked and chopped
rice wine or vinegar
dried chilli flakes (optional)

Although cold noodles are really a preserve of the Japanese, Chinese chefs also make the occasional cool dish during the hot and humid summer months. This recipe is believed to have originated in Shanghai but found its way to north-western China over time.

1 Soak the prawns in warm water for 10 minutes. Drain and remove any pieces of shell. Wash and drain again. Chop roughly, then put into a serving bowl. Stir in the soy sauce, rice wine or vinegar, sesame oil and spring onions.

2 Plunge the noodles into a bowl of boiling water, or according to the packet instructions, until softened. Drain, then transfer to a serving bowl. Drizzle sesame oil all over, then set aside to cool.

3 To serve, toss the prawns and cucumber with the noodles at the table, and serve with side dishes of rice wine or vinegar (with optional chilli flakes) and pickled vegetables, so diners can help themselves.

SERVES 2

150g/5oz mung bean noodles
200g/7oz/scant 1 cup minced/ ground pork
30ml/2 tbsp dark soy sauce
5ml/1 tsp caster/superfine sugar
10ml/2 tsp cornflour/cornstarch
5ml/1 tsp chilli paste
2.5ml/½ tsp ground black pepper
45ml/3 tbsp vegetable oil
2 garlic cloves, finely chopped
2 spring onions/scallions, finely chopped
1 red chilli, seeded and finely chopped, to garnish

Variation

If you can't find Xinkiang vinegar, use dark wine vinegar instead.

PORK MINCE & GLASS NOODLES

This Chongqing dish of mung bean noodles (translucent vermicelli) and pork is fondly known as 'ants climbing trees', so-called because the cooked meat looks rather like ants clambering over a silky mound. Flavoured with garlic, chilli and soy, it is a truly delicious combination.

1 Soak the noodles in warm water for 20 minutes, or until they swell to almost double their dry size. Drain and set aside.

2 Put the pork in a large bowl and add the soy sauce, sugar, cornflour, chilli paste and pepper. Mix well together.

3 Heat the oil and fry the garlic until golden, then add the onions. Fry for 1 minute. Add the pork, stirring with a spoon to break it up.

4 Stir-fry for 2–3 minutes, or until the pork is well cooked through. Add 20ml/4fl oz/1/2 cup water and the soaked noodles. Toss for 20–30 seconds, or until the noodles are just tender and have absorbed the sauce. Serve, garnished with the chopped red chilli.

STIR-FRIED NOODLES WITH PORK

One of the most basic noodle dishes, this Shaanxi staple is perfect comfort food when you are pushed for time; fresh wheat noodles need only to be briefly blanched, or you could even use instant ones and discard the flavour sachet. Beansprouts are the perfect crunchy complement to the soft noodles, to give the dish its yin and yang balance.

SERVES 4

- 250g/9oz fresh wheat noodles
- 115g/4oz lean pork, fat removed
- 30ml/2 tbsp groundnut/peanut oil
- 2 garlic cloves, chopped
- 30ml/2 tbsp oyster sauce
- 2.5ml/½ tsp ground black pepper
- 65g/2½ oz beansprouts

1 Plunge the noodles into a pan of boiling water for 1 minute, to blanch briefly, then drain. Slice the pork into thin strips.

2 Heat the oil in a wok and fry the garlic for 30 seconds, then add the pork strips, oyster sauce and pepper. Stir-fry for 2 minutes, or until the pork is cooked through.

3 Add the beansprouts and noodles, then stir-fry for 2 minutes over a high heat. Add 90ml/6 tbsp water. Stir to blend well and serve hot.

Cook's Tip

For vegetarians, substitute pork with the equivalent amount of half and half sliced mushrooms or whole button/white mushrooms and dried tofu.

BEEF & CHIVE NOODLES

SERVES 4

300g/11oz dry egg noodles
30ml/2 tbsp sesame oil
5ml/1 tsp ground Sichuan peppercorns
30ml/2 tbsp dark soy sauce
5ml/1 tsp cornflour/cornstarch
200g/7oz beef sirloin, sliced into thin strips
30ml/2 tbsp groundnut/peanut oil
4 garlic cloves, chopped
25g/1oz fresh ginger, shredded
75g/3oz Chinese chives, cut into 5cm/2in lengths
120ml/4fl oz/½ cup water

TO SERVE
2 fresh green chillies, chopped
30ml/2 tbsp dark soy sauce
15ml/1 tbsp grated ginger
30ml/2 tbsp Xinkiang black vinegar
fresh coriander/cilantro

Sichuan noodle dishes have a reputation for being hearty, as they are meant to be complete meals in themselves. This one uses Chinese chives, which are a favourite for their crunch, and is accompanied by piquant flavourings.

1 Prepare the accompaniments. Put the chillies into a small dish and mix in the soy sauce. Put the ginger into a small dish with the black vinegar. Put the fresh coriander into a small dish.

2 Cook the noodles in a pan of boiling water for 5 minutes or according to the packet instructions. Drain and set aside, raking them with chopsticks or a fork to separate the strands.

3 Put the sesame oil into a bowl and blend in the peppercorns, soy sauce and cornflour. Add the beef and toss. Marinate for 10 minutes.

4 Heat the oil in a wok and fry the garlic and ginger for 30 seconds. Add the beef and marinade and stir-fry for 2 minutes. Add the noodles and chives, then cook, stirring, for 1 minute. Add the water and stir until the sauce is thick. Serve with the accompaniments.

WESTERN CHINA
VEGETABLES

CRISP & FRESH, PICKLED & FRIED

The vegetables in western China tend to be pickled or stir-fried in a multitude of dishes. Various types of aubergines, ranging from white to deep purple, slender to plump, and tiny to large, are available all year round. They are deep-fried, then stir-fried with a medley of flavoursome ingredients in the classic dish Shredded Aubergine.

Crunchy beansprouts pop up almost everywhere, eaten raw or stir-fried. Bamboo shoots are prolific here because of the sub-tropical climate, and have a chameleon-like quality, absorbing other flavours while at the same time imparting their own distinctive scent.

Chives are found in three forms throughout China: green chives (jiu cai) with flat slim-bladed leaves; yellow chives (jiu huang), which are grown under a cloche or in the dark; and flowering chives (also known as garlic chives) with sturdy round stems tipped with pointed green buds. All feature prominently in Sichuan and Hubei cooking and are much loved for their garlicky flavour.

Mustard greens are often pickled to be used as a robust foil for other ingredients. Most versatile, they turn up in many a vegetarian soup, as a salting agent or as a stir-fried vegetable in their own right. Fresh coriander and celery are used imaginatively, not merely as garnishes but as featured players in bold salads.

It is, however, the Sichuan bean, similar to the green bean, that has become truly representative of classic Sichuan vegetarian cooking.

SPICY CUCUMBER SALAD

A Hubei staple, this fresh-tasting pickle is flavoured with mustard, chillies and ginger, though there are many taste variations on the theme throughout the region. Leave the flavours to blend for an hour before serving, but then eat it while it is fresh, with grilled meats and chicken.

1 Quarter the cucumber lengthways and cut out the soft core. Slice each strip into 1cm/½in-thick pieces on the diagonal. Sprinkle with salt and leave for 30 minutes.

2 Pound the garlic and ginger to a fine paste using a mortar and pestle. Transfer to a bowl and add the brown sugar, rice wine or vinegar and mustard. Stir well.

3 Squeeze out the moisture from the cucumber pieces and pat dry. Put into a serving bowl. Cut the chillies into thin strips and add to the cucumber. Add the garlic and ginger dressing and mix well. Cover and leave for 1 hour. Serve, sprinkled with sesame seeds.

SERVES 4

1 whole cucumber
5ml/1 tsp salt
4 garlic cloves, peeled and chopped
3 thick slices fresh root ginger, peeled and chopped
5ml/1 tsp soft light brown sugar
30ml/2 tbsp rice wine or vinegar
5ml/1 tsp prepared English or Dijon mustard
4 fresh red chillies, seeded
15ml/1 tbsp sesame seeds

Variation

You can make this recipe using half cucumber and half mooli or daikon, salted, squeezed and drained as for the cucumber.

SERVES 4

300g/11oz Chinese or English celery sticks
10ml/2 tsp salt
75g/3oz fresh coriander/cilantro
5ml/1 tsp ground Sichuan peppercorns
5ml/1 tsp caster/superfine sugar
30ml/2 tbsp rice wine or vinegar
25ml/1½ tbsp sesame oil
25g/1oz/2 tbsp roasted peanuts, coarsely chopped
15ml/1 tbsp sesame seeds, lightly toasted

Cook's Tip

If you prefer your celery less salty, rinse it under running water first.

PICKLED CELERY SALAD

Fresh coriander might not be an obvious salad ingredient but its flavour goes marvellously with celery in this dish from Hubei. It is the simplest of salads, sharp with vinegar and aromatic with ground Sichuan peppercorns.

1 Slice the celery thickly into 1cm/½in-wide pieces on the diagonal. (You can include the leaves, if you wish.) Put it in a colander and sprinkle with the salt. Leave for 25 minutes.

2 Remove the thickest, toughest stalks from the coriander and chop the remainder roughly.

3 Put the Sichuan peppercorns into a bowl and add the sugar, rice wine or vinegar and sesame oil. Whisk to dissolve the sugar.

4 Squeeze out as much moisture as you can from the celery and pat dry with kitchen paper. Place the celery in a bowl, add the fresh coriander and the peppercorn dressing and toss well.

5 Transfer to a serving plate and top with chopped peanuts and sesame seeds, then serve.

SPICY GREEN BEANS

This dish has spawned many regional versions purporting to be 'Sichuan-style' but few come close to the original, which uses a special bean grown in the province, called the 'four-season bean'. However, green beans come close. Sichuan preserved vegetables are bought as a dry product, pickled in salt, then soaked and drained before use.

SERVES 4

15g/½ oz/1 tbsp dried shrimp, soaked for 15 minutes
450g/1lb green beans, trimmed
25g/1oz/2 tbsp Sichuan preserved vegetables, soaked for 15 minutes
vegetable oil, for deep-frying
30ml/2 tbsp groundnut/peanut oil
2 spring onions/scallions, chopped
25g/1oz fresh root ginger, grated
pinch of salt
2.5ml/½ tsp caster/superfine sugar
30ml/2 tbsp chilli bean paste (dou banjiang)
10ml/2 tsp sesame oil
5ml/1 tsp rice wine or vinegar

1 Finely chop the drained shrimp and preserved vegetables. Heat the vegetable oil in a wok over a medium heat. Plunge the beans into the oil for 1–2 minutes or until lightly blistered. Lift out and drain well on kitchen paper.

2 In a clean wok, heat the groundnut oil over high heat and fry the spring onion and ginger for 30 seconds. Add the shrimp and preserved vegetable and stir-fry for 1 minute.

3 Add the salt, paste, sesame oil, wine and the fried beans, stir for 30 seconds then add a splash of water, stir for a minute and serve.

PICKLED MUSTARD GREENS

SERVES 6–8

- 1 litre/1¾ pints/4 cups water
- 45ml/3 tbsp crushed rock or sea salt
- 5 fresh red chillies, stalks removed but left whole
- 2.5ml/½ tsp ground Sichuan peppercorns
- 15ml/1 tbsp rice wine or vinegar
- 15ml/1 tbsp soft light brown sugar
- 25g/1oz fresh root ginger, grated
- 450g/1lb mustard greens, cut into 5cm/2in pieces

Cook's Tips

Dry the greens thoroughly before brining. Sometimes only the tender leaves are pickled. Tenderstem broccoli, purple sprouting broccoli or chard could also be used as a substitute.

Mustard greens, called qing cai in Mandarin or gai choy in Cantonese, are most often sun-dried, rubbed with salt, and pickled in spices and sugar, as in this Guizhou recipe. Large, fleshy and bright jade, the greens have a crisp and slightly bitter edge when stir-fried, but when pickled they have a robust flavour and texture. They can be left to mature for months in earthenware or ceramic crocks, and are then known as ya cai in Mandarin.

1 Bring the water to a boil in a pan, add the salt and stir to dissolve. Allow to cool completely before pouring into a clean large pickling jar or non-metal bowl. Add the chillies, peppercorns, rice wine or vinegar, sugar and ginger, and stir well. Put in the mustard greens.

2 Put a clean plate on top and weight down with a heavy object to ensure the vegetables are completely immersed. Cover tightly with clear film or a large plate and store in a cool, dark place for at least four days; they are best after a week. To serve, drain and squeeze out any excess liquid, and cut the greens into shreds.

MIXED MUSHROOM STIR-FRY

Yunnan chefs are adept at cooking the many varieties of mushrooms found in the region, the most popular being dried mushrooms, straw mushrooms and oyster mushrooms. You can use any mixture, or even just one type.

1 Drain and rinse the canned mushrooms. Cut off the hard stalks from the soaked dried mushrooms. Cut all the mushrooms into similar-sized pieces.

2 Heat the oil in a wok and fry the ginger and garlic for 30 seconds, until golden brown, then add the mushrooms. Stir-fry for 2 minutes.

3 Put the cornflour into a bowl and blend in 60ml/4 tbsp water. Add the oyster sauce to the wok with the soy sauce, pepper and cornflour mixture. Stir until the sauce is thick and serve hot, garnished with fresh coriander leaves.

SERVES 4

- 200g/7oz canned straw mushrooms
- 200g/7oz dried Chinese mushrooms, soaked for 30 minutes in warm water
- 200g/7oz canned button/white or oyster mushrooms
- 30ml/2 tbsp groundnut/peanut oil
- 2 slices fresh root ginger, chopped
- 3 garlic cloves, chopped
- 5ml/1 tsp cornflour/cornstarch
- 30ml/2 tbsp oyster sauce
- 15ml/1 tbsp soy sauce
- 2.5ml/½ tsp ground black pepper
- fresh coriander/cilantro leaves, to garnish

STIR-FRIED BAMBOO SHOOTS

SERVES 4

450g/1lb cooked bamboo shoots, thinly sliced
30ml/2 tbsp groundnut/peanut oil
2 garlic cloves, crushed
30ml/2 tbsp oyster sauce
30ml/2 tbsp sesame oil
15ml/1 tbsp yellow bean sauce
5ml/1 tsp caster/superfine sugar
5ml/1 tsp cornflour/cornstarch
fresh coriander/cilantro leaves, to garnish

Cook's Tip

Bamboo shoots are sold in many forms: fresh, canned and vacuum-packed cooked, fermented, pickled with chillies, as young shoots in water, and so on.

Bamboo shoots are cooked throughout China and are much loved for their taste and firm texture that never goes mushy. This recipe uses the bold flavours of oyster sauce and yellow bean sauce to give the bamboo shoots richness.

1 If you are using canned bamboo shoots, soak them in fresh water for 1 hour. Drain well and pat lightly dry with kitchen paper.

2 Heat the oil in a wok over a high heat. Add the garlic and fry for 45 seconds, then add the bamboo shoots. Stir-fry vigorously for 1 minute, then stir in the oyster sauce, sesame oil, yellow bean sauce and sugar.

3 Fry for 1 minute more, then add 105ml/7 tbsp water. Simmer for 2–3 minutes, or until the sauce is reduced.

4 Blend the cornflour with 15ml/1 tbsp water, then add this to the wok and cook until the sauce is thickened and glossy. Serve hot, garnished with fresh coriander.

STIR-FRIED CHIVE STEMS

Garlic stems, also called Chinese chives or garlic chives, are quite different from common chives, being thicker and juicier, rather like green beans, and tipped with small pale green heads. The chives have a pronounced green onion and garlic flavour, so there is no need to add garlic here.

SERVES 4

200g/7oz firm tofu
30ml/2 tbsp groundnut/peanut oil
450g/1lb Chinese chives, cut into 5cm/2in lengths
30ml/2 tbsp light soy sauce
2.5ml/½ tsp ground black pepper
15ml/1 tbsp sesame oil

1 Cut the tofu into four squares and again into thin slices, each about 5mm/¼in thick.

2 Heat the oil in a wok over a high heat. Add the tofu and fry for 1 minute, or until lightly browned on both sides.

3 Push the tofu to one side, add the chives and stir-fry for 1 minute, taking care not to break up the tofu. Add the soy sauce, pepper, sesame oil and 60ml/4 tbsp water. Stir for 1 minute more, or until the water has evaporated and the chives are just tender. Serve hot.

Cook's Tip

Take care not to over-stir the ingredients in the wok or you will break up the tofu pieces.

SERVES 4

450g/1lb courgettes/zucchini
30ml/2 tbsp groundnut/peanut oil
25g/1oz fresh root ginger, grated
2 garlic cloves, crushed
2.5ml/½ tsp finely ground Sichuan peppercorns
15ml/1 tbsp light soy sauce
2.5ml/½ tsp caster/superfine sugar
15ml/1 tbsp oyster sauce

STIR-FRIED SPICY COURGETTES

Courgettes can be stir-fried if you use the young, firm ones. Do not peel them, as most of the nutrients are just under the skin, which is not fibrous. With older courgettes, however, it is best to remove the skin.

1 Slice the courgettes into thick strips, about 2cm x 7.5cm/¾in x 3in. Bring a small pan of water to the boil and plunge in the courgettes. Cook for 1 minute to blanch them. Drain.

2 Heat the groundnut oil in a wok and fry the ginger and garlic for 1 minute, then add the blanched courgettes. Stir-fry over a high heat for 1 minute, then add the peppercorns, soy sauce, sugar and oyster sauce.

3 Cook, stirring, for 1 more minute, then add 30ml/2 tbsp water. Bring to a quick boil and serve hot.

SHREDDED AUBERGINE

This dish of fried aubergine strips is traditionally served alongside fish. It is one of the most mouthwatering of western regional dishes, and is believed to have been a favourite of Empress Dowager Cixi whenever she travelled west to Zhongqing. She was frightened of being poisoned, so she would bring her own aubergines from the palace gardens. The reason for this paranoia was that she was not averse to poisoning anyone who crossed her!

SERVES 4

- 450g/1lb aubergines/eggplants or Asian brinjals
- vegetable oil, for deep-frying
- 30ml/2 tbsp groundnut/peanut oil
- 25g/1oz fresh root ginger, finely grated
- 2 garlic cloves, crushed
- 2 spring onions/scallions, chopped
- 30ml/2 tbsp light soy sauce
- 30ml/2 tbsp Shaoxing wine or dry sherry
- 5ml/1 tsp hot chilli paste or sauce
- 5ml/1 tsp cornflour/cornstarch
- 30ml/2 tbsp water

1 Cut the aubergines or brinjals into strips about 6 x 2cm/2½ x ¾in. Heat the vegetable oil in a wok over a medium heat or in a deep-fryer and fry the strips, in batches if necessary, for 1–2 minutes, or until browned. Lift out and drain on kitchen paper.

2 Heat the groundnut oil in a clean wok and fry the ginger, garlic and spring onions for 2 minutes. Add the soy sauce and wine or sherry and cook, stirring, for 1 minute, then add the aubergine and chilli paste or sauce and stir-fry for 2 minutes.

3 Blend the cornflour with 30ml/2 tbsp water, then add to the wok. Cook, stirring, until the sauce thickens and coats the aubergines. Serve.

POCK-MARKED TOFU

SERVES 4

2 packets firm tofu (about 650g/1lb 7oz), cut into 2cm/ ¾in cubes
30ml/2 tbsp groundnut/peanut oil
15ml/1 tbsp finely chopped garlic
1 fresh red chilli, finely chopped
5ml/1 tsp black bean sauce
30ml/2 tbsp sesame oil
30ml/2 tbsp chilli bean paste (dou banjiang)
200ml/7fl oz/scant 1 cup strong meat or vegetable stock
1 green bell pepper, finely diced
30ml/2 tbsp peas, thawed if frozen
5ml/1 tsp cornflour/cornstarch
sliced spring onions/scallions, to garnish

Probably the best-known Sichuan export, this dish has fascinating etymology. Legend has it that it was first cooked by a woman more than 100 years ago in Chengdu. Her husband was a chef who was always experimenting with new dishes, and when she cooked it for him he liked it so much that he named it in her honour.

1 Spread out the tofu on a double layer of kitchen paper to drain for 10 minutes – this makes them less prone to crumbling later.

2 Heat the oil in a wok over a medium-high heat. Add the garlic and chilli, and fry for 40 seconds. Add the black bean sauce, sesame oil and chilli bean paste. Stir for 1 minute, then add the stock. Bring to the boil, then add the tofu, green pepper and peas. Cook for 2 minutes, stirring gently, so that the tofu doesn't break up.

3 Put the cornflour in a small bowl and blend with 15ml/1 tbsp water. Add to the wok, then stir until the sauce has thickened slightly. Serve immediately, garnished with spring onion slices.

WESTERN CHINA
SWEET TREATS

SUGARY TREATS & DELICATE CREATIONS

The products that go into sweet dishes include red or kidney beans, silver ear fungus (called bai mu erh in Mandarin), sesame seeds, tangerine peel, rock sugar and very little else. Tangerine peel is used widely in Hunan cooking, not just for sweet dishes but also with savoury meats and poultry dishes where its citrus flavour is known for cutting the fat. Even Chinese herbalists sell it as an important medicinal herb for treating various illnesses.

Sesame seeds have a versatility all their own, and they are often ground for making the well-known dessert drink, Sesame Cream, which is enjoyed as a late-night snack. Both the white and black varieties are used in similar ways. They turn up often as a coating ingredient for battered and deep-fried foods.

Red beans are cooked and mashed with sugar as a filling for the famous pancakes that originated in Shanghai, though they are popular in western China, too. Used much like almond paste, it has a similar taste and texture to sweet chestnut purée and the Middle Eastern tahini.

Unlike many European desserts where wheat flour is the basic ingredient, rice flour plays the main role in this region. Rice flour balls are a favourite offering, believed to be of peasant origin, and are a featured dish in Hunan during festive days. Known as tong yuan, they are often tinted a delicate pink, as the colour symbolizes prosperity. The sugar syrup is also tinged with the citrus flavour of tangerine peel, which is very much a Hunan speciality.

SESAME CREAM

This is a universal Chinese dessert, which is actually more like a thick drink, and is sold by itinerant hawkers as a late-night snack. You find it in every province, especially Sichuan, where it is also made with black sesame seeds. It is very sweet, so you may want to adjust the amount of sugar.

SERVES 4

350g/12oz/3 cups sesame seeds
115g/4oz/generous ½ cup caster/superfine sugar
120ml/4fl oz/½ cup evaporated milk
15ml/1 tbsp cornflour/cornstarch

1 Put the sesame seeds into a food processor or blender with 350ml/12fl oz/1½ cups water and process until you get a smooth cream.

2 Put the sesame mixture in a pan with 600ml/1 pint/2½ cups water and bring to the boil. Simmer for 10 minutes over a low heat.

3 Add the sugar and evaporated milk, and stir until the sugar dissolves. Put the cornflour in a small bowl and gradually blend with 30ml/2 tbsp water, then add to the sesame mixture and cook until creamy and smooth.

Variation

You can also use nuts for this recipe as they will grind down to the same consistency. Cashew nuts and almonds both work well and have very distinctive flavours.

SERVES 4

50g/2oz dried white fungus or silver-ear fungus
150g/5oz rock sugar

Variation
You could also add a few stoned/pitted Chinese dates or slices of preserved and sweetened winter melon.

SUGARED SILVER-EAR FUNGUS

Many Chinese sweets use esoteric ingredients that are not well known in the West, such as the white or silver-ear fungus called bai mu erh in Mandarin (pictured on page 602). Also called tremella mushrooms, the silver-ear have a gelatinous texture yet are delightfully crunchy.

1 Trim and discard the hard parts of the fungus, then cut into small pieces, wash and drain. Soak in warm water for about 20 minutes, until soft.

2 Put the fungus and sugar in a pan with 800ml/$1\frac{1}{4}$ pints/$3\frac{1}{4}$ cups water. Bring to the boil and simmer for 40 minutes, or until the fungus is jelly-like in texture.

3 Serve cold or warm.

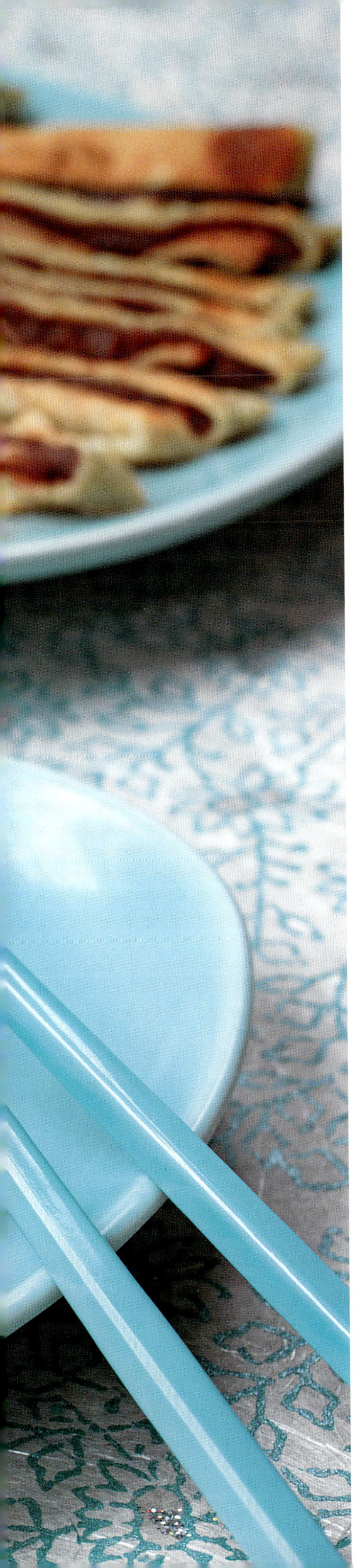

RED BEAN PASTE PANCAKES

Pastes made with red beans and almonds are commonly used in Chinese sweet snacks and festive buns. Red bean paste is a typically Sichuan filling, used in many different ways, but this pancake is by far the most popular. They are eaten throughout China: in Shanghai these are called Shanghai pancakes and in Hong Kong they are named wo bing or wok pancakes. The custard powder gives the batter a good colour when fried.

MAKES 6 PANCAKES

150g/5oz/1¼ cups plain/all-purpose flour
2.5ml/½ tsp custard powder
1 egg, lightly beaten
vegetable oil, for greasing and shallow frying
115g/4oz red bean paste

1 Put the flour in a bowl and add the custard powder and beaten egg, then pour in 400ml/14fl oz/1⅔ cups water and mix to form a batter with the consistency of thin cream. Strain into another bowl to remove any lumps.

2 Oil a sheet of baking parchment and a non-stick frying pan. Heat the pan and pour in 45ml/3 tbsp batter, swirling around the pan so that you get a round, thin pancake.

3 Cook until the underside is speckled with brown, then lift out and put on the baking parchment. Cover with a dish towel. Use the rest of the batter to make more pancakes.

4 When all the pancakes are cooked, spread a thin layer of bean paste in the centre of each (brown side up). Fold one side in to cover the filling and then fold in the other to overlap. Tuck both ends under to seal and make a thin parcel.

5 Heat about 60ml/4 tbsp oil in the pan for shallow frying and cook each pancake, turning over once, until brown and crisp. Cool slightly and cut into slices to serve.

Variations

- Almond and chestnut purées also make excellent fillings, each with a different taste.
- Sprinkle the fried pancakes, while they are still hot, with sesame seeds for extra crunch.

RED BEAN & TANGERINE BROTH

Tangerine peel is used widely in Hunan, not just for sweet dishes but also in meat and poultry recipes. Here it adds flavour to a broth of aduki beans and ginkgo nuts. Ginkgo nuts are known for their restorative properties and are often added to sweet brews.

SERVES 4

150g/5oz dried aduki beans, soaked overnight until soft
1 small piece tangerine peel, 5cm/2in square, plus extra strips to garnish if liked
115g/4oz canned ginkgo nuts
about 175g/6oz/scant 1 cup caster/superfine sugar

1 Drain and rinse the beans, then put them in a medium pan and add 1 litre/1¾ pints/4 cups water. Bring to the boil and simmer for 15 minutes.

2 Add the tangerine peel and simmer for 10 minutes more, or until the beans are soft. Use a wooden spoon to mash them until they become a grainy paste.

3 Add the ginkgo nuts and their liquor, and the sugar, then cook for 5 minutes to make a broth. Taste and add more sugar if necessary, according to taste. Serve, garnished with decorative peel if you like.

Cook's Tips

- If you have a pressure cooker, you can soak the beans in boiling water for 1 hour and then cook them in the pressure cooker for just 20 minutes.
- This broth is the basis of a sweet drink that is often served as a digestive after a surfeit of meat.

MAKES ABOUT 20 BALLS

200g/7oz/1¾ cups rice flour, plus extra for dusting
15g/½oz/2 tbsp tapioca flour
2.5ml/½ tsp salt
175ml/6fl oz/¾ cup tepid water
pinch of red colouring
150g/5oz rock sugar
5cm/2in square piece of tangerine peel

RICE-FLOUR BALLS IN SYRUP

These little rice balls in a fragrant broth are known as tong yuan. Hunan cooks give the balls a delicate pink tint on special occasions, as the colour symbolizes prosperity. The sugar syrup is flavoured with tangerine peel.

1 Sift the two flours and the salt into a bowl and add the tepid water to make soft dough. Dissolve the red colouring in a little water and mix into the dough.

2 Divide the dough into two pieces and roll each on a floured board into a sausage shape about 2cm/1in thick. Pinch off small pieces the size of large grapes and shape them into round balls.

3 Put 800ml/1¼ pints/3¼ cups water in a large pan and bring to the boil. Add the rock sugar and tangerine peel.

4 Drop in the balls and cook for 15 minutes. They will float to the surface when cooked. Serve hot.

PEARL BALLS

Although pearls are symbolic of longevity and beauty, this Sichuan dessert earned its name from the glistening sheen of the glutinous rice grains that coat these little dumplings. Short grain glutinous rice grows best in mountainous areas, of which there are many in Sichuan province. These balls are filled with chestnut purée, making it a tasty fusion dish, which goes particularly well with ice cream.

SERVES 4

- 90g/3½oz/scant ½ cup short grain or ordinary glutinous rice
- 225g/8oz/generous 1 cup glutinous rice flour, plus extra for dusting
- 15ml/1 tbsp rice flour
- 200ml/7fl oz/scant 1 cup warm water
- 115g/4oz/⅓ cup chestnut purée

1 Soak the rice for several hours or overnight in plenty of water. Sift the glutinous rice flour and rice flour together into a bowl and add the warm water. Stir to make a soft, pliable dough.

2 Divide the dough into two or three pieces and roll out on a floured board into sausage shapes about 2.5cm/1in wide. Cut off pieces the size of cherry tomatoes.

3 Flatten each piece and make a dent in the centre. Place 5ml/1 tsp chestnut purée in the centre and seal into balls. Roll to shape evenly like marbles.

4 Drain the glutinous rice grains thoroughly and put on a flat plate. Roll each dough ball around the rice to coat.

5 Arrange on a slightly oiled plate that is large enough to hold them without touching each other; they will swell slightly when steamed.

6 Put the plate in a wok or steamer over simmering water. Steam for 25 minutes, then serve warm.

Cook's Tip

You can make the balls festive by tinting the glutinous rice red, blue or green with a little food colouring, if you like.

NUTRITIONAL INFORMATION

42 Chicken & bamboo shoot soup Energy 94kcal/393kJ; Protein 9g; Carbohydrate 4g, of which sugars 0g; Fat 4g, of which saturates 1g; Cholesterol 22mg; Calcium 9mg; Fibre 1g; Sodium 537mg

43 White fungus & chicken soup Energy 169kcal/701kJ; Protein 9g; Carbohydrate 7g, of which sugars 0g; Fat 12g, of which saturates 2g; Cholesterol 22mg; Calcium 11mg; Fibre 1g; Sodium 452mg

44 Chicken, pea & tomato soup Energy 187kcal/799kJ; Protein 12g; Carbohydrate 8g, of which sugars 5g; Fat 11g, of which saturates 2g; Cholesterol 33mg; Calcium 22mg; Fibre 2g; Sodium 1016mg

45 Chicken & prawn ball soup Energy 169kcal/706kJ; Protein 19g; Carbohydrate 2g, of which sugars 0g; Fat 8g, of which saturates 1g; Cholesterol 144mg; Calcium 55mg; Fibre 0g; Sodium 884mg

46 Tofu & minced pork soup Energy 244kcal/1014kJ; Protein 23g; Carbohydrate 2g, of which sugars 0g; Fat 16g, of which saturates 3g; Cholesterol 155mg; Calcium 345mg; Fibre 1g; Sodium 448mg

47 Sour-and-hot lamb soup Energy 128kcal/534kJ; Protein 11g; Carbohydrate 5g, of which sugars 1g; Fat 7g, of which saturates 3g; Cholesterol 38mg; Calcium 20mg; Fibre 1g; Sodium 904mg

48 Prawn & crab wontons Energy 451kcal/874kJ; Protein 30g; Carbohydrate 13g, of which sugars 1g; Fat 31g, of which saturates 4g; Cholesterol 225mg; Calcium 207mg; Fibre 1g; Sodium 762mg

49 Sesame-coated chicken Energy 168kcal/701kJ; Protein 19g; Carbohydrate 1g, of which sugars 0g; Fat 10g, of which saturates 2g; Cholesterol 102mg; Calcium 56mg; Fibre 1g; Sodium 259mg

50 Little dragon dumplings Energy 482kcal/2027kJ; Protein 28g; Carbohydrate 55g, of which sugars 1g; Fat18g, of which saturates 3g; Cholesterol 129mg; Calcium 145mg; Fibre 3g; Sodium 493mg

53 Lotus leaf parcels Energy 309kcal/1289kJ; Protein 16g; Carbohydrate 10g, of which sugars 0g; Fat 22g, of which saturates 6g; Cholesterol 192mg; Calcium 39mg; Fibre 1g; Sodium 590mg

54 Beef & mushroom dumplings Energy 177kcal/766kJ; Protein 10g; Carbohydrate 21g, of which sugars 1g; Fat 6g, of which saturates 2g; Cholesterol 19mg; Calcium 42mg; Fibre 1g; Sodium 153mg

57 Beef cakes Energy 304kcal/1268kJ; Protein 10g; Carbohydrate 25g, of which sugars 1g; Fat 19g, of which saturates 4g; Cholesterol 20mg; Calcium 44mg; Fibre 1g; Sodium 232mg

63 Raw fish salad Energy 263kcal/1093kJ; Protein 23g; Carbohydrate 5g, of which sugars 5g; Fat 16g, of which saturates 3g; Cholesterol 56mg; Calcium 47mg; Fibre 1g; Sodium 309mg

64 Sweet-and-sour prawns Energy 266kcal/1114kJ; Protein 21g; Carbohydrate 15g, of which sugars 6g; Fat 12g, of which saturates 1g; Cholesterol 219mg; Calcium 99mg; Fibre 2g; Sodium 308mg

65 Prawn cutlets Energy 332kcal/1386kJ; Protein 28g; Carbohydrate 11g, of which sugars 0g; Fat 20g, of which saturates 3g; Cholesterol 335mg; Calcium 365mg; Fibre 0g; Sodium 443mg

66 Fresh scallops & pak choi Energy 162kcal/674kJ; Protein 13g; Carbohydrate 7g, of which sugars 1g; Fat 8g, of which saturates 1g; Cholesterol 24mg; Calcium 57mg; Fibre 1g; Sodium 344mg

67 Fish & tofu mock crab cakes Energy 270kcal/1123kJ; Protein 21g; Carbohydrate 18g, of which sugars 1g; Fat 17g, of which saturates 2g; Cholesterol 98mg; Calcium 178mg; Fibre 0g; Sodium 257mg

68 Mongolian seafood steamboat Energy 163kcal/687kJ; Protein 29g; Carbohydrate 3g, of which sugars 1g; Fat 4g, of which saturates 1g; Cholesterol 172mg; Calcium 200mg; Fibre 1g; Sodium 581mg

70 Garlic eel cutlets Energy 324kcal/1344kJ; Protein 20g; Carbohydrate 6g, of which sugars 2g; Fat 24g, of which saturates 5g; Cholesterol 169mg; Calcium 38mg; Fibre 1g; Sodium 260mg

71 Trout in wine sauce Energy 300kcal/1251kJ; Protein 22g; Carbohydrate 6g, of which sugars 2g; Fat 20g, of which saturates 3g; Cholesterol 75mg; Calcium 30mg; Fibre 1g; Sodium 546mg

73 Steamed fish with ginger Energy 161kcal/671kJ; Protein 15g; Carbohydrate 4g, of which sugars 3g; Fat 10g, of which saturates 1g; Cholesterol 60mg; Calcium 130mg; Fibre 1g; Sodium 278mg

74 Monkfish in yellow bean sauce Energy 192kcal/805kJ; Protein 18g; Carbohydrate 3g, of which sugars 1g; Fat 12g, of which saturates 1g; Cholesterol 16mg; Calcium 24mg; Fibre 1g; Sodium 211mg

75 Crispy fish Energy 197kcal/833kJ; Protein 31g; Carbohydrate 11g, of which sugars 3g; Fat 3g, of which saturates 1g; Cholesterol 56mg; Calcium 67mg; Fibre 0g; Sodium 355mg

77 Red cooked fish Energy 245kcal/1023kJ; Protein 23g; Carbohydrate 7g, of which sugars 2g; Fat 13g, of which saturates 2g; Cholesterol 42mg; Calcium 58mg; Fibre 1g; Sodium 279mg

78 Hot-and-sour carp Energy 217kcal/899kJ; Protein 11g; Carbohydrate 6g, of which sugars 2g; Fat 17g, of which saturates 2g; Cholesterol 43mg; Calcium 43mg; Fibre 1g; Sodium 613mg

79 Carp in ginger sesame sauce Energy 210kcal/873kJ; Protein 13g; Carbohydrate 2g, of which sugars 1g; Fat 16g, of which saturates 2g; Cholesterol 42mg; Calcium 99mg; Fibre 2g; Sodium 521mg

84 Chicken with walnuts Energy 359kcal/1459kJ; Protein 29g; Carbohydrate 6g, of which sugars 5g; Fat 25g, of which saturates 2g; Cholesterol 70mg; Calcium 36mg; Fibre 2g; Sodium 157mg

85 Chicken with hoisin sauce Energy 178kcal/751kJ; Protein 25g; Carbohydrate 8g, of which sugars 4g; Fat 5g, of which saturates 1g; Cholesterol 70mg; Calcium 21mg; Fibre 2g; Sodium 254mg

87 Tea-smoked chicken Energy 623kcal/2599kJ; Protein 57g; Carbohydrate 1g, of which sugars 0g; Fat 43g, of which saturates 12g; Cholesterol 258mg; Calcium 25mg; Fibre 0g; Sodium 673mg

88 Five-spice smoked chicken Energy 126kcal/529kJ; Protein 18g; Carbohydrate 1g, of which sugars 0g; Fat 5g, of which saturates 1g; Cholesterol 53mg; Calcium 6mg; Fibre 0g; Sodium 716mg

90 Phoenix chicken Energy 466kcal/1947kJ; Protein 52g; Carbohydrate 7g, of which sugars 2g; Fat 26g, of which saturates 5g; Cholesterol 197mg; Calcium 31mg; Fibre 1g; Sodium 739mg

91 Kwei-fei chicken Energy 534kcal/2225kJ; Protein 44g; Carbohydrate 2g, sugars 1g; Fat 34g, of which saturates 9g; Cholesterol 193mg; Calcium 36mg; Fibre 0g; Sodium 1216mg

92 Oil-soaked chicken Energy 202kcal/839kJ; Protein 9g; Carbohydrate 9g, of which sugars 2g; Fat 14g, of which saturates 2g; Cholesterol 48mg; Calcium 13mg; Fibre 0g; Sodium 899mg

93 Steamed chicken with wine Energy 173kcal/727kJ; Protein 28g; Carbohydrate 2g, of which sugars 1g; Fat 5g, of which saturates 1g; Cholesterol 79mg; Calcium 16mg; Fibre 0g; Sodium 427mg

94 Braised chicken & chestnuts Energy 296kcal/1216kJ; Protein 24g; Carbohydrate 8g, of which sugars 3g; Fat 19g, of which saturates 4g; Cholesterol 114mg; Calcium 30mg; Fibre 2g; Sodium 479mg

95 Braised quails Energy 550kcal/293kJ; Protein 49g; Carbohydrate 16g, of which sugars 3g; Fat 32g, of which saturates 5g; Cholesterol 44mg; Calcium 70mg; Fibre 0g; Sodium 1185mg

97 Braised duck in peppery soy sauce Energy 657kcal/2719kJ; Protein 31g; Carbohydrate 1g, of which sugars 0g; Fat 59g, of which saturates 17g; Cholesterol 149mg; Calcium 35mg; Fibre 0g; Sodium 917mg

98 Peking duck Energy 113kcal/476kJ; Protein 13g; Carbohydrate 3g, of which sugars 3g; Fat 6g, of which saturates 2g; Cholesterol 63mg; Calcium 8mg; Fibre 0g; Sodium 54mg

104 Stewed spare ribs Energy 301kcal/1250kJ; Protein 24g; Carbohydrate 6g, of which sugars 3g; Fat 19g, of which saturates 6g; Cholesterol 84mg; Calcium 16mg; Fibre 0g; Sodium 820mg

105 Pork & turnips Energy 210kcal/880kJ; Protein 25g; Carbohydrate 4g, of which sugars 4g; Fat10g, of which saturates 2g; Cholesterol 72mg; Calcium 32mg; Fibre 1g; Sodium 758mg

107 Mu shu pork Energy 540kcal/2239kJ; Protein 28g; Carbohydrate 10g, of which sugars 1g; Fat 43g, of which saturates 7g; Cholesterol 288mg; Calcium 53mg; Fibre 0g; Sodium 384mg

108 Sweet-and-sour lamb Energy 243kcal/1014kJ; Protein 17g; Carbohydrate 14g, of which sugars 9g; Fat 14g, of which saturates 3g; Cholesterol 56mg; Calcium 30mg; Fibre 1g; Sodium 151mg

109 Cassia lamb Energy 210kcal/873kJ; Protein 16g; Carbohydrate 1g, of which sugars 0g; Fat 16g, of which saturates 6g; Cholesterol 215mg; Calcium 31mg; Fibre 0g; Sodium 274mg

110 Cumin & caraway lamb Energy 337kcal/1401kJ; Protein 17g; Carbohydrate 12g, of which sugars 8g; Fat 25g, of which saturates 5g; Cholesterol 56mg; Calcium 51mg; Fibre 1g; Sodium 162mg

113 Tung-Po mutton Energy 312kcal/1299kJ; Protein 22g; Carbohydrate 12g, of which sugars 5g; Fat 20g, of which saturates 5g; Cholesterol 74mg; Calcium 39mg; Fibre 2g; Sodium 806mg

114 Sliced beef & bamboo shoots Energy 253kcal/1056kJ; Protein 21g; Carbohydrate 7g, of which sugars 3g; Fat 11g, of which saturates 2g; Cholesterol 52mg; Calcium 21mg; Fibre 2g; Sodium 805mg

116 Stir-fried venison Energy 220kcal/918kJ; Protein 22g; Carbohydrate 8g, of which sugars 0g; Fat 11g, of which saturates 2g; Cholesterol 44mg; Calcium 34mg; Fibre 0g; Sodium 766mg

117 Oxtail stew Energy 462kcal/1928kJ; Protein 46g; Carbohydrate 2g, of which sugars 1g; Fat 27g, of which saturates 10g; Cholesterol 169mg; Calcium 26mg; Fibre 0g; Sodium 1309mg

118 Liver in five spices Energy 223kcal/934kJ; Protein 25g; Carbohydrate 4g, of which sugars 1g; Fat 11g, of which saturates 2g; Cholesterol 293mg; Calcium 22mg; Fibre 0g; Sodium 681mg

119 Shredded kidneys in wine Energy 159kcal/664kJ; Protein 14g; Carbohydrate 2g, of which sugars 1g; Fat 10g, of which saturates 2g; Cholesterol 359mg; Calcium 21mg; Fibre 0g; Sodium 391mg

120 Four treasures meat Energy 288kcal/1202kJ; Protein 25g; Carbohydrate 3g, of which sugars 2g; Fat 19g, of which saturates 5g; Cholesterol 305mg; Calcium 24mg; Fibre 1g; Sodium 247mg

127 Mandarin pancakes Energy 68kcal/288kJ; Protein 2g; Carbohydrate 13g, of which sugars 0g; Fat 1g, of which saturates 0g; Cholesterol 0mg; Calcium 23mg; Fibre 1g; Sodium 1mg

128 Bean paste cakes Energy 356kcal/1485kJ; Protein 6g; Carbohydrate 34g, of which sugars 1g; Fat 22g, of which saturates 5g; Cholesterol 13mg; Calcium 68mg; Fibre 3g; Sodium 291mg

131 Steamed breads Energy 77kcal/326kJ; Protein 2g; Carbohydrate 17g, of which sugars 0g; Fat 0g, of which saturates 0g; Cholesterol 0mg; Calcium 32mg; Fibre 1g; Sodium 1mg

132 Beijing eel noodles Energy 637kcal/2674kJ; Protein 22g; Carbohydrate 75g, of which sugars 3g; Fat 29g, of which saturates 6g; Cholesterol 105mg; Calcium 53mg; Fibre 6g; Sodium 539mg

133 Minced lamb noodles Energy 351kcal/1470kJ; Protein 16g; Carbohydrate 39g, of which sugars 2g; Fat 15g, of which saturates 4g; Cholesterol 47mg; Calcium 36mg; Fibre 3g; Sodium 584mg

134 Stir-fried noodles & lamb Energy 342kcal/1434kJ; Protein 16g; Carbohydrate 38g, of which sugars 2g; Fat 15g, of which saturates 4g; Cholesterol 47mg; Calcium 28mg; Fibre 3g; Sodium 337mg

135 Noodles with minced beef Energy 342kcal/1439kJ; Protein 15g; Carbohydrate 44g, of which sugars 2g; Fat 13g, of which saturates 2g; Cholesterol 44mg; Calcium 36mg; Fibre 3g; Sodium 556mg

140 Pickled Chinese cabbage Energy 20kcal/80kJ; Protein 1g; Carbohydrate 2g, of which sugars 2g; Fat 0g, of which saturates 0g; Cholesterol 0mg; Calcium 16mg; Fibre 1g; Sodium 251mg

141 Sweet-and-sour cabbage Energy 36kcal/150kJ; Protein 2g; Carbohydrate 6g, of which sugars 5g; Fat 0g, of which saturates 0g; Cholesterol 0mg; Calcium 47mg; Fibre 3g; Sodium mg

143 Cold aubergine salad Energy 108kcal/446kJ; Protein 2g; Carbohydrate 3g, of which sugars 10g; Fat 2g, of which saturates 2g; Cholesterol 0mg; Calcium 36mg; Fibre 2g; Sodium 249mg

144 Steamed egg custard Energy 177kcal/735kJ; Protein 14g; Carbohydrate 1g, of which sugars 1g; Fat 13g, of which saturates 3g; Cholesterol 232mg; Calcium 391mg; Fibre 0g; Sodium 267mg

145 Fried leeks with hot sauce Energy 98kcal/405kJ; Protein 2g; Carbohydrate 4g, of which sugars 2g; Fat 8g, of which saturates 1g; Cholesterol 0mg; Calcium 20mg; Fibre 2g; Sodium 182mg

146 Fried beans in garlic sauce Energy 137kcal/565kJ; Protein 3g; Carbohydrate 5g, of which sugars 4g; Fat 12g, of which saturates 2g; Cholesterol 0mg; Calcium 42mg; Fibre 3g; Sodium 95mg

147 Stir-fried beansprouts Energy 73kcal/303kJ; Protein 42g; Carbohydrate 5g, of which sugars 3g; Fat 4g, of which saturates 1g; Cholesterol 0mg; Calcium 30mg; Fibre 6g; Sodium 252mg

148 Braised bamboo shoots Energy 130kcal/537kJ; Protein 3g; Carbohydrate 4g, of which sugars 3g; Fat 4g, of which saturates 2g; Cholesterol 0mg; Calcium 30mg; Fibre 2g; Sodium 337mg

149 Braised tofu Energy 152kcal/629kJ; Protein 8g; Carbohydrate 3g, of which sugars 1g; Fat 11g, of which saturates 1g; Cholesterol 0mg; Calcium 458mg; Fibre 1g; Sodium 323mg

150 Vegetarian stew Energy 114kcal/475kJ; Protein 3g; Carbohydrate 7g, of which sugars 1g; Fat 9g, of which saturates 1g; Cholesterol 0mg; Calcium 57mg; Fibre 1g; Sodium 819mg

152 Boiled peanuts Energy 641kcal/2663kJ; Protein 29g; Carbohydrate 16g, of which sugars 8g; Fat 52g, of which saturates 10g; Cholesterol 0mg; Calcium 69mg; Fibre 8g; Sodium 3mg

153 Soy sauce potatoes Energy 224kcal/932kJ; Protein 3g; Carbohydrate 20g, of which sugars 1g; Fat 15g, of which saturates 2g; Cholesterol 0mg; Calcium 7mg; Fibre 2g; Sodium 437mg

158 Caramelized apples Energy 448kcal/1899kJ; Protein 4g; Carbohydrate 95g, of which sugars 81g; Fat 9g, of which saturates 1g; Cholesterol 58mg; Calcium 116mg; Fibre 4g; Sodium 113mg

161 Caramelized taros Energy 360kcal/1516kJ; Protein 3g; Carbohydrate 64g, of which sugars 35g; Fat 12g, of which saturates 1g; Cholesterol 0mg; Calcium 82mg; Fibre 4g; Sodium 8mg

162 Date pancakes Energy 178kcal/749kJ; Protein 3g; Carbohydrate 24g, of which sugars 12g; Fat 8g, of which saturates 2g; Cholesterol 32mg; Calcium 32mg; Fibre 1g; Sodium 13mg

165 Sweet sesame rolls Energy 351kcal/1463kJ; Protein 9g; Carbohydrate 39g, of which sugars 9g; Fat 17g, of which saturates 2g; Cholesterol 6mg; Calcium 218mg; Fibre 1g; Sodium 126mg

166 Taro cream Energy 490kcal/2053kJ; Protein 2g; Carbohydrate 69g, of which sugars 41g; Fat 25g, of which saturates 10g; Cholesterol 23mg; Calcium 32mg; Fibre 4g; Sodium 7mg

182 Fish ball & noodle soup Energy 375 kcal/1558kJ; Protein 20g; Carbohydrate 49g, of which sugars 7g; Fat 10g, of which saturates 7g; Cholesterol 100mg; Calcium 273mg; Fibre 1g; Sodium 2285mg

183 Carp & mooli soup Energy 215kcal/894kJ; Protein 16g; Carbohydrate 3g, of which sugars 2g; Fat 16g, of which saturates 2g; Cholesterol 50mg; Calcium 100mg; Fibre 1g; Sodium 873mg

184 Tofu & spinach soup Energy 150kcal/620kJ; Protein 7g; Carbohydrate 2g, of which sugars 1g; Fat 13g, of which saturates 2g; Cholesterol 6mg; Calcium 215mg; Fibre 2g; Sodium 628mg

185 Pork & soya bean soup Energy 242kcal/1101kJ; Protein 15g; Carbohydrate 16g, of which sugars 2g; Fat 14g, of which saturates 2g; Cholesterol 24mg; Calcium 31mg; Fibre 4g; Sodium 132mg

186 Ham & bamboo shoot soup Energy 173kcal/715kJ; Protein 10g; Carbs 2g, of which sugars 1g; Fat 14g, of which saturates 3g; Cholesterol 83mg; Calcium 20mg; Fibre 1g; Sodium 896mg

187 Spare rib & bitter melon soup Energy 181kcal/755kJ; Protein 18g; Carbohydrate 2g, of which sugars 1g; Fat 12g, of which saturates 4g; Cholesterol 70mg; Calcium 72mg; Fibre 3g; Sodium 771mg

189 Salted duck egg congee Energy 192kcal/809kJ; Protein 7g; Carbohydrate 22g, of which sugars 0g; Fat 9g, of which saturates 2g; Cholesterol 255mg; Calcium 45mg; Fibre 1g; Sodium 547mg

190 Quail's egg sesame toast Energy 171kcal/1713kJ; Protein 12g; Carbohydrate 8g, of which sugars 1g; Fat 10g, of which saturates 2g; Cholesterol 168mg; Calcium 47g: Fibre 1g; Sodium 254mg

193 Sweet turnip dumplings Energy 130kcal/545kJ; Protein 3g; Carbohydrate 16g, of which sugars 3g; Fat 6g, of which saturates 1g; Cholesterol 29mg; Calcium 37g: Fibre 1g; Sodium 187mg

194 Steamed prawn dumplings Energy 52kcal/221kJ; Protein 6g; Carbohydrate 7g, of which sugars 0g; Fat 0g, of which saturates 0g; Cholesterol 66mg; Calcium 29g: Fibre 0g; Sodium 166mg

197 Pumpkin cake Energy 267kcal/1115kJ; Protein 8g; Carbohydrate 40g, of which sugars 2g; Fat 8g, of which saturates 1g; Cholesterol 32mg; Calcium 126g: Fibre 1g; Sodium 542mg

P202 Seaweed fish Energy 238kcal/1002kJ; Protein 25g; Carbohydrate 11g, of which sugars 0g; Fat 11g, of which saturates 1g; Cholesterol 21mg; Calcium 23g: Fibre 1g; Sodium 345mg

P203 Wine-braised fish & leeks Energy 302kcal/1269kJ; Protein 36g; Carbs 11g, of which sugars 4g; Fat 13g, of which saturates 2g; Cholesterol 62mg; Calcium 91g: Fibre 1g; Sodium 648mg

P205 Fish in black bean sauce Energy 272kcal/1137kJ; Protein 18g; Carbohydrate 10g, of which sugars 2g; Fat 18g, of which saturates 2g; Cholesterol 16mg; Calcium 19g: Fibre 0g; Sodium 611mg

P206 Smoked pomfret Energy 185kcal/776kJ; Protein 23g; Carbohydrate 1g, of which sugars 0g, Fat 10g, of which saturates 2g; Cholesterol 46mg; Calcium 93g: Fibre 0g; Sodium 610mg

P207 Fish head casserole Energy 236kcal/978kJ; Protein 18g; Carbohydrate 3g, of which sugars 2g; Fat 17g, of which saturates 2g; Cholesterol 42mg; Calcium 65g: Fibre 2g; Sodium 137mg

P208 Fish in vinegar sauce Energy 209kcal/880kJ; Protein 27g; Carbohydrate 8g, of which sugars 2g; Fat 7g, of which saturates 1g; Cholesterol 101mg; Calcium 78g: Fibre 0g; Sodium 603mg

P209 Eels in hoisin sauce Energy 446kcal/ 1855kJ; Protein 29g; Carbohydrate 6g, of which sugars 2g; Fat 34g, of which saturates 7g; Cholesterol 253mg; Calcium 47g: Fibre 0g; Sodium 855mg

P210 Fried prawn balls Energy 252kcal/1054kJ; Protein 30g; Carbohydrate 11g, of which sugars 0g; Fat 10g, of which saturates 1g; Cholesterol 329mg; Calcium 139g: Fibre 0g; Sodium 815mg

P212 Fried fish balls Energy 212kcal/875kJ; Protein 10g; Carbohydrate 14g, of which sugars 7g; Fat 13g, of which saturates 4g; Cholesterol 50mg; Calcium 141g: Fibre 0g; Sodium 1398mg

P213 Prawns & ginkgo nuts Energy 179kcal/749kJ; Protein 20g; Carbohydrate 6g, of which sugars 0g; Fat 8g, of which saturates1g; Cholesterol 219mg; Calcium 95g: Fibre 1g; Sodium 410mg

P214 Dry-fried prawns Energy 111kcal/464kJ; Protein 8g; Carbohydrate 2g, of which sugars 2g; Fat 8g, of which saturates 1g; Cholesterol 98mg; Calcium 45g: Fibre 0g; Sodium 1076mg

P215 Phoenix prawns Energy 117kcal/490kJ; Protein 9g; Carbohydrate 3g, of which sugars 0g; Fat 8g, of which saturates 1g; Cholesterol 98mg; Calcium 44g: Fibre 1g; Sodium 831mg

P216 Dragon well prawns Energy 169kcal/708kJ; Protein 21g; Carbohydrate 1g, of which sugars 1g; Fat 8g, of which saturates 1g; Cholesterol 219mg; Calcium 94g: Fibre 0g; Sodium 497mg

219 Braised tofu with crab Energy 472kcal/1966kJ; Protein 46g; Carbs 4g, of which sugars 2g; Fat 30g, of which saturates 2g; Cholesterol 121mg; Calcium 1684g: Fibre 1g; Sodium 592mg

224 Beggar's chicken Energy 1219kcal/5136kJ; Protein 61g; Carbohydrate 176g, of which sugars 16g; Fat 34g, of which saturates 8g; Cholesterol 172mg; Calcium 416g: Fibre 14g; Sodium 1451mg

226 Rice wine chicken Energy 289kcal/1211kJ; Protein 40g; Carbohydrate 5g, of which sugars 2g; Fat 13g, of which saturates 3g; Cholesterol 159mg; Calcium 48g: Fibre 0g; Sodium 600mg

227 Chicken & ginseng stew Energy 260kcal/1090kJ; Protein 39g; Carbohydrate 1g, of which sugars 0g; Fat 11g, of which saturates 3g; Cholesterol 159mg; Calcium 33g: Fibre 0g; Sodium 597mg

229 Prime minister's chicken stew Energy 277kcal/1159kJ; Protein 34g; Carbohydrate 1g, of which sugars 1g; Fat 15g, of which saturates 5g; Cholesterol 438mg; Calcium 50g: Fibre 0g; Sodium 589mg

230 Stir-fried diced chicken Energy 207kcal/869kJ; Protein 28g; Carbohydrate 4g, of which sugars 2g; Fat 9g, of which saturates 1g; Cholesterol 79mg; Calcium 15g: Fibre 0g; Sodium 320mg

231 Chicken with chestnuts Energy 460kcal/1945kJ; Protein 33g; Carbohydrate 56g, of which sugars 12g; Fat 13g, of which saturates 2g; Cholesterol 88mg; Calcium 99g: Fibre 9g; Sodium 395mg

232 Snow flower chicken Energy 284kcal/1196kJ; Protein 27g; Carbohydrate 39g, of which sugars 0g; Fat 2g, of which saturates 0g; Cholesterol 70mg; Calcium 15g: Fibre 0g; Sodium 252mg

234 Braised chicken with taro Energy 429kcal/1805kJ; Protein 41g; Carbohydrate 32g, of which sugars 2g; Fat 16g, of which saturates 4g; Cholesterol 159mg; Calcium 72g: Fibre 4g; Sodium 668mg

235 Chicken in scallion sauce Energy 267kcal/1114kJ; Protein 30g; Carbohydrate 2g, of which sugars 1g; Fat 15g, of which saturates 2g; Cholesterol 88mg; Calcium 23g: Fibre 0g; Sodium 569mg

236 Chicken with cloud ears Energy 169kcal/710kJ; Protein 16g; Carbohydrate 8g, of which sugars 2g; Fat 8g, of which saturates 1g; Cholesterol 44mg; Calcium 22g: Fibre 1g; Sodium 478mg

238 Marinated duck Energy 375kcal/1574kJ; Protein 51g; Carbohydrate 7g, of which sugars 6g; Fat 16g, of which saturates 5g; Cholesterol 275mg; Calcium 50g: Fibre 0g; Sodium 4083mg

244 Frog's legs in bean sauce Energy 289kcal/1206kJ; Protein 28g; Carbohydrate 3g, of which sugars 2g; Fat 19g, of which saturates 3g; Cholesterol 105mg; Calcium 12g: Fibre 0g; Sodium 185mg

245 Pork in preserved beancurd Energy 224kcal/935kJ; Protein 25g; Carbs 3g, of which sugars 2g; Fat 12g, of which saturates 3g; Cholesterol 71mg; Calcium 42g: Fibre 1g; Sodium 80mg

246 Lychee pork Energy 267kcal/1118kJ; Protein 17g; Carbohydrate 19g, of which sugars 7g; Fat 14g, of which saturates 2g; Cholesterol 47mg; Calcium 18g: Fibre 1g; Sodium 573mg

249 Pork, cabbage & mushrooms Energy 166kcal/697kJ; Protein 23g; Carbohydrate 9g, of which sugars 2g; Fat 4g, of which saturates 1g; Cholesterol 63mg; Calcium 25g: Fibre 1g; Sodium 607mg

250 Pork with Chinese chives Energy 174kcal/725kJ; Protein 14g; Carbohydrate 4g, of which sugars 4g; Fat 11g, of which saturates 2g; Cholesterol 39mg; Calcium 75g: Fibre 1g; Sodium 296mg

251 Stewed pork & vegetables Energy 326kcal/1357kJ; Protein 23g; Carbohydrate 10g, of which sugars 9g; Fat 22g, of which saturates 8g; Cholesterol 71mg; Calcium 97g: Fibre 5g; Sodium 879mg

253 Tung-Po pork Energy 307kcal/1282kJ; Protein 20g; Carbohydrate 13g, of which sugars 12g; Fat 20g, of which saturates 7g; Cholesterol 71mg; Calcium 24g: Fibre 0g; Sodium 600mg

254 Fuzhou pork Energy 320kcal/1335kJ; Protein 18g; Carbohydrate 14g, of which sugars 4g; Fat 22g, of which saturates 7g; Cholesterol 62mg; Calcium 42g: Fibre 1g; Sodium 218mg

256 Pork chops in brown sauce Energy 443kcal/1850kJ; Protein 39g; Carbohydrate 18g, of which sugars 4g; Fat 24g, of which saturates 6g; Chol 172mg; Calcium 41g: Fibre 1g; Sodium 839mg

259 Lion's head pork balls Energy 300kcal/1256kJ; Protein 23g; Carbohydrate 14g, of which sugars 3g; Fat 16g, of which saturates 5g; Cholesterol 74mg; Calcium 47g: Fibre 1g; Sodium 600mg

260 Sweet–and-sour spare ribs Energy 386kcal/1612kJ; Protein 25g; Carbs 19g, of which sugars 10g; Fat 24g, of which saturates 7g; Cholesterol 137mg; Calcium 31g: Fibre 1g; Sodium 374mg

262 Salt & pepper spare ribs Energy 383kcal/1595kJ; Protein 29g; Carbohydrate 9g, of which sugars 1g; Fat 26g, of which saturates 8g; Cholesterol 106mg; Calcium 14g: Fibre 0g; Sodium 594mg

263 Shredded beef with celery Energy 302kcal/1258kJ; Protein 28g; Carbohydrate 7g, of which sugars 5g; Fat 18g, of which saturates 4g; Cholesterol 57mg; Calcium 60g: Fibre 2g; Sodium 475mg

265 Lamb in hot bean sauce Energy 377kcal/1566kJ; Protein 23g; Carbohydrate 6g, of which sugars 6g; Fat 28g, of which saturates 9g; Cholesterol 84mg; Calcium 19g: Fibre 1g; Sodium 585mg

266 Stir-fried kidneys Energy 219kcal/910kJ; Protein 17g; Carbohydrate 3g, of which sugars 1g; Fat 14g, of which saturates 3g; Cholesterol 490mg; Calcium 18g: Fibre 0g; Sodium 270mg

273 Fish & salt egg congee Energy 223kcal/944kJ; Protein 14g; Carbohydrate 33g, of which sugars 1g; Fat 5g, of which saturates 1g; Cholesterol 35mg; Calcium 29g: Fibre 1g; Sodium 651mg

274 Fried rice with beansprouts Energy 300kcal/1260kJ; Protein 12g; Carbohydrate 37g, of which sugars 1g; Fat 13g, of which saturates 2g; Cholesterol 11mg; Calcium 37g: Fibre 3g; Sodium 833mg

275 Yangzhou fried rice Energy 326kcal/1369kJ; Protein 19g; Carbohydrate 37g, of which sugars 1g; Fat 13g, of which saturates 3g; Cholesterol 238mg; Calcium 98g: Fibre 2g; Sodium 431mg

276 Fried rice with mixed meats Energy 434kcal/1821kJ; Protein 22g; Carbs 40g, of which sugars 3g; Fat 22g, of which saturates 5g; Cholesterol 209mg; Calcium 65g: Fibre 2g; Sodium 1078mg

279 Taoist vegetarian rice noodles Energy 417kcal/1713kJ; Protein 8g; Carbohydrate 5g, of which sugars 2g; Fat 20g, of which saturates 2g; Cholesterol 0mg; Calcium 113g: Fibre 3g; Sodium 521mg

280 Dumpling noodles Energy 285kcal/1208kJ; Protein 17g; Carbohydrate 46g, of which sugars 2g; Fat 5g, of which saturates 1g; Cholesterol 67mg; Calcium 49g: Fibre 4g; Sodium 847mg

283 Hangzhou pork noodles Energy 283kcal/1196kJ; Protein 15g; Carbs 42g, of which sugars 3g; Fat 8g, of which saturates 1g; Cholesterol 24mg; Calcium 35g: Fibre 3g; Sodium 124mg

284 Braised noodles Energy 367kcal/1545kJ; Protein 25g; Carbohydrate 41g, of which sugars 4g; Fat 13g, of which saturates 2g; Cholesterol 179mg; Calcium 421g: Fibre 3g; Sodium 1703mg

287 Jia Jiang noodles Energy 355kcal/1495kJ; Protein 20g; Carbohydrate 49g, of which sugars 7g; Fat 10g, of which saturates 1g; Cholesterol 36mg; Calcium 60g: Fibre 4g; Sodium 678mg

288 Liver & kidney in fine noodles Energy 368kcal/1541kJ; Protein 27g; Carbs 45g, of which sugars 1g; Fat 8g, of which saturates 2g; Cholesterol 310mg; Calcium 23g: Fibre 3g; Sodium 675mg

294 Stir-fried mixed vegetables Energy 112kcal/465kJ; Protein 3g; Carbohydrate 5g, of which sugars 3g; Fat 9g, of which saturates 1g; Cholesterol 0mg; Calcium 46g: Fibre 3g; Sodium 342mg

295 Stir-fried beans & onions Energy 72kcal/297kJ; Protein 2g; Carbohydrate 5g, of which sugars 4g; Fat 5g, of which saturates 1g; Cholesterol 0mg; Calcium 49g: Fibre 3g; Sodium 2mg

296 Bamboo shoots with sausage Energy 153kcal/631kJ; Protein 5g; Carbohydrate 3g, of which sugars 3g; Fat 13g, of which saturates 2g; Cholesterol 0mg; Calcium 221g: Fibre 2g; Sodium 194mg

298 Bamboo shoots & mushrooms Energy 94kcal/388kJ; Protein 2g; Carbohydrate 4g, of which sugars 2g; Fat 8g, of which saturates 1g; Cholesterol 0mg; Calcium 21g: Fibre 3g; Sodium 274mg

299 Jade button mushrooms Energy 111kcal/461kJ; Protein 3g; Carbohydrate 5g, of which sugars 3g; Fat 8g, of which saturates 1g; Cholesterol 0mg; Calcium 34g: Fibre 4g; Sodium 543mg

300 Mushrooms & beancurd skin Energy 33kcal/140kJ; Protein 3g; Carbohydrate 3g, of which sugars 1g; Fat 1g, of which saturates 0g; Cholesterol 0mg; Calcium 70g: Fibre2g; Sodium 252mg

301 Tofu & preserved beancurd Energy 187kcal/779kJ; Protein 9g; Carbohydrate 10g, of which sugars 8g; Fat 12g, of which saturates 1g; Cholesterol 0mg; Calcium 376g: Fibre 5g; Sodium 12mg

302 Buddha's vegetarian stew Energy 224kcal/929kJ; Protein7 g; Carbohydrate 15g, of which sugars 5g; Fat 16g, of which saturates 2g; Cholesterol 0mg; Calcium 67g: Fibre 4g; Sodium 464mg

305 Steamed eggs with mushrooms Energy 168kcal/696kJ; Protein 8g; Carbohydrate 3g, of which sugars 2g; Fat 14g, of which saturates 3g; Cholesterol 179mg; Calcium 77g: Fibre 1g; Sodium 826mg

306 Oyster omelette Energy 140kcal/580kJ; Protein 5g; Carbohydrate 4g, of which sugars 2g; Fat 12g, of which saturates 1g; Cholesterol 21mg; Calcium 62g: Fibre 1g; Sodium 611mg

312 Five-flavoured soup Energy 409kcal/1741kJ; Protein 7g; Carbohydrate 96g, of which sugars 94g; Fat 2g, of which saturates 1g; Cholesterol 10mg; Calcium 72g: Fibre 8g; Sodium 54mg

313 Sweet potato & ginkgo nuts Energy 193kcal/822kJ; Protein 1g; Carbohydrate 49g, of which sugars 34g; Fat 0g, of which saturates 0g; Cholesterol 0mg; Calcium21g: Fibre 2g; Sodium 71mg

314 Mung beans in syrup Energy 480kcal/2043kJ; Protein 19g; Carbohydrate 105g, of which sugars 57g; Fat 1g, of which saturates 0g; Cholesterol 0mg; Calcium 127g: Fibre 11g; Sodium 62mg

315 Red beans in syrup Energy 305kcal/1299kJ; Protein 17g; Carbohydrate 61g, of which sugars 28g; Fat 1g, of which saturates 0g; Cholesterol 0mg; Calcium 101g: Fibre 18g; Sodium 36mg

330 Egg drop & ginger soup Energy 44kcal/184kJ; Protein 3.3g; Carbohydrate 0.2g, of which sugars 0.1g; Fat 2.9g, of which saturates 0.8g; Cholesterol 95mg; Calcium 18mg; Fibre 0.1g; Sodium 166mg

331 Liver & matrimony vine soup Energy 113kcal/472kJ; Protein 11.3g; Carbohydrate 0.9g, of which sugars 0.9g; Fat 7.2g, of which saturates 1.3g; Cholesterol 130mg; Calcium 31mg; Fibre 0.4g; Sodium 600mg

333 Prawn wonton soup Energy 178kcal/748kJ; Protein 19g; Carbohydrate 15.2g, of which sugars 0.8g; Fat 4.9g, of which saturates 0.8g; Cholesterol 156mg; Calcium 132mg; Fibre 0.6g; Sodium 1267mg

334 Stuffed squid soup Energy 279kcal/1175kJ; Protein 34.9g; Carbohydrate 13.7g, sugars 0.3g; Fat 9.4g, saturates 2.5g; Cholesterol 419mg; Calcium 31mg; Fibre 0.2g; Sodium 220mg

337 Chicken broth of prosperity Energy 254kcal/1065kJ; Protein 29.9g; Carbohydrate 7.9g, of which sugars 0.9g; Fat 11.8g, of which saturates 2.6g; Cholesterol 217mg; Calcium 31mg; Fibre 0g; Sodium 1086mg

338 Beef ball soup Energy 247kcal/1031kJ; Protein 24.3g; Carbohydrate 16.8g, of which sugars 7g; Fat 9.6g, of which saturates 3.8g; Cholesterol 58mg; Calcium 38mg; Fibre 1.8g; Sodium 1546mg

344 Yam cake Energy 481kcal/2025kJ; Protein 9.9g; Carbohydrate 79.6g, of which sugars 2.6g; Fat 14.6g, of which saturates 2.9g; Cholesterol 37mg; Calcium 121mg; Fibre 3g; Sodium 648mg

347 Radish cake Energy 263kcal/1099kJ; Protein 7g; Carbohydrate 44.2g, of which sugars 2.7g; Fat 6.3g, of which saturates 0.9g; Cholesterol 32mg; Calcium 111mg; Fibre 1.9g; Sodium 560mg

348 Braised beancurd skin parcels Energy 263kcal/1099kJ; Protein 7g; Carbohydrate 44.2g, of which sugars 2.7g; Fat 6.3g, of which saturates 0.9g; Cholesterol 32mg; Calcium 111mg; Fibre 1.9g; Sodium 560mg

351 Crystal dumplings Energy 244kcal/1022kJ; Protein 3.6g; Carbohydrate 38.2g, of which sugars 5.2g; Fat 8.7g, of which saturates 1.1g; Cholesterol 0mg; Calcium 21mg; Fibre 1.3g; Sodium 1134mg

352 Chive dumplings Energy 140kcal/589kJ; Protein 1.8g; Carbohydrate 25.9g, of which sugars 0.9g; Fat 3.9g, of which saturates 0.6g; Cholesterol 24mg; Calcium 58mg; Fibre 1.3g; Sodium 295mg

354 Pork & prawn dumplings Energy 228kcal/957kJ; Protein 18.2g; Carbohydrate 20.2g, of which sugars 1.3g; Fat 8.8g, of which saturates 2.5g; Cholesterol 86mg; Calcium 57mg; Fibre 1.3g; Sodium 622mg

355 Deep-fried wontons Energy 326kcal/1357kJ; Protein 16.3g; Carbohydrate 18.3g, of which sugars 0.6g; Fat 21.3g, of which saturates 4.4g; Cholesterol 50mg; Calcium 33mg; Fibre 0.6g; Sodium 319mg

357 Pork & nut dumplings Energy 216kcal/906kJ; Protein 6.7g; Carbohydrate 24.3g, of which sugars 0.7g; Fat 10.9g, of which saturates 2.1g; Cholesterol 17mg; Calcium 10mg; Fibre 0.4g; Sodium 294mg

358 Roast pork dumplings Energy 73kcal/309kJ; Protein 2.4g; Carbohydrate 15.6g, of which sugars 0.2g; Fat 0.5g, of which saturates 0.2g; Cholesterol 6mg; Calcium 4mg; Fibre 0g; Sodium 194mg

364 Fish-stuffed vegetables Energy 226kcal/951kJ; Protein 31.8g; Carbohydrate 8.4g, of which sugars 2.2g; Fat 7.5g, of which saturates 1g; Cholesterol 119mg; Calcium 381mg; Fibre 4g; Sodium 584mg

366 Steamed fish with sour plum Energy 188kcal/791kJ; Protein 20.4g; Carbs 9.3g, of which sugars 9.2g; Fat 8g, of which saturates 2.4g; Cholesterol 45mg; Calcium 51mg; Fibre 1.7g; Sodium 658mg

367 Braised carp in ginger sauce Energy 211kcal/883kJ; Protein 22.2g; Carbs 5.4g, of which sugars 1.9g; Fat 11.4g, of which saturates 1.9g; Chol 84mg; Calcium 62mg; Fibre 0g; Sodium 590mg

368 Sweet-and-sour snapper Energy 332kcal/1389kJ; Protein 25.4g; Carbohydrate 14.2g, of which sugars 1.1g; Fat 19.8g, of which saturates 2.6g; Cholesterol 46mg; Calcium 61mg; Fibre 0.2g; Sodium 884mg

370 Red prawns on the shell Energy 154kcal/643kJ; Protein 11.3g; Carbs 13.4g, of which sugars 10.6g; Fat 6.5g, of which saturates 0.9g; Cholesterol 35mg; Calcium 93mg; Fibre 1.8g; Sodium 934mg

371 Salt & pepper prawns Energy 172kcal/717kJ; Protein 20.1g; Carbohydrate 2.7g, of which sugars 2.4g; Fat 9g, of which saturates 1.1g; Cholesterol 219mg; Calcium 97mg; Fibre 0.3g; Sodium 1197mg

372 Butterfly prawns Energy 156kcal/653kJ; Protein 12.5g; Carbohydrate 7.3g, of which sugars 0.5g; Fat 8.8g, of which saturates 1.3g; Cholesterol 157mg; Calcium 64mg; Fibre 0.3g; Sodium 316mg

374 Wenchang steamed crab Energy 119kcal/495kJ; Protein 17.1g; Carbohydrate 0.4g, of which sugars 0.3g; Fat 4.8g, of which saturates 0.5g; Cholesterol 63mg; Calcium 1mg; Fibre 0g; Sodium 642mg

375 Chilled pickled crab Energy 45kcal/187kJ; Protein 6.8g; Carbohydrate 0g, of which sugars 0g; Fat 1.9g, of which saturates 0.2g; Cholesterol 25mg; Calcium 1mg; Fibre 0g; Sodium 1788mg

377 Steamed scallops with black bean sauce Energy 75kcal/319kJ; Protein 12.3g; Carbohydrate 3.9g, of which sugars 0.9g; Fat 0.8g, of which saturates 0.2g; Cholesterol 24mg; Calcium 19mg; Fibre 0.3g; Sodium 91mg

378 Stir-fry squid & mangetout Energy 141kcal/589kJ; Protein 8.5g; Carbs 6.0g, of which sugars 3.6g; Fat 9.1g, of which saturates 1.3g; Chol 98mg; Calcium 27mg; Fibre 1.1g; Sodium 173mg

379 Stir-fry mussels with ginger Energy 97kcal/404kJ; Protein 5.7g; Carbs 2.4g, of which sugars 0.2g; Fat 6.3g, of which saturates 0.8g; Chol 18mg; Calcium 18mg; Fibre 0.3g; Sodium 355mg

384 Chicken with cashew nuts Energy 297kcal/1244kJ; Protein 32g; Carbohydrate 12.5g, of which sugars 9g; Fat 13.6g, of which saturates 2.5g; Cholesterol 79mg; Calcium 51mg; Fibre 2.4g; Sodium 131mg

385 Plum sauce chicken Energy 270kcal/1132kJ; Protein 20.4g; Carbohydrate 16g, of which sugars 8.8g; Fat 14.3g, of which saturates 2.4g; Cholesterol 91mg; Calcium 23mg; Fibre 0.3g; Sodium 188mg

387 Chicken with shrimp paste Energy 411kcal/1721kJ; Protein 31.5g; Carbohydrate 30g, of which sugars 0g; Fat 19.4g, of which saturates 2.5g; Cholesterol 104mg; Calcium 88mg; Fibre 0g; Sodium 302mg

388 Chicken & banana rolls Energy 402kcal/1689kJ; Protein 20.4g; Carbohydrate 46.1g, of which sugars 10.5g; Fat 16.4g, of which saturates 2.3g; Cholesterol 100mg; Calcium 20mg; Fibre 0.6g; Sodium 83mg

389 Chicken with ginger wine Energy 394kcal/1634kJ; Protein 33g; Carbs 0.5g, of which sugars 0.4g; Fat 27.6g, of which saturates 8g; Cholesterol 171mg; Calcium 20mg; Fibre 0.1g; Sodium 136mg

390 Soy-braised chicken Energy 445kcal/1846kJ; Protein 33g; Carbohydrate 8.2g, of which sugars 3.5g; Fat 31.2g, of which saturates 8.4g; Cholesterol 171mg; Calcium 18mg; Fibre 0g; Sodium 1026mg

393 Jade & silver chicken Energy 182kcal/763kJ; Protein 22.9g; Carbohydrate 4.4g, of which sugars 0.9g; Fat 7.3g, of which saturates 1.3g; Cholesterol 63mg; Calcium 28mg; Fibre 1g; Sodium 261mg

394 Hainan chicken rice Energy 802kcal/3333kJ; Protein 52.7g; Carbohydrate 41.1g, of which sugars 0.9g; Fat 47g, of which saturates 12.8g; Cholesterol 256mg; Calcium 34mg; Fibre 0.2g; Sodium 201mg

397 Duck stuffed with glutinous rice Energy 504kcal/2092kJ; Protein 21.7g; Carbohydrate 14.1g, sugars 6.3g; Fat 40.3g, saturates 7.9g; Cholesterol 119mg; Calcium 28mg; Fibre 1.3g; Sodium 755mg

398 Cantonese roast duck Energy 306kcal/1274kJ; Protein 20.8g; Carbohydrate 1.5g, of which sugars 1.5g; Fat 23.7g, of which saturates 7g; Cholesterol 144mg; Calcium 13mg; Fibre 0g; Sodium 116mg

400 Soy-braised duck Energy 119kcal/498kJ; Protein 10.2g; Carbohydrate 4.6g, of which sugars 3.4g; Fat 6.9g, of which saturates 1.5g; Cholesterol 50mg; Calcium 35mg; Fibre 1.1g; Sodium 412mg

401 Crispy quail Energy 462kcal/1938kJ; Protein 77.1g; Carbohydrate 0.2g, of which sugars 0.2g; Fat 15.1g, of which saturates 3.9g; Cholesterol 0mg; Calcium 99mg; Fibre 0g; Sodium 212mg

406 Spare ribs in black bean sauce Energy 722kcal/3012kJ; Protein 61.8g; Carbohydrate 2.6g, of which sugars 1g; Fat 51.9g, of which saturates 18.1g; Cholesterol 215mg; Calcium 59mg; Fibre 0.7g; Sodium 897mg

407 Stir-fried pork with ginger Energy 179kcal/747kJ; Protein 25.3g; Carbs 2.8g, of which sugars 2.1g; Fat 7.4g, of which saturates 1.9g; Cholesterol 71mg; Calcium 21mg; Fibre 0.7g; Sodium 614mg

408 Cantonese roast pork Energy 158kcal/664kJ; Protein 24.3g; Carbohydrate 4g, of which sugars 4g; Fat 4.6g, of which saturates 1.6g; Cholesterol 71mg; Calcium 18mg; Fibre 0g; Sodium 141mg

410 Sweet-and-sour pork Energy 727kcal/3035kJ; Protein 32.7g; Carbohydrate 76.5g, of which sugars 39.4g; Fat 32.8g, of which saturates 5.8g; Cholesterol 272mg; Calcium 85mg; Fibre 2.7g; Sodium 1048mg

411 Pork in preserved beancurd Energy 215kcal/898kJ; Protein 24.9g; Carbohydrate 5.7g, sugars 1.9g; Fat 10.4g, of which saturates 2.3g; Cholesterol 71mg; Calcium 51mg; Fibre 0.2g; Sodium 82mg

413 Mist of harmony Energy 551kcal/2276kJ; Protein 20.4g; Carbohydrate 2.6g, of which sugars 2.6g; Fat 51g, of which saturates 17.9g; Cholesterol 96mg; Calcium 12mg; Fibre 0g; Sodium 98mg

414 Minced pork rolls in beancurd skins Energy 387kcal/1608kJ; Protein 23.8g; Carbohydrate 8.6g, of which sugars 2.4g; Fat 28.9g, of which saturates 6.1g; Cholesterol 114mg; Calcium 158mg; Fibre 0.9g; Sodium 361mg

416 Cantonese beefsteak Energy 365kcal/1518kJ; Protein 34.2g; Carbohydrate 5g, of which sugars 1.5g; Fat 22.2g, of which saturates 6.7g; Cholesterol 87mg; Calcium 17mg; Fibre 0g; Sodium 322mg

417 Tangerine peel beef Energy 242kcal/1005kJ; Protein 20.3g; Carbohydrate 3.1g, of which sugars 3.1g; Fat 16.5g, of which saturates 4.5g; Cholesterol 51mg; Calcium 17mg; Fibre 0.4g; Sodium 65mg

418 Sautéd beef in oyster sauce Energy 160kcal/669kJ; Protein 17.5g; Carbohydrate 2.9g, sugars 2.7g; Fat 8.8g, of which saturates 2g; Cholesterol 44mg; Calcium 10mg; Fibre 0.6g; Sodium 485mg

420 Mutton and beancurd sticks Energy 209kcal/870kJ; Protein 19.5g; Carbohydrates 2.2g, of which sugars 2g; Fat 13.6g, of which saturates 5g; Cholesterol 67mg; Calcium 137mg; Fibre 0g; Sodium 877mg

421 Flower kidneys with ginger Energy 118kcal/491kJ; Protein 6.6g; Carbohydrate 6.4g, of which sugars 2.9g; Fat 6.6g, of which saturates 1g; Cholesterol 144mg; Calcium 15mg; Fibre 0.7g; Sodium 196mg

426 Rice with mixed vegetables Energy 199kcal/834kJ; Protein 4.6g; Carbohydrate 43.4g, of which sugars 6.6g; Fat 0.7g, of which saturates 0.1g; Cholesterol 0mg; Calcium 23mg; Fibre 1.6g; Sodium 232mg

427 Rice soup from Shantou Energy 354kcal/1483kJ; Protein 16.1g; Carbohydrate 69.8g, of which sugars 0g; Fat 1g, of which saturates 0.2g; Cholesterol 23mg; Calcium 22mg; Fibre 0g; Sodium 394mg

429 Clay pot rice with dried oysters Energy 472kcal/1971kJ; Protein 18.1g; Carbohydrate 71.7g, of which sugars 1g; Fat 12g, of which saturates 1.5g; Cholesterol 14mg; Calcium 90mg; Fibre 0.1g; Sodium 2544mg

430 Seafood fried rice Energy 386kcal/1629kJ; Protein 13.1g; Carbohydrate 62.6g, of which sugars 0.7g; Fat 11.1g, of which saturates 2.1g; Cholesterol 144mg; Calcium 73mg; Fibre 0.3g; Sodium 619mg

433 Classic Cantonese fried rice Energy 473kcal/1997kJ; Protein 25.3g; Carbohydrate 65.3g, of which sugars 2.5g; Fat 14.3g, of which saturates 2.9g; Cholesterol 238mg; Calcium 114mg; Fibre 1.3g; Sodium 1317mg

434 Glutinous rice in a lotus leaf Energy 596kcal/2488kJ; Protein 23.6g; Carbohydrate 79.5g, of which sugars 2.7g; Fat 19.3g, of which saturates 3.9g; Cholesterol 44mg; Calcium 45mg; Fibre 0.9g; Sodium 979mg

436 Oyster sauce noodles Energy 536kcal/2237kJ; Protein 20.4g; Carbohydrate 83.5g, of which sugars 1.9g; Fat 11.9g, of which saturates 1.7g; Cholesterol 44mg; Calcium 24mg; Fibre 0.4g; Sodium 133mg

437 Chilli noodles Energy 208kcal/879kJ; Protein 18.9g; Carbohydrate 26.6g, of which sugars 7.1g; Fat 3.5g, of which saturates 0.9g; Cholesterol 39mg; Calcium 101mg; Fibre 2.3g; Sodium 975mg

439 Buddhist vegetarian noodles Energy 509kcal/2116kJ; Protein 12.7g; Carbohydrate 73g, of which sugars 9.9g; Fat 18.6g, of which saturates 2.2g; Cholesterol 0mg; Calcium 200mg; Fibre 3.3g; Sodium 726mg

440 Silver threads of longevity Energy 307kcal/1274kJ; Protein 3.3g; Carbohydrate 34.8g, of which sugars 3.4g; Fat 16.7g, of which saturates 2.2g; Cholesterol 0mg; Calcium 15mg; Fibre 0.6g; Sodium 663mg

441 Lobster noodles Energy 501kcal/2110kJ; Protein 29.9g; Carbohydrate 56.9g, of which sugars 4g; Fat 18.8g, of which saturates 3.5g; Cholesterol 123mg; Calcium 83mg; Fibre 2.6g; Sodium 559mg

446 Braised Chinese leaves Energy 58kcal/239kJ; Protein 1.3g; Carbohydrate 4.6g, of which sugars 4.5g; Fat 3.8g, of which saturates 0.5g; Cholesterol 0mg; Calcium 42mg; Fibre 1.8g; Sodium 362mg

447 Greens with oyster sauce Energy 89kcal/369kJ; Protein 3.6g; Carbohydrate 4.2g, of which sugars 4g; Fat 6.5g, of which saturates 0.8g; Cholesterol 0mg; Calcium 214mg; Fibre 2.7g; Sodium 297mg

448 Stir-fried kai lan Energy 108kcal/448kJ; Protein 5g; Carbohydrate 5.9g, of which sugars 3.7g; Fat 6.4g, of which saturates 0.8g; Cholesterol 0mg; Calcium 53mg; Fibre 2.9g; Sodium 131mg

449 Lettuce with conpoy sauce Energy 131kcal/549kJ; Protein 12.4g; Carbohydrate 3.5g, of which sugars 1.8g; Fat 6.7g, of which saturates 1g; Cholesterol 24mg; Calcium 43mg; Fibre 0.9g; Sodium 94mg

450 Stir-fried bitter gourd Energy 80kcal/331kJ; Protein 1.6g; Carbohydrate 5.6g, of which sugars 5.4g; Fat 5.8g, of which saturates 0.7g; Cholesterol 0mg; Calcium 21mg; Fibre 0.8g; Sodium 696mg

452 Water convolvulus stir-fry Energy 138kcal/574kJ; Protein 12.1g; Carbohydrate 8.6g, of which sugars 5.2g; Fat 6.2g, of which saturates 0.7g; Cholesterol 98mg; Calcium 97mg; Fibre 2.7g; Sodium 104mg

453 Beansprouts with salt fish Energy 185kcal/772kJ; Protein 13.2g; Carbohydrate 6.5g, of which sugars 3.7g; Fat 12.1g, of which saturates 1.5g; Cholesterol 0mg; Calcium 68mg; Fibre 2.3g; Sodium 2157mg

454 Abacus beads Energy 201kcal/844kJ; Protein 7.9g; Carbohydrate 25.7g, of which sugars 0.8g; Fat 7.8g, of which saturates 1.1g; Cholesterol 65mg; Calcium 41mg; Fibre 1.1g; Sodium 425mg

460 Lotus seeds in syrup Energy 531kcal/2209kJ; Protein 5g; Carbohydrate 42.8g, of which sugars 42.4g; Fat 38.9g, of which saturates 5.6g; Cholesterol 0mg; Calcium 43mg; Fibre 3.4g; Sodium 143mg

461 Almond jelly Energy 181kcal/768kJ; Protein 4.8g; Carbohydrate 41.1g, of which sugars 41.1g; Fat 0.8g, of which saturates 0.5g; Cholesterol 3mg; Calcium 69mg; Fibre 0g; Sodium 24mg

462 Egg tarts Energy 131kcal/549kJ; Protein 3g; Carbohydrate 12.5g, of which sugars 3.9g; Fat 8g, of which saturates 3.1g; Cholesterol 37mg; Calcium 50mg; Fibre 0.4g; Sodium 104mg

465 Bean paste buns Energy 112kcal/477kJ; Protein 4.5g; Carbohydrate 24.1g, of which sugars 5g; Fat 0.4g, of which saturates 0.1g; Cholesterol 0mg; Calcium 36mg; Fibre 1.5g; Sodium 3mg

466 Water chestnut cake Energy 190kcal/800kJ; Protein 2.2g; Carbohydrate 29g, of which sugars 28.4g; Fat 8.1g, of which saturates 1.3g; Cholesterol 2mg; Calcium 60mg; Fibre 0.5g; Sodium 18mg

482 Spicy fish soup Energy 138kcal/572kJ; Protein 8g; Carbohydrate 1g, of which sugars 0g; Fat 11g, of which saturates 2g; Cholesterol 7mg; Calcium 5mg; Fibre 0.2g; Sodium 9mg

483 Hot-and-sour soup Energy 65kcal/275kJ; Protein 9g; Carbohydrate 5g, of which sugars 2g; Fat 1g, of which saturates 0g; Cholesterol 22mg; Calcium 73mg; Fibre 0g; Sodium 655mg

484 Corn soup Energy 185kcal/777kJ; Protein 14g; Carbohydrate 15g, of which sugars 2g; Fat 8g, of which saturates 2g; Cholesterol 138mg; Calcium 28mg; Fibre 1.3g; Sodium 448mg

487 Pork balls in clear soup Energy 180kcal/745kJ; Protein 12g; Carbohydrate 4g, of which sugars 1g; Fat 14g, of which saturates 2g; Cholesterol 32mg; Calcium 12mg; Fibre 0.2g; Sodium 734mg

488 Chicken & pickled green soup Energy 73kcal/307kJ; Protein 8g; Carbohydrate 1g, of which sugars 1g; Fat 4g, of which saturates 1g; Cholesterol 22mg; Calcium 4mg; Fibre 0.1g; Sodium 286mg

489 Sweet potato cakes Energy 75kcal/315kJ; Protein 1g; Carbohydrate 11g, of which sugars 1g; Fat 3g, of which saturates 0g; Cholesterol 0mg; Calcium 8mg; Fibre 0.7g; Sodium 11mg

490 Sesame seed pastries Energy 590kcal/2451kJ; Protein 13g; Carbohydrate 33g, of which sugars 11g; Fat 46g, of which saturates 7g; Cholesterol 61mg; Calcium 343mg; Fibre 4.3g; Sodium 130mg

493 Glutinous rice balls with sesame paste Energy 335kcal/1402kJ; Protein 5g; Carbohydrate 65g, of which sugars 19g; Fat 6g, of which saturates 1g; Cholesterol 2mg; Calcium 51mg; Fibre 1.6g; Sodium 8mg

494 Jicama dumplings Energy 123kcal/513kJ; Protein 1g; Carbohydrate 16g, of which sugars 1g; Fat 6g, of which saturates 1g; Cholesterol 5mg; Calcium 19mg; Fibre 0.8g; Sodium 227mg

497 Pork & cabbage dumplings Energy 95kcal/401kJ; Protein 4g; Carbohydrate 14g, of which sugars 1g; Fat 3g, of which saturates 1g; Cholesterol 5mg; Calcium 64mg; Fibre 0.7g; Sodium 291mg

502 Chrysanthemum fish hot pot Energy 100kcal/422kJ; Protein 15g; Carbs 6g, of which sugars 1g; Fat 2g, of which saturates 0g; Cholesterol 41mg; Calcium 142mg; Fibre 0.6g; Sodium 1396mg

505 Clay-pot fish stew Energy 238kcal/995kJ; Protein 20g; Carbohydrate 11g, of which sugars 2g; Fat 12g, of which saturates 1g; Cholesterol 12mg; Calcium 324mg; Fibre 0.6g; Sodium 506mg

506 Braised grouper in chilli sauce Energy 430kcal/1796kJ; Protein 41g; Carbohydrate 18g, of which sugars 4g; Fat 21g, of which saturates 3g; Cholesterol 0mg; Calcium 281mg; Fibre 0.2g; Sodium 688mg

509 Braised fish with garlic Energy 257kcal/1075kJ; Protein 21g; Carbohydrate 11g, of which sugars 2g; Fat 14g, of which saturates 2g; Cholesterol 37mg; Calcium 54mg; Fibre 0.3g; Sodium 397mg

510 Tofu fish in a spicy sauce Energy 340kcal/1418kJ; Protein 31g; Carbohydrate 6g, of which sugars 2g; Fat 22g, of which saturates 3g; Cholesterol 21mg; Calcium 280mg; Fibre 0.1g; Sodium 2189mg

511 Five-spice carp Energy 318kcal/1326kJ; Protein 21g; Carbohydrate 9g, of which sugars 1g; Fat 22g, of which saturates 3g; Cholesterol 75mg; Calcium 61mg; Fibre 0 g; Sodium 483mg

513 Sweet-and-sour carp Energy 334kcal/1402kJ; Protein 21g; Carbohydrate 30g, of which sugars 11g; Fat 14g, of which saturates 2g; Cholesterol 75mg; Calcium 67mg; Fibre 0.2g; Sodium 620mg

514 Fish in hot sweet-and-sour sauce Energy 347kcal/1450kJ; Protein 33g; Carbohydrate 17g, of which sugars 5g; Fat 17g, of which saturates 2g; Cholesterol 78mg; Calcium 28mg; Fibre 1.5g; Sodium 571mg

517 Crispy hot whitebait Energy 672kcal/2783kJ; Protein 25g; Carbohydrate 8g, of which sugars 1g; Fat 61g, of which saturates 0g; Cholesterol 0mg; Calcium 1077mg; Fibre 0.3g; Sodium 534mg

518 Dragon phoenix eels Energy 269kcal/1120kJ; Protein 22g; Carbohydrate 6g, of which sugars 3g; Fat 17g, of which saturates 3g; Cholesterol 53mg; Calcium 49mg; Fibre 0.5g; Sodium 360mg

520 Jade prawns Chengdu-style Energy 243kcal/1015kJ; Protein 24g; Carbohydrate 8g, of which sugars 1g; Fat 12g, of which saturates 2g; Cholesterol 219mg; Calcium 104mg; Fibre 0.8g; Sodium 680mg

521 Wine-marinated prawns Energy 151kcal/632kJ; Protein 20g; Carbohydrate 3g, of which sugars 2g; Fat 6g, of which saturates 1g; Cholesterol 219mg; Calcium 103mg; Fibre 0.6g; Sodium 487mg

522 Prawns in Sichuan pepper sauce Energy 124kcal/513kJ; Protein 9g; Carbohydrate 1g, of which sugars 1g; Fat 9g, of which saturates 2g; Cholesterol 98mg; Calcium 43mg; Fibre 0.1g; Sodium 489mg

525 Paper-wrapped prawns Energy 288kcal/1214kJ; Protein 10g; Carbohydrate 18g, of which sugars 2g; Fat 20g, of which saturates 3g; Cholesterol 98mg; Calcium 46mg; Fibre 0 g; Sodium 563mg

526 Chilli squid Energy 127kcal/529kJ; Protein 8g; Carbohydrate 5g, of which sugars 2g; Fat 8g, of which saturates 2g; Cholesterol 113mg; Calcium 18mg; Fibre 0.4g; Sodium 57mg

533 Kung Po chicken Energy 286kcal/1194kJ; Protein 21g; Carbohydrate 14g, of which sugars 10g; Fat 16g, of which saturates 3g; Cholesterol 53mg; Calcium 24mg; Fibre 0.7g; Sodium 506mg

534 Garlic chicken in chilli oil Energy 270kcal/1125kJ; Protein 24g; Carbohydrate 3g, of which sugars 2g; Fat 18g, of which saturates 4g; Cholesterol 118mg; Calcium 16mg; Fibre 0.3g; Sodium 369mg

535 Chicken with bamboo shoot Energy 202kcal/847kJ; Protein 28g; Carbohydrate 3g, of which sugars 1g; Fat 9g, of which saturates 2g; Cholesterol 79mg; Calcium 17mg; Fibre 0.9g; Sodium 337mg

536 Chilli chicken Energy 270kcal/1126kJ; Protein 28g; Carbohydrate 1g, of which sugars 1g; Fat 16g, of which saturates 3g; Cholesterol 79mg; Calcium 19mg; Fibre 0.1g; Sodium 2527mg

537 Chilli chicken with peanuts Energy 285kcal/1185kJ; Protein 18g; Carbohydrate 5g, of which sugars 3g; Fat 21g, of which saturates 4g; Cholesterol 44mg; Calcium 17mg; Fibre 0.9g; Sodium 40mg

539 Hot-and-sour chicken Energy 174kcal/729kJ; Protein 24g; Carbohydrate 4g, of which sugars 3g; Fat 7g, of which saturates 2g; Cholesterol 118mg; Calcium 25mg; Fibre 0.3g; Sodium 308mg

540 Chicken & cloud ear stir-fry Energy 271kcal/1131kJ; Protein 27g; Carbohydrate 4g, of which sugars 1g; Fat 16g, of which saturates 3g; Cholesterol 79mg; Calcium 13mg; Fibre 0.1g; Sodium 69mg

541 Braised chicken with tripe Energy 414kcal/1723kJ; Protein35g; Carbohydrate 3g, of which sugars 1g; Fat 28g, of which saturates 7g; Cholesterol 174mg; Calcium 63mg; Fibre 0.1g; Sodium 695mg

542 Chicken in vinegar sauce Energy 143kcal/599kJ; Protein 19g; Carbohydrate 4g, of which sugars 2g; Fat 5g, of which saturates 1g; Cholesterol 53mg; Calcium 13mg; Fibre 0.5g; Sodium 822mg

544 Wine-braised chicken Energy 231kcal/967J; Protein 28g; Carbohydrate 5g, of which sugars 2g; Fat 10g, of which saturates 2g; Cholesterol 79mg; Calcium 13mg; Fibre 0.4g; Sodium 344mg

545 Duck with bamboo piths Energy 287kcal/1207kJ; Protein 17g; Carbohydrate 28g, of which sugars 26g; Fat 13g, of which saturates 3g; Cholesterol 83mg; Calcium 34mg; Fibre 1.9g; Sodium 517mg

546 Aromatic crispy duck Energy 602kcal/2491kJ; Protein 20g; Carbohydrate 5g, of which sugars 0g; Fat 64g, of which saturates 16g; Cholesterol 108mg; Calcium 22mg; Fibre 0.1g; Sodium 301mg

549 Braised duck with tofu Energy 179kcal/743kJ; Protein 11g; Carbohydrate 4g, of which sugars 2g; Fat 13g, of which saturates 3g; Cholesterol 41mg; Calcium 174mg; Fibre 0.5g; Sodium 179mg

554 Cold garlic pork Energy 223kcal/933kJ; Protein 24g; Carbohydrate 4g, of which sugars 3g; Fat 12g, of which saturates 3g; Cholesterol 72mg; Calcium 18mg; Fibre 0.3g; Sodium 885mg

556 Pork ribs in peppercorn sauce Energy 321kcal/1767kJ; Protein 23g; Carbohydrate 7g, of which sugars 6g; Fat 34g, of which saturates 10g; Cholesterol 80mg; Calcium 21mg; Fibre 1.3g; Sodium 634mg

557 Pork in hot-and-sour sauce Energy 327kcal/1364kJ; Protein 27g; Carbohydrate 17g, of which sugars 5g; Fat 17g, of which saturates 3g; Cholesterol 130mg; Calcium 28mg; Fibre 0.7g; Sodium 109mg

559 Twice-cooked pork Energy 426kcal/1866kJ; Protein 24g; Carbohydrate 20g, of which sugars 4g; Fat 31g, of which saturates 9g; Cholesterol 71mg; Calcium 106mg; Fibre 4.5g; Sodium 507mg

560 Cold spicy beef Energy 160kcal/672kJ; Protein 25g; Carbohydrate 3g, of which sugars 2g; Fat 5g, of which saturates 2g; Cholesterol 66mg; Calcium 16mg; Fibre 0.1g; Sodium 1096mg

561 Sesame beef Energy 255kcal/1062kJ; Protein 25g; Carbohydrate 2g, of which sugars 2g; Fat 16g, of which saturates 5g; Cholesterol 69mg; Calcium 33mg; Fibre 0.3g; Sodium 512mg

562 Crispy chilli beef Energy 353kcal/1472kJ; Protein 25g; Carbohydrate 18g, of which sugars 7g; Fat 20g, of which saturates 4g; Cholesterol 66mg; Calcium 19mg; Fibre 0.7g; Sodium 500mg

565 Red-cooked beef Energy 295kcal/1234kJ; Protein 39g; Carbohydrate 5g, of which sugars 3g; Fat 14g, of which saturates 3g; Cholesterol 113mg; Calcium 26mg; Fibre 0.1g; Sodium 367mg

566 Five-spice beef in bean sauce Energy 178kcal/745kJ; Protein 27g; Carbohydrate 3g, of which sugars 1g; Fat 6g, of which saturates 2g; Cholesterol 57mg; Calcium 21mg; Fibre 0.1g; Sodium 153mg

567 Boiled fiery beef Energy 399kcal/1653kJ; Protein 27g; Carbohydrate 0g, of which sugars 0g; Fat 16g, of which saturates 5g; Cholesterol 69mg; Calcium 33mg; Fibre 0.3g; Sodium 512mg

569 Mixed smoked meats Energy 280kcal/1179kJ; Protein 51g; Carbohydrate 2g, of which sugars 0g; Fat 7g, of which saturates 2g; Cholesterol 176mg; Calcium 56mg; Fibre 0g; Sodium 657mg

570 Rabbit in hot bean sauce Energy 274kcal/1422kJ; Protein 23g; Carbohydrate 8g, of which sugars 5g; Fat 17g, of which saturates 4g; Cholesterol 53mg; Calcium 45mg; Fibre 0.9g; Sodium 676mg

571 Hot-and-sour kidneys Energy 186kcal/776kJ; Protein 14g; Carbohydrate 9g, of which sugars 2g; Fat 11g, of which saturates 2g; Cholesterol 333mg; Calcium 23mg; Fibre 1g; Sodium 451mg

576 Black rice porridge Energy 246kcal/10267kJ; Protein 15g; Carbohydrate 29g, of which sugars 1g; Fat 7g, of which saturates 2g; Cholesterol 16mg; Calcium 10mg; Fibre 0.2g; Sodium 1097mg

577 Pineapple rice Energy 403kcal/1692kJ; Protein 13g; Carbohydrate 48g, of which sugars 4g; Fat 19g, of which saturates 4g; Cholesterol 116mg; Calcium 61mg; Fibre 1.1g; Sodium 422mg

579 Glutinous rice in bamboo leaves Energy 548kcal/2288kJ; Protein 20g; Carbohydrate 80g, of which sugars 1g; Fat 15g, of which saturates 3g; Cholesterol 32mg; Calcium 29mg; Fibre 0.5g; Sodium 1377mg

580 Clay-pot rice with salt fish Energy 706kcal/2927kJ; Protein 30g; Carbohydrate 92g, of which sugars 0g; Fat 27g, of which saturates 3g; Cholesterol 35mg; Calcium 80mg; Fibre 0.5g; Sodium 1968mg

583 Dan dan noodles Energy 531kcal/2231kJ; Protein 17g; Carbohydrate 70g, of which sugars 4g; Fat 22g, of which saturates 3g; Cholesterol 18mg; Calcium 46mg; Fibre 2.9g; Sodium 815mg

584 Cold noodles Energy 501kcal/2118kJ; Protein 18g; Carbohydrate 88g, of which sugars 4g; Fat 11g, of which saturates 1g; Cholesterol 0mg; Calcium 60mg; Fibre 3.6; Sodium 622mg

585 Pork mince & glass noodles Energy 658kcal/2743kJ; Protein 26g; Carbohydrate 71g, of which sugars 5g; Fat 29g, of which saturates 4g; Cholesterol 63mg; Calcium 37mg; Fibre 0.3g; Sodium 1152mg

586 Stir-fried noodles with pork Energy 358kcal/1506kJ; Protein 14g; Carbohydrate 50g, sugars 2g; Fat 13g, of which saturates 2g; Cholesterol 18mg; Calcium 23mg; Fibre 2.1g; Sodium 334mg

587 Beef & chive noodles Energy 374kcal/1582kJ; Protein 22g; Carbohydrate 56g, of which sugars 3g; Fat 9g, of which saturates 3g; Cholesterol 48mg; Calcium 44mg; Fibre 2.7g; Sodium 706mg

592 Spicy cucumber Energy 42kcal/174kJ; Protein 2g; Carbs 4g, sugars 3g; Fat 2g, saturates 0g; Chol 0mg; Calcium 40mg; Fibre 0.9g; Sodium 555mg

593 Pickled celery salad Energy 98kcal/405kJ; Protein 2g; Carbohydrate 3g, of which sugars 2g; Fat 9g, of which saturates 1g; Cholesterol 0mg; Calcium 73mg; Fibre 1.2g; Sodium 1044mg

594 Spicy green beans Energy 292kcal/1204kJ; Protein 5g; Carbohydrate 5g, of which sugars 3g; Fat 28g, of which saturates 4g; Cholesterol 0mg; Calcium 207mg; Fibre 1g; Sodium 762mg

595 Pickled mustard greens Energy 26kcal/111kJ; Protein 2g; Carbohydrate 5g, of which sugars 3g; Fat 0g, of which saturates 0g; Cholesterol 0mg; Calcium 53mg; Fibre 2.5g; Sodium 183mg

596 Mixed mushroom stir-fry Energy 238kcal/993kJ; Protein 8g; Carbohydrate 34g, of which sugars 1g; Fat 9g, of which saturates 2g; Cholesterol 0mg; Calcium 50mg; Fibre 0.6g; Sodium 731mg

597 Stir-fried bamboo shoots Energy 168kcal/693kJ; Protein 2g; Carbohydrate 6g, of which sugars 3g; Fat 15g, of which saturates 3g; Cholesterol 0mg; Calcium 21mg; Fibre 2g; Sodium 317mg

598 Stir-fried chive stems Energy 167kcal/690kJ; Protein 7g; Carbohydrate 3g, of which sugars 3g; Fat 14g, of which saturates 2g; Cholesterol 0mg; Calcium 353mg; Fibre 2.1g; Sodium 542mg

599 Stir-fried spicy courgettes Energy 102kcal/420kJ; Protein 3g; Carbohydrate 5g, of which sugars 4g; Fat 8g, of which saturates 2g; Cholesterol 0mg; Calcium 32mg; Fibre 1.1g; Sodium 425mg

600 Shredded aubergine Energy 195kcal/805kJ; Protein 1g; Carbohydrate 5g, of which sugars 33g; Fat 18g, of which saturates 3g; Cholesterol 0mg; Calcium 21mg; Fibre 2.4g; Sodium 38mg

601 Pock-marked tofu Energy 276kcal/1143kJ; Protein 14g; Carbohydrate 6g, of which sugars 3g; Fat 22g, of which saturates 3g; Cholesterol 0mg; Calcium 837mg; Fibre 1g; Sodium 365mg

606 Sesame cream Energy 695kcal/2890kJ; Protein 18g; Carbohydrate 37g, of which sugars 33g; Fat 54g, of which saturates 9g; Cholesterol 10mg; Calcium 677mg; Fibre 6.9g; Sodium 75mg

607 Sugared silver-ear fungus Energy 109kcal/464kJ; Protein 1g; Carbohydrate 29g, sugars 20g; Fat 0g, saturates 0g; Cholesterol 0mg; Calcium 22mg; Fibre 0g; Sodium 5mg

609 Red bean paste pancakes Energy 186kcal/784kJ; Protein 5g; Carbohydrate 29g, of which sugars 7g; Fat 6g, of which saturates 1g; Cholesterol 39mg; Calcium 47mg; Fibre 1.5g; Sodium 17mg

610 Red bean & tangerine broth Energy 323kcal/1376kJ; Protein 8g; Carbohydrate 75g, sugars 49g; Fat 1g, of which saturates 0g; Cholesterol 0mg; Calcium 49mg; Fibre 5.3g; Sodium 7mg

611 Rice-flour balls in syrup Energy 54kcal/228kJ; Protein 13g; Carbohydrate 4g, sugars 0g; Fat 0g, of which saturates 0g; Cholesterol 0mg; Calcium 3mg; Fibre 0.2g; Sodium 50mg

612 Pearl balls Energy 354kcal/1482kJ; Protein 6g; Carbohydrate 76g, of which sugars 2g; Fat 2g, of which saturates 2g; Cholesterol 0mg; Calcium 32mg; Fibre 2.4g; Sodium 7mg

INDEX

This edition is published by Lorenz Books
an imprint of Anness Publishing Ltd
www.lorenzbooks.com; info@anness.com
 A CIP catalogue record of this book is available from the British Library.

Publisher: Joanna Lorenz
Editor and layout: Lucy Doncaster
Photography: Martin Brigdale
Food stylists: Katie Giovanni and Lucy McKelvie
Index: Marie Lorimer
Cover design: Adelle Mahoney

Parts of this book have been previously published in The Food and Cooking of: Shanghai and East China; Cantonese and South China; Sichuan and West China; and Mandarin and North China.

COOK'S NOTES

- Quantities are given in both metric and imperial measures and in standard cups and spoons. Follow one set of measures, but not a mixture, because they are not interchangeable.
- Standard spoon and cup measures are level. 1 tsp=5ml, 1 tbsp=15ml, 1 cup = 250ml/8fl oz.
- Australian standard tablespoons are 20ml. Australian readers should use 3 tsp in place of 1 tbsp for measuring small quantities of gelatine, flour, salt, etc.
- American pints are 16fl oz/2 cups. American readers should use 20fl oz/2.5 cups in place of 1 pint when measuring liquids.
- Electric oven temperatures are for conventional ovens. Since fan ovens vary, you should check with your manufacturer's instruction book.
- The nutritional analysis is calculated per portion (i.e. serving or item), unless otherwise stated. If the recipe gives a range, such as Serves 4–6, then the nutritional analysis will be for the smaller portion size. Measurements for sodium do not include salt added to taste.

Additional picture credits: Shutterstock: 5, 11, 14, 17, 25, 31, 35, 36, 173, 174, 320, 321, 323, 468, 471, 472; iStock: 2–3, 8, 9, 12, 13, 15, 16, 18, 19, 20, 26, 28–9, 32, 33, 34, 37, 168–9, 171, 172, 175, 176, 177, 316–17, 319, 324, 325, 473, 474, 475; Alamy: 21, 476, 477.

CAPTIONS
2–3 Dim sum, traditionally served with tea, is one of the most iconic Chinese foods and is especially popular in southern China, where it originated.
28–9 The Great Wall of China snaking its way some 21,200km (13,200 miles) through the frozen landscape of northern China.
168–9 The traditional architecture in Hongcun village in Anhui, eastern China, follows ancient feng shui principles.
316–17 One of the most iconic cityscapes in the world, Hong Kong is a key player on the world stage and has long been a centre of commerce and a foodie hub.
468–9 A yurt village in front of Karakul Lake – the highest lake of the Pamir plateau – in Xinjiang Uighur Autonomous Region of western China.